Videoconferencing Technology in K–12 Instruction:
Best Practices and Trends

Dianna L. Newman
University at Albany/SUNY, USA

John Falco
The College of St. Rose, USA

Stan Silverman
New York Institute of Technology, USA

Patricia Barbanell
Schenectady City School District, USA

INFORMATION SCIENCE REFERENCE

Hershey · New York

Acquisitions Editor:	Kristin Klinger
Development Editor:	Kristin Roth
Senior Managing Editor:	Jennifer Neidig
Managing Editor:	Sara Reed
Copy Editor:	Susanna Svidunovich
Typesetter:	Jeff Ash
Cover Design:	Lisa Tosheff
Printed at:	Yurchak Printing Inc.

Published in the United States of America by
Information Science Reference (an imprint of IGI Global)
701 E. Chocolate Avenue, Suite 200
Hershey PA 17033
Tel: 717-533-8845
Fax: 717-533-8661
E-mail: cust@igi-pub.com
Web site: http://www.igi-pub.com/reference

and in the United Kingdom by
Information Science Reference (an imprint of IGI Global)
3 Henrietta Street
Covent Garden
London WC2E 8LU
Tel: 44 20 7240 0856
Fax: 44 20 7379 0609
Web site: http://www.eurospanonline.com

Library of Congress Cataloging-in-Publication Data

Videoconferencing technology in K-12 instruction : best practices and trends / [edited by] Dianna L. Newman ... [et al.].

p. cm.

Summary: "This book combines relevant and cutting-edge information on the current and future use of videoconferencing technology in the field of education. It serves as the foundation for future research and implementation of K-12 technology, professional development, and integration efforts. Educators will gain scientific evidence, case studies, and best practices from this book"--Provided by publisher.

Includes bibliographical references and index.

ISBN 978-1-59904-331-9 (hardcover) -- ISBN 978-1-59904-333-3 (ebook)

1. Videoconferencing--United States. 2. Teleconferencing in education--United States. I. Newman, Dianna L.

LB1044.9.V53V53 2008

371.33'58--dc22

2007007287

British Cataloguing in Publication Data
A Cataloguing in Publication record for this book is available from the British Library.

All work contributed to this book set is new, previously-unpublished material. The views expressed in this book are those of the authors, but not necessarily of the publisher.

Table of Contents

Section I
What is K-12 Videoconferencing?

Section II
Bringing Providers to the Camera

Detailed Table of Contents

Section I
What is K-12 Videoconferencing?

This chapter introduces the concept of videoconferencing in K-12 education by providing an overview of what it is and why it should be used. Key terms are defined, and an overview of benefits to uses are presented. When discussing "What is videoconferencing?", six types of videoconferences which are frequently found in K-12 educational settings are described, and the key roles of stakeholders are introduced. These six types include: point-to-point or provider-classroom videoconferencing; collaborative classroom videoconferencing; multi-point videoconferencing; mass audience or electronic field trips videoconferencing; homebound videoconferencing; and one-to-one videoconferencing. Potential benefits of each type are also presented. Following this discussion, the author discusses "Why do it?" by addressing, in lay language, the results of multiple studies that have documented the benefits of K-12 videoconferencing from the points of view of teachers, students, and providers.

Section II
Bringing Providers to the Camera

The Virtual Outreach Program at the Michigan State University Museum progressed through three stages of videoconference program development while taking museum resources on the virtual "road." This chapter documents the shift from an experts-based model to one focused on learning content through object-based learning and dynamic inquiry in a collaborative community. Revisions in pedagogy, philosophy, and content are explored at each level and supported by the literature and best-practice standards that shaped these changes. Throughout, the museum virtual field trip is presented as a partnership between the classroom, museum experts, and distance-learning providers, working together to create meaningful virtual learning experiences for K-12 students.

This chapter presents an overview of videoconferencing technology in K-12 instruction from the perspective of a program (content) provider. The chapter provides an overview of the development process, issues, and challenges, and future goals of a distance learning program which provides lessons to K-12 classrooms across the country. Specific topic areas include technology and equipment, establishing partnerships, working with K-12 school districts and educators, expanding a program, and staffing needs. Using the analogy of a road trip, the author takes us on a journey through the development, piloting, and use of a distance education videoconferencing program, and how it is now being sustained and enhanced.

This chapter explores the modality and benefits of videoconferencing from the content provider's perspective. The content provider as "field expert" is discussed along with the benefits of providing nationwide outreach to K-12 educators and students via a cost-effective, interactive media. Applications of videoconferencing are addressed in addition to the perceptions of the provider in such areas as the needs of the K-12 educational community, methods and tools for presenting successful virtual field trips, and evidence of impact through informal teacher feedback and a professional study conducted in 2000. The author also addresses how providers can reach out to and collaboratively work with other organizations to enhance and build capacity.

This chapter discusses various points of view regarding the process of developing a videoconferencing lesson that focuses on an architectural landmark, the Solomon R. Guggenheim Museum. This lesson was the result of collaboration among provider educators from the Solomon R. Guggenheim Museum, and three teachers. The project involved a working partnership that lasted a year and a half, culminating with the launch of the videoconference lesson. Information on establishing the goals, developing the program, and assessing outcomes are provided. This chapter includes input from the museum and from teachers at the participating schools about the collaboration process and its value to participants.

Chapter VI

In K-12 videoconferencing, we often allow the pressures and challenges of our jobs to interfere with being able to enjoy our work. In this chapter, I have recounted some of my own personal experiences that show that it is quite possible to love your job and to find humor and enjoyment in each day. By making your enthusiasm obvious, combining a variety of different disciplines into programming and making the most out of "technical difficulties," you can become a more effective and believable content provider and learn to take real pleasure in creating a positive and unique experience for students through technology.

Section III
Bringing Teachers to the Camera

Chapter VII

This chapter presents the process of videoconferencing with external providers from the teacher's side of the camera. It summarizes the steps necessary to conduct a videoconference, including how to contact and select external providers, as well as how to prepare, conduct, and follow up on a videoconference. It carefully examines how to develop lasting relationships with experts in the field, and how to use their resources to create an interactive research-based classroom environment. For classroom teachers, videoconferencing is a relatively new educational tool, and the extent of its implementation is constantly expanding and virtually endless. Utilizing examples of specific experiences, the chapter provides the reader with an overview of videoconferences that exist and can be used by P-12 educators.

Chapter VIII

This chapter provides a three-step framework for improving student learning in videoconferencing. Using the Understanding by Design model, educators can design videoconferencing instruction that focuses on specific student learning. As they pre-assess their curriculum and instruction goals and shape the videoconference plan, as they assess students' learning before, during, and after the videoconference, and as they scaffold the learning to meet these goals and assessment needs, they will automatically build in structured, successful learning experiences. While discussing the transfer of the understanding by design model to videoconferencing settings, the author provides specific examples of each step of this process that will help other educators use the system in their own instructional practices.

Chapter IX

The chapter introduces collaborative classroom projects implemented through videoconferencing technology as a means of enhancing and enriching classroom instruction. The various applications of collaborative classroom videoconferencing are discussed in the light of social constructivist learning theory. Special attention is devoted to teacher professional development training in designing and implementing collaborative classroom videoconference projects. Distinctive types of collaborative classroom implementation projects with supporting examples, as well as effective outcomes associated with student learning, are presented and discussed. The chapter concludes with a summary of the best practices in the utilization of collaborative classroom projects; directions and recommendations for future research are also offered.

Section IV
Building and Supporting a System of Videoconferencing

Chapter X

The purpose of this chapter is to examine the role of leadership in interactive videoconferencing. Interactive videoconferencing provides the opportunity for schools to bring content-area experts from anywhere in the world into the classroom to engage students in real-time learning. The effective integration of interactive videoconferencing into classroom practice requires leadership. This leadership is rooted in a belief in providing world-class, student-centered learning through interactive videoconferencing. It is a vision that is results-driven in terms of measuring student learning, and realized through instructional leadership that is committed to collaboration, professional development, appropriate technical support and infrastructure, and the use of research to support practice.

Chapter XI

Due to the increases in connectivity capacities prevalent in our nation's schools, educational administrators are utilizing a variety of resources in their classrooms, including the interactive videoconferencing. For videoconferencing to be successful, however, planning for technological infrastructure must occur prior to program implementation. It is important for both schools and providers to be aware of the infrastructure requirements needed in order to provide students with knowledge and learning via videoconference experiences. The purpose of this chapter is to identify the key components of the technological infrastructure needed to support videoconferencing within K-12 in the schools, such as connectivity needs and essential hardware requirements including computers, cameras, audio essentials, and operating controls; in addition, the chapter provides, in easy-to-read language, an overview of many of the key technical terms used in the videoconferencing literature, and provides teachers with a graphical display of use.

Chapter XII

The purpose of this chapter is to identify policy issues for videoconferencing at the elementary through college levels. As videoconferencing becomes a part of our educational landscape in schools across the country, it is important to understand what policy implications need to be addressed in regards to this educational resource. Issues such as ownership, content, and access are some of the areas that suggest policy discussion. Federal, state, and international policies that guide the use of videoconferencing will be discussed. In sum, this chapter attempts to investigate policy issues and trends related to videoconferencing that informs the educational (PreK-12), business (training), and academic (higher education) communities that use this resource.

Section V
Videoconferencing and Teacher Preparation

Chapter XIII

Videoconferencing is one form of distance learning that can enhance teacher-education programs by linking students in higher education with Pre-K–12 schools. As part of a Preparing Tomorrow's Teachers to use Technology grant (PT3), a teacher-education program utilized distance learning to link college classes with an urban school. Mediated observations of specific literacy practices were integrated into a traditional introductory literacy course. Preservice teachers observed urban teachers teaching literacy. Immediately following these observations, the preservice teachers were granted the opportunity to reflect on the lesson by conversing with the teachers via distance learning. Initial findings suggest that students acquired positive attitudes toward teaching in urban classrooms and preferred this virtual field experience to a traditional in-school placement.

Chapter XIV

The purpose of this chapter is to provide a brief history of videoconferencing when used as virtual field trips in educational settings, and to discuss some of the various aspects in which they can be implemented. In addition, this chapter focuses on the unique benefits to students and teachers as noted in the literature that videoconferencing field trips can bring to the learning community, and some of the challenges that many educators, eager to use this technology, have experienced. Speculation as to what the future will hold for virtual field trips and where the technology will possibly take us is also discussed.

This chapter focuses on the enhancement of teacher preparation through various types of videoconferences and through various types of engagement within a videoconference. These can include: expert; university to school; peer-to-peer and meetings; multiple sessions; mentoring/observation; learning about videoconferencing; and interviewing/job searching. Both preservice students and their professors can benefit from involvement in videoconferencing. Teacher-preparation students become more engaged in the content through interactive activities, streaming video, blogs, discussion areas of programs, Webinars, shared applications, tele-education aspects of videoconferencing, and follow-up discussion boards. Instructors can improve the quality of their instruction to maximize learning by transforming their teacher-preparation classes into ones in which students have more in-depth and comprehensive experiences to prepare them for future teaching.

This chapter introduces ways in which videoconferencing can be used to support professional development which is being provided to educators. It looks at the ways in which adults learn, the need for quality professional development in education, and the different types of professional development which are being provided. It then goes on to discuss ways in which videoconferencing can be used to make the transfer of knowledge more effective. After reading this chapter, educators will be able to identify ways in which they can utilize videoconferencing to make professional development more beneficial and cost-efficient. It also shows educators how they can break away from ineffective traditional modes of providing in-service training and move toward more high-quality, comprehensive, and embedded professional development, which addresses the individual needs of teachers and buildings.

Section VI
The Impact of Videoconferencing: Does it Help?

The use of videoconferencing as a means of bringing external informal educators into the K-12 classroom is an area of increasing interest in the field of education. To date, however, few studies have documented the impact of the process on students' cognitive and affective outcomes. This chapter presents findings from a series of studies that compared student outcomes for those who received technology-supported videoconferencing with those who did not receive videoconferencing. Findings indicate that students who participated in videoconferencing had higher scores on cognitive indicators, were more motivated to learn the material, and were more interested in learning about related topics.

This chapter examines evidence that there is significant value added to K-12 educational outcomes that emerge as a result of provider use of interactive videoconferencing and supporting resources in their content delivery. It includes discussion of the outcomes of several presentation approaches that have been analyzed with regard to effectiveness and impact on student understanding. The aim of the chapter is to offer a solid foundation for understanding the impact of interactive videoconferencing on student learning, and to present an overview of approaches to structuring interactive programs to enable comprehensive, systemic change in student encounters with and understanding of curriculum content.

This chapter will focus largely on the author's experiences in promoting the creative use of videoconferencing in schools in Northern Ireland over the past ten years. It will also describe certain groundbreaking projects that educators in other parts of the United Kingdom (UK) and Ireland have undertaken in this field. Although until recently there has been little in the way of a systemic approach in Northern Ireland to the introduction and integration of videoconferencing into K-12 classrooms, there have been some striking examples of good practice. The examples chosen demonstrate the potential of videoconferencing to be inclusive of different needs and learning styles, and to extend and enrich the learning experiences available in the classroom. They are intended to show how videoconferencing can have a powerful effect on learning and teaching, and to give more educators the motivation and confidence to explore and develop this user-friendly valuable education resource.

Section VII
The Future of K-12 Videoconferencing

With the advent of broadband telecommunications and affordable equipment, videoconferencing has emerged to replace expensive and elaborate distance learning systems that had been developed in the early 1980's. Yet, as we enter the close of the first decade of the 21st century, videoconferencing has not fulfilled its potential. The following chapter describes and poses solutions to the issues of access, equity, *student achievement, pedagogical strategies, and the integration of emerging communication and media technologies that, if deployed, can transform videoconferencing to become a high performance tool for teaching and learning. In addition, as we embrace the millennial generation with unique characteristics that distinguish it from generations that have gone before, we must acknowledge the global, diverse, and politically-charged world. As a result, there is also an urgency to deploy videoconferencing with its fullest capacities; this urgency is an embedded theme in the writings that follow.*

Foreword

THE EVOLUTION OF VIDEOCONFERENCING

Videoconferencing is a teaching/learning medium with a long history in education. Replicating as many advantages as possible of face-to-face interaction has dominated attempts to design learning across barriers of distance and time. Using a high-bandwidth visual/auditory medium to convey not just verbal information, but non-verbal cues (e.g., facial expression, body posture, voice tone and inflection) is an obvious extension of the intellectual and emotional dimensions of human instruction.

At the time of its development, television ("broadcast" videoconferencing) was a major advance in distance education technology (Dede, Brown-L'Bahy, Kelehut, & Whitehouse, 2004). As early as 1934, the State University of Iowa used television to deliver course content. Early research into learning via television indicated mixed results, with several studies showing that it was similar to conventional instruction. Two generations ago, echoes of current debates about technology as a tool for learning were heard regarding the use of broadcast media in distance education (Nasseh, 1997).

Similar concerns about "talking heads" have dogged videoconferencing from its beginning, since presentational/assimilative instruction is a relatively weak form of pedagogy. In predominantly one-way videoconferencing, teachers communicate with students across distance in ways essentially similar to face-to-face, lecture-based pedagogies; this type of instruction does not take into account the full strengths of media for informing, sharing, and expressing. The exclusive use of conventional, presentational models of instruction can lead to a deficit perspective on videoconferencing: A remote participant is perceived to have "almost" as good a cognitive, affective, and social experience as those immediately present with the teacher.

And yet, this limited form of videoconferencing is still extensively used as a means to access expertise not available locally. In part, this popularity is due to the fact that teaching by telling and learning by listening are familiar forms of instruction that don't require teachers reconceptualizing their pedagogical approach. Also, the dramatic drop in costs of Internet-based videoconferencing equipment and services, compared to older forms of satellite-based and digital telephony forms of videoconference, has created a resurgence of interest in this medium.

Fortunately, in recent years advanced developments in technology-based and distance education are generating novel instructional strategies based on the capabilities of new interactive media and the learning styles of Internet-generation students. The private sector uses sophisticated forms of videoconference for coordinating global workplaces in a "flat" world (Friedman, 2005). Outside of school, kids use highly interactive forms of webconferencing for personal communication and expression (Lenhart & Madden, 2005; Roberts, Foehr, & Rideout, 2005). Research is documenting that presentational face-to-face instruction is not the "gold standard" for many students, who sit silent and passive in lectures, but instead "find their voice" in various forms of mediated interaction (Dede et al., op cit).

Creative educators are developing many innovative, interactive forms of videoconferencing that build on these trends in society. This book documents intriguing, exemplary methods of using videoconferencing to engage students and improve their educational outcomes. The affordability and ubiquity of Internet-based videoconferencing makes these innovations scalable across a wide range of settings. This is truly an exciting time in the history of the videoconferencing medium, and I hope you will join these authors in developing novel, powerful educational applications.

Chris Dede, EdD
Wirth Professor in Learning Technologies
Harvard Graduate School of Education
Education 323
Longfellow Hall
Cambridge, MA 02138
chris_dede@gse.harvard.edu

REFERENCES

Dede, C., Brown-L'Bahy, T., Ketelhut, D., & Whitehouse, P. (2004). Distance learning (Virtual learning). In H. Bidgoli (Ed.), *The internet encyclopedia* (pp. 549-560). New York: Wiley.

Friedman, T. L. (2005). *The world is flat: A brief history of the twenty-first century.* New York: Farrar, Straus, and Giroux.

Lenhart, A., & Madden, M. (2005). *Teens content creators and consumers.* Washington, DC: Pew Internet & American Life Project.

Nasseh, B. (1997). *A brief history of distance education.* SeniorNet. Retrieved on January 16, 2007, from http://www.seniornet.org/edu/art/history.html

Roberts, D. F., Foehr, U. G., & Rideout, V. (2005). *Generation M: Media in the lives of 8–18 year-olds.* Washington, DC: Henry J. Kaiser Family Foundation.

Preface

INTRODUCTION

The use of videoconferencing is a growing factor in education and instructional technology. The majority of schools and higher education institutions now access, or plan on obtaining, some form of videoconferencing technology. Equipment ranges from low-end Webcams attached to classroom computers to mobile high-end carts complete with cameras, microphones, high definition monitors, and wireless access as well as interactive electronic field trips supplemented by online archived resources. Current and prospective uses in K-12 classrooms also are wide-ranging; they include direct, supplemental, and enrichment-based videoconferencing that may be student-to-external providers, student-to-student, student-to-teacher, and teacher-to-teacher. Higher education also is now beginning to understand the value of videoconferencing and its potential in preservice and in-service education. Uses now being piloted include preservice teacher preparation and in-service for practicing professionals. Examples of applications are: live preservice teacher observation of master teacher practices, supervision of student teaching, and cross-building/district coaching and modeling. External and informal educators are determined to not be left behind in this movement; many see videoconferencing as a way of expanding their mission and meeting the need of the millennium generation. Faced with only limited resources, they have a need for best practices in developing and offering videoconferencing services to schools that will have both provider and receiver goals.

Multiple resources are being developed that will assist teachers, administrators, and higher-education faculty to plan the use of the equipment or assist in the design and implementation of curriculum that uses videoconferencing; however, there currently is no text or "one source" available that discusses how videoconferencing is, will, or could impact the total field of education. This book proposes to provide the reader with that resource; our goal is to bring together, in one volume, perceptions, practices, and evidence supporting the use of videoconferencing in educational settings. To meet that end, we have solicited chapters from key stakeholders in the process. This includes: advice and best practices from some of the most active and advanced external providers in the United States; input from teachers who, after in-depth use, have found videoconferencing to be of extreme value in their classrooms; information from administrators and policy-makers on how to support and sustain the process; research-based data that document positive outcomes; and novel uses by teacher preparation programs that will prepare the next generation of educators. Each of these chapters offers a separate, unique voice on the role of videoconferencing in K-12 education, and provides the reader with an overview of best practices and future trends.

ORGANIZATION OF THE BOOK

This book is organized around key themes relating to the concepts and practices of K-12 education and videoconferencing. Following is a brief summary of each of the sections.

Section I: What is K-12 Videoconferencing?

In Chapter I, Newman introduces the concept of videoconferencing in K-12 education by providing an overview of what it is and why it should be used. In discussing "What is videoconferencing?", she presents the six major types of videoconferences that are found in the K-12 settings, provides an overview of their major characteristics and the roles of participants, and briefly discusses the benefits of each type. When addressing "Why should videoconferencing be used?", Newman summarizes the benefits of involvement in the voices of teachers, students, and providers.

Section II: Bringing Providers to the Camera

This section presents key aspects of videoconferencing from the points-of-view of external providers who are actively involved in the process. Their unique view offers a series of models and best practices that can be used by other providers, and also offers educators with a look at the process from the other side of the camera.

In Chapter II, Leach, Morrissey, and Alvarado present a model that can be used by other providers in developing their videoconferencing capacity. Based on their experiences with *The Virtual Outreach Program* at the Michigan State University Museum, they document the shift from an experts-based model to one which is focused on learning content through object-based learning and dynamic inquiry in a collaborative community. Revisions in pedagogy, philosophy, and content are explored at each level and supported by the literature and best practice standards that shaped these changes. Throughout this chapter, the museum virtual field trip is presented as a partnership between the classroom, museum experts, and distance-learning providers, working together to create meaningful virtual learning experiences for K-12 students.

In Chapter III, Fawn Warner, from the *Discovery Center of Springfield*, expands on this theme by providing an overview of the development process, issues and challenges, and future goals of a distance-learning program that provides lessons to K-12 classrooms across the country. Specific topic areas include technology and equipment, establishing partnerships, working with K-12 school districts and educators, expanding a program, and staffing needs.

In Chapter IV, Patty Petrey Dees from the *Center for Puppetry Arts* explores the roles and benefits of videoconferencing from the content provider's perspective. The content provider as "field expert" is discussed, along with the benefits of providing nationwide outreach to K-12 educators and students via a cost-effective, interactive media. Applications of videoconferencing are addressed in addition to the perceptions of the provider in such areas as the needs of the K-12 educational community, methods and tools for presenting successful virtual field trips, and evidence of impact through informal teacher feedback and a professional study conducted in 2000.

In Chapter V, Sharon Vatsky, from the *Solomon R. Guggenheim Museum*, discusses a collaborative provider-teacher process of developing of a videoconferencing lesson that focused on her organization's unique architectural structure. This project involved a working partnership between Vatsky and three teachers that lasted a year and a half, culminating with the launch of a videoconference lesson. In this chapter, she describes the process of collaboration and the added value that the inclusion of educators brought to the process.

In Chapter VI, Emily Diekemper Hansen, from the *Indianapolis Zoo*, provides the final voice of providers in this volume by offering a delightful look at what it means to be an external expert on a day-to-day basis. Noting that we often allow the pressures and challenges of our jobs to interfere with being able to enjoy our work, she recounts some of her own personal experiences that show that it is quite possible to love your job and to find humor and enjoyment in each day while creating a positive and unique experience for students through technology.

Section III: Bringing Teachers to the Camera

This section highlights the role of videoconferencing from the teachers' point of view. Written by those who are "in the trenches", these chapters offer advice to educators on how to start the process and offer best practices in implementation.

In Chapter VII, Jennifer Hahn, a *middle school teacher in a suburban district*, presents the process of videoconferencing with external providers from the teacher's side of the camera. She summarizes the steps necessary to conduct a videoconference, including how to contact and select external content providers and how to prepare for, conduct, and follow-up on its use. She also examines the benefits of developing lasting relationships with experts in the field, and how to use their resources to create an interactive research-based classroom environment.

In Chapter VIII, Tuttle, a former *instructional technology specialist for a school district*, provides a framework for improving student learning in K-12 classroom videoconferencing. He describes how educators can use the "Understanding by Design" model to scaffold learning and assessment before, during, and after the videoconference, and provides specific examples of each step.

In Chapter IX, Bidjerano and Wilkinson, *specialists in learning theory and instructional design*, discuss collaborative classroom videoconferencing as a means of enhancing and enriching classroom instruction in light of social constructivist learning theory. Distinctive types of collaborative classroom implementation projects with supporting examples, as well as affective outcomes associated with student learning, are presented and discussed. The chapter concludes with a summary of the best practices in the utilization of collaborative classroom projects.

Section IV: Building and Supporting a System of Videoconferencing

This section provides readers with an overview of the infrastructure needed for successful K-12 video-conferencing. In these chapters, three long-term experts in the field offer their advice on how to develop and sustain an active videoconferencing program that will aid all children.

In Chapter X, John Falco examines the role of leadership, especially the specific aspect of building level administrators, in supporting and sustaining effective videoconferencing programs. Written in the voice of a *knowledgeable administrator*, he describes how interactive videoconferencing can provide an opportunity for schools to bring content-area experts from anywhere in the world into the class-room to engage students in real-time learning. Based on his extensive experience with technology and videoconferencing, he describes best practices in instructional leadership that reflect a commitment to collaboration, professional development, appropriate technical support and infrastructure, and inclusion of external resources.

In Chapter XI, Bose and De Angelo provide the readers with a clear and concise look at what is needed in terms of equipment and classroom design if videoconferencing is to be efficient and effective. They define and discuss key components of the *technological infrastructure* needed to support videoconferencing within the schools' K-12, such as connectivity needs and essential hardware requirements, including computers, cameras, audio essentials, and operating controls, and how to decide which equipment and methods are best for different settings.

In Chapter XII, Bowman, Hernadez, and Miller-Vice take the reader back to the broader but equally important implications of *policy issues* related to the use and future of videoconferencing at the elementary through college levels. This includes issues such as ownership, content, and access, as well as current and future state, federal, and international policies that guide the use of videoconferencing. Noting that the future is at hand, they advise us to be aware of these key issues and to provide input into decisions that will affect the education of future generations.

Section V: Videoconferencing and Teacher Preparation

When we think about videoconferencing and K-12 education, we cannot omit the preparation and training of those who are or will be teachers. These chapters deal with the role of videoconferencing in preservice teacher preparation and in-service professional development, offering innovative uses and examples of best practice in the transfer of knowledge on how to teach.

In Chapter XIII, Barnett, Truesdell, Kenyon, and Mike describe an innovative and powerful role for videoconferencing in enhancing teacher education programs. They describe how Buffalo State College uses videoconferencing to *link preservice teachers in a higher education program* with Pre-K–12 urban schools. Mediated observations of real classrooms are integrated into a traditional on-campus course via videoconferencing allowing preservice teachers to observe teachers in the field without having to travel off-site or be an influence in the classroom. In addition, teachers at the field site are available to debrief students and help them reflect on successful practices.

In Chapter XIV, Spaulding and Ranney provide an *overview of videoconferencing* that can be used by higher education faculty when describing the process to preservice teachers. They offer a brief history of videoconferencing and discuss some of the various ways in which it can be implemented, noting some of the benefits that it can bring to the learning community, and some of the challenges that many educators, eager to use this technology, have experienced.

In Chapter XV, Tuttle expands on the potential uses of videoconferencing when *preparing higher education students* for the field of teaching. Through the use of multiple real-life examples, he focuses on the various types of videoconferences and the types of engagements that can occur that will inform the teaching process. He advocates for the transformation of teacher preparation classes into ones in which students have more in-depth and comprehensive experiences that will prepare them, through videoconferencing, for their future teaching.

In Chapter XVI, Mountain addresses the use of videoconferencing as a means of supporting *in-service teacher professional development*. She begins by addressing how adults learn, the need for quality professional development in education, the different types of professional development being provided, and examples of how videoconferencing can be used to make this process more effective and cost-efficient. She concludes with a call for more embedded professional development, offered via videoconferencing, as a means of serving the needs of individual teachers and buildings.

Section VI: The Impact of Videoconferencing: Does it Help?

This section provides readers with in-depth evidence of the benefits of videoconferencing in K-12 educational settings. Based on years of experience, hundreds of uses, and thousands of students, the authors put forth evidence and examples of the impact of videoconferencing on student learning.

In Chapter XVII, Newman begins the discussion by presenting findings from a series of quasi-experimental studies that compared student outcomes for those who received technology-supported videoconferencing with those who did not. Her findings indicate that students who participated in videoconferencing had higher scores on *cognitive indicators*, were more motivated to learn the material, and were more interested in learning about related topics than were students who received parallel instruction via traditional classroom techniques.

In Chapter XVIII, Barbanell addresses the *value-added outcomes* that result from use of provider-based interactive videoconferencing and supporting resource. She offers a solid foundation for understanding the impact of the process on student learning, and presents an overview of approaches to structuring interactive programs to enable comprehensive, systemic change in student encounters with and understanding of curriculum content.

In Chapter XIX, Martin expands these discussions by relating her experiences in promoting the creative use of videoconferencing in schools in Northern Ireland over the past ten years. Rich in examples, this chapter demonstrates the potential of videoconferencing in assisting educators in being *inclusive of different needs* and learning styles and in extending and enriching students' learning experiences. Readers who want a full overview of the potential of this medium will find this chapter helpful.

Section VII: The Future of K-12 Videoconferencing

In Chapter XX, our final voice is heard. Silverman describes and offers potential *solutions to the issues* of access, equity, student achievement, pedagogical strategies, and the integration of emerging communication and media technologies that, if deployed, can transform videoconferencing to become a high performance tool for teaching and learning. Noting that the millennial generation, with unique characteristics that distinguish it from generations that have gone before, must have the skills and knowledge to live and work in a global, diverse, and politically-charged world, he urges us to deploy videoconferencing to its fullest capacity and to seek out new ways that will further expand our horizons.

SUMMARY

It is our hope that you find this volume useful and that it helps to expand your knowledge and value of the process of videoconferencing in K-12 education. We believe this tool is transforming education in ways that we have only begun to realize, and that the future of education will be found on both sides of the camera. We welcome your feedback on this material, your examples of how you use videoconferencing now and in the future, and most importantly, any new and creative uses that you might develop.

Dianna L. Newman
John Falco
Stan Silverman
Patricia Barbanell
Editors

evalpub@uamail.albany.edu

Acknowledgment

No book is possible without the assistance of other people. We would like to take this opportunity to thank the authors who contributed to this volume for their insights, experiences, and willingness to share their knowledge. We must also acknowledge the hundreds of providers, teachers, students, and administrators who have been brave enough and curious enough to embark on the journey of videoconferencing. They have been our muses and, as early adopters, have jumped into the world of videoconferencing and have kept us all grounded in the importance of the teaching and learning environment. They have reinforced for all involved that a good instructional environment happens because of caring and knowledge participants. Each success was a celebration, and each failure was treated as a noble failure from which we gained great insights and suggestions for new approaches. The teachers and their students are the true pioneers; we are only their biographers.

We would also like to thank Meg Stocking at IGI Global for her expertise in guiding us through this process and for her marvelous sense of humor and helpful attitude. A very special "thank you" goes to Kristina Osborne, our internal reader, secretary, and timekeeper; this process was made manageable by her hard work.

Finally, but not least, we would each like to thank our families, coworkers, and friends for their support, patience, and laughter during this process. As Emily Diekemper Hansen notes in her chapter, work should be fun, and you gave us the opportunity to make it so. A special "thank you" from Dianna Newman to Gary Clure for listening and supporting this effort, and to her children, she will go and get those birthday presents now. Additionally, Patricia Barbanell would like to thank Mark Edelstein, her husband, who remains, as always, one of the "Good Guys."

Section I
What is K–12 Videoconferencing?

Chapter I
Videoconferencing and the K–12 Classroom:
What is it? and Why do it?

Dianna L. Newman
University at Albany/SUNY, USA

ABSTRACT

This chapter introduces the concept of videoconferencing in K-12 education by providing an overview of what it is and why it should be used. Key terms are defined, and an overview of benefits to uses are presented. When discussing "What is videoconferencing?", six types of videoconferences which are frequently found in K-12 educational settings are described, and the key roles of stakeholders are introduced. These six types include: point-to-point or provider-classroom videoconferencing; collaborative classroom videoconferencing; multi-point videoconferencing; mass audience or electronic field trips videoconferencing; homebound videoconferencing; and one-to-one videoconferencing. Potential benefits of each type are also presented. Following this discussion, the author discusses "Why do it?" by addressing, in lay language, the results of multiple studies that have documented the benefits of K-12 videoconferencing from the points of view of teachers, students, and providers.

INTRODUCTION

The impact of technology and technology-supported curriculum and instruction is an area of increased interest for educators, providers, and funders. It is estimated that approximately six billion dollars have been invested in providing K-12 buildings with technology in the past decade (Ringstaff & Kelley, 2002). One of the most interactive modes of online learning is videoconferencing. Unlike other forms of technology-based instruction, videoconferencing requires the participants' real-time physical presence to communicate with learners at distant sites. Videoconferencing has been defined as "a live connection between people in separate locations for the purpose of communication, usually involving audio and often text as well as video" (Tufts University, Educational Media Center, n.d., Glossary). As noted by Bose and DeAngelo (see Chapter XI in this volume), this method of videoconferencing is possible in most K-12 schools with varying technological complexity; schools need only a modern computer, a communication connection, a video camera, and videoconferencing software. As a result, classrooms are able to become part of active online learning communities, allowing all students to benefit from a mutual learning context (Menlove, Hansford, & Lignugaris-Kraft, 2000). Proponents of the medium believe that using videoconferencing in the classroom community has many advantages; most notably, these include its capacity to import external resources to the classroom and its ability to accommodate communities of diverse learning styles (Motamedi, 2001). In fact, many state that, when combined with well-planned instruction, it is the combination of synchronous, visual, interactive elements supported by videoconferencing that is the real key to its success (Greenberg, 2004; Omatseye, 1996).

WHAT IS K-12 VIDEOCONFERENCING?

Several major types of videoconferencing communities may be found in K-12 educational settings: These include point-to-point or provider-classroom videoconferencing; collaborative classroom videoconferencing; multi-point videoconferencing, electronic field trips; support for homebound students; and one-to-one support. Each of these types of videoconferencing has unique user characteristics and patterns of interaction that reflect variations in goals, participants, and outcomes. Following is a brief discussion of each[1] that will allow potential users to become oriented to the field. A summary of their characteristics and uses is presented in Table 1.

Point-to-Point or Provider-Classroom Videoconferencing

In *point-to-point* or *provider-classroom* videoconferencing, an external expert or *provider* communicates directly with a classroom of students via videoconferencing modalities. The goal of the communication is to allow students to have access to resources that normally would not be available in a school setting, but to do it in a way that allows for synchronous provider-student interactions and direct sharing of information. Newman, Barbanell, and Falco (2006) note several benefits of provider-classroom videoconferencing: It promotes equal access to resources and increases the quality of educational opportunity for learners in remote or economically-disadvantaged schools; it allows access to subject matter experts and career role models for students across gender, ethnic, and racial divisions; it eliminates security issues related to travel; and it overcomes time and budgetary constraints typically associated with off-site field trips.

Provider organizations that support these virtual field trips (VFTs) may consist of museums, zoos, historical sites, scientific organizations, government officials, and so forth; the presenter may be a member of the educational staff of the organization, a single expert in the field, a group of program sponsors, or others who have unique information that can be shared with a group of students through visual and auditory interactions. Providers sponsored by distance education programs, such as those at museums, art institutes, or zoos, usually have a series of replicable but adaptable curriculum units based on their internal archives, areas of expertise, and mission. In many cases, these curriculum units have been developed with the assistance of K-12 educators to ensure that they meet state and/or national standards. As a result, teachers may easily integrate these external provider-based videoconferences into their instructional practices in ways that can support

Table 1. Videoconferencing in educational settings: An overview of key characteristics

Provider-Based Point-to-Point Videoconferencing

Description: An external expert or provider videoconferences directly with a single classroom of students.

Participants and Their Roles

    Provider: serves as an external expert; helps the teacher bring outside resources into the classroom; depending on the type of conference, students' role may range from passive to very active; and the teacher serves as facilitator of the process and is responsible for helping the provider embed the videoconference into current instruction and curriculum.

Types

    Provider-Centered: The provider controls the flow and use of content; students are recipients of knowledge;

    Provider-Guided Inquiry: Through pre-developed kits or exercises, the provider helps students reach pre-set goals; students are guided to knowledge; and

    Student-Centered: The provider and teacher facilitate students in developing their own knowledge; they serve as resources while students actively engage in project work.

Value-Added Outcomes: Inclusion of external resources; facts become "alive"; equity of access; enhanced motivation for learning; less expensive than real field trips; and limited security issues.

Examples: A second-grade classroom visits a bird sanctuary and learns about climates and weather; a sixth-grade classroom visits a historical museum, sees material related to WWII, and presents papers on how it impacted their family history; a high-school class views a major art museum and works with the provider to translate art into mathematics.

Collaborative Classroom Videoconferencing

Description: Two geographically-distanced classrooms share resources, curriculum, and activities via videoconferencing.

Participants and Their Roles

    Students serve as the main participants in the process as both providers and receivers of information; teachers serve as facilitators of the process, being coordinators, co-instructors, and co-receivers of the students' input.

Types

    Students-to-Students: Students, generally of equal ability, share the same curriculum and goals

    Tutoring: Students of different grade levels and/or different ability levels work with each other to enhance advanced and basic skills

    Students with Special Needs: Students with unique needs in inclusion and self-contained classrooms work with those of like needs to enhance academic, social, and behavioral skills

    After-School: At-risk students receive, via videoconferencing, additional assistance in academic, social, and cultural goals through tutoring, interactions with outside experts, and collaborative exchanges

Value-Added Outcomes: Increased verbal skills; increased exposure to diversity and other cultures; improved peer interactions; and access to other teachers and building experts.

Continued on following page

Table 1. continued

Examples: Two seventh-grade classrooms collaboratively study and share science projects by pairing students across the classrooms; a group of advanced eighth-grade students tutor a group of fifth-grade students on multiplication of fractions; children who are hearing-impaired in two different settings videoconference their math work with each other; children with English Language Arts problems in an urban setting videoconference as part of their after-school program with children in another city.
Multi-Point Videoconferencing
Description: Three or more sites videoconferencing synchronously
Participants and Their Roles: Provider serves as external expert; students serve as receivers, presenters, or collaborators; teachers serve as classroom managers, facilitators, co-teachers, presenters, or responders.
Types
Multi-Point Provider: One provider communicating with two or more interactive classrooms sharing and facilitating the use of resources at all sites; provider may have multiple interactions together or separately with the classrooms
Multi-Point Collaborative Classroom: Three or more groups of students at different sites are simultaneously sharing information with each other or viewing each other's resources.
Value-Added Outcomes: Increased oral and problem solving opportunities; increased access to diversity; greater opportunity to share resources.
Example: A zoo educator videoconferences with two classrooms, presenting information on animals that live in the rainforest; students then work on projects with the provider and share those projects with the provider and with each other; students in schools in Pennsylvania, North Carolina, and Israel practice speaking Hebrew with each other on a weekly basis.
Electronic Field Trips
Description: An expert provider simultaneously broadcasts to multiple sites for a limited amount of time and for a limited number of times; this is a provider-centered approach necessitated by the material/content.
Participants and Their Roles: The external provider offers unique external expert(s) whose appearance allows for a "one-time only" experience, assisting the teacher in translating information to classroom needs; students serve as receivers of information, with limited opportunity for questioning; the teacher has complete control of tying videoconference to curriculum, classroom management during the videoconference, but no part in teaching during the videoconference; in some settings, a select group of teachers may work with the provider before the videoconference to ensure a fit between standards, classroom language, and provider goals.
Value-Added Outcomes: Allows students the opportunity to experience a unique opportunity that otherwise, because of cost or lack of availability, could not be experienced.
Example: The Holocaust Museum gathers a group of survivors together to discuss what childhood was like in concentration camps; a major science museum takes children to an underwater reef where they explore plant life.

Continued on following page

Table 1. continued

Homebound
Description: Students who are unable to access the traditional school building participate, via videoconferencing, with teachers, classmates, and external providers from their home setting.
Participants and Their Roles: Teachers' roles can range from that of a tutor to a regular classroom instructor; the home-bound student is both a receiver and communicator of instruction and learning; depending on the duration of the setting, the student may have more frequent interactions of longer duration; in long-term situations, classroom students become collaborative learners, tutors, and co-receivers of instruction.
Value-Added Outcomes: Students deprived of teacher and student interactions receive oral and visual synchronous learning opportunities; less expensive than on-site tutoring; facilitates inclusion and assists in meeting short-term and long-term needs of special students.
Example: Students with short-term physical disabilities continue to be involved in their classroom activities and main-tain their academic progress; students with long-term immune deficiencies become and stay part of a cohort of learners, increasing their opportunities to be involved with peers and experience outside events.
One-to-One Connections
Description: Students, either on- or off-site who need one-to-one access to experts within the school system or at other sites; on-site settings serve students in advanced learning, independent study, or individual learning settings; off-site use serves a mobile population or those who are isolated from the school's internal experts.
Participants and Their Roles: Students are recipients of special services that help meet their individual social, academic, and career needs; educators and external providers serve as facilitators of learning and student decision-making; parents serve as corecipients of information.
Value-Added Outcomes: Increased access to external resources for advanced students at a lower cost; early inclusion in school for students who are relocating, resulting in increased academic performance and less social stress; in-creased access to community members assisting the district in providing diversity and community involvement.
Examples: A student studying psychology of the child can interview and interact with a specialist at a university set-ting; children of military families who will be relocating into a community can begin the academic year with the rest of their class; parents and children can "visit" potential colleges asking specific questions about majors and talking to faculty; community members can regularly "meet" with students whom they are mentoring, helping to keep them enrolled in school.

their traditional curriculum. Newman (2005a) found that provider-based videoconferencing could be used to support classroom instruction in several ways, including as an advanced orga-nizer, for enrichment of regular instruction, for exposure to primary resources, and as summary overviews.

When investigating the relationship between provider roles, provider-student interactions, and perceived outcomes of the videoconferencing experience, Newman and Goodwin-Segal (2003) and Newman (2005a) found three dominant modes of point-to-point provider-classroom videoconfer-encing. The first, which they labeled *provider-centered*, is currently the most frequently used

Vignette 1.

Barbara, a seventh grade science teacher, brought 2 one-hour videoconferences to her class from a variety of content providers, including the Smithsonian Environmental Research Center (SERC) and Mote Marine Laboratory, a nonprofit research organization located in Florida. She prepared her students for the videoconferences by using pre-conference materials, and required her students to research the topics to be presented and write down specific questions to ask the content providers prior to the videoconferences. During the videoconferences, the providers showed the students video clips, educated them about different types of sea creatures and their natural habitats, discussed what steps should be taken to help protect marine animals, and engaged students in an interactive game that required them to answer questions about what they had just learned. Barbara explained that she takes the role of the classroom manager if needed (i.e., reminding the students of videoconferencing etiquette or engaging in classroom management and discipline); however, students generally were so engaged that it was unnecessary for her to intervene during the videoconferences. Barbara noted that students perceived the videoconferences to be "an authentic source of information," and that they were excited to hear expert perspectives on the topics. In Barbara's words, "videoconferencing definitely has helped me enhance my teaching."

and reflects many of the components of a teacher-centered classroom. In this type of point-to-point videoconferencing, the provider directs the flow of content and communication. While the delivery is "live", the majority of the students are passive recipients; only a few are involved in asking and answering questions, and there is limited, if any, student activity other than listening and viewing archival materials. The role of the teacher in this scenario tends to be that of classroom manager and technology monitor. The second type of provider-based point-to-point videoconferencing which was identified was labeled *provider-guided inquiry*. In this scenario, students might passively receive information from a provider for the first part of the program, and then participate in a follow-up exercise led by the provider and supported by the on-site teacher. Using kits sent by the provider or materials prepared by the teacher according to provider directions, students are led through a series of predetermined activities by the external expert, who oversees their work, corrects their mistakes, and lead them to the desired outcome. Students are allowed to ask and answer questions about the assigned tasks and

to discuss the topics with other students while they are following directions and working toward the set outcomes. The role of the teacher in an inquiry-based videoconference expands to that of a task monitor and guide as well as classroom manager.

The final type of point-to-point provider-classroom videoconference identified by Newman and Goodwin-Segal (2003) is *student-centered* and reflects the most hands-on interactive learning; it is also the most difficult but most rewarding in terms of student learning. During student-centered videoconferencing, students are actively involved in solving a problem with the presenter, in designing or making something, or in participating in a teacher-led activity to which the provider is responding and/or serving as an expert aide. This type of videoconference reflects a constructivist classroom setting that has been enhanced to include an outside expert who helps with hands-on problem-solving. While the videoconference is in progress, students are asking and answering questions of each other, the teacher, and the provider. The provider and teacher allow students to make mistakes, respond to student-suggested solutions to problems, and involve all students in developing scenarios, generating hypotheses, and solving problems. The role of the teacher is that of a co-instructor who helps encourage all students to question the provider, other students' work, and their own work. To an outside observer, it may appear that "reality television" has come to the classroom. In terms of access to an external expert, that perception is true; in a student-centered videoconference, one can truly see students interacting with an outside expert as they generate knowledge, share information, and gain in-depth skills in questioning and problem-solving.

Collaborative Classroom Videoconferencing

A second type of K-12 videoconferencing incorporates the concept of collaborative classrooms. The overall goal of a collaborative classroom is to engage students in the process of instruction and assessment, thereby modeling and supporting higher-level thinking and problem-solving (Jonassen, 2002); evidence suggests that this interaction results in greater satisfaction with learning, higher levels of thinking, greater retention, improved oral skills, and more self-responsibility for learning (Davis, 1993; Totten, Sills, Digby, & Russ, 1991; Woolfolk, 2004). In *collaborative classroom videoconferencing,* two classrooms, at geographically-distanced sites, use videoconferencing technology as a means of accessing, sharing, and transmitting information between each other. Collaboration is no longer just within the classroom; it is now synchronous across two distant classroom communities who are sharing instruction, resources, and assessment (Newman, 2005). Four major types of collaborative classroom videoconferencing have been identified as successful within K-12 settings; each serves a distinct group of users and has unique characteristics.

Student-to-student collaborative videoconferencing is utilized when two classrooms or groups of students geographically distanced use videoconferencing as part of their regular instructional process; the goal is to share instructional and learning opportunities across classrooms that are studying similar content, usually with learners who are similar in ability level and grade placement. Students accrue multiple benefits from this type of videoconferencing: They are more motivated to learn the material; they increase their verbal and presentation skills; they are involved more frequently in problem-solving and higher-level thinking; and, if culturally-diverse groups are involved, they see facts through others' interpretations, becoming more aware of global similarities and differences. Newman (2004) found that teachers also benefited from the opportunities to compare and enhance their curriculum offerings and frequently replicated the process over several semesters and academic years. The second type of collaborative videoconference, *tutoring collaborations,* reflects synchronous, visual, and audio sharing of information among students across grade and ability barriers. In these settings, students who are more advanced or at a higher ability level collaborate, via videoconferencing, with students who are learning more basic concepts. Advantages have been found for both groups: Advanced students have the opportunity to review, enlarge, and enhance their knowledge base as they select and develop methods of sharing knowledge; students who are gaining basic knowledge are more motivated to learn the material and see it as more relevant because it is presented by other students. Without the use of videoconferencing, formation of interactive tutoring sessions would require either the use of student groups within the same building, which might result in potential student stereotyping, or transportation of one or both groups to another site, resulting in increased costs and loss of learning time.

The third type of collaborative classroom is now assisting many K-12 districts in serving students with special needs. In *special needs collaborations,* geographically-distanced groups are formed to support the academic, social, physical, and emotional needs of students who are in inclusion and self-contained classrooms. These groups of learners may be composed of students who have similar needs and ability levels; through videoconferencing, these students can now work together to master skills and knowledge under the guidance of either teachers or advanced students. By using videoconferencing, students can access resources, sometimes for the first time or on a more regular basis, than is otherwise possible. Specialists can reach more students; students have more opportunities to learn and rehearse skills by working with others with similar disabilities; and students' boundaries are expanded to encompass more real-life experiences.

The fourth type of collaborative videoconferencing, *after-school collaboration*, builds on the success of special needs collaborations and No Child Left Behind (NCLB) mandates for after-school remediation to support at-risk students. After-school programs frequently serve students and families who are in need of additional academic support, social assistance, or who have limited access to cultural experiences. Multiple types of videoconferencing experiences can be formed in these settings to meet these needs, including student-to-student, tutorial, and special needs/ability level groupings. Through the use of videoconferencing, schools can help these students eliminate geographical and structural boundaries that have limited their interactions with other students and curtailed their learning opportunities.

Multi-Point Videoconferencing

Multi-point videoconferencing expands classroom videoconferencing to three or more sites. Participant groups may be all students, or a combination of students and content providers. Variations in the types of participants, the order and timing of the videoconferences within curriculum units, and the depth and breadth of participant involvement

make almost every multi-point videoconference a unique experience. Newman, Barbanell, and Falco (2006) identify two major categories of these types of experiences: *multi-point provider-classroom videoconferencing* and *multi-point collaborative classroom videoconferencing*. In the former, point-to-point videoconferencing is expanded so that a provider simultaneously works with two or three classrooms, sharing not only the organization's resources but also facilitating the sharing of resources among and across the distanced classrooms. This process works best when students of equivalent ability level are studying similar material. The role of the provider varies; in some settings, artifacts and discussions may serve as advance organizers, while in others, the provider may guide both groups in sharing their thoughts, theories, or products across classrooms as well as with the provider. In multi-point collaborative classroom communities, three or more classrooms of students are simultaneously sharing information, resources, and student-generated products under the guidance of the teacher; each classroom serves as both provider and audience to other classrooms. This model can be used successfully among students studying the same content and in tutorial settings. Newman and her colleagues (Newman, 2005a, 2005b; Newman, Barbanell, & Falco, 2006) have noted several successful methods of adapting these models to individual settings.

Electronic Field Trips

A fourth type of videoconferencing, termed an *electronic field trip* or *EFT,* represents an extreme variation of videoconferencing. This method is less frequent in occurrence than multi-point or collaborative classrooms, but is equally important in broadening students' access to external and rare resources. Most providers have some unique resources or archives that can only be accessed for a limited time period (e.g., NASA satellite launches, explorations of wetlands, special viewings of Egyptian artifacts, or gatherings of World War II Veterans). As a result, there is a need to increase access to as wide an audience as is possible while maintaining at least some interactivity with the receiving communities. By using videoconferencing technologies, a provider can broadcast simultaneously to a large number of classrooms at a preset time; these broadcasts are more structured than point-to-point and collaborative interactions and are presented only a few times. Some may only be available once in a lifetime. By nature provider-centered, these videoconferences do allow for some student questioning via small selective samples of on-site students or phone or email contacts. These questions and answers, though limited, help to transfer the content and information to the language of students and the classroom. Studies have shown that a key benefit of K-12 students' participation in EFTs was their exposure to "real" people and events, which helped to connect facts to people and occurrences; this resulted in not only more interest and retention of information but also in more transfer of knowledge to other settings

(Newman, 2003; Newman, Catapano, & Spaulding, 2002; Worthington & Ellefson, n.d.)

Homebound Videoconferencing

A special use of videoconferencing is support for homebound students. *Homebound videoconferencing* builds on collaborative classroom and special needs models. Due to unique circumstances and special needs, some students in K-12 settings are unable to access even the traditional classroom setting and their local district's experts and specialists. By using videoconferencing technologies located in the school and in their home, these students can interact with their peers, their teachers, and outside experts on a regular basis. In situations where the separation from the traditional classroom is short in duration, continued access to and involvement with regular curriculum and instruction allows the student to keep up with the class and alleviates remediation frequently needed when students return. In these settings, the technology used for communication may be on the "low end", making use of computers and

Table 2. Support for learning standards and standards-based assessment

Statement:	% Agree
Videoconferencing supports standards-based performance indicators.	78
Videoconferencing assists students in preparing for standardized assessments.	45
Videoconferencing improves student performance on standardized assessments.	44

Table 3. Support for inquiry-based outcomes

Statement:	% Agree
Videoconferencing supports direct instructional practices.	82
Videoconferencing supports inquiry-based learning.	84
Videoconferencing supports student generation of questions and analysis of solutions.	81
Videoconferencing supports students in reflecting on their learning.	71
Videoconferencing assists students in organizing information.	63
Videoconferencing helps students analyze and solve problems more effectively.	66

webcams, supported by email and Internet resources. When the separation from the classroom is of longer or of permanent duration, the use of videoconferencing between the school setting and the home becomes even more crucial, in that it provides not only academic support but also social and emotional bridges for students who are homebound. In these long-term settings, students' only opportunities to interact in a synchronous visual manner on a regular basis, with peers of their age group or with those with similar issues or interests, may be through videoconferencing. Currently, homebound videoconferencing support in these long-term settings is based primarily on teacher-student interactions that occur on a daily or weekly schedule, supported where possible by as-needed peer-to-student, expert-to-student, and specialist-to-student interactions. As videoconferencing becomes more common, however, and teachers and students become more fluent in its use, these interactions are beginning to include continuous whole-class videoconferencing, where the student is present via technology through the entire instructional sequence, including group activities, and through multi-point connections, takes part in provider-classroom activities as well.

One-to-One Connections

The use of videoconferencing to support one-to-one connections is also important in K-12 education. While homebound support addresses the special communication and access needs of students who cannot come to the classroom, schools are now finding that through videoconferencing, they have a new way to serve students who need access to special resources via *one-to-one connections* or conversations. These connections are now being used to serve two types of students—those *off-site* and those *on-site*. Situations where the student is off-site and may need access to the school and its resources might include migrant family mobility, military family relocations, rural isolation, and parent-choice home schooling. Other situations may represent uses where the student is on-site, that is, at the school building, but needs access to special experts or resources to aid in independent or individualized work. This could include access to a scientist, special archives, an author, or a business specialist. In addition, many districts are now finding one-to-one videoconferencing to be an effective and fiscally-responsible means of supporting increased access to local community members as part of service projects, more frequent mentor-mentee contacts for disadvantaged students, preliminary college recruitment for students and parents, and extended language and cultural exchanges that support building a global identify.

WHY DO VIDEOCONFERENCING?

The integration of videoconferencing into K-12 education requires changes to the system, changes

Table 4. Support for underlying educational principles

Statement	% Agree
Videoconferencing helps students build skills that transfer to multiple settings.	79
Videoconferencing helps students develop attitudes of self-direction and responsibility.	67
Videoconferencing allows for the development of individual strengths, talents, and abilities.	70
Videoconferencing increases student motivation.	87

Table 5. Student perceptions of videoconferencing

Questions about the broadcast:	% Agree
The program was interesting to me.	92
The program was easy to understand.	94
I learned a lot from the program.	88
I would like to learn more about what I saw or learned during the program.	79
I learned more about the topic through the program than I would have in an ordinary class.	78
The topic of the program fit in with what I am learning in school right now.	81
The program made me more interested in the topic.	78

that will require both districts and providers to reconsider polices and procedures pertaining to use of external resources, the importance and degree of technological resources they must make available, the curriculum and instructional philosophies which they chose to advocate, and their expectations of students and what they believe an educated citizen should be. If these changes are to occur, it is necessary to begin a discussion of "Why should we videoconference?", as well as to validate the expected outcomes presented in the prior section with responses of those in the field. The following section provides a brief overview of teacher, student, and provider perceptions of the impact of videoconferencing based on surveys, interviews, observations, and comparison-group studies reported by Newman (2005a). Additional support is provided by Barbanell (see chapter XVIII), Martin (see chapter XIX), and Newman (see chapter XVII) in this volume.

Videoconferencing and Student Learning

Triangulated results of several studies conducted by Newman (2005a, 2005b; Newman, Gilgora, King, & Guckemus, 2005) indicate that use of integrated, standards-based videoconferencing embedded within regular classroom use does have an impact on student learning. As noted in Table 2, when queried after multiple uses, the

majority of teachers consistently indicated that videoconferencing assisted in instruction by supporting standards-based performance indicators. In addition, approximately half of all teachers agreed that it helped with performance-based assessment, noting that videoconferencing assisted students in preparing for assessments and, more importantly, improved student performance on these assessment measures. Interviews with teachers indicated that the most successful use of videoconferencing, in terms of support for standards-based learning, occurred when providers had clear indicators of what standards teachers needed to be addressed by a particular program, and when providers and teachers communicated before the videoconference on how the program was being used to supplement the curriculum.

Similar findings were noted when teachers were queried over time about the ability of videoconferencing to support student outcomes related to inquiry-based learning (see Table 3). Over two-thirds of the teachers agreed that videoconferencing had resulted in higher levels of problem-solving, and high levels of discussion and questioning; it also helped students reflect on multiple sources of information, yielding more internal organization of data as well as a greater ability to analyze and solve problems. Observers noted that during videoconferencing students tended to ask higher levels of questions (based on Bloom's taxonomy) than during regular

Table 6. Support for reform movements

Reform movement supported by videoconferencing:	% Agree
Inquiry-based learning: Videoconferencing facilitates the integration of active learning and inquiry teaching within lessons and promotes literacy critical thinking, and inquiry and analytical skills.	77
Alignment of curriculum and instruction with standards: The concepts presented and activities advocated by videoconferencing are aligned with state and national standards.	83
Expanded use of resources: Videoconferencing expands teachers' resources for curriculum development and instruction.	75
Improved student achievement: Videoconferencing has the potential to increase student achievement in academic areas.	77
Reasons for the support:	
Implementing videoconferencing has had a positive impact on my students' learning.	72
I believe there is a definite need for educators to integrate videoconferencing into curriculum design and instruction.	69
I welcome opportunities to use videoconferencing as a catalyst for changing curriculum design and instruction.	81

Table 7. Student activities during videoconferencing that support reform movements: Guided inquiry and constructivist learning

Activity	Presenter Guided	Presenter Teacher Guided	Student Centered	% Agree
Watching the program	***	***	***	93
Answering questions	**	*	***	62
Asking questions	**	***	***	58
Participating in an activity with the presenter(s)		***		51
Discussing the topic with others	*	*	***	33

Continued on following page

Table 7. continued

Participating in an activity with my teacher(s)		**	**	26
Working in a group	*		***	24
Solving a problem with the presenter			**	23
Working independently				18
Talking with my friends	*		**	15
Taking notes			**	14
Designing or making something			***	14
Solving a problem with my teacher				11
Writing about the topic				10
Doing things not related to the program				8
Working on an experiment				9
Working on other homework				3

Table 8. Student involvement in reform movements: Collaborative and cooperative learning

Type of Interaction	% Participation
Worked alone	40
Worked with my teacher	47
Worked with a partner	23
Worked with a small group	31
Worked with my whole class	43

classroom discussions, and that when providers involved students in observation and reflection, students became more attentive and engaged. This was particularly true in settings where the provider led students in conducting hands-on activities in the classroom during the videoconference. During interviews, teachers supported the importance of this involvement, noting that inquiry-based learning was now considered an important student outcome and that they wanted

more videoconferences that would support this type of learning.

As a follow-up to these findings, teachers noted that the use of videoconferencing supported several underlying educational principles (see Table 4). At least two-thirds of all teachers who used videoconferencing noted that it helped students to transfer knowledge and to develop lifelong learning skills such as self-direction and responsibility, aided in creating the underlying positive effect needed for continued learning, and helped to meet the individual needs of students. During interviews, teachers noted that videoconferencing was a mode of instruction that could be utilized by students of all ability levels and that, if possible, they would prefer to discuss their students' strengths and weaknesses with the provider ahead of the broadcast. Providers supported this desire, noting that they could and would adapt their material to meet specific needs. Observations of repeated videoconferences by the researcher indicated that providers who were student-centered were easily able to make these adaptations and perceived the benefit of doing so both for the student and for their organization.

As noted in Table 5, self-reported outcomes from students supported the findings reported from teachers. Almost all students reported positive outcomes from involvement, both in terms of effect and learning. Most noted that the program was interesting, that it made them more interested in learning about the topic as it was presented, and also that it made them more interested in learning more. Similarly, they reported that because of videoconferencing, the material was easier to understand, that they learned from the program, and that they would like to learn more. The majority of students also perceived the videoconference

as supporting instruction, noting that it fit into what their teacher was covering in the classroom. Observations by researchers noted that, when the latter finding was not supported by students, the purpose of the videoconference tended to be more of a reward or "fun" experience, but that when teachers took the time to integrate the broadcast both before and after use, students were able to transfer the knowledge to on-site instruction.

The findings from these studies are further supported by a series of studies conducted by Newman (see Chapter XVII in this volume), which investigated the impact of videoconferencing on student achievement via a series of quasi-experimental comparison group studies. In each of these studies, similar standards-based curriculum was provided to two groups of students; however, one group of students received part of the material via videoconferencing, while the other group received parallel material via the teacher. All students in each study received the same teacher-developed assessment at the end of the unit. Results indicated that students who received interactive videoconferencing as part of instruction had greater interest and retention and tended to receive higher scores on the assessment measure than did students who received the traditional on-site only material.

Table 9. Impact of videoconferencing on providers

Provider Reported Benefits Resulting from Videoconferencing
Enhanced mission statement
Global outreach
Inclusion of previously-inaccessible audiences
Reduced travel time
Increased use of needs assessments
Identification of new uses for resources and archives
Development of new curriculum that stays current with K-12 needs

Videoconferencing and Educational Practices

A major concern of educational administrators and teachers who have been practicing for multiple years is the ability of a new initiative to support mandated reform movements. All programming, but especially new approaches, require a shift in resources, and that shift must be weighed against external demands and availability. As a result, a second question that should be addressed is, "Does the use of videoconferencing benefit schools' need to meet selected educational reform initiatives, and if so, what kinds of videoconferencing would best facilitate this need?"

Four major reform efforts were studied as part of Newman's effort to document the effects of videoconferencing; these included: inquiry-based learning, alignment of curriculum and instruction with standards-based learning, an expanded use of divergent resources, and the improvement of student achievement. Presented in Table 6 is a summary of selected findings, reported by teachers who had used videoconferencing, for each of these initiatives (Newman, 2004, 2005a, 2005b). Data indicate that teachers who have used videoconferencing perceive that it does support major initiatives, especially the use of expanded resources. Also of note are teachers' perceptions pertaining to videoconferencing's support of two NCLB initiatives, improved student achievement, and inquiry-based learning. When queried as to why they perceived this support, over half of the teachers noted the presence of specific outcomes related to student learning, and the majority noted videoconferencing's impact on changing curriculum and instructional design. These findings were supported during interviews with teachers who noted that, as a result of training in videoconferencing and its subsequent use, they had redesigned specific curriculum units to include more resources, greater differentiated instruction, and more hands-on and problem-solving activities.

When student data were analyzed in a manner similar to that presented by Newman and Goodwin-Segal (2003), findings supported the use of student-centered videoconferences with outside experts and the use of student-centered activities within those videoconferences. As noted in Table 7, approximately 60% of the students participating in successful videoconferences reported that they were involved in programs that assisted in building advanced problem-solving skills, reflective thinking, and improved questioning. This finding is supported by student-to-student interactions documented by independent observations that are reported in Table 8.

Benefits to Providers

If providers are to make major investments in videoconferencing, they also must perceive benefits to their organization and to their mission (see Table 9). Barbanell, Newman, and Falco (2003) indicate that these can include enhanced educational offerings, increased awareness of current audience needs, and more frequent use of archives. These findings are supported by Newman (2005b) who, as a result of intensive case studies and interviews with providers, identified several major outcomes of building videoconferencing capacity on the part of providers. Providers reported that working with videoconferencing helped them to reinforce, enhance, and expand their mission statements. This included promoting content-based literacy and fostering advanced knowledge in their fields of expertise. Videoconferencing with K-12 classrooms also expanded their existing distance learning programs to reach audiences beyond their local geographical area, allowing them to go "global" and work with children from many different states and countries. While many had been doing some of this work via mailed kits and online offerings, the use of interactive videoconferencing allowed them to utilize real archives and expand the coverage of special topics that had previously been labeled "non-transportable". Providers also expressed satisfaction with the development of ongoing relationships with receiving teachers and buildings. The increased understanding that they gained of the needs of the current educational community, especially the role of state and national standards, helped them to improve not only their videoconferencing curriculum units, but also their on-site programs. Many reported that they now use more constructivist approaches in their gallery and on-site visits, and are receiving more positive feedback from on-site field trips and more requests for follow-up assistance and information. Providers also noted that the continued use of videoconferencing improved their presentation skills; having to adapt to the demands of videoconferencing (e.g., time-delays for student responses, the inclusion of children with different ability levels, from different backgrounds, and with different cultural values) helped them to broaden their skills and to be more receptive of and responsive to all visitors' needs.

CONCLUSION

As this chapter indicates, videoconferencing is now a growing part of the K-12 education landscape. Both schools and providers have begun to implement the process; major methods and approaches have been developed and piloted, and are now being used in a increasing number of buildings and settings. Educational leaders have begun to recognize the unique potential of this form of technology and the associated benefits in terms of expanded access to external resources, support for meeting current state and national standards, and alternative ways of improving academic performance in problem-solving and higher-level thinking. Equally important, educators are seeing the use of videoconferencing as a way to support the development of a global society, decreasing digital and cultural divides, and supporting active, student-centered learning

environments. Many provider agencies also are examining the potential of videoconferencing as a way of enhancing their outreach to distant audiences and of supporting and sharing their collections of resources and archives with young audiences.

As these needs and uses grow, many of the key stakeholders—providers, teachers, administrators, and teacher-preparation faculty—are requesting information on how they can prepare themselves and their organization to meet this new demand. Providers want information on how to do videoconferencing and its benefits to their organizations; educators want information on the roles of teachers and how to build the necessary infrastructure that will support the instructional process; teacher-preparation units want information on how to prepare the next generation for this new tool and how it can better help them to bridge the gap between theory and practice; all three groups need evidence that will help them make and support their decision to be involved. The following chapters provide the readers with core knowledge and examples in those areas.

REFERENCES

Abrahamson, C. (1998). Issues in interactive communications in distance education. *College Student Journal, 32*(1), 33-43.

Barbanell, P., Newman, D. L., & Falco, J. (2003, March). *New vision, new realities: Methodology and mission in developing interactive videoconferencing programming.* Paper presented at the Museums and the Web Annual Conference, Charlotte, NC.

Davis, B. G. (1993). *Tools for teaching.* San Francisco: Jossey-Bass.

Gokhale, A. A. (1995). Collaborative learning enhances critical thinking. *Journal of Technology Education, 7,* 1045-1064.

Greenberg, A. (2004, February). Navigating the sea of research on videoconferencing-based distance education: A platform for understanding research into the technology's effectiveness and value. *Wainhouse Research.* Retrieved September 9, 2005, from http://www.wainhouse.com/files/papers/wr-navseadistedu.pdf

Jonassen, D. H. (2002). Engaging and supporting problem solving in online learning. *The Quarterly Review of Distance Education, 3,* 1-13.

Menlove, R., Hansford, D., & Lignugaris-Kraft, B. (2000). Creating a community of distance learners: Putting technology to work. *Conference Proceedings of the American Council on Rural Special Education (ACRES),* Alexandria, VA, (pp. 247-253).

Motamedi, V. (2001). A critical look at the use of videoconferencing in United States distance education. *HighBeam Research.* Retrieved on September 15, 2005, from http://www.highbeam.com

Newman, D. L. (2003). *The virtual informal education Web project: Formative evaluation of the Schenectady City School District technology innovation challenge grant* (Schenectady Component, Year 3 Report (2002-2003) - Tech. Rep.). Albany, NY: Evaluation Consortium University at Albany, SUNY.

Newman, D. L. (2004). *The virtual informal education web project: Formative evaluation of the Schenectady City School District technology innovation challenge grant* (New York Institute of Technology Component, Year 4 Report - Tech. Rep.). Albany, NY: Evaluation Consortium University at Albany, SUNY.

Newman, D. L. (2005a). *The virtual informal education web project: Formative evaluation of the Schenectady City School District technology innovation challenge grant* (Schenectady

Component, Year 5 Report - Tech. Rep.). Albany, NY: Evaluation Consortium University at Albany, SUNY.

Newman, D. L. (2005b). *Beyond the barriers: Benefits of K-12 teacher participation in collaborative classroom videoconferencing training.* A paper presented at the Annual Conference of the Society for Technology in Teacher Education (SITE), Phoenix, AZ.

Newman, D. L., Barbanell, P., & Falco, J. (2006). Videoconferencing communities: Documenting online face-to face user interactions. In N. Lambropoulos & P. Zaphiris (Eds.), *User-centered design of online learning communities* (pp. 122-140). Hershey, PA: Idea Group Publishing.

Newman, D. L., Catapano, N., & Spaulding, D. T. (2002). *The virtual informal education Web project: Formative evaluation of the Schenectady City School District technology innovation challenge grant* (Ball State Report, March, 2002—Tech. Rep.). Albany, NY: University at Albany/SUNY, Evaluation Consortium.

Newman, D. L., Gligora, M. A., King, J., & Guckemus, S. (2005, April). *Breaking down the classroom walls: The impact of external videoconferencing on children's cognition.* Paper presented at the annual meeting of the American Educational Research Association, Montreal, Canada.

Newman, D. L., & Goodwin-Segal, T. (2003). *Evaluation of a technology integration challenge grant program: Using technology to connect museums and classrooms.* A paper presented at the 2003 Annual Meeting of the American Educational Research Association, Chicago.

Omatseye, J. N. (1999). Teaching through tele-conferencing: Some curriculum challenges. *College Student Journal, 33*(3), 346-353.

Penn, M. (1998). Videoconferencing one-to-one but far from home. *Technology Connections, 5*(2), 22-23.

Ringstaff, C., & Kelley, L. (2002). The learning return on our educational technology investment. Retrieved April 8, 2004, from http://www.wested. org/online_pubs/learning_return.pdf

Silverman, S., & Silverman, G. (1999). The educational enterprise zone: Where knowledge comes from. *T H E Journal, 26, 56-57.*

Totten, S., Sills, T., Digby, A., & Russ, P. (1991). *Cooperative learning: A guide to research.* New York: Garland.

Tufts University, Educational Media Center (n.d.). Glossary. Retrieved September 15, 2005, from http://www.tufts.edu/orgs/edmedia/gloss.shtml

Woolfolk, A. (2004). *Educational psychology (9th ed.).* Boston: Pearson Education, Inc.

Worthington, V., & Ellefson, N. (n.d.). Electronic field trips: Theoretical rational. *LETSNet, Michigan State University.* Retrieved on September 15, 2005, from http://commtechlab.msu.edu/sites/ letsnet/noframes/bigideas/bl/blthor.html

ENDNOTE

[1] An in-depth discussion of the first four types of videoconferencing and supporting evidence may be found in Newman, Barbanell, and Falco (2006).

Section II
Bringing Providers to the Camera

Chapter II
Taking Videoconferencing to the Next Level:
Creating a Model for Museum Virtual Field Trips

Denice Blair Leach
Michigan State University Museum, USA

Kristine Morrissey
Michigan State University Museum, USA

Gel Alvarado
Michigan State University Museum, USA

ABSTRACT

The Virtual Outreach Program at the Michigan State University Museum progressed through three stages of videoconference program development while taking museum resources on the virtual "road." This chapter documents the shift from an experts-based model to one focused on learning content through object-based learning and dynamic inquiry in a collaborative community. Revisions in pedagogy, philosophy, and content are explored at each level and supported by the literature and best-practice standards that shaped these changes. Throughout, the museum virtual field trip is presented as a partnership between the classroom, museum experts, and distance-learning providers, working together to create meaningful virtual learning experiences for K-12 students.

INTRODUCTION

What do a mammoth tooth, a log cabin, and a dinosaur bone have in common? A lot, it seems, if you happen to find yourself at the Michigan State University Museum's (MSUM) Virtual Outreach Program (VOP). These objects are part of an effort to connect K-12 students with museum objects to enhance learning and creative thinking. In its first two-year phase, the Virtual Outreach Program served participants nationwide. During this time, the program evolved through different "levels" of videoconference field trip development and delivery, with the ultimate goal of aligning videoconference programs with the museum's educational philosophies and successful on-site programming, which encourages understanding, interpretation, and respect for natural and cultural diversity.

Prior to the inception of the Virtual Outreach Program, two limitations of the museum's education programs were geography and access. While the MSUM staff provided a wide variety of research-based programs for K-12 schools, sharing these programs with students and teachers who could not physically come to the museum was a challenge. There was a real difficulty in connecting educators with museum experts, especially in rural districts and the Upper Peninsula, where schools are often located too far from museums for traditional field trips. Similarly, urban schools often lack the resources to provide transportation to visit museums. When Michigan's Regional Educational Media Centers put out a call to the state's museums with an offer to provide equipment and work with them to develop electronic fieldtrips for the growing number of schools equipped for videoconferencing, the Museum's Education Division saw the opportunity to overcome the limitations of geography and take their guiding philosophy, which encourages students to learn through *creative expression, critical thinking,* and *personal connection,* on the virtual "road."

The possibilities for new audiences, the lure of technology, and school demand for outreach programs all affected the decision to pursue a distance learning program. As a result, in September, 2003, the Michigan State University Museum launched the Virtual Outreach Program, a distance education outreach using videoconferencing equipment and providing point-to-point programs called "virtual field trips." When a grant from the Institute of Museum and Library Services provided the support for strategic planning and creating the infrastructure necessary to do videoconferencing, general excitement and anticipation about the possibilities for bringing museum resources and experts into classrooms throughout Michigan and the nation began to grow.

This chapter describes the evolution of the Virtual Outreach Program's pedagogy and techniques, beginning with an experts-based presentation style and culminating with a current focus on learning content through presenting and practicing object-based learning and dynamic inquiry. The discussion reviews the three stages of programming, the rationale behind the changes in each stage, and the literature and best-practice standards that shaped these changes. Articulating these stages has provided a model to guide development, pushed our thinking and experimentation with technologies and with techniques, and encouraged us to continue evolving. While there is vast literature in formal and informal education and a growing literature in distance learning, the model we present attempts to define the intersection between the three fields, suggesting that museum-based virtual field trips can be most successful when drawing from all three fields. The chapter provides a platform for discussion between content providers and schools.

A FAST LEARNING CURVE

The Michigan State University Museum provides many different on-site and community-based programs for K-12 audiences. Typical of many museums, these programs range from single on-site visits to multiple visit immersion and off-site programs. The initial intention was to expand the current programming into virtual versions. It seemed natural to take what was already succeeding and adapt it for a virtual audience. Two of the most popular expert-based programs for on-site visitors were a dinosaur program and another about the fossil record in Michigan. Guided by the MSUM's educational philosophy as a university museum, these programs were reshaped as virtual field trips to give distant classrooms access to collections and experts. The dinosaur program engaged students in a dialogue related to the ways in which scientists learn about dinosaurs by examining fossils, and the Michigan fossils program allowed students to talk with a paleontologist about the various geological ages that affected the types of fossils found in the state.

In this first stage, or level, of providing videoconferencing programs, the technology promised to introduce a new edge to our existing programs, making them not only accessible but also unique. Students were excited about the chance to interact with real scientists, and the VOP staff was equally enthusiastic about the ease of bringing experts and museum objects into the distant classrooms. We quickly realized, however, that the technology also shaped the presentation, and not always in desirable ways. The technical structure of videoconferencing threatened to coerce presenters into a traditional lecture style eschewed for in-house programs. Standing in one position in front of the camera reinforced the role of the presenter as the focus of the program, in charge of the interaction. The audience was positioned on the other side, watching and occasionally asking questions, a style contrary to any definition of interactive learning and not what we aimed for in our on-site programs. The technology flattened both our images and our interactions, and students on the other end of the connection were sometimes observed slipping into what one presenter called a "TV-watching mode." While the use of camera close-ups and other multimedia enriched the program content beyond what the on-site programs contained, the additional value of the multimedia only minimally compensated

for what was missing in not being physically present with the audience. Elements of context, sensory perception, and dimensionality were compromised. We had not broken the technology barrier, and distance learning felt truly distant.

Recognizing the limitation of these initial forays into virtual education, the need to expand the project by raising it to a new level of performance and expectation was clear. This first level of programs was characterized by the following:

- Content presented by experts
- Interaction characterized by question and answer at the end of the talk
- Objects used to illustrate content were not the in classroom but were with the expert
- One-time experience

When compared to the on-site museum programs, the virtual field trips seemed to lack at least two important components necessary for a truly interactive learning experience: dynamic presenter-student interaction, and integration into the ongoing learning environment through sustained connection between the classroom and the provider. During on-site programs, there is a more authentic dialogue, and presenters are more likely to use probing questions to assess prior knowledge and encourage inquiry. This process of dialogue promotes active learning, but it is also time-consuming. With too much information and objects to share with students in forty to forty-five minute blocks, there was little time committed to a learning dialogue. This made it difficult to determine students' understanding of content.

The other prime limitation of these initial efforts was that the virtual programs were conceived as one-time, stand-alone experiences. Although teachers could, and did, request the same program more than once, it was always for a new group of students. This precluded creating relationships between the presenter and students that would allow the classroom group to view the presenter as a class resource person. Without some fundamental changes in the programming, the virtual field trip experiences could not live up to our expectations.

BACK TO THE DRAWING BOARD

Based on what we learned from this assessment, we decided to go back to the drawing board. It was time to create a new vision that went beyond the initial goal of getting experts and objects into distant classrooms. Brainstorming and planning sessions with core Virtual Outreach Program staff began, with the goal of moving the programs to the level of exemplary learning experiences. The three main objectives of these sessions were to conduct a literature review, study other providers' programs as models, and ultimately, to revise our pedagogy and instructional technique to match our philosophy and learning goals.

In determining how to revise the program, we turned to the literature and best practices from the fields of classroom learning, museum education, and distance education. A successful virtual field trip required grounding in each of these fields, each acting as one of a triad of determinants that affect how programs are developed and eventually delivered. Each leg of the triangle must work in concert with the others to create meaningful virtual learning experiences for students.

The *level one* programming described above derived its strength from elements typical of museum education (one leg of the triangle), by using objects, providing authentic content expertise, and including at least a minimal level of inquiry as evidenced in the question-and-answer section for the programs. However, it drew only minimal guidance from classroom education and was missing almost entirely an incorporation of distance learning practices that could address some of the constraints and limitations that the videoconferencing technology imposed. As it existed at level one, it was clear that our programming could be improved by strengthening the alignment with classroom and distance learning.

A successful model for a museum virtual field trip would have to include the best practices from each of these three areas. To this end, we began reviewing literature on classroom, museum, and distance education, the three essential partner elements in the virtual learning experience. From these, specific principles and theory guided the development of the next level of programming and strengthened the three legs of the model.

Figure 1. Museum virtual field trip is a three-way partnership

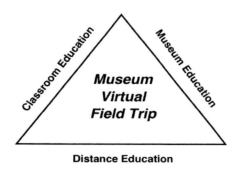

Classroom Education

Classroom education practices naturally vary widely, but certain constants emerge within the literature that directly relate to museum and distance education. Research consistently advocates learning that imparts inquiry-based and interdisciplinary skills. Inquiry unites the learning process with "a state of mind—that of inquisitiveness" (National Research Council, 2006, p. xii). Promoting students' curiosity through inquiry can create fundamental shifts in pedagogy and learning. Theorist Lev Vygotsky advocates allowing students to be actively involved in their own education, instead of viewing them as passive "receivers of instruction" (Blanck, 1990, p. 50). Our program's question-and-answer sessions and practice of using objects only to illustrate points tended to perpetuate this passivity, reflecting what Newmann, Secada, and Wehlage (1995) describe as "transmitting prior knowledge to students and asking them to accept it as authoritative and to reproduce it in fragmented statements" (p. 10). An inquiry-based framework for learning provides activities for students to build and demonstrate understanding and to express their knowledge creatively. Could videoconferencing programs integrate these types of learning experiences in a virtual environment?

Incorporating inquiry-based instruction into the virtual field trip is possible by giving students opportunities not merely to reproduce the knowledge of others but to create their own knowledge (Newmann et al., 1995). Although some of the information from which students learn must come through the knowledge of others, engaging in real-world object-based learning activities allows students to build their own knowledge bases through first-hand observation. The museum is uniquely positioned to offer students chances to interact with authentic objects. There are, however, better ways, to engage students with artifacts than simply displaying and identifying the objects for them (Visual Understanding in Education, 2006).

Encouraging students to study an artifact, describe it in their own words, analyze this description, and then create and evaluate theories about the object encourages personal connections in learners' minds. Non-object based construction of knowledge also may occur during virtual field trips, when students are asked to think about a certain issue or problem and engage in discussion with others about the topic. What is important for both types of knowledge building is allowing students to explore their ideas about a given subject and practice higher-order thinking skills, activities well suited to virtual learning.

Virtual field trips have the potential to engage students, both in the videoconferencing experience and in a participant-driven learning process. For many students, the lack of personal relevance in the standard school curriculum limits their interest in academic activities. Involving students in educational experiences that challenge them to take part in real-world activities naturally seems to stimulate interest. Barbara Rogoff has done significant work on sociocultural learning theory, emphasizing the theory of *intent participation*. Intent participation is characterized by allowing students to learn by "observing and listening-in on activities of adults and other children" (Rogoff et al., 2003, p. 176). Instead of practicing a "hierarchical participation structure" as found in the traditional classroom, intent participation provides a "collaborative, horizontal participant structure" (Rogoff et al., 2003, p. 185). Teachers and students learn from each other by taking part in learning activities together, with the more experienced learners guiding and supporting the knowledge acquisition of the less experienced, a process called *scaffolding*.

Intent participation changes not so much *what* is taught, but *how* something is taught. Traditional classroom learning involves a teacher "transmitting" knowledge to students, which students receive in isolated "chunks" that often do not seem to have relevance to any practical application. Rogoff suggests that children's learning activities should not be far-removed from the practice of tasks in real-life applications, arguing:

In intent participation, learners engage collaboratively with others in the social world. Hence, there is no boundary dividing them into sides. There is also no separation of learning into an isolated assembly phase, with exercises for the immature, out of the context of the intended activity. (Rogoff et al., 2003, p. 182)

Key constructs from these pedagogies, including the inquiry-based approach, intent participation, and scaffolding, supplied a necessary connection to classroom practice and the needs of educators and students. Constants in classroom learning, building a knowledge base through active learning and providing opportunities for students to shape and share their knowledge in a collaborative environment, combined in the new framework for our virtual field trips. Following this review of classroom education, we also considered how museum education could help transform our virtual programming.

Museum Education

Museums practice a wide range of strategies for sharing information and develop diverse pedagogies for public education; however, within the variety of approaches, museum education efforts are generally concentrated on three main areas: the *things* of the museum, the *place* of the museum, and the *people* of the museum. Each of these areas requires the attention of museum educators to share the resources and experiences of the museum with visitors.

Because most museums, by design, focus on the objects maintained in their collections, the *things* of the museum are central to museum education. Accordingly, museums offer visitors the opportunity to interact with authentic objects. Genuine artifacts possess what Andreas Huyssen (1995) calls an "aura" of enchantment associated with their relationship to history and status as repositories of memory (p. 33). This enchantment is part of the excitement of interacting with and learning about objects, an excitement we wished to capture in our videoconference programs. Object-based learning often includes "hands-on" experiences, for example, touching objects or manipulating exhibit activities. While the object is central to these types of activities, Hein and Alexander (1998) stress that the real benefit from engaging with objects is the link that it forges to mental activity through "requir[ing] the learner to struggle with ideas, that is, to think" (p. 38). The use of objects as part of a virtual field trip should go beyond the "show and tell" to include meaningful interaction with the object on the part of the learner.

The *place* of the museum, as the environment in which learning occurs, sets the stage for learning. Place includes factors such as physical comfort, effects of the environment on learning, and the appropriateness of the context for the particular type of learning activity (Falk & Dierking, 2000). The effects of the physical setting cannot be overlooked, especially in a virtual environment. Although the connection is virtual, learners and facilitators are physically present in different spaces, and during a videoconference, the sites involved should meet physical needs on both ends of the connection. Videoconference programs may commence by addressing comfort, just as one would do in a traditional physical setting, by asking questions like, "Can everyone see the screen? Can everyone hear me?"

The position of learners in one place while the facilitator is in another presents a unique challenge that can be addressed by thoughtful and creative use of physical space and technology. It is interesting to observe how people tend to transfer the behavioral scripts with which they are comfortable, such as for museums or classrooms, to new physical experiences. In 2005, Helen Roy, an instructor in the Michigan State University Less Commonly-Taught Languages Program, participated in the Virtual Outreach Program by teaching the Ojibwe language to students at Spotted Eagle High School in Milwaukee, Wisconsin. Toward the end of the first semester, the students became so comfortable with the spatial orientations of the videoconference that they would bring their portfolios to the videoconferencing unit when the session was over, holding them in front of the camera for Roy to see, exactly like students in a regular classroom might show their teacher something after class. The videoconferencing equipment acted as a bridge for the gap between the students' physical classroom and the physical studio space, and for a few brief moments, the line between the two seemed to blur. Videoconferencing can change people's perceptions about place, and these changes may be used to advance learning.

The presence of individuals and groups in the museum learning environment leads to the production of educational strategies that address the needs of the *people* of the museum. These needs are varied and largely individual. Falk and Dierking (2000) highlight the intimate nature of learning. No matter what people's educational needs or styles are, the authors suggest that learning will always be experienced through the internal filters of motivation and personal interests, affecting the manner in which individuals construct and use knowledge in a variety of situations. Hein's (1995) theories about knowledge and learning emphasize the importance of supplying constructivist learning opportunities in museums, which he defines as those that are learner-driven and encourage people to create understanding in their own minds. Hein suggests that constructivist museums allow visitors to form independent conclusions about the meaning of objects and exhibits.

Dialogue is a crucial element of museum learning. Museum visitor groups interact with each other while experiencing the museum, but even when people visit alone, they connect with the collective experience of designers, curators, educators, and others, who are not physically pres-

ent, through exhibit content, label text, and design. This community around the individual helps him or her to connect with what is being experienced. Social interaction not only enhances learning but is a prerequisite to learning, as Vygotsky asserts (Blanck, 1990; Rogoff et al., 2003). In their observations of conversations that take place in museums, Leinhardt and Knutson see discourse as "the real moment of co-construction of meaning" (2004, p. xv). Building on these models of socially-mediated learning from Vygotsky and others, dialogue and the related creation of community became central goals for our virtual field trips.

The examples above underscore only a few of the wide variety of educational needs that museum educators attempt to meet. Including a variety of presentation styles in virtual programming will help maximize the potential for learning by individuals who take part in activities. This translates into a need to include objects and activities that provide students with a range of media and learning opportunities, offering visual, auditory, and tactile stimuli as part of the virtual field trip.

Distance Education

The review of best practices in distance education involved both literature and the examples of outstanding videoconference providers. While programs designed for a virtual audience can incorporate teaching elements of classroom education, they also need to include certain methods tailored specifically to the virtual environment, what Li and Akins call "e-pedagogy" (Li & Akins, 2005, p. 52; Merrill, 2004). Many researchers argue that distance learning should incorporate a learner-centered process, with the teacher acting as a leader or guide rather than a lecturer (DuCharme-Hansen & Dupin-Bryant, 2005; Merrill, 2004; Smyth, 2005). Activities where learners take more of the initiative in the learning process while videoconferencing lead to increased student autonomy and a more constructivist pedagogy

(Smyth, 2005). For example, Schrum (1996) observes, "In most traditional courses, educators build in time to encourage small-group discussions, problem-solving, or hypothesis building. Unfortunately, that component is frequently left out of distance education courses" (p. 3). These researchers seem to suggest that best practices for distance education can be similar to those for creative and engaging regular classroom instruction with added attention to what works best via the medium of videoconferencing.

Virtual program design should allow for learning activities that may be slightly different than normal classroom tasks but that will help overcome distance and technological barriers. Distance education programs can incorporate a variety of engaging tasks, such as discussions and online chatting, which will enrich the experience and build interaction between participants (Li & Akins, 2005). Greenberg (1998) stresses the importance of developing places where presenters and students can share information, including electronic "white boards," Web sites, and e-mail. These technologies can be used during videoconferences, but time allotted for activities like these may be limited during programs. If so, providing opportunities for participants to communicate before or after videoconferences deepens connections to resource people and information. Developing accessible variety in distance "languages" extends a communication highway between participants.

Expert facilitation is crucial to successful distance education because presenters are the impetus behind creating an engaging and collaborative environment for students (Merrill, 2004). Besides providing content and resource expertise for students, presenters also should facilitate the social processes in program delivery (Merrill, 2004). This includes helping students establish relationships in the virtual learning community (DuCharme-Hansen & Dupin-Bryant, 2005). Achieving this goal is possible using various pedagogical strategies, while remembering that

what works well for one classroom may not work for another. Greenberg (1998) observes, "Good distance education practice depends upon creative, well-informed teachers," which involves understanding the needs of particular educators and students (p. 39).

In addition to the literature, other videoconferencing providers became models as we sought to reinvent our programming. For instance, "Gadget Works," provided by the Center of Science and Industry (COSI) in Columbus and Toledo, Ohio, nationally known for their virtual programming, provides an example of how to integrate objects and hands-on activities into videoconferences. During a professional conference for virtual programming providers, presenters from COSI engaged an audience in a simulation of a "Gadget Works" program. The participants examined wind-up toys and learned how they work through observation and physically disassembling and reassembling the objects. One of the best aspects of this program was the way each person performed the activity individually but was also simultaneously involved in group discussion with fellow students and the presenter, exemplifying the creation of "community." This activity demonstrated that activities do not need to be elaborate to be meaningful and effective.

As a second example, the "Your Place or Mine" distance learning program offered by the Tennessee Aquarium in Chattanooga was designed to help students understand how and why animals live in particular habitats. This field trip expertly illustrated how to integrate the museum or other institution's physical spaces into videoconferences. During the program, instead of remaining stationary, the presenter moved throughout the spaces of the zoo, which allowed the audience essentially to "move" with her. Students participating in the program experienced the space, not only by seeing the various animals, but also by transcending the gap between "here" and "there" in virtual space as described above. This added dimension of moving through the exhibit spaces offered a possible remedy for the static immobility of studio programs.

A New Framework

From this review of literature and best practices as exemplified by outstanding distance learning providers, a series of core principles developed. Moving our programs to the next level involved translating these principles into a new philosophy and pedagogy, which in turn transformed our program content. A new set of criteria became what we called *level two*. This level included:

- Inquiry-based activities
- Constructivist approach
- Content connected directly to curriculum
- Interaction characterized by engagement (observation and comparison)
- Objects in classroom
- Classroom integration pre- and post-program
- Use of multiple media (document camera, video, and other technologies)

In the move from level one to level two, we incorporated exemplary teaching methods researched during the literature review that we discovered were translatable into videoconferencing practice. By looking for overlaps between distance learning methods, museum education, and classroom practice, intersections were revealed that offered the benefits of interdisciplinary thinking to our model, because the techniques worked in all three arenas. Once solid techniques from each discipline were developed that fit and functioned together, a more stable model with clearer outlines emerged.

The program topics designed in level two were selected to bridge research interests of the museum and university and the curriculum needs of K-12 audiences. The programs included a myriad of formats matching diverse learning styles and delivered before, during, and after the videoconference presentations. Programs emphasized inquiry using national science and social studies education standards, incorporating them into our three core principles to promote content and skills acquisition: critical thinking, creative expression, and personal connection.

Figure 2. An emerging model with input from three disciplines

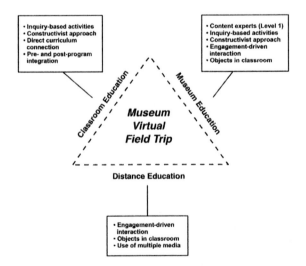

The overarching goal was to engage students in active, inquiry-based activities that incorporated the principles of intent participation and social learning community building.

One of the first programs developed using the level two framework was "MSI: Museum Scene Investigation," which focused on an early nineteenth-century fur trader's cabin in the permanent collection of the Michigan State University Museum. This program was designed to use the cabin as a context to teach inquiry skills and content about Michigan's early history. "MSI" invited students to look for clues about the lives of the people who built the cabin by examining various parts of the cabin's structure and formulating theories about the building's use and significance in nineteenth-century Michigan. The students used primary source materials, including Historic American Buildings Survey (HABS) photographs and floor plan sketches of the building made while it was *in situ*, in addition to photographs and documentation of the process of acquiring and moving the cabin to the MSUM.

The most significant element of the "MSI" program was the focus on inquiry skills that were taught and practiced through pre- and post-program integration components. Educators received an activity package including student "investigator's handbooks" and a curriculum guide. Using the guide, educators provided their students with an introductory lesson about close examination of artifacts, followed by a group exercise using the skills learned to conduct a practice investigation on classroom objects. The second preprogram lesson introduced the topic of the fur trade, while the third lesson gave students the opportunity to discover how cabins are constructed. The virtual field trip took place *after* these activities were completed. By the time students participated in the videoconference, they had acquired somewhat of an "expert level" understanding of cabins and were ready to participate in the museum investigation. During the program, students wrote their observation notes on the "MSI field investigation packet," which provided scaffolding for the learning process by including written prompts for investigation questions. After the information-gathering and conclusion-making processes, students received the "solution" to the investigation, which gave the reasons why changes had been made to the structure and a brief history of the building. Following the program, educators could choose to do two additional discovery activities provided as part of the program package, including an oral history from a woman who lived near the cabin as a child in the 1840s.

The second new program developed using our level two framework was called "A Sense of Adaptation." Using their five senses, first and second grade students explored a series of animal adaptations, acting as "scientists" making observations. This virtual field trip integrated a variety of hands-on objects sent to the classroom and interactive activities during the program. The presenter used everyday objects to help students understand how animals adapt to their environments. For example, touching a peacock feather allowed students to decide whether or not they thought that peacocks could fly. Folding a paper napkin demonstrated the difference in thickness between a chicken egg and an ostrich egg. Other activities illustrated types of animal camouflage and the various sounds that insects make.

This program was extremely engaging, with the students in constant dialogue with the presenter and each other. As they worked through each physical sense, students were encouraged to support their conclusions about each animal's adaptation characteristics with concrete evidence learned in the program or from previous experience. The culminating activity of the program put students' inquiry skills to the test. Given live crickets in ventilated containers, students observed their crickets and drew diagrams of the insects' body parts on paper. After they discussed their observations with the presenter, students were issued another challenge: Imagine what kinds of adaptations your cricket would need if it were suddenly transported to a different habitat. With the opportunity to apply some of the things learned in the virtual field trip to an immediate problem, students demonstrated high levels of creativity and reasoning. Extensive opportunities for feedback from teachers and students during the program helped the presenter to adjust the activities to allow for the types of learning occurring in individual classrooms as videoconferences progressed[1].

With "MSI" and "A Sense of Adaptation," the Virtual Outreach Program moved closer to programs that would be considered exemplary by current distance learning standards. Although some of our level one framework programs continued to be offered, they were recast as *experts talk* field trips, reflecting their question-and-answer formats. However, the presenters of these *experts* programs also developed new pre- and post-field trip activities that were made available to educators. Together, both types of programs offered choices to educators for virtual field trips that they believed would best meet their students' learning needs.

A PLAN FOR THE FUTURE

Although working within the new framework for level two prompted beneficial change in the virtual programming, concern about the depth of connection with students that our programs allowed still existed. Lack of sustained contact with classrooms, along with limited student engagement, constrained the learning process. The pre- and post-program materials offered some continued connection, mostly in the form of brief discussions before a program or the occasional post-field trip e-mail or telephone call, but the one-time connection was an unfortunate reality. Additionally, the museum galleries had not been used as extensively as possible to allow people to experience the "place" of the museum. These

limitations were addressed as we moved into what became the third level of virtual programming.

During this transition, all of the goals from level two were retained as a foundation for the next stage. Characteristics of successful on-site programs continued to influence the virtual practices. In particular, highly successful immersion field trips that brought students into the museum for a week of curriculum-based museum experiences reinforced an interest in going beyond the one-time experience. From the on-site programs, we knew that a strong connection to the curriculum was important if educators were to make use of virtual field trip opportunities, but so was a constructivist approach, characterized by methods that connected students' learning to real-world applications. Developing learning communities and strategies for more effective contextualized inquiry-based activities became a primary focus. By enhancing the use of objects and multi-media technologies, students could be more fully engaged before, during, and after the programs. Through sustained contact, museum experts could become classroom partners and resource people, within learning networks created between classrooms, museums, and distance educators.

With increased contact comes the possibility for more collaborative learning opportunities with students. Raider-Roth (2005) explores how the existence of trust in school "relational contexts" affects students' learning and confidence in their own knowledge. She identifies elements present in trusting relationships between teachers, students, and their peers, including the types of environments in which trust develops. Raider-Roth argues, "In constructing this kind of trust [regarding their own knowledge], they [students] act politically by sharing and suppressing knowledge based on their understandings of classroom relationships" (Raider-Roth, 2005, p. 622). To foster sharing through trust and collaboration, Hung and Nichani (2002) advocate the cultivation of classroom "learning communities," in which a learning environment is created "where each person's contributions are respected" and where "mechanisms for the community to synthesize diverse views" exist (p. 178). During virtual field trips, the "classroom" is extended to include the distance learning provider and others outside the school, thus underscoring the need to create trusting relationships that will encourage participation and the sharing of knowledge.

One of the main characteristics of participatory, collaborative learning is the free exchange of ideas between participants. In levels one and two, the virtual field trip programs largely focused on the presenters, and the discussion and inquiry activities were presenter-driven. How could a true learner-centered forum for dialogue be created? Hung, Tan, and Chen (2005) define dialogue in learning as a "thread" or "common denominator" for interactions between learners of all knowledge levels (p. 40). In an environment of exchange, teachers become "models, coaches, or facilitators"

to help students explore their own knowledge and make connections through dialogue (Hung & Nichani, 2002, p. 181). Students who have opportunities to engage in dialogue, especially with people who offer different viewpoints, experience "multiple ways of seeing and knowing" (Robinson & Kakela, 2006, p. 204). While effective learning discussions provide opportunities for expression and debate, the best dialogues lead students to use their own knowledge to solve problems. Hung, Tan, and Chen (2005) assert, "Discussion should center on a complex, ill-structured problem or case that engages the participants in higher-order thinking and requires them to present their multiple views with sound arguments" (p. 43). Focusing dialogue on meaningful, authentic activities makes it even more effective as a tool for engaging students.

Once established, learning networks and dialogue open the door for contextualized, authentic learning activities. Videoconferencing can provide programs as part of a larger learning unit,

Figure 3. Stable model includes overlapping strategies

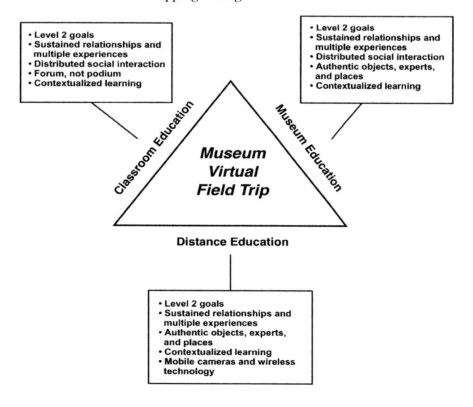

focusing on real scenarios or problems. Students may use real tools, genuine artifacts, and real experts as educational resources (Floyd, 2002; Hung & Nichani, 2002). This includes the use of museum objects (such as teaching models or replicas) and specialized equipment provided to classrooms for use in guided practice. Additionally, authentic places, even those experienced virtually, may become an extension of the classroom world. Museum galleries, laboratories, and office spaces may eventually be considered as familiar as the students' school environments.

Framing virtual field trip experiences to allow for activities like those outlined above provides an outlet for creative expression, critical thinking, and personal connection, by encouraging students' confidence in their own ideas and ability to share them with others. Further, these practices promise to build a community between classrooms, museums, and distance learning providers, all dedicated to knowledge building. Weaving these new goals into the existing framework developed at Level Two resulted in the following additional goals and strategies for *level three*:

- Sustained relationships and multiple experiences
- Distributed social interaction between the presenter and the audience to reinforce collaborative learning
- Dynamic and contextualized presentations (some in museum galleries)
- Programs that create a forum for dialogue rather than a podium for lecturers
- Contextualized learning with programs as part of a larger learning unit focusing on an authentic scenario or problem
- Use of mobile cameras and wireless technology to use galleries and research labs as context for programs

Retaining selected elements from levels one and two, the level three models finally emerged as stable and complete, a model for museum virtual field trips reflecting sound educational theory and more mature videoconferencing practice.

Level three will expressly highlight sustained relationships and the forging of learning networks between classrooms, museum experts, and distance learning educators. To test and realize the vision of level three, the VOP developed a program called Learning and Developing Distance Education Resources for Science (LADDERS)[2]. In partnership with the Cranbrook Institute of Science, a fellow distance learning provider in Bloomfield Hills, Michigan, LADDERS involves the creation of a series of virtual field trip modules, correlated to core components of the middle-school science curriculum. To encourage repeat and ongoing experiences, each program is independent but builds on other programs, using a consistent format, vocabulary, and pedagogy in each virtual field trip. These repeat visits attempt to overcome the limitations imposed by single-visit programs.

LADDERS will give students direct experience and practice with inquiry, both as a skill and an understanding. For example, middle-school students studying the "Organization of Living Things" may participate in a videoconference with a scientist who discusses how she relies on inquiry in her work. Students will observe earthworms and then document behaviors observed and hypothesize reactions to stimuli, following the types of experiments and observations conducted by Charles Darwin, an avid, curious naturalist and scientist and a model of inquiry in science. After the program, students may continue their observations, create and test hypotheses, and post questions and observations on an electronic bulletin board, providing a forum for continuing dialogue between classrooms and virtual educators. This experience would be followed with a student-lead videoconference program with another class that conducted similar experiments, to discuss their results and to design further research. The LADDERS model advances the vision of level three by creating inquiry experiences and sustained learning networks where technology provides the forum for communication.

If successful, LADDERS will enhance understanding and appreciation for the role of inquiry in the fields of life and earth sciences. Students and educators will have opportunities to practice inquiry, ask scientific questions, weigh hypotheses based on evidence, and discuss current issues together. LADDERS promises to be both a viable *high-tech* and *high-touch* model that encourages personal connections and individual engagement, while providing ways to overcome many of the distance learning challenges encountered in videoconferencing.

CONCLUSION

In the Virtual Outreach Program's quest to take videoconferencing to the next level, we hoped to create strong and effective links between classrooms, museum experts, and us, the virtual field trip provider. Each videoconference is an invitation into a classroom, not only to share resources but also to join students in authentic and empowering intellectual inquiries. Through strong partnerships that link the major stakeholders, the museum virtual field trip can become an effective educational tool to improve pedagogies, encourage learner engagement, and transform educational practice.

Videoconferencing, at its best, can provide excellent learning experiences for K-22 students. The desire to reach this goal provides the motivation for professionals to explore, discuss, study, and experiment with new ways to integrate formal and informal learning environments for learners in virtual spaces. As we work together to build new connections through videoconferencing, we are simultaneously opening new "localities" where innovation and imagination can freely grow.

The progress through the levels of programming, as described above, pushed our own learning process and focused the program's educational philosophy. Taking time to "step back" from the demands of providing programs and concentrate on improving our videoconferencing pedagogy allowed us to take advantage of the wealth of information available in the literature and learn from the examples of excellent providers. Because others may be contemplating instituting outreach programs using videoconferencing technology or have concerns about the educational effectiveness of the programs they are already providing, we offer this model for museum virtual field trips. Perhaps the discussion of our journey through this endeavor will guide others by helping them to avoid some of the pitfalls that we encountered and to share in the successes.

REFERENCES

Blanck, G. (1990). Vygotsky: The man and his cause. In L. C. Moll (Ed.), *Vygotsky and education: Instructional implications and applications of sociohistorical psychology* (pp. 31-58). Cambridge, MA: Cambridge University Press.

DuCharme-Hansen, B. A., & Dupin-Bryant, P. A. (2005). Distance education plans: Course planning for online adult learners. *TechTrends, 49*(2), 31-39.

Falk, J. H., & Dierking, L. D. (2000). *Learning from museums: Visitor experiences and the making of meaning.* Walnut Creek, CA: AltaMira.

Floyd, M. (2002). More than just a field trip: Making relevant curricular connections through museum experiences. *Art Education, 55*(5), 39-45.

Greenberg, G. (1998). Distance education technologies: Best practices for K-12 settings. *Technology and Society Magazine, 17*(4), 36-40.

Hein, G. E. (1995). The constructivist museum (electronic version). *Journal for Education in Museums, 16*, 21-23. Retrieved August 3, 2006, from http://www.gem.org.uk/pubs/news/hein1995.html

Hein, G. E., & Alexander, M. (1998). *Museums: Places of learning.* Washington, DC: American Association of Museums.

Hung, D., & Nichani, M. R. (2002). Bring communities of practice into schools: Implications for instructional technologies from Vygotskian perspectives. *International Journal of Instructional Media, 29*(2), 171-183.

Hung, D., Tan, S. C., & Chen, D.T. (2005). How the Internet facilitates learning as dialog: Design considerations for online discussions. *International Journal of Instructional Media, 32*(1), 37-46.

Huyssen, A. (1995). *Twilight memories: Marking time in a culture of amnesia.* New York: Routledge.

Leinhardt, G., & Knutson, K. (2004). *Listening in on museum conversations.* Walnut Creek, CA: AltaMira.

Li, Q., & Akins, M. (2005). Sixteen myths about online teaching and learning in higher education: Don't believe everything you hear. *TechTrends, 49*(4), 51-60.

Merrill, H. S. (2004). Best practices for online facilitation. *Adult Learning, 14*(12), 13-16.

National Research Council (2000). *Inquiry and the national science education standards.* Washington, DC: National Academy Press.

Newmann, F. M., Secada, W. G., & Wehlage, G. G. (1995). *A guide to authentic instruction and assessment: Vision, standards, and scoring.* Madison, WI: Wisconsin Center for Education Research.

Raider-Roth, M. B. (2005). Trusting what you know: Negotiating the relational context of classroom life. *Teachers College Record, 107*(4), 587-628.

Robinson, C. F., & Kakela, P. J. (2006). Creating a space to learn: A classroom of fun, interaction, and trust. *College Teaching, 54*(1), 202-206.

Rogoff, B., et al. (2003). Firsthand learning through intent participation. *Annual Review of Psychology, 54,* 175-203.

Schrum, L. (1996). Teaching at a distance: Strategies for successful planning and development. *Learning and Leading with Technology, 23*(March), 30-33.

Smyth, R. (2005). Broadband videoconferencing as a tool for learner-centered distance learning in higher education. *British Journal of Educational Technology, 36*(5), 805-820.

Visual Understanding in Education (2006). What is VTS? Retrieved April 18, 2006, from http://www.vue.org/whatisvts.html

ENDNOTES

[1]   The development of this model was supported through the efforts and ideas of Nick Visscher, Virtual Outreach educator at the MSU Museum.

[2]   The Virtual Outreach Program and Learning and Developing Distance Education Resources in Science (LADDERS) were made possible in part by a grant from the U.S. Institute of Museum and Library Services.

Chapter III
The Journey into Distance Learning:
Test Drives, Roadblocks, and Destinations

Fawn Warner
Discovery Center of Springfield, USA

ABSTRACT

This chapter presents an overview of videoconferencing technology in K-12 instruction from the perspective of a program (content) provider. The chapter provides an overview of the development process, issues, and challenges, and future goals of a distance learning program which provides lessons to K-12 classrooms across the country. Specific topic areas include technology and equipment, establishing partnerships, working with K-12 school districts and educators, expanding a program, and staffing needs. Using the analogy of a road trip, the author takes us on a journey through the development, piloting, and use of a distance education videoconferencing program, and how it is now being sustained and enhanced.

INTRODUCTION

Discovery Center of Springfield (DCS) is a non-profit, hands-on science and technology center located in Springfield, Missouri. Considered a small science center, our annual general visitor count is in the neighborhood of 36,000; however, we reach another 15,000 people through outreach and special programs each year. We have been working with videoconferencing technology since 2001 in a variety of capacities; our primary goal in this endeavor is to deliver educational lessons to K-12 classrooms. In the distance learning community, we are most often referred to as "content providers", and the practice of providing educational programming through videoconferencing technology is called "distance learning". These two terms will be used on a regular basis as our program is discussed.

DCS received a federal technology innovation challenge (TIC) grant in June of 2001. This three-year grant allowed us to gradually create a distance learning program by hiring an information technology coordinator and a distance learning coordinator, purchasing the necessary hardware and equipment, setting up a high-bandwidth network, creating curriculum, and forging local partnerships to promote this new technology. This gradual implementation has allowed us to carefully expand the program while maintaining quality; in the final year of the grant (2004-2005), we delivered 60 videoconferences. The following year we delivered 180 lessons, and in our fifth year of working with videoconferencing technology, we delivered 230 educational lessons to 20 different U.S. states and Mexico City, Mexico.

As content providers, schools and organizations connect via videoconferencing technology to us, and we deliver an educational lesson to students or adults at their site. Our lessons are approximately an hour long, with topics ranging from DNA to the culture of Mexico (currently a total of 26 topics). Most topics are accompanied by a kit of supplies and props, which is shipped to the classroom educator when the lesson is reserved (approximately two weeks in advance). In addition, we have formed partnerships with other organizations in the community to bring their educational content to our distance learning program.

We also serve as distance learning program recipients. Discovery Center has received lessons through distance learning for field trips, professional development, and other audiences who are visiting the Center. For example, third graders who are learning about astronomy may conclude their curriculum unit by visiting the Discovery Center and taking part in a videoconference delivered by NASA. The myriad of topics available through distance learning can fit almost any curriculum

theme or topic. Many people describe distance learning as going on a journey without ever physically leaving the classroom, which is why these offerings are often referred to as electronic field trips (or e-trips).

Finally, DCS utilizes videoconferencing technology to add sustainability to the organization as a whole by offering the technology to businesses and other organizations who rent meeting space in the Center. As part of the TIC grant, DCS also created professional development workshops for teachers and other organizations who are interested in distance learning. These workshops generate income through registration fees and increased future business.

Purpose of Chapter

Our discussion here will cover our experiences with two goals in mind: first, to outline a process for developing and expanding a successful distance learning program, and second, to give educators and other content recipients insight as to what goes on "behind the scenes" when working with a content provider. Our experiences will be related in three sections: Test-Drives (development), Roadblocks (issues and solutions), and Destinations (plans and goals for the future).

TEST DRIVES

Initial Program Development

The initial investment to implement videoconferencing technology can be daunting, especially for smaller organizations. The TIC grant, which was awarded to DCS in June, 2001, provided $500,000 in funding toward educational technology. For many small non-profit organizations and school districts, grants are probably the most likely source of funding for videoconferencing technology at present. The TIC grant was a federal program through the U.S. Department of

Education. The TIC program no longer exists; however, many different technology grants are available. A quick search of Grants.gov with the keywords "education technology" reveals over 700 grant opportunities. Businesses such as phone companies or law firms who are already using the technology may be another viable source of funding and expertise. Universities can often assist through faculty and staff who specialize in distance learning. Groups such as these also may be able to lend equipment.

At the outset of the TIC grant award, DCS hired a distance learning coordinator, who was charged with overseeing the program, including administration of the advisory board, topic and curriculum development, lesson delivery, and marketing the distance learning program as a whole. The focus of the TIC grant was on distance learning implementation within the state of Missouri. This focus created strong roots for the program within the region and allowed DCS to create partnerships with organizations within the state who are potential stakeholders in promoting education technology. The effectiveness of this focus will be revisited in the next section of the chapter: "Ongoing Development."

An advisory board provided guidance on implementation of the grant, combining board members who had experience in distance learning with board members who had a vested interest in education technology. Advisory board members included:

- Administrators (principals and superintendents) from both private and public schools
- Staff members from larger science and technology centers that already had distance learning programs in place
- A science curriculum facilitator and director of information services from a large public school district
- The director of an existing university-based distance learning education grant program

- The owner of a private education technology consulting firm
- The dean of the college of education at a state university
- Science educators from various levels of K-12 education
- DCS staff who were involved in the program, including the information technology coordinator, education director, and CEO

This group met on a quarterly basis to review and facilitate progress in the development of the program. The group assisted in identifying appropriate partnerships and marketing opportunities, methods for collecting feedback on the program, and future possibilities for utilizing videoconferencing technology to further the mission of the Discovery Center. Advisory board members who worked in videoconferencing provided guidance on purchasing equipment, installing the necessary network lines, and designing distance learning classrooms. Advisory board members who worked in school districts helped identify and troubleshoot issues in working with school districts to incorporate videoconference technology.

In year one of the grant, the distance learning coordinator offered 12 different topics through distance learning. The curriculum for these topics was developed based on current topics that Discovery Center was covering in other educational programs and exhibits. The adaptation of existing curriculum allowed us to begin offering lessons much earlier than if curriculum was being built from scratch. Another advantage that we had in this process was the fact that the distance learning coordinator was a certified science teacher, so she was very familiar with curriculum design and implementation.

The first kits, which contain hands-on manipulatives to go along with activities taught during the distance learning lesson, were created during years one and two of the grant period. These kits have proven themselves over time as a valuable component of our program, and are one of the primary elements that set DCS distance learning lessons apart from other distance learning lessons currently being offered.

A large amount of time was spent researching other content providers' programs to ensure that we did not duplicate lessons, and to garner ideas for how to present program information. By working with other content providers rather than competing against them, we were able to gather useful information on best practices and establish a good reputation for the Discovery Center Distance Learning Program within the distance learning community. This effort is still paying off, as discussed in the chapter sections: "Ongoing Development" and "Roadblocks."

In keeping with the focus of implementing distance learning within the state of Missouri, program curricula was aligned to state curricula frameworks and testing requirements. Aligning lessons with curriculum requirements is extremely important to the vitality of the program, as the needs of teachers, administrators, and school districts as a whole are centered on these parameters. Now that teachers are required to fit such an immense amount of information into each school year, most teachers are not interested in educational enrichment programs that do not have a specific tie to their teaching goals.

In addition to lesson development for students, we also developed and presented a professional development workshop for educators. This short workshop introduced the concepts of videoconferencing and distance learning to teachers and administrators, and explored some of the educational opportunities available through the technology. In addition to helping teachers from the region become familiar with the concept of distance learning, it also generated word-of-mouth advertising for Discovery Center and its programs. The feedback gathered from educators who attended these workshops also provided insight into issues in implementing distance learning in the classroom and the teachers' attitudes toward the technology.

While the professional development workshop focused on training educators in person in small group settings, we also began offering "faculty presentations" free of charge, via videoconferencing. These 30- to 45-minute presentations give a quick introduction to the concept of distance learning and outline the educational programs that we offer. Now, five years later, we still offer free faculty presentations as a way to reach schools and organizations who may be new to the concept of distance learning, or who are experienced with distance learning but unfamiliar with Discovery Center distance learning offerings.

The distance learning coordinator also took the primary role in marketing the Discovery Center's Distance Learning Program and TIC grant. Again, in maintaining the focus on the state of Missouri, marketing efforts were primarily facilitated through regional and state-wide organizations. Articles and invitations to professional development workshops were placed in Science Teachers of Missouri (STOM) and the Missouri Distance Learning Association (MODLA) newsletters. Information on the grant award and topics being offered were listed in Discovery Center's annual program guide and the quarterly member newsletter. A press release spurred articles in several regional newspapers, and presentations were made at several state-wide education and technology conferences over the course of the grant period. Once lessons had been developed and were ready to implement, we began to list them online with various marketing Web sites that specialize in providing distance learning information to educators. The original Web sites where we listed our topics include:

- Pacific Bell/SBC Global Network, www.kn.packbell.com
- Distance Learning Exchange, www.dle.state.pa.us
- Videoconference Advance, www.vcadvance.com
- The Global Schoolhouse, www.globalschoolnet.org

These Web sites allow educators and organizations to see lesson details for a variety of different content providers so that they can "shop" for the lesson that best meets their needs. DCS also created a distance learning section within its own Web site, to which all of the online listings above refer. DCS's Web site also includes a reservation request form, which is the primary method used by schools and organizations to reserve our lessons.

Most education-related organizations recognize the importance of forming partnerships. Two ongoing partnerships that developed early on for our program are with Dickerson Park Zoo (DPZ) and the Missouri Department of Conservation (MDC). DCS partners with both of these organizations to expand the scope of topics which we are able to offer via videoconferencing. DPZ brings live animals and a zoo educator to DCS to deliver distance learning lessons on various animal-related topics. MDC brings artifacts and an educator to deliver a lesson called *Native American Use of Bison*. Neither of these partner organizations has access to videoconferencing technology of their own, so this partnership allows them to reach more students than they normally would be able to, while allowing DCS to increase its offerings and to bring more educational value to classrooms across the country.

TIC grant funding also allowed DCS to hire an information technology coordinator. This position was vital to the implementation of the program, as it oversaw the setup of a firewall and installation of the network and fiber-optic lines, after research and purchase of the necessary equipment. As the network was being set up, various videoconferencing-capable areas were connected throughout the Center, including classrooms, exhibit halls, and a small studio space designed specifically to deliver lessons to remote classrooms. This allowed us to utilize different spaces for different purposes, even utilizing exhibits located on the museum floor as props to further demonstrate concepts being covered. The information technol-ogy coordinator also identified school districts in the state that had videoconferencing capability, and even traveled to regional school districts to help make sure their videoconferencing systems were in working order. The IT coordinator also presented technical information in the professional development workshops that the distance learning coordinator created. Once DCS began to deliver lessons, the IT coordinator conducted test connections with schools that were scheduled to receive a lesson to ensure that the connection had no technical difficulties as well as good audio and video feeds.

In addition, to measure the success of the TIC grant, an outside evaluator was contracted to collect data on the distance learning lessons delivered through videoconferencing and the educator professional development workshops and presentations. This evaluator assisted in developing data collection tools, such as surveys. (For a sample survey, see appendix A.) Data collected were presented to the advisory board on a regular basis and also were included in a mandatory report to the TIC grant board at the end of each year. Aside from the needs of the grant, the data and feedback which were gathered played a very important role in strategically designing and refining DCS's distance learning program to meet the needs of educators and students.

These major developmental processes created a strong foundation for our distance learning program. By developing the program on a gradual basis and utilizing a myriad of partnerships and educational resources, we were able to ensure a high-quality product that can serve to build sustainability for the distance learning program specifically, and for the organization as a whole.

Ongoing Program Development

Like most education-based programs, our distance learning program continues to grow and evolve. Over the five years of the program, we have employed four different distance learning coordinators. This has been both a challenge and a benefit for the program, as our curriculum has been reviewed and updated by a variety of educators with a variety of specialties. As a result, some of the original 12 lessons have been removed, new lessons have been added, and we have continued to grow our partnerships to bring our total current number of lessons available to 26. We have also increased our marketing efforts, and refocused our efforts from state-based to international-based goals. This change has made the biggest impact on our program, tripling the number of lessons we delivered between year three and year four, and bringing a new level of recognition to Discovery Center of Springfield as a whole.

Curriculum development for our distance learning program will likely never be "finished." We have continually updated our curriculum, moving from alignment with state standards to alignment with national standards. Alignment with national standards insures that our lesson topics, curriculum, and activities are applicable not only to classrooms within the state of Missouri, but to schools nationwide. This realignment greatly increased the value and reach of our program, as it allowed every school district in the country to easily see how our lessons catered to their curriculum. The national curriculum standards also help us determine which lessons to keep and which to remove from our offerings. As mentioned previously, if a lesson cannot be tied directly to curriculum requirements, it is far less likely to be requested.

Our videoconferences are very hands-on: Each lesson that we deliver includes a pre-lab activity that is facilitated in the classroom by the educator, three to five activities that students complete during the hour-long videoconference connection, and a post-lab activity that is facilitated in the classroom by the educator. Each of these activities within each separate lesson has been reviewed for functionality and educational effectiveness based on educator and student feedback, and many activities have been refined

or changed to fit the distance learning format. We also have added several "optional" activities to our lessons, which allow us to offer the same topic to a wide grade range. For example, our ecology lesson is available for grades two through eight, but second graders do entirely different activities than eighth graders. See appendix B for a sample lesson description.

Of the 26 lessons that we offer, 16 of them include kits. The kits also have undergone a continual process of review and improvement in an effort to provide fun, interactive activities that require very few consumable supplies. This helps cut the supply costs for the distance learning program, increasing sustainability. When DCS started its distance learning program five years ago, kits were a relatively new concept in the field. Many classroom educators complained that distance learning took away the hands-on component from students, so content providers starting offering kits as a way to ensure that in addition to topic expertise, hands-on activities became another valuable component of the distance learning experience for students. Now, five years later, kits appear to be a growing trend in distance learning program development. Although there are some logistical challenges in managing kits (see "Roadblocks" section below), they actually provide further flexibility for content providers as they develop activities for lesson topics. By shipping all the necessary supplies to the classroom, content providers do not have to rely on the classroom teacher to round up items like rubber bands and toothpicks, and by shipping specialty items such as gram scales, deer skulls, or DNA models, classrooms benefit from having access to educational materials they do not normally have on hand. In addition to supplies and manipulatives, our kits also include write-ups for a pre-lab and post-lab, vocabulary, and an outline of the actual lesson to be taught. Teachers that we work with in our program continually point to our kits as a huge value because the kit provides them with everything they need so that it is very easy for them to prepare the students to take part in the videoconference.

In addition to expanding existing lessons, we have added new topics in a variety of ways. As we add new topics to other educational programs that we offer, such as Center-based or classroom outreach, we utilize the same topic (and therefore much of the same curriculum research efforts) in distance learning. Our partner, Dickerson Park Zoo, has also gradually added additional topics over the past few years, including four new lessons for the 2006-2007 year. In addition, we are working to form partnerships with other organizations in the community, such as the Watershed Committee of the Ozarks, to bring their education expertise to our offerings.

As new lessons, activities, or educators are introduced to DCS's program, we conduct practice runs, which we call "test-drives." A test-drive allows our distance learning educators to try out new activities or topics in a semi-realistic setting prior to actually teaching a class. We do this by utilizing two videoconferencing units on-site at DCS. One is located in the studio, from which the educator teaches; the other is located in a classroom. The educator connects to the classroom and runs their Test-Drive from the studio, while other educators and museum staff participate as the "class" from the classroom. This process is a benefit for both the educator running the test-drive and the educators watching the test-drive, as it provides the opportunity to refine a variety of lesson elements, including:

- Camera angles and lighting
- Prop placement and handling
- Word usage, vocal volume, and tone
- Activity processes, meaning the ordering of steps and instructions, and determining how much time the class should be allowed to complete each step
- Overall impact of the lesson

During a typical test-drive, educators will often take turns conducting the same activity from the studio so that all educators can gain experience with leading the activity, but also see what the presentation looks like to the audience. This is a great method for new educators to gain basic training and experience so that they feel more comfortable with the format of distance learning before they actually teach a live class. Experienced distance learning educators also benefit from test-drives, as they gain new ideas from both the other educators and the lessons that they do not normally see being taught.

Just as the rest of our program grows, so too does the need for scheduling administration. Although the distance learning coordinator originally handled all scheduling of lessons in addition to teaching them, the volume of requests we receive now makes it impossible for one person to do both the bulk of the teaching and the scheduling. Now, all distance learning reservation requests are handled by our programs facilitator, and we have a separate distance learning educator who teaches the majority of the lessons we offer. As we mentioned, the majority of our reservation requests come through the request form on our own Web site at http://www.discoverycenter.org/distance. php. This is quite convenient, as it allows us to have complete control over the information that we are gathering from school partners. When a request is submitted, it is automatically emailed to the programs facilitator, who works with the appropriate DCS educator and the requesting teacher to schedule the test connection, shipping of the kit, and the actual videoconference. Requests that come through other Web sites such as CILC.org are also emailed to the programs facilitator and handled in the same way. No matter how much information is collected via reservation request form, completion of a reservation usually still requires between one and five emails or phone calls. Although this process can be somewhat time-intensive, it insures that the needs of the school partner are met and that everyone has a good understanding of what the expectations for both the provider and the recipient are. This one-on-one interaction allows us to make sure we are meeting any special needs.

Although the TIC grant has ended and we no longer are conducting required evaluations, we still seek feedback from the schools that we serve. DCS's Web site includes an online feedback form that we specifically ask classroom teachers who have received a distance learning lesson to fill out. This feedback is anonymous and gives the teacher the opportunity to tell us what they liked and did not like. The information collected in the form is emailed to the education director and the DCS educator who taught the lesson so that it can be used to improve lesson content and teaching methods. The DCS's education director also makes phone calls to schools that receive multiple programs to ensure that the teachers and

program coordinators at the schools are happy with the lessons that they have received.

Since the end of the TIC grant, DCS has continued to expand its marketing efforts and partnerships across the nation. Just as in all other areas of the program, shifting our focus from state-based to nation-based has made an incredibly positive impact on the overall success of our distance learning program. Our relationships with schools and other partners have been invaluable in establishing good repute within the distance learning community. Many schools talk with other schools to find out which content providers are best to work with, or even which specific lessons seem to have the most impact. As distance learning becomes more mainstream, several school districts, and even some states, have established system-wide distance learning programs. Many of the schools that we serve

Figure 1. DCS delivered during the 2005-2006 school year by state

•	Alabama	13
•	Arizona	1
•	Colorado	5
•	Connecticut	3
•	Florida	14
•	Illinois	1
•	Indiana	15
•	Massachusetts	45
•	Maine	1
•	Mexico (country)	2
•	Michigan	11
•	Missouri	35
•	Mississippi	2
•	North Carolina	1
•	New Hampshire	2
•	New Jersey	12
•	New York	36
•	Ohio	17
•	Pennsylvania	2
•	Texas	11
•	Virginia	11
•	Washington	1
•	Wisconsin	1

are repeat customers, receiving between 5 and 40 programs per school year. By looking at the number of lessons that DCS delivered during the 2005-2006 school year by state, it is plain to see that some states are far ahead of others in the move toward utilizing technology in the classroom.

As the distance learning community grows, the number of online resources and Web sites available for posting program information grows as well. One of the most valuable resources DCS has partnered with is the Center for Interactive Learning and Collaboration (CILC). Based out of Indiana, CILC started out serving Indiana's state-based distance learning program. More recently, CILC has shifted to a national focus, serving both content providers and content recipients to facilitate the growth of distance learning technology. CILC, which is a non-profit organization, provides a variety of services including an online searchable database of distance learning program offerings, videoconferencing technology planning and implementation consulting, professional development opportunities, distance learning program development consulting, and event management services. Because CILC's Web site is so well known, listing our programs on their site gave us access to potential school partners who would not have known about us otherwise. As content providers, we can contribute a large portion of the dramatic increase in lessons delivered to having our programs listed on CILC's Web site, CILC.org. In addition to providing a huge marketing opportunity, CILC's Web site also provides us with an excellent resource for researching other organizations and their distance learning programs so that we can ensure any new topics we create are not already being offered by other organizations. CILC also has given us the opportunity to advertise our program at CILC conference booths and presentations. CILC has their own lesson feedback form that schools can fill out after receiving a distance learning lesson. The results of feedback forms which are submitted generate a rating system that other content

recipients can see when searching through the programs database. This helps lend credibility to our topics on an individual basis, and to our program as a whole. And finally, one of the most valuable features of our partnership with CILC is the insight that CILC staff and other content providers can provide on a variety of topics, including program and lesson development, scheduling processes, and even providing references on school districts who request programs. As is addressed in "Roadblocks," just as schools need to be assured of the quality and professionalism of the distance learning content providers with whom they work, it is also important for content providers to have references to check on school districts who are requesting multiple lessons. Overall, the online community for distance learning that CILC has created helps to keep the field of distance learning open, friendly, and honest.

Working with other content providers also has opened the door to partnership opportunities. A new partnership that DCS is just beginning is with MOTE Marine Labs in Sarasota, Florida. MOTE provided some of the very first distance learning programs for students who were on-site at DCS. Over the years, we have taken part in multiple paid programs from MOTE, as well as some incredible live shark-feedings, which MOTE provided at no cost. This type of programming is an excellent example of the power of distance learning: Here in landlocked Missouri, many of the children who participated in the MOTE programs have never seen a live shark or the ocean. Now, through a grant from the Institute of Museum and Library Services, MOTE is implementing a new program in distance learning that combines their distance learning programs with small, hands-on traveling exhibits. Because of our past experience of working with MOTE to present their programs to Discovery Center visitors, MOTE has asked us to partner with them on this grant. The Discovery Center will receive these new traveling exhibits and the associated distance learning programs on a pilot basis to gather feedback from audiences on the quality of the programs. Again, this is a wonderful opportunity for both DCS and our visitors, as many people from our region have very little exposure to sea life or ocean habitats. Ongoing partnerships such as these will help increase our presence in the distance learning community, and also allow more of our on-site visitors to become familiar with the concept and value of distance learning.

ROADBLOCKS

Controversies, Problems, and Solutions

Distance learning is a relatively new concept in the field of education, so there are often many roadblocks to overcome when implementing, maintaining, and expanding distance learning programs. In an effort to keep things simple, we can look at two main categories for distance learning roadblocks: technology and program coordination.

As with anything technology-related, it is vital to have access to staff or consultants who know what they are doing. Distance learning technology is not something that you can implement without a good amount of funding, so it is important to make sure things are done properly the first time. It is difficult to address specific issues that may come up with distance learning technology, since everyone's networks are unique, and there is a wide variety of equipment from which to choose. In our own experience, we have worked with schools that have everything that they need in place, including the expensive camera and microphone, but the district's IT coordinator refuses to configure the firewall to allow streaming audio and video. On the other hand, there are plenty of school districts out there who would be happy to meet the networking requirements if they could only get the funding to buy the necessary camera and microphone.

Because of the infinite combinations of network and equipment combinations, compatibility issues sometimes arise when connecting with schools and other organizations via videoconferencing. We have found that an easy defense for day-of-program technology issues is conducting a test connection prior to the actual lesson. If at all possible, the test connection should be scheduled at least a week in advance of the lesson so that if problems do arise, there is ample time to troubleshoot and fix any issues.

Troubleshooting can be another issue by itself. Even classroom teachers who are utilizing the technology for the first time and are having difficulty connecting with us are absolutely sure that the problem is on our end, despite the fact that we often complete two or three successful connections to different locations on any given day. The difficulty arises in trying to troubleshoot situations such as this without making the school partner feel that you are blaming them for the problems. Typical connection problems and some easy things to check follow:

- No connection can be made.
  - Many organizations are not aware that there are two different types of connection: IP (over computer lines) and ISDN (over phone lines). If the content provider is using one type of connection and the recipient is using the other type, a bridge is required. Most schools have their own bridging service, but it is still a good idea to retain the services of a bridging service of your own. Our partnership with CILC gave us access to Norlight Telecommunications, who provides on-demand bridging services when we need them.
  - If the provider and the recipient are using the same connection type, check to make sure the correct IP address or phone number is being dialed.

     o   Oftentimes, a non-connection requires the involvement of the IT coordinators from both the provider and recipient organizations.

- There is a connection, but there is no picture and/or sound.
  - o These issues are usually easily resolved by checking cable connections and input setups on both the provider and recipient side. If both the provider and the recipient have compatible equipment, the provider can try taking control of the far-side camera to adjust inputs.
  - o Sound issues can often be identified by conducting a tone test. Most videoconferencing systems have built-in troubleshooting features, including a tone test. If you run a tone test, and you can hear the tone, but the recipient cannot, then the issue is likely on their end. If the recipient runs a tone test, and you can hear it, but they cannot, the problem is definitely on their end. Of course, these scenarios can be reversed as well.

An entire book could be written on troubleshooting distance learning technology. Another great way to help identify where the problem lies is to dial in to a different location and test picture and sound. Many organizations such as universities or bridge providers have test sites that are available for connection 24-7. If you can gain access to one of these sites, you will always have an easy way to make sure that your own system is up to par. Perhaps the most valuable weapon in troubleshooting technology is to learn about your equipment by reading the manual and becoming familiar with the menus and features within the software.

As equipment gets older, maintenance can become an issue as well. Five years later, we are still utilizing the same equipment with which we started our distance learning program. We have had very few issues with our videoconferencing equipment, but due to the overall cost of replacing equipment should something go wrong, we invested in a service contract once the warranties on our camera systems ran out. Having a backup set of equipment has been another nice advantage for us. Even if something little such as an s-video cable or a microphone malfunctions, we always have a spare on hand so that lessons can go on as scheduled.

The lighting and sound in your distance learning classroom or studio is another important element in videoconferencing. As a distance learning recipient, it is important to have a classroom space large enough to accommodate at least 25 to 30 students, and at least for our particular lessons, a tabletop workspace works best. As content providers, however, we have found that the smaller the space is from which we deliver lessons, the better it is for us. This allows us to have as much control over lighting and sound as possible. At DCS, we have created a distance learning studio that measures approximately 10 feet by 12 feet and has both regular overhead fluorescent lighting as well as track lighting that can be adjusted. This small space helps eliminate echoes and shadows without having to spend large amounts of money on sound proofing and lighting features, and also gives us enough space to store the props and supplies needed to teach our lessons.

Ask any three organizations that are involved in distance learning as to which type of connection is better, IP or ISDN, and you are likely to get three different answers. Some organizations have one or the other, and a few even have both. As mentioned above, IP connections run over Internet lines while ISDN connections utilize phone lines. Many school districts, including the entire state of Indiana, have ISDN connections, but most districts also have easy access to a bridging service, which is utilized to join providers and recipients with different connection types together. Bridging services can introduce a new set of issues to the distance learning arena. Troubleshooting becomes a little more difficult when utilizing a bridge, because a third party and their equipment are now involved. Different bridges handle billing of their fees in different ways as well. Some organizations have their own bridging technology or pay a yearly fee for unlimited use of a bridge. In our case, we pay a per-use fee every time we use our bridging service. In most cases, we bill the cost of that fee to the recipient in an effort to keep our overhead costs down.

Program coordination includes all the logistics behind setting up and running a distance learning program, including determining program format, working with schools and other partners, adapting new teaching methods, scheduling and tracking kits, and tapping resources to expand the program. At first glance, these elements can seem overwhelming, but by implementing a distance learning program gradually and adjusting it for growth as you go, many issues can either be avoided, or chalked up to great learning experiences. As with any educational program, flexibility is most important.

In general, distance learning programs geared toward K-12 classrooms create their lessons based on the school schedule, limiting them to between 45 minutes and an hour in length. There are other format decisions that must be made, however. The first is how lessons are scheduled. DCS offers its lessons on-demand, meaning schools and other recipients request a specific day and time for their program, and we do our best to meet that request. Other organizations have set scheduling, where they determine the date and time that they will offer a specific lesson, and recipients sign up for these scheduled slots. Determining a scheduling method relies heavily on many factors, including staff and educator availability, demand for lessons, schedules of other educational programs that must be accommodated, availability of lesson materials and props, and availability of equipment and teaching space. Content providers must also decide if their lessons are appropriate

for multi-point connections, which means that multiple schools or classrooms are connected to one provider at a time. Due to the highly interactive nature of our lessons, DCS has chosen to schedule only single-point (only one classroom) connections unless special permission is given in advance. This allows us to ensure the quality of the program for the teacher and students which are involved.

Unique scheduling issues come along when working with recipients and partners across the country. Time zones are difficult to handle for both content providers and content recipients. When scheduling distance learning, you may find yourself repeatedly asking the question, "Is that program supposed to start at 10:30 the provider's time, or 10:30 the recipient's time?" The best way to avoid issues with crossing time zones is to always label times stated with the time zone they apply to. For example, do not send a confirmation for a 10:30 test connection; send the confirmation for a 10:30 a.m. CST test connection. Weather in different parts of the country can have an effect as well. Content providers in Florida may never think to address what to do in the event that a DL program is cancelled due to snow in Iowa. As providers in Missouri, we did not directly feel the effects of Hurricane Katrina, until it caused a few of our scheduled lessons with schools in Florida to be cancelled. Just remember to be flexible when acts of God are involved.

In fact, it is not only beneficial but necessary for your sanity to *always* be flexible when working with school districts. Some schools have been taking part in distance learning for several years and have the steps all worked out. Other schools are new to the game and are still working on organization and logistics. Just as there are probably some content providers who are difficult to work with, there are also some school districts that are difficult to work with, and they are not always the small or inexperienced districts. This is where your partnerships with other content providers come in handy. If a certain school district is repeatedly troublesome, overly demanding, or raises some other sort of red flag to you, ask around. Chances are that someone else has had contact with this same district and can either confirm that their experience was much the same, or give some suggestions on how you might adjust your practices to enjoy the same positive results that they had with your new red-flag friends.

Kit tracking issues tie in with both scheduling and working with schools. If you choose to include kits as part of your distance learning program, make sure that you have a good system in place for keeping track of where kits are and whether they are ready to ship out or not. In the spring, which is the busiest time of year for distance learning at DCS, kits often arrive back at the Center one day and need to be shipped back out to another school the very next day. If a kit goes missing, it can wreak havoc on your entire distance learning schedule. If you have established good relationships with your recipient schools, tracking down missing kits becomes much easier. It is a good idea to ship out kits with a tracking number so that you can ensure that the kit makes it to its proper destination. If your partner schools do the same, you can also track kits on their way back to you when necessary. Depending on the content of your kits, it is probably a good idea to establish damage policies. Only after the same school completely ruined two of our kits by not repacking them properly did we create a damage policy. Schools now seem to be much more careful in following the repacking instructions.

In most areas of the country, very few people have experience with distance learning technology. Therefore, training educators to adapt to this method of program delivery can be a challenge. Audience interaction takes a new approach, as educators are speaking to an audience they cannot see in detail, facilitating classroom discussion without being able to address students by name ("you, in the third row, with the green shirt"), and are unable to physically interact with students or assist with material handling in the classroom.

As previously mentioned, our test-drives seem to be a successful mode of gaining experience. DCS educators tell us that observing other educators while they are teaching distance learning lessons is also helpful. It seems, however, that most educators need about two months or so of actually delivering lessons to remote classrooms before they become completely comfortable with teaching through a camera.

DESTINATIONS

Plans and Goals

As distance learning becomes more mainstream, the Discovery Center's primary goal is to continue to stay on the forefront as a provider of high-value educational programs. As our Center expands as a whole, we will explore new ways to utilize our distance learning program to further our mission of inspiring people of all ages with a lifelong love of learning and an appreciation for the world and our place in it. Our specific plans for the future include:

- Resurrecting and implementing new professional development distance learning workshops as both a content provider and a content recipient
- Establishing new partnerships with other content providers and school districts
- Expanding the capabilities of our lessons through emerging technologies such as wireless videoconferencing equipment
- Creating a larger presence for distance learning within our own state through increased marketing and grant partnerships to fund equipment and scholarships

Based on our experiences to date, our suggestions for overarching goals that a distance learning program can serve include:

- Expanding the size, type, and geographic location of your organization's audiences
- Providing an avenue to partner with organizations with whom you would normally have nothing in common
- Exposing educators to new teaching styles, tools, and ideas
- Adding sustainability to the organization as a whole

For us at the Discovery Center of Springfield, distance learning is one of the most successful programs we have ever implemented. We are excited about the educational opportunities that it holds, and are curious to see where the developing technology will take us. By building our program gradually as we have outlined above, we were able to alleviate some of the growing pains and missteps, but were also able to take the time to learn from the mistakes we did make. Just like all educational programs, distance learning certainly has its issues. We would encourage organizations to utilize the development models they have successfully employed in the past, but to remember to try a few new methods as well. One of the greatest things about distance learning is that the people and organizations who are working in the field are very helpful and friendly; seeking advice and guidance from others may be your best asset when starting a new program, whether you are a content provider or a content recipient.

REFERENCES

CILC: Center for Interactive Learning and Collaboration (n.d.). Retrieved August 22, 2006, from http://www.cilc.org

Distance Learning (n.d.). Retrieved August 22, 2006, from http://www.discoverycenter.org/distancelearning.php

Search Grant Opportunities (n.d.). Retrieved August 22, 2006, from http://www.grants.gov/search/basic.do

APPENDIX A: SAMPLE SURVEY

"Dial-In" Video Conference Activity
Teacher Survey Questionnaire 2003-04
Discovery Center Technology Challenge Grant Evaluation

I.   Dial-In Presentation
(Please place an "X" in the box that most appropriately expresses your opinions. Strongly Disagree = 1, Disagree = 2, Neutral = 3, Agree = 4, Strongly Agree = 5)

Title of Course: _____

Name of Dial-In Site: Discover Center of Springfield

Date of Presentation: _____

Sample survey continued on following page

Sample survey continued

This dial-in video conference…	Strongly Disagree	Disagree	Neutral	Agree	Strongly Agree
1. **Allowed** students to learn new information in a different way					
2. **Provided** an interesting "hands-on" lab activity in which students could interact					
3. **Made** connections to "real life" helping students think about the world in a new way					
4. **Had** a clear connection with presenter and students able to see/hear each other					
5. **Provided** students with feedback to their questions in a way that was easily understood					
6. **Has** prompted me to learn more about the Discovery Center by visiting their Web site (www.discoverycenter.org)					
7. **Was** too easy for my students; I would have preferred it to be more challenging					
8. **Was** too difficult for my students; they had a hard time understanding the concepts which were presented					
9. **Covered** instructional goals/objectives within my district's curriculum					
10. **Impacted** my students' learning in a positive manner					
11. **Enhanced** what my students are learning in the classroom					
12. **Was** a presentation which was worth my classroom time					
13. **Has** prompted me to participate in another video conference activity with the Discovery Center, based on my experience today					

14. Please describe anything you would change about today's video conference.

II. Personal Information
(Please place an "X" in the appropriate space and/or supply information as requested.)

1. What is your current position as an educator?

___Teacher   _____ Administrator
___ Other (Please specify: _____)

2. Please circle the grade level(s) you currently teach.

K   1   2   3   4   5   6   7   8   9   10   11   12

3.   What is the highest level of education you have completed?
      (please indicate only one)

___ Bachelors   ___ Bachelors + additional graduate hours
___ Masters   ___ Masters + additional graduate hours
___ Specialist
___ Ph.D./Ed.D.

4.   What is your gender: ___ Female   ___ Male

5.   What is the number of students in your class(es)?   _____

6.   How many students attended the video conferencing activity today?   _____
     7.   Would you characterize your school as   _____ Urban   or   _____ Rural?
          (please indicate only one)

     8.   Would you characterize your school as   _____ Public   or   _____ Private?
          (please indicate only one)

     9.   Does your school receive Title I funding?   _____ YES   _____ NO

APPENDIX B: SAMPLE PROGRAM

Sample Distance Learning Program: MAGNET MANIA

Program Description: Students will create their own forces of attraction and repulsion with static electricity and magnets, create magnetism with electricity, experiment with different variables for magnetic strength, relate magnetism to the earth, be exposed to the concept of electrons and atoms, and make their own compass. Audience: Grades 2-8.

Objectives:

•   Students will be able to assess a magnet's strength and observe limits
•   Students will demonstrate the effects of static electricity and relate to charged particles
•   Students will experience the forces of repulsion and attraction
•   Students will build their own electromagnet and experiments with changing some of the variables
•   Students will relate magnetism to the flow of electrons and earth's magnetic field, and make their own compass

Standards Alignment:

•   **National Science NS.K-4: PHYSICAL SCIENCE** As a result of the activities in grades K-4, all students should develop an understanding of light, heat, electricity, and magnetism.

- **National Science NS.5-8: PHYSICAL SCIENCE** As a result of their activities in grades 5-8, all students should develop an understanding of motions and forces and transfer of energy.

Kit Contents:

- 6 pre-lab bags, each with assorted metal and non-metal items
- 6 bags of nuts
- 1 bag of magnets (12 pieces)
- 30 balloons (1 per student)
- VC homemade electromagnet lab kit:
  - 1 bag of 15" insulated copper wires
  - 1 bag of 20" insulated copper wires
  - 1 bag of 25" insulated copper wires
  - 1 bag of 6 large iron nails
  - 6 bags of 10 paper clips in each (and 1 baggie of extras)
- 6 "6-volt" batteries
- 6 compasses
- 1 spool of sewing thread
- 6 rulers
- 6 floating magnets
- 6 bowls
- 15 straight pin taped to card stock (1 per 2 students)
- 1 film canister of iron filings
- 1 3-D magnetic field demonstrator

Chapter IV
Making the System Work:
The Content Provider and Videoconferencing in the K–12 Classroom

Patty Petrey Dees
Center for Puppetry Arts, USA

ABSTRACT

This chapter explores the modality and benefits of videoconferencing from the content provider's perspective. The content provider as "field expert" is discussed along with the benefits of providing nationwide outreach to K-12 educators and students via a cost-effective, interactive media. Applications of videoconferencing are addressed in addition to the perceptions of the provider in such areas as the needs of the K-12 educational community, methods and tools for presenting successful virtual field trips, and evidence of impact through informal teacher feedback and a professional study conducted in 2000. The author also addresses how providers can reach out to and collaboratively work with other organizations to enhance and build capacity.

INTRODUCTION

Videoconferencing has permeated rural and urban K-12 school systems across the nation and beyond. This virtual world has opened doors for non-traditional educators and professionals working in various fields of industry, science, history, and the arts to share specialized knowledge and interact with students in a real-time environment. In a recent article in *Learning and Leading in Technology*, the author notes, "Many traditional field trip resource locations such as museums, zoos, and historical sites are creating video-conferencing sessions for the K-12 audience" (Pachnowski, 2002, p. 10). The Center for Puppetry Arts, the largest nonprofit organization dedicated to puppetry in the United States, has provided arts-based videoconferencing programs to K-12 audiences since 1997. This chapter will explore the Center for Puppetry Arts' role as an effective content provider by discussing the following issues: use and perceptions of the provider, meeting educational community needs, tools for successful virtual field trips (VFTs), and evidence of impact through a professional study.

BENEFITS OF VIDEOCONFERENCING TECHNOLOGY

Benefits to the Provider

The Center has found videoconferencing to be a viable, cost-effective way to fulfill its global outreach mission of nurturing the world community of artists and expanding the puppetry art form. Prior to 1998, the Center's traditional, physical outreach was regionally and financially limited. Artists traveled in vans to schools within a 300-mile radius of Atlanta and worked face-to-face with students and teachers. The Center mainly served Georgia and South Carolina school systems. This limited regional focus was mainly due to travel and transportation costs associated with the program. The program also required four full-time staff members, a team which was difficult to maintain due to the physical demands of the job and the time spent away from home. The Center realized that it was unable to develop the national and global educational reach which had been set forth in its mission statement due to these constraints. Videoconferencing provided a viable solution by eliminating the boundaries of time and the cost associated with "physical outreach." It required fewer staff to administer programs, eliminated the overhead costs associated with travel and transportation, and allowed the Center to develop a national and international audience base, reaching 35 states and three countries by 2005 (Figure 1). The Center also was able to develop unique, hands-on puppetry arts programming complementing state and national curriculum standards in technology, fine arts, social studies, life sciences, and language arts for the K-12 audience.

Virtual Field Trips (VFTs) as Teaching Tools

One question often raised by potential funding sources and educators as a challenge to VFT programs and the teaching modality itself is the following, "Is it as effective a teaching tool as a

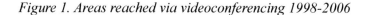

Figure 1. Areas reached via videoconferencing 1998-2006

live person in the classroom?" Alan Greenburg (2004), author of *Navigating the Sea of Research on Video Conferencing-Based Distance Education*, quotes research analyst Thomas L. Russell (2001) on this issue. Russell concludes, "From the perspective of learning outcomes, distance education technology is no better—and no worse—than the traditional classroom for delivering instruction" (p. 5). Many providers, students, and teachers, however, will argue that the benefits of this technology far surpass what one live person can do in a traditional classroom setting. They note that, for the educational community, the benefits are seemingly endless: professional development, enhanced programs, access to experts in other fields such as arts and humanities, cultural exchange and discourse in the classroom, and the opportunity to evolve into the role of content provider for field experts and teachers.

Professional Development

Videoconferencing is a viable tool for professional development of administrators and teachers. Kellah Edens (2001) author of *Bringing Authentic K-12 Classrooms and Teachers to a University Classroom through Videoconferencing*, states, "It can allow interactive interchanges with teachers and administrators impossible due to conflicts of meeting times of regular university classes and teachers' required meeting times with students at their own schools" (p. 30). Videoconferencing also can be used for instruction and accreditation for preservice and current teachers. The Center has conducted nearly 100 hands-on teacher workshops since 1998. These workshops demonstrate how to integrate puppetry arts into other classroom curricula through the use of video conferencing technology. Edens (2001) also notes, "Recommendations based on new technology standards also have been made to prepare teachers to teach in the digital age. These recommendations emphasize the importance of the integration of appropriate technologies throughout students' undergraduate

and teacher education coursework" (p. 26). Edens references the National Technology Standards (NETS) issued by the International Society for Technology in Education (ISTE), which can be found at http://www.cnets.iste.org/. As of May, 2004, 49 of the 50 states are applying the use of these standards by students, teachers, and administrators (ISTE, 2004).

The Center's teacher and K-12 workshops fully integrate NETS standards. During teacher workshops, interaction via the technology allows teachers as active participants to understand the program format and exposes them to the creative teaching methodologies demonstrated by the presenter. Teachers also engage in a dialogue with the presenter at the end of the workshop and discuss the teaching techniques employed during the workshop, potential student reaction and impact, and the "ease of use" entailed with the equipment and technology itself. The workshops foster a sense of comfort toward a new technology that many teachers find intimidating. A support system is created through peer interaction (teacher and expert) which forms a sense of community using the technology (Amirian, 2003). The use of the modality for instruction also demonstrates richer classroom curricula to teachers and can serve as a catalyst for teachers to become content providers themselves.

Teachers as Content Providers

With a "comfort factor" established, teachers as content providers are bridging a gap in the educational community. Videoconferencing has become a viable tool for school systems to share and use teachers as content providers when educators are not available locally, especially in rural areas. In an article in *U.S. News and World Report*, "Skipping the Formaldehyde: Virtual Frogs, Videoconferencing Teachers - and Vital Lessons," Mulrine (2003) writes, "Increasingly educators are taking advantage of virtual learning—some to supplement lessons, other to provide vital courses in math, science, and the fine arts that students in small, poor, or rural schools might not have otherwise" (p. 64). Lance Ford, a school district technology coordinator, notes in this same article that half of the districts in his school system use videoconferencing to bring high school and college courses to students due to teacher shortages (Mulrine, 2003). School administrators, teachers, and students all benefit from the use of this technology in this scenario.

VFTs and Field Experts as Content Providers

Videoconferencing is also a tool that fosters a broader cultural exchange for students by exposing them to experts in various fields through virtual or electronic field trips (VFTs). Schools are increasingly finding that virtual field trips are cost-effective and reduce issues involved with actual field trips, such as student transportation, safety, and time issues (Pachnowski, 2002). VFTs allow teachers to bring field experts into their classroom. Merrick (2005), author of *Videoconferencing for Primary and Secondary Schools: Where Are We?*, states "A 20-minute IVC (interactive video conference) presentation by an expert in any field can provide, in a novel and motivating way, richer content than can be presented in the same amount of time by the in-class instructor through traditional lectures" (p. 1). VFTs allow students to speak to an astronaut at NASA, or discuss puppetry manipulation techniques and themes of the production *Edgar Allan Poe* with the associate producer at the Center for Puppetry Arts. Students can also connect with other countries and participate in cross-cultural exchanges. Schools can visit the Great Barrier Reef off the coast of Australia, or connect with other classrooms around the world and converse directly with peers. The SBC knowledge network explorer's (KNE) videoconferencing directory (http://www.kn.pacbell.com/wired/vidconf/vidconf.html) lists over 1,200 content providers offering K-12 virtual field trips

around the globe. Type in "videoconferencing" in any Internet search engine and it will elicit a variety of videoconferencing directories like KNE.

"Clearinghouse" organizations have also developed in recent years to assist educators in locating reputable VFT content providers that meet K-12 curriculum needs. Interactive Digital Solutions (ID Solutions/www.e-idsolutions.com) and the Center for Interactive Learning and Collaboration (CILC/ www.cilc.org) are two examples. These groups also work directly with content providers by providing such free services as posting program offerings and schedules, offering curriculum guidelines, and providing online program evaluations.

The Modality's Appeal to Students

Besides fostering cultural exchange in students, videoconferencing is also a modality that appeals to current and future K-12 digital audiences. The Henry J. Kaiser Family Foundation recently conducted a study with the Children's Digital Media Center which documents the usage of interactive media in children ages zero to six years. The study notes that nearly half (48%) of children six and under have used a computer, 30% have played video games, and 83% of children aged 0-6 have used screen media (Rideout, Vandewater, & Wartella, 2003, p. 4). Students today belong to the electronic media generation. Thus, teaching methods and modalities must evolve to keep up with the demands of the growing digital-based audience. Students find videoconferencing to be a stimulating environment because it is an interactive media. Reactions from Eden's (2001) study involving preservice teachers, first-grade, and fifth-grade classes garnered the following reactions from students: "It was a great learning tool," and "The real live people gave me a great understanding that we do not normally have" (p. 30). Overall, teachers noted that the students viewed the opportunities to experience videoconferencing technology as "extremely exciting" (p. 30).

PROGRAM DEVELOPMENT

Aligning Programs to Curriculum Standards: The First Step

Successful content providers develop programs that meet the needs of the educational community. It is simply not enough for a videoconference topic to sound interesting. Teachers search for content that supplements their curriculum (Pachnowski, 2002). They simply do not have time to research benchmarks or standards for a program offered by a content provider. It is critical for the content provider to incorporate state and national curriculum standards into both live programs and pre/post program materials. Prospective content providers should review state and/or national benchmarks and standards *prior* to developing content. This research can often serve as a catalyst for developing relevant content that directly complements curricula.

State and national curriculum standards can be accessed easily at a variety of Web sites. EducationWorld.com (http://www.educationworld.com) is a user-friendly Web site that lists both national and state standards. The Center's VFT programs highlight specific national curriculum standards in technology, language arts, life sciences, social studies, visual arts, and performing arts (see Appendix). Study guides should provide pre- and post-activities that cite specific curriculum standards, including those standards which will be met during the live VFT. Study guides should be online and downloadable from your Web site or emailed to participating teachers.

Tips for Pre- and Post-Communication for VFTs

Both your Web site and email are invaluable tools to initiate and foster communication with all parties involved in the VFT. Teacher preparation letters sent via email are an effective way to provide preprogram communication. The teacher letter should confirm the program time (very important when working with different time zones), date, program topic, grade level, number of participating students, and link to download the study guide. It can include any preprogram instructions, student expectations, and provide a brief summary of the live program. In addition, a technical letter containing the studio phone number, contact name, equipment and connectivity (ISDN, IP, Internet2, or other) specifications is also suggested and should be emailed to the corresponding technician responsible for facilitating the connection. Pre-communication with the technical contact is very important. A test connection is highly recommended at least one week prior to the actual program connection to work out any problems that may arise.

The Applications of Traditional Classroom Teaching Methods in VFTs

Videoconferencing challenges presenters to introduce a variety of teaching methods to provoke interactivity with the students. One question often asked is, "Are classroom teaching methods applicable in the virtual classroom? Can they even serve as a resource?" This technology may improve motivation in some students if used with "already-familiar" teaching methods (Greenburg, 2003, p. 7). For example, during the Center's *Butterflies* program, oral repetition is used in addition to a visual stimulus to reinforce vocabulary words associated with the lifecycle of the butterfly. Colored visual imagery of the butterfly's life cycle is accompanied with the corresponding text: egg, caterpillar, chrysalis, and butterfly (Figure 2). The presenter sends the images via a document camera or computer, zooming in on each stage of the butterfly's life as students repeat the words after the instructor. It is a simple but effective call-and-response technique often used in traditional classrooms that works well with the multimedia aspects of videoconferencing.

It is important to incorporate a variety of teaching practices including hands-on projects, the use of kinesthetics, and other visual and auditory experiences to engage students often labeled "non-traditional" learners (students that do not respond in a traditional classroom setting or to traditional teaching methods such as lectures). All K-8 programs presented by the Center include a hands-on puppet-making activity that directly reinforces the curriculum content of the program. Students use a variety of sensory skills while following the presenter's instructions to construct their puppet. The hands-on arts element of physically constructing the puppet aids in the learning retention of students (Wenzel, 2000). Besides the "hands-on" approach, incorporating physical movement, such as wiggling side to side to mimic a caterpillar as it sheds its skin, can be particularly useful for engaging primary students. The elementary program format used by the Center balances the experiences of a hands-on art activity, physical movement corresponding to the lesson, and the use of multimedia aids to capture and maintain the attention of the younger audiences. Different learning styles are addressed during the program while curriculum standards are being met as well.

Interactivity: The Key to Successful VFTs

Successful VFTs must appeal to a variety of learners and meet curriculum standards. Most importantly, programs must be designed for interactivity. Interactivity is the most important element of a successful VFT (Greenburg, 2003). The "talking heads" of university distance learning classrooms, which were prevalent 15 years ago, have been replaced by animated presenters that expect and encourage constant discourse of the content being presented. The challenge that content providers face today is *not* to present a "lecture" via this technology, but to provide an experience that actively engages students and creates excitement for learning. Many techniques can be used to gain the interest and interaction of the audience.

To begin, content providers must know their audience in order to develop age-appropriate content and interaction. The techniques of physical movement are particularly successful with K-2 audiences. Unless students are participating in a particular theatre or dance workshop, middle- and high-school students are not the most receptive to

Figure 2. Example

kinesthetics. Hands-on art projects or activities are also highly recommended for K-5 programs. Primary students are particularly receptive to hands-on elements; therefore, all K-5 VFTs offered by the Center involve hands-on puppet-building to reinforce the curriculum content covered during the live programs (Wenzel, 2000).

Some content providers also include hands-on elements for middle- and high-school grade levels, including one Center program. *Discovering Puppetry in Other Cultures* has been highly successful with this age group. In this sixty-minute program, students build a Chinese Hand Puppet based on a warrior figure from China's Sung Dynasty. Students compare and contrast the social and historical elements of puppetry in China with other countries such as Japan and Mali. The program fosters interactivity through the hands-on puppet-building and discussion of puppets from the Center's museum collection. A document camera sends visual imagery to students to stimulate discussion, and DVD performance excerpts are incorporated to illustrate the use of puppetry in these cultures.

The Use of Multi Media

The use of multimedia in VFTs is a simple yet effective method of providing visual and auditory stimulation for nearly all audiences. Greenburg (2004) quotes research done by Modupe Irele (1999) as stating, "... in a video conferencing-based learning situation, a combination of media increases the chances of positive learning outcomes by increasing the range of learning styles that can be accommodated" (2004, p. 7). The Center has experienced that the use of short excerpts (30 seconds to seven minutes) from CDs, DVDs, or VHS clips can introduce an idea and therefore encourages a dialog between the audience and presenter. For example, high-school students view four DVD excerpts ranging in length from three minutes to seven minutes from the Center's performance *Edgar Allan Poe*. Students participate in a discussion with the presenter, the Center's associate producer, after viewing each excerpt. The presenter guides and initiates the discussion with particular curriculum content questions for the group, such as "What is exposition, and how was it portrayed in this excerpt?" Alternatively,

Figure 3. Example

the group is asked, "Which of Poe's themes are explored in this clip?"

For primary students, the *Butterflies* program includes a 30-second DVD clip of butterflies demonstrating camouflage techniques and protective markings. Excerpts are kept short to maintain the attention of a younger audience. The clip introduces a life science concept to the students visually and aurally. Students then add colors and markings to their butterfly puppets. This activity reinforces the material shown in the clip by incorporating a tactile, hands-on experience (Figure 3).

Multimedia also can include the use of computers, green screens, audio and visual mixers, the Internet, auxiliary camera sources, and a variety of visual aids, to name a few. An effective content provider incorporates the most effective multimedia to supplement or complement the program content. Multimedia should facilitate interaction with the presenter, but not override the entire presentation.

Developing VFT Content

What if an organization that is interested in providing programming through VFTs does not possess the educational or technological staff to assist with the research? An organization may need guidance in developing content, curriculum, and/or program format. Fee-based consultants are available, but can be costly. Content providers can forge partnerships with teachers in their area to assist with ideas for program development. Educational advisory and review committees are a great way to bring together teachers from various curriculum backgrounds and grade levels. In addition, a small honorarium or stipend will often garner interest from teachers, especially during summer break. "Clearinghouse" sites provide a plethora of information on content providers, program descriptions, program formats, standards and benchmarks, evaluations of programs, and study guides. Organizations should research suc-

cessful content providers to educate themselves on the programming that is already available.

Aspiring content providers also can learn a lot from existing providers. These experienced presenters can provide consultation in many areas: equipment necessities, vendor preferences, maintenance service, connectivity options, operating budgets, staffing needs, marketing programs, and successful content and teaching techniques. Copresenting a collaborative program with an experienced provider also can be the first step in "learning the ropes."

Collaborative Programming

Collaborative programs with other organizations provide yet another avenue to explore when developing engaging content. Many organizations do not possess the funding, staff, or building space necessary to open a videoconferencing studio. The Center was in this position in 1996/1997. The Center worked with Zoo Atlanta, which possessed studio space and videoconferencing equipment at that time, to provide programs through the state's videoconferencing network, until funding was secured for its own studio in 1998. The Center and Zoo Atlanta worked as copresenters and developed several programs together that adhered to state science and fine art standards for lower-primary audiences: Wacky Rabbits (PreK/1st), Monkey Business (K/1st), Giraffes (2nd/3rd), Talking Birds (2nd/3rd), and Turtle Excursion (2nd/3rd). Titles were based on science topics, but involved hands-on puppet-building that directly complemented the life science curricula being covered during the program. Once the Center established its own studio in 1998, the two organizations continued their partnership by presenting from their own studios as multi-point presenters to multi-point audiences. The programs were viewed as highly successful by both organizations as confirmed by positive teacher evaluations and waiting lists for participation in the programs.

The Center also established partner programs with the Marine Science Extension Service and the Savannah Regional Ecology Lab. These partnerships continued to foster the fusion of life science, technology, and fine arts; however, the Center wanted to expand its partnerships to include other curriculum areas. The Center forged a partnership with The Atlanta History Center to provide a program entitled: *The Aztecs: Pre-Columbian Mexico to the Present Day*. The History Center's permanent exhibit contained artifacts tracing Aztec culture to Mexican immigrants presently living in the Atlanta area. The History Center wanted to develop a program to reach out to the Hispanic population. The Puppetry Center also wanted to explore the history of puppetry in Mexico with audiences. The program allowed the two organizations to meet both their goals. The History Center did not have a videoconferencing studio, so the representative traveled to the Puppetry Center to copresent the program. This program mostly served a point-to-point audience.

Point-to-Point vs. Multi-Point

What are the advantages and disadvantages of point-to-point and multi-point conferences? This is a question that challenges all content providers. Some school districts or state networks, such as the Digital Dakota Network (DDN) in South Dakota, prefer that content providers interact with multiple sites; as a result, the Center interacts with seven to ten sites in South Dakota during one program, serving up to 250 students at one time. The financial savings is the most obvious benefit for the school district; large numbers of students are served for a small amount of money. The district pays one program fee versus 10 program fees. The cost for each student to participate in a Center program can be less than $2.00. Schools view this as a major economical benefit of videoconferencing. This process also enables the content provider to serve large numbers of students at once. This could be beneficial for an institution with a small staff that may have time to conduct only one VFT versus ten. Content providers, however, are faced with the challenge of maintaining the interest and interactivity of ten different classrooms. This can be difficult for even the most experienced content provider. It requires a skilled presenter who can *effectively present the content* while initiating the interaction between multiple sites. This format proves to be even more challenging when working with a primary audience. A content provider can quickly lose younger students' attention without consistent interaction.

What is the ideal number of participants for a multi-point conference? It varies, depending on the program topic, format, and preference of the content provider. Providers may want to allow three or four classrooms to participate if the program topic is discussion-based and geared toward interaction between students at different locations. On the other hand, content providers may prefer point-to-point connections where students in one classroom are the sole focus of the presenter and vice versa. Point-to-point conferences have several positives and negatives. On the positive side, point-to-point conferences stimulate the most interaction between presenter and students. Technical problems are also easier to resolve when working with one site. If a class is late or unprepared, it does not interrupt the experience for other sites as it would in a multi-point conference. There are, however, several drawbacks of point-to-point videoconferencing to consider: no peer communication between students, higher cost ratio per student than with a multi-point videoconference, and smaller audience numbers reached by the provider.

The ability to facilitate both types of conferences is a key component to becoming a good content provider. Content providers should encourage feedback through formal evaluations, informal emails from participating teachers, or direct discussion with teachers. Consideration of this feedback can be used to guide providers in choosing the best format for their program.

A CASE EXAMPLE: A HISTORY OF THE DEVELOPMENT OF A VFT PROGRAM

The Founding of the Program

The Center has built a strong K-12 audience base through its VFTs since the program's inception in 1997. The history of the development of the Center's Distance Learning Program is important to understanding the evidence of impact which is presented later in this chapter. As mentioned previously, the Center's journey into virtual education began in 1997 when the Center trained and copresented programs with Zoo Atlanta. The Center joined the state of Georgia's ISDN-based videoconferencing network, the Georgia State-wide Academic and Medical Systems Network (GSAMS), in the fall of 1998, and began working

with K-5 schools. The state network of Georgia, established in 1992, was one of the first of its kind in the nation and, at one time, served as a model to other states interested in establishing their own videoconferencing networks. At the time, there were over 100 K-12 sites on the network. The Center developed its original K-5 programming for multi-point audiences and worked with teacher groups and the Center's Educational Advisory Committee to evaluate subject matter and curriculum needs. The Coca-Cola Foundation provided funding to purchase videoconferencing equipment and develop programming for the first three years. The Center was responsible for providing the salary and benefits of one part-time staff member, the distance learning specialist (who also served as the education director).

Within the next several years, the Center expanded its offerings to include middle- and high-school programs as well as teacher workshops. Demand for programming grew rapidly over the next three years. The Center served just over 5,600 students in 1998-1999 versus over 17,000 in 2005-2006 (Figure 4). The state network allowed the Center to have a global reach, but it operated on a fee-based system for its bridging service.

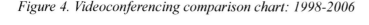

Figure 4. Videoconferencing comparison chart: 1998-2006

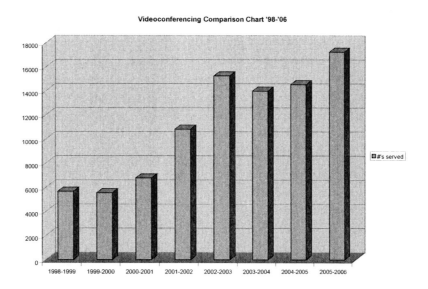

The ISDN network also was quickly becoming defunct due to IP migration.

It was no longer the nations "premier" video-conferencing network, and had been far surpassed by networks and technological developments in other states.

There were other drawbacks to being part of the state network as well. It had no supporting financial or programming infrastructure for content providers. Content providers that were not in the school system, such as field experts in non-profit arts and science museums, were subject to large maintenance and connectivity fees to be part of the network. These organizations were also restricted from charging program fees to Georgia schools; all programs were free. It became a "Catch 22" situation for content providers. By 2004, all field expert content providers left the network. Schools also could no longer afford the fees associated with the network, and most K-12 sites dropped the network entirely.

The Center began offering more programs to out-of-state schools in 2003-2004 to begin building its national audience base and recouping some operating and programming expenses. One additional part-time staff member was added to assist with VFT presentations and school bookings. The Center experienced a slight decrease in numbers of participating students due to out-of-state schools preferring point-to-point interaction (averaging 20 participants) versus Georgia schools that were booked as multi-point conferences (averaging 100 participants). Participation was still high in Georgia; however, all participants came from only five local counties. The Center was no longer reaching a regionally-diverse audience. Out-of-state requests continued to rise, but the Center had to pay a large bridging fee that amounted to nearly 50 % of the programming fee for every connection made outside the state. Programs had reached 27 states by 2004, but the outreach came with a price tag which the Center could no longer afford. The Center was faced with a decision in

December 2004: close the program, or leave the state network.

The Center secured new IP-capable equipment through a donation from TANDBERG, an international videoconferencing vendor, and decided to leave the state network in 2004-2005 in order to move forward with its own IP network that was still ISDN-capable. The Center chose to offer both IP and ISDN connectivity options, because many school systems were ISDN-based with plans to transition to IP networks within the next two years. ISDN was provided through standard BRI lines that functioned perfectly. The Center connected IP via an ADSL-dedicated loop, considered risky by many due to DSL technology. The connection proved to dispel the belief that DSL cannot provide a quality videoconference connection. The connections were better in overall audio and video quality than those provided by the state. In addition, the monthly cost of an ADSL connection was a tenth of the state's monthly fee charged to the Center for use of the ISDN-based network.

Connectivity Options: The Migration to IP

The 2004-2005 school year saw an increase in IP networks and connections. The 2005-2006 school year showed that IP networks were continuing to gain in popularity as the technology continued to develop and to provide greater bandwidth and stable connections. A recent white paper written by Wainhouse Research notes, "Wainhouse Research estimates that in 2004, IP became the most common network used for hosting videoconferencing calls" (Weinstein, 2006, p. 1). ISDN, however, cannot be disregarded completely due to its continued use by many schools systems in states such as Texas and New York. There is usually a larger financial cost on both ends when dealing with ISDN, however (Weinstein, 2006). Long-distance line charges are paid by the participating school to connect with the content provider. Monthly

ISDN-BRI lines charges are paid by the content provider to provide ISDN connections. For content providers, IP is not as costly in most circumstances (Weinstein, 2006). The monthly fee paid by the Center for the IP connectivity is only 25% of the cost of the monthly fee paid for the ISDN-BRI lines. IP can also eliminate the use of a bridging service to connect to some schools that operate on closed networks. The Center has experienced that direct connections (without the use of a bridge) from content provider to the participating site produce higher quality connections.

ISDN is quickly being replaced by updated technologies, and school systems acknowledge the need to move forward with IP, Internet 2, and other developing technologies. Content providers must decide if ISDN connectivity is still necessary or not for the particular audience that they are trying to reach. The 2005-2006 school year continued to exceed the previous year in the number of videoconference programs and the number of students that were served due to the Center's use of both technologies. As the 2006-2007 school year begins, the Center believes that it is still necessary to provide ISDN connectivity, since about 35-40% of all connections from its K-12 audience still involve ISDN.

Evidence of Impact

The Center has employed a variety of evaluative tools to gauge the success and impact of its programs. Teacher feedback is invaluable and can assist content providers in improving programs. Unsolicited feedback is often received via email from participating teachers. Why email? Perhaps it is because teachers are not restricted by the parameters of a formal evaluation tool. The Center has discovered that email often provides the most honest criticism from teachers, both positive and negative. The Center does provide a formal evaluation form for teachers to express feedback on the programs; however, very few are returned. Teachers are busy and have little

time for additional paperwork. Most content providers will agree that it is difficult to obtain post-program evaluations. Evaluation tools can be made readily available to teachers by posting them online, attaching them to program study guides, or making them downloadable on a Web site either via the study guide or independent of it. Also, making a verbal request at the end of the VFT or by follow-up email after a program can improve the number of evaluations that are returned. The Center receives a high return of program evaluations from agencies that assist K-12 schools in booking VFTs. The Center for Interactive Learning and Collaboration (CILC) is one such agency. They provide their own online evaluation forms to participating schools. A copy of the completed evaluation is sent to the provider via email. These types of evaluation forms involve rating a presenter on a scale of some sort, and the form provides an area for the participants' overall comments. The Center receives more generic responses using a formal evaluation tool, but the structured questions and answers allow for more conducive and measurable results.

A Formal VFT Program Assessment

Measurable results can be especially beneficial when trying to prove the success of a program to the funding community. Potential funders encourage and often require the formal assessment of a program. The Center conducted a formal assessment of its videoconferencing program in 1999-2000. At that time, the Center needed to secure future financial assistance for the program due to the high costs associated with the state videoconferencing network. The Center received a grant from The Community Foundation for Greater Atlanta to finance this critical project. The Center's education director who founded the Distance Learning Program, Patty Petrey Dees, worked with the Educational Advisory Committee to select a scholar to develop the assessment instruments for the program. This expert worked with the education director to develop the content and the implementation of the assessment tools.

Next, the director secured a partnership with three school districts in metro-Atlanta counties. Their selection was based on their consistent use of the Center's VFTs and highly-competent video-conferencing coordinators. The videoconferencing coordinators served as on-site facilitators at the schools and were responsible for distributing the assessment tools to teachers. Teachers facilitated pre-assessments in the VFT studio prior to the program and post-assessments in the classroom after the conference. The assessments measured the students' retention of material in a distance education workshop and students' increased interest in other traditions/cultures. Teachers also participated in the assessment, with the on-site facilitator administering the evaluation tool. The Center hoped to prove that 50% of teachers would increase hands-on classroom activities to reinforce learning after participating in a VFT. Teachers then returned assessments to the video-conferencing coordinators. Coordinators faxed the completed assessment tools to the outside evaluator, who analyzed the data and provided the results to the Center in April, 2000.

As a result of this process, the assessment was relatively easy to implement and had very positive results. The assessment involved 10 elementary-school classes from grades 2-5 and included 109 females (47%) and 124 males (53%) for a total of 233 students. Ethnicity included 80% white, 15% African-American, 4.5% Asian-American, and 0.5% other. "Two of three expected outcomes were achieved. Of students' outcomes, one was exceeded by 3% and one was short by 3%, thus a balance is cited concerning retention of material and increased interest. Teacher outcomes exceeded expectations by 33%" (Wenzel, 2000, p. 1). The report also states, "Overall, the assessment results are positive. Results correlate with expectations, with teacher input exceeding student output. It may be noted that numerous factors are involved, including collaboration

between teacher and remote-site facilitators, the divergence of students' previous knowledge and interest, and the novelty of interaction involving a simulated classroom via telecommunications (Wenzel, 2000, p. 2)." The resulted outcomes of the assessment are as follows: Sixty-eight percent of students retained 75% of the material in a distance education workshop, 47% of students increased interest in other traditions/cultures; 83% of teachers increased hands-on classroom activities to reinforce learning (Wenzel, 2000).

Securing Grant Funding

The impact of the formal assessment has been instrumental in securing private grant funding for the entire Center for Puppetry Arts by broadening its potential funding base in the community. The innovative K-12 curriculum-based VFTs, coupled with proven measurable statistics, initiated many new funding opportunities with local and national community arts partners. The Coca-Cola Foundation, which provided the Center's first grant in 1998 to purchase the videoconferencing equipment and develop programming, has continued providing financial support based upon the proven success of the program. Lucent Technologies, BellSouth, and Cingular Wireless were also early funders of the program. The 1999-2000 assessment brought forth additional funding dollars for the Distance Learning Program from such private companies as the UPS Foundation, the South Share Foundation, and TANDBERG. The assessment also insured the continuation of private and public funding for the Center on the state and national level. Most notably, in 2000, the Center received an award from the highly-respected Ford Foundation as one of the only 28 arts organizations across the country for excellence in management and programming innovation. The Foundation recognized the Center as having one of the most extensive arts education programs in the nation. This recognition by such prestigious foundations has promoted the Center's reputation on a national and international level. Georgia's state art agency recognizes the Center's Distance Learning Program as a model for other arts and nonprofit organizations wishing to establish a videoconferencing studio. The Center has consulted with school districts and numerous other non-profit agencies interested in establishing a videoconferencing program. The Center is also considered a content leader in K-12 VFTs. Presentations and/or demonstrations at state and national technology conferences such as the National Education in Computing Conference (NECC) and Keystone Conference (national K-12 videoconferencing conference) allow the Center to connect with peer providers and broaden its audience base. The Center is recognized as a top provider on such Web sites as CILC (http://www.cilc.org), ID Solutions (http://www.e-idsolutions.com/), TWICE/Polycom (http://www.twice.cc/fieldtrips.html), and TANDBERG Connections (http://www.tandberg.net/ind_focus/education/connections.jsp). Most recently, the Center's VFT program was one of two recipients of the *2006 Teachers' Choice Award* for *Best Content Provider - Fine Arts Museum (*http://www.twice.cc/fieldtrips.html)

CONCLUSION

The Center for Puppetry Arts began videoconferencing and offering collaborative VFTs in 1997. With the establishment of its own studio in 1998, the Center has grown to be a top content provider in K-12 VFTs serving nearly 90,000 students and teachers as of 2006. Videoconferencing allows the Center to fulfill its mission of educating the public on puppetry through an interactive modality that is both economically "sound" and innovative. The Center is no longer restricted by time or cost, and serves K-12 students, teachers, and other community agencies throughout North America. Professional development workshops and curriculum-based content infuses the puppetry arts with life science, social studies, language arts,

and fine arts curriculum to introduce teachers to innovative teaching techniques that incorporate a variety of learning styles. The Center continues to measure its programming impact through the formal assessment of the program conducted in 1999-2000 and ongoing teacher evaluations. Private and public funding agencies recognize the success of the Center's videoconferencing program; however, funding for the nonprofit sector continues to shrink as competition for funds continues to grow. The Center plans to promote future growth by continuing to infuse the educational needs and resources within the community into its programming. The Center believes that its dynamic and highly-interactive VFT content will secure its future as a national leader in K-12 education.

REFERENCES

Amirian, S. (2003, October). Pedagogy and videoconferencing: A review of recent literature. In *Proceedings of the First NJEDge.NET Conference,* Plainsboro, New Jersey.

Edens, K. M. (2001). Bringing authentic K-12 classrooms and teachers to a university classroom through videoconferencing. *Journal of Computing in Teacher Education, 17*(3), 26-31.

Greenburg, A. (2003). Best practices in live content acquisition by distance learning organizations: Enhancing primary- and secondary-school classrooms by tapping content resources via two-way interactive video. *Wainhouse Research.* Retrieved February, 2006, from http://www.wainhouse.com/files/papers/wr-content-acq.pdf

Greenburg, A. (2004). Navigating the sea of research on video conferencing-based education: A platform for understanding research into the technology's effectiveness and value. *Wainhouse Research.* Retrieved February, 2006, from http://www.wainhouse.com/files/papers/wr-navseadistedu.pdf

Hamza, M., Checker, C., & Perez, B. (2001). Creative leaps in distance education technologies. *International Society for Technology in Education, SIGTel Bulletin, Archives*. Retrieved March, 2006, from http://www.iste.org/Content/Navigation-Menu/Membership/SIGs/SIGTel_Telelearning_/SIGTel_Bulletin2/Archive/20012/2001_June_-_Hamza.htm

Irele, M. (1999). Cost-benefit analysis in distance education. *Lucent Technologies and the World Campus, Pennsylvania State University.*

International Society for Technology in Education (2004). Use of NETS by state. National education technology standards (NETS) and the states (updated May 19, 2004). Retrieved April, 2006, from http://cnets.iste.org/docs/States_using_NETS.pdf

Merrick, S. (2005). Videoconferencing primary and secondary: The state of the art. *Innovate, 2*(1). Retrieved April, 2006, from http://www.tandberg.net/ind_focus/education/index.jsp

Mulrine, A. (2003). Skipping the formaldehyde: Virtual frogs, videoconferencing teachers - and vital lessons. *U.S. News and World Report, 135*(13), 64.

Pachnowski, L. M. (2002). Virtual field trips through technology. *Learning and Leading with Technology, 29*(6), 10-13.

Rideout, V., Vandewater, E., & Wartella, E. (2003). Zero to six: Electronic media in the lives of infants, toddlers, and preschoolers. *The Henry J. Kaiser Family Foundation*, 1-38. Retrieved April, 2006, from http://www.kff.org/entmedia/upload/Zero-to-Six-Electronic-Media-in-the-Lives-of-Infants-Toddlers-and-Preschoolers-PDF.pdf

Russell, T. L. (2001). *The no significant difference phenomenon: A comparative research annotated bibliography on technology in education, 5th ed.* Montgomery, AL: IDECC.

Weinstein, I. M. (2006). The ISDN to IP migration for videoconferencing: Real world options that make both dollars and sense. *Wainhouse Research*. Retrieved March, 2006, from http://www.tandberg.net/ind_focus/education/index.jsp

Wenzel, G. C. (2000). Center for Puppetry Arts GSAMS outcomes: Survey assessment instrument results for distance education. Retrieved February 2006, from http://www.puppet.org/edu/distance.shtml

APPENDIX:
SAMPLE OF A VIDEOCONFERENCING PROGRAM

Program: Butterflies

Content Provider	Center for Puppetry Arts
Contact Information	Patty Petrey Dees Distance Learning Program Director distancelearning@puppet.org 1404 Spring St., NW @ 18th St. Atlanta, GA 30309 United States Phone: (404) 881-5117 Fax: (404) 873-9907
Target Audience	K,1,2
Primary Disciplines	Fine Arts, Sciences
Secondary Disciplines	Technology/Information Science
Program Description	Each student will construct a Butterfly Marionette while participating in learning activities about the lifecycle of the butterfly, what makes a butterfly an insect, and coloring and camouflage. Video clips and photographs of the different stages in the life of a butterfly are included. This is a great arts and science lesson all in one! Puppet materials are easy-to-find, low-cost items that can mostly be found around the classroom. The materials list, templates, and curriculum-based study guide can be downloaded from our website.
Program Format	1. This program begins by showing the students an example of the type of puppet we will be making-- a marionette. 2. We identify our focus butterfly-- the monarch-- and do our first puppet building step. Students also "stretch" their wings by stretching their arms (kinesthetic activity). 3. We do an interactive learning activity on the lifecycle of the monarch butterfly. Students participate in a kin esthetic activity by doing a "wiggle jiggle" dance mimicking a monarch shedding its skin (kinesthetic activity). 4. We work on our second section of puppet building by adding colors and markings to the butterfly's wings. Symmetry is discussed and visual aids (document camera) give examples. 5. We do an interactive learning activity on the coloring, camouflage, and protective markings of butterflies. Students view a DVD clip of butterflies using protective devices. 6. Students work on the third section of puppet building-- adding the insect body parts. A kinesthetic activity teaches students the names of the body parts. 7. We discuss the characteristics of all insects. 8. We finish the puppet and demonstrate manipulation techniques. Students manipulate their puppets to the visual and oral instruction.
Objectives	- Students will develop and appreciation for the global art form of puppetry. - Students will identify the characteristics of insects. - Students will discuss protective devices (how butterflies use coloring and camouflage to protect themselves from predators). - Students will explore the lifecycle of the butterfly. - Students will create a working puppet. - Students will recognize the use of arts in other disciplines—specifically life science.

Continued on following page

Table continued

| National Standards to which this program aligns | **National Technology**
NT.K-12.1 BASIC OPERATIONS AND CONCEPTS

Students demonstrate a sound understanding of the nature and operation of technology systems.

Students are proficient in the use of technology.

NT.K-12.2 SOCIAL, ETHICAL AND HUMAN ISSUES

Students understand the ethical, cultural, and societal issues related to technology.

Students practice responsible use of technology systems, information, and software.

Students develop positive attitudes toward technology uses that support lifelong learning, collaboration, personal pursuits, and productivity.

NT.K-12.3 TECHNOLOGY PRODUCTIVITY TOOLS

Students use technology tools to enhance learning, increase productivity, and promote creativity.

NT.K-12.4 TECHNOLOGY COMMUNICATION TOOLS

Students use telecommunications to collaborate, publish, and interact with peers, experts, and other audiences. Students use a variety of media and formats to communicate information and ideas effectively to multiple audiences.

NT.K-12.5 TECHNOLOGY RESEARCH TOOLS

Students use technology to locate, evaluate, and collect information from a variety of sources. Students use technology tools to process data and report results. Students evaluate and select new information resources and technological innovations based on the appropriateness for specific tasks.

NT.K-12.6 TECHNOLOGY PROBLEM- SOLVING AND DECISION-MAKING TOOLS

Students use technology resources for solving problems and making informed decisions.

Students employ technology in the development of strategies for solving problems in the real world. |
| National Standards to which this program aligns. continued | **National Life Science**
NS.K-4.3 LIFE SCIENCE

As a result of activities in grades K-4, all students should develop understanding of

The characteristics of organisms

Life cycles of organisms
Organisms and environments

National Visual Arts
NA-VA.K-4.1 UNDERSTANDING AND APPLYING MEDIA, TECHNIQUES, AND PROCESSES

Achievement Standard:

Students know the differences between materials, techniques, and processes

Students describe how different materials, techniques, and processes cause different responses

Students use different media, techniques, and processes to communicate ideas, experiences, and stories

Students use art materials and tools in a safe and responsible manner

NA-VA.K-4.2 USING KNOWLEDGE OF STRUCTURES AND FUNCTIONS

Achievement Standard:

Students know the differences among visual characteristics and purposes of art in order to convey ideas

Students use visual structures and functions of art to communicate ideas |

Continued on following page

Table continued

National Standards to which this program aligns. continued	**NA-VA.K-4.3 CHOOSING AND EVALUATING A RANGE OF SUBJECT MATTER, SYMBOLS, AND IDEAS** Achievement Standard: Students explore and understand prospective content for works of art Students select and use subject matter, symbols, and ideas to communicate meaning **NA-VA.K-4.4 UNDERSTANDING THE VISUAL ARTS IN RELATION TO HISTORY AND CULTURES** Achievement Standard: Students know that the visual arts have both a history and specific relationships to various cultures Students identify specific works of art as belonging to particular cultures, times, and places Students demonstrate how history, culture, and the visual arts can influence each other in making and studying works of art **NA-VA.K-4.5 REFLECTING UPON AND ASSESSING THE CHARACTERISTICS AND MERITS OF THEIR WORK AND THE WORK OF OTHERS** Achievement Standard: Students understand there are various purposes for creating works of visual art Students describe how people's experiences influence the development of specific artworks Students understand there are different responses to specific artworks **NA-VA.K-4.6 MAKING CONNECTIONS BETWEEN VISUAL ARTS AND OTHER DISCIPLINES** Achievement Standard: Students understand and use similarities and differences between characteristics of the visual arts and other arts disciplines Students identify connections between the visual arts and other disciplines in the curriculum decisions. Students employ technology in the development of strategies for solving problems in the real world.
Program Length	50 minutes
By Request	This program is available by request/on demand ONLY
Connection Type(s) Available and Program Fees	Point to Point Cost: $145.00 Multi-point Cost: $145.00 for up to 3 sites Receiving Site is responsible for own line charge
Program Fee Notes	Book 8 programs and the 9th is FREE.
Cancellation Policy	We will not charge for programs cancelled due to nature i.e. snow days or if there are technical problems that do not allow a connection. Sites will need to reschedule. Sites will be charged the full fee if cancelled within 48 hours of conference.
Is videotaping allowed?	No
Connectivity Technology	IP – Preferred speed of 384 K ISDN- Minimum Broadcast Speed: 128 K Maximum Broadcast Speed: 384 K
Minimum Technology Specifications for sites connecting to this provider	Schools are required to dial in to us directly. Minimum speed of 128 k is required with a maximum speed of 384 k.

Chapter V
From Concept to Conference:
Developing a Distance Learning Lesson Using a Museum/School Collaboration Model

Sharon Vatsky
Solomon R. Guggenheim Museum, USA

ABSTRACT

This chapter discusses various points of view regarding the process of developing a videoconferencing lesson that focuses on an architectural landmark, the Solomon R. Guggenheim Museum. This lesson was the result of collaboration among provider educators from the Solomon R. Guggenheim Museum, and three teachers. The project involved a working partnership that lasted a year and a half, culminating with the launch of the videoconference lesson. Information on establishing the goals, developing the program, and assessing outcomes are provided. This chapter includes input from the museum and from teachers at the participating schools about the collaboration process and its value to participants.

INTRODUCTION AND OVERVIEW

In the autumn of 2001, the Solomon R. Guggenheim Museum was poised to open the Sackler Center for Arts Education on the lower level of its famed Frank Lloyd Wright-designed landmark museum. In this visionary facility, the presence of videoconferencing technology provided the museum with the ability to reach and engage new audiences. Museum staff, however, had yet to answer several key questions about the videoconference process: How could the museum identify new audiences? What would those audiences find compelling? What was the best way to structure the outreach? How could the museum manage staff and resources to allow for developing and delivering videoconference lessons?

In surveying the museum education landscape, it was apparent that the readiness to delve into new technology similar to that available in the

Guggenheim's new facility ran the gamut from fully capable to nonexistent. Some content providers already were well on their way to integrating videoconferencing into their museum mission. For instance, by 2000, the Philadelphia Museum of Art and the Museum of Modern Art (New York City) had established extensive videoconferencing programs. Other parallel institutions had neither the equipment nor the staff to devote to the new technology. As a result, the Guggenheim was in need of an opportunity to collaborate with another institution to develop its own readiness to embark on a new course in program delivery.

It was at this time that *Project VIEW[1],* a federally-funded Technology Innovation Challenge grant program based in Schenectady, New York, approached the museum and offered an invitation to join a community of schools and content providers who were working to create infrastructure for delivering world-class education to students using interactive educational technology. VIEW involved a development model that simultaneously trained teachers in the use of videoconferencing methods for the classroom and also facilitated content providers' efforts to share their resources through interactive videoconference programming.

For the Solomon R. Guggenheim Museum, the invitation to collaborate could not have come at a more perfect time. Although the museum receives many requests to participate in programs, it rarely is able to accept the offers; however, the VIEW model possessed unique and practical attributes that addressed the then-current needs of the Guggenheim. First, VIEW was committed to alignment of project focus with museum mission; and second, it required the in-depth involvement of teacher teams (consumers) in program development.

Institution-Aligned Project Focus

Under the VIEW model, it is important that partners recognize that the content provider (in this case, the Guggenheim) determines the theme or focus of the videoconferencing lesson. This is a simple yet crucial premise. Once the focus that met the provider's educational philosophy is established, school-based teacher teams can participate in collaborative planning and curriculum design that determine the final specific content and structure of the videoconference. This basic procedure ensures that the topic for the lesson will be one central to the museum's mission and will reflect the needs of the schools.

To this end, the initial phase of the Guggenheim collaboration asked museum education staff to identify a general theme for a pilot lesson. After careful consideration, it was decided that the videoconferencing lesson would focus on the museum's unique Frank Lloyd Wright architecture. The design of the museum is both central to its identity, and, based on visitor surveys, is an important factor in determining why audiences locally, nationally, and internationally decide to make the museum a destination.

The architecture focus was a broad-enough umbrella to subsume various curricular areas and diverse grade levels. Architecture can serve as an effective means of teaching social studies and demonstrating that art forms are a reflection of the cultural milieu in which they were created. For art classes, architecture in general, and Frank Lloyd Wright in particular, provides opportunities to explore aesthetic and functional problem-solving and the design tenet of "form follows function". For middle-school art students, architecture provided a perfect stimulus for a study of three-dimensional design elements and constructive techniques. The Guggenheim's unique architectural design and well-known reputation provided an additional aura of interest.

Development Readiness

Educators from the Guggenheim recognized that they needed some fundamental training in classroom videoconference integration and delivery. Thus, they enthusiastically took advantage of an invitation to observe and participate in videoconference training that not only offered a core education in techniques of integrating videoconference content into classroom curriculum, but also provided the opportunity to view other videoconference programs, including those of the Baseball Hall of Fame, the Albany Institute of History and Art, and the Philadelphia Museum of Art. The following underlying factors were pivotal to the various successes in videoconferencing:

- Focused and structured lessons
- Opportunities for authentic, active engagement and interaction
- Engaging style of the videoconference presenter
- Limit on the size of the student groups to ensure opportunities for maximum participation
- Cooperation of both the presenter and classroom teacher
- Visual interest of "the set", including background and lighting
- Technical support, so image and sound allowed for clear transmission and true interaction

Project-Aligned Teacher Teams

Following training in videoconferencing, the process for assembling a team of teachers began. The selection criteria ensured the recruitment of teachers who were already aware of the exciting curriculum applications that the preselected project focus, the study of architecture, could provide. Many of the teachers who responded already were incorporating the study of architecture in their classrooms. Some were using architecture to teach local history. Others had constructed architectural models with their students. The diversity of the team[2] of teachers across grades levels and subject areas assured that the resulting content would be broadly relevant.

From the teacher's perspective, videoconferencing was an exciting prospect, and it offered an opportunity to incorporate enriched content through technology into classroom presentation. From the outset, teachers assumed that students would be intrigued by the dynamic nature of a videoconference format, and the expertise of Guggenheim personnel added credence to an architectural curriculum project and provided site-based content that offered an additional dimension to supplement learning. On the other

Figure 1.

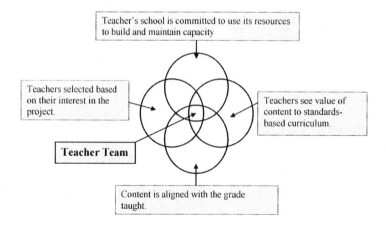

72

hand, although the teachers were enthusiastic, they were concerned about the work commitment and time spent out of the classroom, about whether their schools would have the appropriate technology to actually utilize the product of their work, and whether conflicting scheduling constraints might prevent them from being able to schedule videoconferences for their students.

Collaborative Development of the Lesson

The museum took the role of leader, providing content regarding the museum and its collections. The museum educators knew the history, archives, photographic documentation, and the story they wanted to tell. The teacher's expertise guided the curriculum connections, and provided advice and fine-tuning for the evolving lesson.

The museum found the process of collaborative development an instructive enterprise. During the course of the project, the teachers and museum educators met both in person and through videoconferencing. To introduce the program content to the teachers, the museum educators met with the team at the museum so that they (the teachers) could become immersed in the collection and architecture of the site. They toured the galleries, visited the Sackler Center for Arts Education, and met with Guggenheim educational staff members. Historical videos focusing on the building and other archival materials were viewed, followed by a discussion focusing on how some of these resources might be incorporated into the lesson.

The fact that the project provided financial support for the museum was crucial. Without this funding, it would not have been possible to provide the commitment of staff time needed to develop the project. With funding, the research, development, collaboration, and support of the cultural institution could all be brought to the project. Providing ongoing financial support at varying levels throughout the three-year period allowed for continuing collaboration.

Funding ensured the technical and professional support to troubleshoot problems and draw on the expertise of trained staff. This component would

Figure 2. Teachers Hokanson and Bordick review lesson materials during their visit to the Guggenheim

Figure 3.

Summary of Collaborative Development:

- Team selection: focused on synergy with museum mission

- Content integration: alignment of content focus among team members

- Program articulation: what will be included, what will work

- Mutual contributions: collaborative integration of expertise

- Supporting resource development: teachers and museum generated

- Alignment with audience: age, curriculum, standards

- Project testing and retooling: Multiphase with different audiences

become crucial when experiencing a technical glitch that can derail even the best educational efforts. The technical teams at the Guggenheim Museum were able to consult with the technical experts who were skilled in the technical aspects of the program.

After visiting the museum, the teachers and the museum educators met several times via videoconference technology. There was a short period of adjustment to the videoconferencing communication, but they soon were at ease, conducting the sessions seamlessly as they collaboratively outlined the videoconference and the supporting materials that they were developing.

From the outset, it was determined that the videoconference for students would be both visual and interactive. It would use images of the museum and ask students for their perceptions and interpretation. This inquiry-based approach that posed open-ended questions to the students and encouraged them to respond with multiple interpretations was what made videoconferencing technology exciting and interesting. This same philosophy of using open-ended questions to facilitate discussion has long been in use by the museum's education department, and it

permeates every level of the institution programming. In the project development sessions, the participants reviewed ideas and discussed the viability of activities in the environment of the videoconference.

In this project, all participants felt that an essential part of the videoconference development was the identification and creation of supporting educational materials. Teacher-created materials were placed on a project Web site where other educators could benefit from their work[3], and the resources created by the Guggenheim staff were mounted on the museum's site in a special section devoted to the museum's architecture.[4] The Web sites provided a resource location where teachers could share supplementary and preparatory materials. The materials were selected to be easily used in the classroom and aligned with State and National Learning Standards.

The project also provided the teachers with resources to extend learning opportunities for the students in diverse ways. At the elementary level, for example, the Guggenheim experience created a foundation for students to engage in classroom research experiences. The videoconference was integrated into the curriculum and was

Figure 4. Teachers' videoconference with the Guggenheim

one of several activities including student-made videos, and a classroom museum that extended learning opportunities. One particular project required the students to create structures based on the culture and climate of a particular location in the world. The activity culminated in the creation of a mock television show where student reporters interviewed student architects in sites throughout the world.

TESTING THE LESSON

Over the course of several months, the developing videoconference and supporting lessons were presented to the teachers several times for feedback. As the lesson took shape, it was piloted first with the teachers on the development team who offered suggestions for how the activities could be fine-tuned to make the videoconference more appealing to the students. The next step was to test the lesson with classes of other teachers, first to small groups of students at the elementary- and middle-school levels, and finally to whole classes. At each level, the museum garnered feedback from all participants and continued the process of fine-tuning the videoconference presentation.

This incremental process of development and testing was extremely valuable. Having the experienced critique of a variety of teachers provided the museum with a group of curriculum experts who could evaluate the content and program delivery at every step of development. As the lesson came together, the teachers provided feedback on supporting components, including curriculum links, preparatory lessons, and activities. All work was assessed for age-appropriateness. Input went beyond the pedagogic to include suggestions for ways to enhance the backgrounds and lighting for the videoconference "set". In the end, teachers found the process to be valuable to themselves, their institutions, and the students.

Outcomes

Multiple outcomes were noted by the teachers and project staff as a result of use of the videoconference. Teachers observed that students who participated appeared more stimulated and more motivated. Further, they noted that the hands-on, visual approach is more effective with special-needs students. Overall, students were excited by the personal connections established with museum educators in the videoconferences.

Vignette 1. Expanding elementary curriculum

Felicia Bordick, 3rd Grade Teacher, Glenmont Elementary School, NY
Gale Derosia, Art Teacher, Glenmont Elementary School, NY

The thematic study of architecture provided the focal point for us to collaboratively design original lesson plans to meet the criteria social studies (world cultures) as well as art (cultural study and three dimensional design) objectives. Woven throughout the videoconference project were also lessons in geometry, measuring, and science. The result was that the children were treated to a series of highly cohesive activities that included:

- creating unique structures inspired by natural forms
- building unusual birdhouses that were placed and observed on school grounds
- cooperating on group collages which offered a representation of the need of a particular location and climate
- studying the floor plans of the school building, and then using these floor plans to construct buildings meant for a specific function

For the culmination, individual students were assigned an independent research project to be completed over a six-week period. The project required the study of a location in the world significant for its natural resources, culture, and climate. The goal of the research was to create an original structure that conveyed a basic principle of architecture, 'form follows function'. Once the study and construction were completed, the class wrote their own television show called The Tomorrow Show. Students played the dual roles of architect of the new building as well as the reporter on location. The script, set design, theme song, commercials, and interviews were all student creations with guidance from their teachers.

Although many aspects of the students' year long study of architecture in general, and the Guggenheim in particular, proved inspirational, it was the teleconference with the Guggenheim that sparked the notion to make their own TV show using a video camera. This year long interdisciplinary approach was multifaceted and tapped into student's undiscovered strengths and talents.

Vignette 2. Extending the lesson

Suzanne Hokanson, Art Teacher, Bethlehem Middle School, NY

A connection with the Guggenheim was ideal not to motivate students to use primary sources, but also to provide the opportunity to be able to ask questions of someone who works at the institution. Frank Lloyd Wright is a primary focus for teaching about how architects utilize design elements to create buildings. Students know Wright's buildings from books, but the videoconference experience brought the learning to another level of understanding and made it seem more real and therefore, relevant.

In this project, students begin by drawing a floor plan of their own home. For most students, this is the first time they have been asked to think about relationships among spaces in their homes. They are then broken into teams and asked to design a new building–a home for a famous artist. The team structure helps them better understand how architects collaborate and compromise in the real world. Students create architectural models by building walls of foam core up from the lines of their floor plan. They show the texture of the exterior as well as the landscaping. They make presentation boards that include elevations, renderings, and site plans, plus a short biography of their artist/client. At completion, they present their finished 3-dimensional house to the class who critique them assuming the role of client.

At the conclusion of the videoconference, students visited the Guggenheim. The excited group made hand-bound sketch/memory books for use during the 2-½ hour train trip to NYS that they used to capture some of what they saw and learned at the museum.

On the day of the visit, the museum was closed to the public and the students felt extra special because they were the only visitors in the museum. After touring the site, we had a brainstorming session in the Sackler Center for Arts Education. Sharon Vatsky, our videoconferencing partner, asked the students about their impressions and ideas about what they had seen. Everyone expressed how excited they were to see real artwork! They were impressed with the architecture, especially the Rotunda, the central area of the museum. Their experience was documented using disposable cameras that captured images from this exciting visit.

Finally, the teachers observe that the use of extended curriculum materials deepen learning and make the lesson more effective and memorable for students.

Several "value-added" benefits were also noted. Although the Guggenheim Museum provided both schools with supporting materials as well as the videoconference, it was the teachers who created a unit of study with a series of conceptual lesson plans; that is, in order to maximize the impact of the videoconference, students needed to be prepared and to have already acquired some knowledge of the videoconference theme so that they could participate in a dialogue with the museum presenter. This unit of study enhanced and expanded current curriculum within the classroom as well as the videoconference.

The museum also observed that the videoconference experience helped to compensate for the restrictions that were placed on student travel to museums as a result of enhanced security and restrictive budgetary concerns. The introduction of videoconferences provided the students with an opportunity to meet museum educators and have an interactive conversation with an expert in the field without leaving the classroom. Schools are offered a practical way to make it possible to expose students to the advantages of experiential learning. Further, the videoconference provided a platform on which to build extended learning experiences.

Comments from the Teachers Who Participated in Development

The teachers who participated in this project have contributed the following suggestions to assist teachers who may be considering adding videoconferencing in their classrooms:

- Teachers must prepare the students well in advance. Videoconferencing should be used to enhance ongoing instruction and should be fully integrated into curriculum content. The supporting materials that are provided on the Web can be helpful in this effort. It is important to keep in mind that the videoconference will fail if it is not connected to the curriculum.

- Because videoconferencing is a truly interactive enterprise, the experience will vary depending on the personalities of both stu-

Vignette 3. Museum educator

Sharon Vatsky, Associate Director of Education, Solomon R. Guggenheim Museum

Developing a videoconferencing lesson would have probably stayed on the backburner were it not for my involvement in Project VIEW and the collegial group of teachers they provided as collaborators for the lesson development.

The basis of the lesson included plenty of material both written and visual that focused on the architecture of the Solomon R. Guggenheim Museum. However, although the necessity of conducting a lesson while fidgeting with a remote control, document camera, video clips, and PowerPoint presentation was daunting, videoconferencing provides an extraordinary opportunity to expand audiences; it can be an experience in multitasking overload. The experience of "teaching in a fishbowl", and projecting through the "bowl" requires energy and attention that is more demanding than face-to-face educational encounters.

The rewards however, can be great. Engaged and committed teachers, enthusiastic students, technical support from Project VIEW, and building relationships with the participating teachers have continued even though the project itself ended.

dents and the teacher in a particular class. The videoconference process is dynamic and changes with interaction with the different groups, from conference to conference, and from year to year. Teachers should not expect uniform results or impact.

• It is important to anticipate difficulties and have backup plans. To lessen the possibility of problems, schools should have technical support accessible during the videoconference. This availability of technical support is often directly correlated to the successful outcome of the videoconference. Yet, despite the best efforts of all, the newness of the media often is accompanied by unavoidable difficulties.

• It is important to limit the size of the participating group. The desire to include as many students as possible in this exciting experience can be counterproductive. Students who are out of camera range and, therefore, are unable to fully participate in the videoconference lose the positive benefits that this technology can provide.

Teacher Outcomes

The relationship of the museum with the teachers who participated in this project did not end with the completion of the videoconference. Four of the teachers who were part of the collaborative team chose to continue their videoconference training, learning and developing methods and models, and videoconference techniques between two collaborating classrooms. The teachers also applied for and were awarded a $10,000 grant from "Teaching the Hudson River Valley" to develop curriculum focusing on the architecture of various historic sites along the Hudson[5]. The resulting curriculum expands the architectural units of study and presented the opportunity for another videoconference with the Guggenheim. Videoconferencing also became a tool for com-

munication between the teachers and students at the two participating schools.

Furthermore, the teachers who were involved this collaboration with the Guggenheim have continued their relationship with the museum, including participation in an intensive weeklong summer professional development program for teachers, sponsored by the Guggenheim and other NYC museums. That program, *Connecting Collections*, focuses on using museum-based inquiry in the classroom.

CONCLUSION

The outcomes of the provider-teacher collaboration process were excellent for all participants. Responses from the schools were overwhelmingly enthusiastic, student outcomes were measurably positive, and teacher acclamations were high. Teachers stated:

"Although we were once fearful of videoconferencing, we now look for new ways to incorporate it in our curriculums. Our confidence has helped other teachers in our own district overcome their fears. We have shared our successes with teachers from other districts at area teacher and supervisor conferences. We have always felt that architecture is the perfect paradigm under which all curricular areas can be addressed: mathematics, physical science, history, language arts, problem-solving and decision-making as higher-level thinking skills, as well as art, music, and theater. The unique structure of the Guggenheim Museum has proven to be the perfect vehicle. We feel that this has been a life changing experience. We began our journey with enthusiasm, yet no clear vision of the outcome. With faith in the process and confidence in our fellow teammates, the experience proved to be more than an end in itself. The journey has not ended; reverberations are still being felt" (F. Bordick, G. Derosia, & S. Hokanson, personal communication, February, 2006).

ENDNOTES

[1]   Project VIEW Web site, http://www.projectview.org/aboutprojview.htm

[2]   The teacher team members included:

Bethlehem Middle School, Delmar, NY: Principal: Mr. Steve Lobban; Art Teachers: Suzanne Hokanson and Peter T. Ruggiero; Social Studies Teacher: Ann Ulion; and English/Social Studies Teacher: Thomas Michalek

Glenmont Elementary School, Glenmont, NY: Principal: Dr. Theresa Snyder; Art Teacher: Gail Derosia; 3rd Grade Teacher: Felicia Bordick; 4th Grade Teachers: Tom Hotaling and Betsy Schrade

[3]   http://www.projectview.org/guggenheim/Guggenheimintro.htm

[4]   http://www.guggenheim.org/artscurriculum/lessons/srgm_intro.php

[5]   For detail on Teaching the Hudson Valley grants and institute: www.TeachingtheHudsonValley.org

Chapter VI
Are You Having Fun Yet?

Emily Diekemper Hansen
Indianapolis Zoo & White River Gardens, USA

ABSTRACT

In K-12 videoconferencing, we can sometimes allow the pressures and challenges of our jobs to interfere with being able to enjoy our work. In this chapter, I have recounted some of my own personal experiences that show that it is quite possible to love your job and to find humor and enjoyment in each day. By making your enthusiasm obvious, combining a variety of different disciplines into programming and making the most out of "technical difficulties," you can become a more effective and believable content provider and learn to take real pleasure in creating a positive and unique experience for students through technology.

INTRODUCTION

In K-12 videoconferencing, we can sometimes allow the pressures and challenges of our jobs to interfere with being able to enjoy our work. In this chapter, I have recounted some of my own personal experiences that show that it is quite possible to love your job and to find humor and enjoyment in each day.

By making your enthusiasm obvious, combining a variety of different disciplines into programming, and making the most out of "technical difficulties", you can become a more effective and believable content provider, and learn to take real pleasure in creating a positive and unique experience for students through technology.

One morning, I was sitting in my supervisor's office, helping him to interview a candidate for a seasonal position within our education department. That person would be expected to help out with the variety of programs that we offer, from overnights to summer camp to distance learning. Most people who are coming in for interviews have never heard of distance learning, so they usually smile and nod as I describe the program, just like I did in my own interview seven years ago.

As is typical during most interviews that we conduct, we asked this woman why she thought she would enjoy working at the zoo, what her expectations were, and what she perceived her strengths to be. At the end of these conversations, my supervisor always gives the interviewee an opportunity to ask any questions they might have of us. More often than not, the questions they pose to us have to do with pay scale (we are a non-profit organization) and what hours they would be working.

Today, however, our potential future colleague turned the tables and asked my supervisor and I why *we* do what we do, and what it is about our jobs that make us enjoy them so much. What a good question! Do you ever ask yourself that same question? Why *do* you like being involved in distance learning?

Is work fun for you? If people can watch you work and readily see that you are enjoying yourself, you are doing something right. Making your excitement obvious is a great way to transcend the technology and to remove the barrier of physical distance from your programs.

Though this observation is not groundbreaking news, sometimes we need a little reminder every once in a while as to why we are in our chosen profession. The best way to be good at what you do is to enjoy doing it, even when faced with the many challenges that life will undoubtedly throw at you. This is the story of one distance learning coordinator (me), and how I get through all the stress of my job and still manage to enjoy the work that I do.

MAIN THRUST OF CHAPTER

So, Why Do I Enjoy Distance Learning?

If you are at all like me, as a content provider you have probably been asked, "How much money do you make?" by an eager student, curious to know about career choices, understand the real world, or just be nosey about your personal life. Chances are that you have answered with the same response as I give: "I do this because I love it. I am not in it for the money." But what is there to love?

Most of us are involved in some form or fashion with education. We have committed ourselves to nurturing and enriching the lives of students of all ages, and we are dedicated to providing them with the life skills, experiences, and opportunities that they need to grow, thrive, and develop into our future. Yes, all of that…and we want them to have fun, too.

It is a scary thought for me, when I think about all that responsibility in terms of my work and me. I cannot possibly have such an impact on a student's life; I am just one person, I make mistakes, and I do not know everything. And yet, all of those fallibilities aside, it *is* possible to make a change, spark an interest, and guide these students, *even while being a total goofball*! It can be done. I am living proof.

One of the beautiful things about those of us who work with videoconferencing is that we have very few boundaries. What a gift, to work outside the confines of a classroom, and to have such a bounty of resources at our fingertips, just an ISDN call or an IP address away! You have merely to turn on your equipment and—voila! An expert on anything is right there, talking to your students, at the press of a button (and the occaisonal frantic phonce call to the help desk).

What makes those of us who brave the trenches of technology so unique is that we can reach out and extend our impact across state lines, across oceans, and across the world. We are forerunners in education, pioneers in the field, and savvy enough to find a successful blend of traditional and contemporary teaching methods.

As we continue to forge ahead in this technology-driven world, students are one-upping their instructors with their understanding of computers, machines, and gadgets. But we, as technology specialists, are speaking their language. I have received numerous comments from teachers who are thrilled that, because of a single videoconference, their students "finally get" an idea or a concept that had been previously covered in the classroom. Could it be that it is the technology itself that makes the lesson more effective, that we are bridging the gap between instruction and understanding, even though the physical distance is far greater?

I can still remember the very first time that I was given a homework assignment that required me to use the Internet for research. I will not divulge how many years ago this was, but it was far enough back that the Internet was still sort of new and exciting, even to a high school student. Using the Internet was not easy, and it did not come as second nature to me as it often does to children today. Finding my information was a confusing, intricate, and painfully-slow endeavor, but we are all too well aware of the innovations and advancements that the Internet has made since those days. Elementary school teachers now post homework assignments on Web pages, parents send emails in lieu of face-to-face conferences, and more students know how to do an effective Google search than know how to use an actual phone book or encyclopedia. It is a bit sad, yes, but this is our day and age. This is where we are.

What Brought You into Videoconferencing?

Something must have piqued your interest enough to make you want to do what you do. Maybe you have wanted to be a teacher ever since you were seven, and you are one of the lucky people who is actually able to live out their childhood dream. Or maybe you fell into the technology field as an adult, when it had never previously occurred to you that even in your wildest dreams, you would end up acquiring a skills set that keeps you so up-to-date with current trends.

For me personally, it was a curiosity for nature and science that had been encouraged from an early age that brought me into the zoo world. It was a desire to be around and interact with people that developed during my undergraduate years in college that brought me into the education field, and it was the thrill of being on camera and know-ing that I was sharing my passion with audiences far and wide that wedded me to technology.

Actually, that last part is not entirely true. I have a secret: I sort of fell into distance learning by coincidence. Granted, I had participated in zoo videoconferences on the periphery, running the camera and occasionally filling in for our primary presenter when she was unable to perform the role of "talent", but it was not my first interest or responsibility within our education department.

Through a series of events, however, the reins were handed to me; at first I felt like I was in way over my head. I had had no training as to what kind of network we utilized; I did not know ISDN from IP from I2 from AT&T, and I felt completely out of control. I dreaded the moment that the network was scheduled to go up (always fearing the technological worst), and I held my breath each time we were scheduled to make a connection. I had not actually *asked* to do this particular kind of work, after all, but *someone* had to keep our distance learning program humming along.

Those first few months, we racked up hundreds of minutes on the cell phone (and during peak calling time, no less!) working out problems with various help desks, furtively trying to figure out why I had red lights instead of green lights (green lights being the desirable sign that everything is working properly), figuring out how to string our ISDN fiber and extension cords so that they were safe from the stomping feet of visitors and the chomping teeth of baboons at the same time, and desperately wishing that I had paid far more attention to my predecessor.

Once I got the hang of things, though, and I could visualize the steps necessary to have a successful connection (at least from an equipment standpoint), I began to really enjoy myself. It took several months for me to mellow out, stop panicking every time we encountered a challenge, and to just deal with the little problems as they came about. Eventually we made it, and I was once again a relatively pleasant coworker and not completely frazzled every time I stepped in front of the camera.

How Do You Keep Things Exciting and Keep Your Audience Entertained?

I believe I am at a distinct advantage because, luckily, my programs are a relatively easy sell. I work in a zoo, remember? Most people (children especially) are drawn to animals and are entertained by the topics that I have to share with them. It is fairly easy for me to capitalize on the curiosity and wonder of a child when I am comparing an Amur tiger skull to a housecat skull. I can almost guarantee that I can hold an entire class of first graders spellbound, as long as there is a polar bear swimming laps behind me. I also know from experience that if a dolphin sneaks up behind you and splashes water on you when you are in the middle of a sentence, your audience *will* laugh.

Thanks to the subject matter that I focus on, there have been times when I have thought I was pretty hot stuff. I mean, admit it. Part of the reason why distance learning is so cool is because *you get to be on TV.* You get that little rush every time you catch a glimpse of yourself in your monitor, right? It is the same little rush that makes kids wave and act goofy whenever they see themselves on the TV screen; for this reason, it is always a good idea to let those first-timers get their wiggles out by spending ten seconds waving and making funny faces at themselves so they get it out of their system. You, however, as a working professional, are probably able to contain your excitement just a little bit more than they are, and it helps once you have had some time to get past being camera-shy.

It is still fun, though, right? In the past, I have connected with students from nearby schools who are then able to come to the Zoo for a field trip. Oftentimes, we will be out on grounds in the middle of another program when I will hear someone squeal, "There's the snake lady!" or "Hey! We saw you on TV!" It is such a trip to be a local celebrity with the eight-year-old set.

I can make people laugh, engage my audience, and I have even managed to get high-school students to come out of their shells enough to raise their hands and risk looking un-cool by asking questions. Many times I have wondered if it is really me, though, or just the animals and the topics with which I am fortunate enough to work. I know where I stand; my audience could probably take me or leave me personally, because it is the animals that they really want to see. The animals are the main attraction, not the goofy woman on camera.

Regardless of whether or not I really am as interesting as I think I am, or if they are just putting up with me so they can see more of the elephants in the background, the important thing to remember is that your excitement over where you are and what you do will be contagious for your audience. I truly believe that if you are passionate and committed to your subject matter, your audience will buy into your teaching, and you will have a much more powerful impact. I do not mind being the "snake lady", as long as I am able to maybe change someone's attitude about snakes just enough so that, the next time they see a snake, their initial reaction is not "Eeew."

In the six years that I have been coordinating our DL program here at the zoo, I have also been able to watch my colleagues in action at other institutions. In observing their programs and seeing how other topics are addressed through videoconferencing, I have seen that it is quite possible to be just as enthusiastic about discovering the mathematical aspects of Renaissance artwork, reenacting the passage of Civil War-era slaves on the Underground Railroad through Indiana, and interviewing costume designers for nationally-touring theater companies. You can be equally convincing if you are pretending to be Johnny Appleseed as you can be if you are demystifying some of the "gross" processes that the human body undergoes. Through your energy and dedication to a topic, *any* topic, you will be able to really reach your audience. You are more believable and genuine when your area of expertise actually makes you happy, and you let that show. You can be a role model simply by being interested in your topic and in sharing it with your audience.

I still giggle when I hear people refer to me as "an expert". It is a flattering term, but not one I would ever apply to myself. Speaking from personal experience, I have been forced to become a generalist as opposed to a specialist. With the range of programs we offer, I have to know enough about everything to be able to effectively teach my audience. It all interests me, but it can be frustrating to decide what information is relevant enough to be included in the short time I have with students during a program. It is still all very exciting, though, no matter which fun facts I use, and I never pass up the opportunity to share our observation messages.

The other advantage that we, as content providers, have is that we have the potential to offer something truly unique, something they could not get in school. I do not know of too many classrooms that would have the ability to come lens-to-tongue with an 18-foot-tall giraffe or who could observe a kangaroo get a live root canal, yet videoconferencing allows me to offer these opportunities. I have brought kids from upstate New York to our tropical rainforest in January when there is a foot of snow on the ground outside, and I have encouraged students in southwestern Texas to point out the visible adaptations that our penguins have to survive in the frigid conditions of Antarctica. How else would they ever have the chance to experience these events?

Another beauty of this technology is that, in this day and age, the chance to provide enriching, memorable, and meaningful activities for students in schools is being limited by everything from rising gas prices and strict adherence to state educational standards to slashed field trip budgets and class schedules that are planned down to the last minute. Most teachers would agree that it is a lot easier to get their classes down the hall to the media center to participate in an hour-long videoconference that meets state standards, than it would be to get the same class out of the building and on a bus for a day-long field trip.

Educational Programs at the Zoo

If one were to look at the educational disciplines that our programs cover here at the zoo, it would be easy to see that our main focus is, of course, on the life sciences. While I am eternally fascinated by the way the living world works, and I would be just as happy doing all animals, all the time, it helps to break the mold occasionally and step a little bit outside of the realm of science.

For example, one of our current programs which is most often requested is called *Animath*. Through working in partnership with teachers in the formal education world, I know that multidisciplinary programs are a hot commodity, and classroom educators are always looking for ways to combine and integrate different areas of study into their lesson plans. For this reason, we thought it might be fun (and applicable) to create a program that highlights the many ways that numbers and math are used in a zoo environment. This idea worked.

During this 45-minute program, our zoo instructor might hold up a gallon milk jug and then ask students to estimate how many gallons are in the dolphin pool in the background (approximately 2.5 million). We could place a box turtle on the document camera so the audience gets an up-close look, and then compare its shell to that of a 500-pound Aldabra tortoise sitting nearby; which one would need more square footage in its exhibit? We might ask for ideas as to how a keeper would weigh an elephant, or suggestions for the best way to count out fish for seals and sea lions each day. Both questions are followed by video clips of our keeper staff at work, depicting zoo workers using scales and weights. For older students, we emphasize the importance of math skills when monitoring water chemistry and exhibit temperatures.

The flow of these programs is very much student-driven, which allows them to feel more successful and empowered and more in control of their own learning experience. While there are certain main ideas and concepts that we do have to address at some point during each presentation, the students' comments determine where the discussions go throughout the course of the connection. This helps to keep the program fresh and a little more exciting for the presenter, especially if it is a program that is requested frequently. It is also nice to have that feeling of instructional freedom when you do not have to stick to a canned script. And, as an added bonus, we even try to update our jokes for those teachers who have requested the program multiple years in a row!

Another popular program that we offer every winter as a holiday special is *The Mitten*, based on the children's book by author Jan Brett. Geared towards a younger audience (usually kindergarten through second grade), we read this short story and then compare the storybook characters to their real-life counterparts and discuss the similarities and differences between the animals on the page and the live animals in our studio.

Although we might present *The Mitten* more than fifty times in one school year (and by the end of its annual run, I can recite the book forwards, backwards, upside-down, and in Spanish), I never get tired of reading it. The excitement on the faces of the students when they see a close-up shot of a live hedgehog's wet little nose, or the awe they express when they see how big a bear's head really is (and how there is no way it could *ever* fit into a mitten) when I hold up a bear skull, *that* is what makes it worthwhile to keep turning those pages.

Although this particular program does have a more predictable flow, the energy does not fade from one class to the next, and that helps to keep my enthusiasm revved as well. I try to always remember that even if I have already read the book four times on a particular day, it is still the first time the students in my fifth presentation

have seen the program, and they deserve the same level of investment from me as a presenter as the students received during the first program.

Teachers always express gratitude for these types of multidisciplinary programs. In addition to combining science with math and reading, we have created multilingual offerings (my meager Spanish-speaking ability somehow got me into offering *Animales en Espanol*, a classification program that teaches Spanish vocabulary), programs that combine science and art (did you know we have elephants, dolphins, parrots, and penguins who paint?), and worked with instructors to "custom-design" geography-based connections that highlight animals from the very specific parts of the world that they have been focusing on in class.

For us, offering these multidisciplinary programs has created win-win situations; the classroom teacher has the opportunity to reinforce what has already been taught (or to introduce a lesson in a unique way), and I get a better sense for what is going on in schools and what topics are relevant. I can then respond to those needs and create programs that are even more useful, timely, and germane.

The practice of integrating multiple disciplines into your programs also can open the door to some unique and exciting partnerships with other institutions. There is no end to the number of ways that you can join forces with schools, science centers, museums, living-history museums, theaters, zoos, and other content providers. The possibilities are endless, and all it takes is some creative thinking and a fun, open attitude towards collaboration. While these projects do require additional work and coordination (and perhaps the talents of a crafty grant writer), they can flesh out some of the best ways to use distance learning technology, as well as to inspire us to think of new ways.

If you can consider "pop culture" as a discipline, you would be well-advised to align yourself not only with state standards and current educational trends, but you had also better know who SpongeBob Squarepant's best friend is (Patrick Star), the name of Harry Potter's snowy owl (Hedwig), who Dora the Explorer's cousin is (Diego), and the difference between PS2, PSP, X-Box 360, and Nintendo DS (I am still working on that one). If you can find a way to weave these modern elements into your presentations, you are letting students know that you understand them and you are in tune with what is important and interesting in their lives. You are hip, you are cool, and they will identify with you more and pay more attention to you if you can show them that you have been listening to what they have been saying.

Dealing with the Setbacks of Technology

One reality that we all must face and accept when working with technology is that, at some point, the technology will fail. Videoconferencing within the K-12 education world brings together people of all abilities and levels of comfort, from the techno-wizard who installs entire systems to the "techno-weenie" who is afraid to even press a button on the remote control.

I was that scared "techno-weenie" when I first started. Forget being camera-shy; I was afraid to touch anything *behind* the camera, not be in front of it. For people who are not familiar with equipment and do not know input from output, that sparkling new videoconferencing system in the front of the classroom can be very daunting. Oftentimes, what prevents teachers and educators from making the most out of the wonderful resource at hand is this: They are too nervous to use that equipment to its full potential.

From the content provider end, it only gets trickier. Not only do we have to convince educators to subscribe to our goods and services and market our programs to schools, but once the deal is sealed, the program is scheduled, and the confirmations have been sent out, we actually have to *deliver*. That, too, can be the tricky part.

We have experienced just about every technological glitch that could occur, and I am almost proud to say that we are inventive enough to have come up with some new problems that have confounded even the most seasoned technicians from help desks far and wide.

From school firewalls that only accept incoming calls to bridges that only dial out, from power outages due to fire inside the school building and pickup trucks that hit the power lines outside the school building, from the media specialist (the only one who knows how to operate the equipment) being sick to snow delays, schools have called with all manners of technical problems. And those are just problems that we have encountered from sites with a dedicated space. When mobility enters the equation, there is a whole new set of potential problems that can occur.

Let me explain a little bit more about our current set-up. While most people probably experience videoconferencing from a dedicated room (inside a building, no less!), nicely equipped with a large-screen TV, several cameras, and equipment that never moves (let alone never gets unplugged so as to put the delicate cords and cables at risk of being damaged), we are fortunate to have a "mobile unit". This 500-pound behemoth of a cart is mobile only in the sense that we are able to push it from one end of the Zoo to another. Have you ever been to any zoo, anywhere? They are big places. They get crowded in the summertime. They get icy in the wintertime. It sometimes rains at zoos. The paths are bumpy and not really designed for rolling around carts loaded with tens of thousands of dollars of A/V equipment.

And yet, we fearlessly go where the animals are. In order to set up these connections, we go over rocks, around trees, across bridges, under train tracks, over the river, and through the woods. What makes the setup process even more fun is that, for each different location across the zoo from which we can run our broadcasts, we have to switch our fiber connection in a central room, conveniently located all the way across the zoo from our education building. It sometimes takes longer to set up for a program than it does to actually deliver the content.

But we make it happen. We power up the system, get our laptop running, and rewind the videotapes; we make sure that our lights are green, and we are ready to go. The time comes for the connection to go up, and we eagerly await the moment when our connecting site pops up on the screen…and we get nothing. Houston, we have a problem.

Troubleshooting under normal circumstances can be difficult enough. Troubleshooting a technical problem via a cell phone with sketchy reception, while 150 students who are each trying to out-scream two macaws in an immersive rainforest exhibit (think dark, hot, 100% humidity, equipment strategically placed to be out from under dripping water) and have clustered themselves around the three square feet of space that you have roped off for yourself, can be a completely different exercise in patience. Why is it, too, that someone always wants to yell as they read aloud the signs requesting, "Quiet please! Videotaping in progress!"?

We have learned many good lessons the hard way over the years, and occasionally we have had to cancel programs altogether. While schools can present their own set of hardships, we too have made those phone calls that start out with "I am really sorry, but…", except our excuses are oftentimes a little more exotic, and take it a step further than "the dog ate my homework".

"I am so sorry, but the baboon seems to have chewed right through my fiber, and by the time we get a backup spool out here, our connection time will have run out."

"They had to drain the penguin pool because there was a Freon leak, and unfortunately there are no penguins on exhibit today."

"I know it was sunny ten minutes ago, but those black clouds are quickly heading our way and we are fairly certain that our safety manager would not want us to be outdoors in the rain with

all of our electrical equipment…wait, can you repeat that last part? I could not hear you over the thunder."

"I know we had a Kodiak bear program scheduled for this morning, but the bear got a splinter lodged in his mouth yesterday after chewing on a log and is currently at the vet hospital having it removed and will not be on exhibit during our *Bear Basics* program today".

"I am so sorry. The help desk cannot actually tell me what the problem is at the moment because they have never seen something like this happen before, but they did say that 'things are all messed up' and they are working on it."

Those are the "biggies", the problems that render your programs unsalvageable. It is frustrating on both ends, because the teacher is stuck staring down a room full of disappointed students, and back here on the content provider end, we feel like we have failed. Whether the problems are technology-based, like the nebulous "network problems" excuse, or more specific ("we cannot broadcast from the giraffe barn today because one of the giraffes is in labor"), we are all inconvenienced by these situations.

I believe that teachers may sometimes forget that while they have responsibility for a very unpredictable group (their students), I too am working with an unpredictable group on my end (animals). I have had to apologize to teachers that, through no fault of my own, we spent 45 minutes looking at a rock, which really did have a sleeping tiger behind it. I promise. And really, the polar bear does do more than sleep…on that rock…I promise…

Those are the moments that fill me with dread, watching the lions snooze peacefully in the sun. It is difficult to keep a classroom enthralled with footage of a sleeping lion. Since lions sleep 20 hours a day, it is unlikely that he is about to wake up just because I have rolled out my camera.

Far be it from me to give advice to teachers; I will say that it always helps to have a backup plan, and that certainly goes for content providers as well. I have to remind students and teachers that no, I cannot *make* the lions wake up from their nap, and no, I cannot *force* the fifteen-foot anaconda to come down off of that tall rock. That is why I turn to the magic of video! Backup footage has saved many a program, especially when we have footage that you might not get to see every afternoon on Animal Planet, such as one-time special events we have captured on film, or special zoo procedures that have taken place.

For example, since animal feeds are often done out of the view of the public eye (face it…most people do not want to see blood and guts when they come to the zoo), we have recorded many of these meals to use during our programs. I do not know why it is that second graders are endlessly fascinated with Things Being Eaten, but if something gets chomped, it is the coolest thing ever. I would not be able to show an event like that every single time we did a live broadcast, so not only is backup footage helpful when we have AWOL animals, but it also provides the chance to see something really special (or even better, something really gross).

And in the end, even if your technology is seamless, the connection is beautiful, animals are frolicking front and center, and everything is working smoothly, you will still make mistakes. There will be interruptions. You will lose your train of thought, say the wrong thing, and not know the answer to a question.

Take those moments as they come, and try not to be too distracted by them. If something happens off camera, keep going. The less you react to a mistake, the less your audience will know anything has happened, and you will spend less time trying to recover. Trust me, coming from someone who has fallen down, spaced out, dropped things, tripped, lost her microphone, and

must ignore the thousands of people filing past (and on occasion, directly into) our broadcast space on a daily basis, being able to keep your concentration and pick up where you left off is a good skill to master.

While on camera, I have been bitten, slimed, and have had a variety of animals produce a variety of bodily substances both in the background and directly onto my person. It is hard to finish a sentence and sound intelligent and professional, when all you really want to say is, "Gaak!" But it is all in a day's work, and since I never know what the day will bring, it is always exciting, and it is almost always fun.

CONCLUSION

And so, we are back to the potential future colleague who asked me what I like about my job. She may not have immediately grasped the technology aspect of what I do, but she did, however, understand the "spark" that you see when you are able to reach out and touch someone. It does not matter that my "sparks" often have to travel hundreds of miles, and that there are two television screens and some fiber optic line between us; I can still reel my audience in and captivate them, and I can still feel that physical rush and surge of excitement and fulfillment when you just *know* that your audience gets it.

It is my most sincere hope that all of my colleagues who join me in the videoconferencing world can enjoy their work as much as I do, and that you get as much joy out of sharing what excites you as I do. We will all have problems and we will all be faced with various challenges each day, but if, at the end of the day, you can say that you really do have fun, then you are truly a success.

Section III
Bringing Teachers to the Camera

Chapter VII
Use and Perceptions of External Content Providers:
A Teacher's Journey through the Process

Jennifer Hahn
Bethlehem School District, USA

ABSTRACT

This chapter presents the process of videoconferencing with external providers from the teacher's side of the camera. It summarizes the steps necessary to conduct a videoconference, including how to contact and select external providers, as well as how to prepare, conduct, and follow up on a videoconference. It carefully examines how to develop lasting relationships with experts in the field, and how to use their resources to create an interactive research-based classroom environment. For classroom teachers, videoconferencing is a relatively new educational tool, and the extent of its implementation is constantly expanding and virtually endless. Utilizing examples of specific experiences, the chapter provides the reader with an overview of videoconferences that exist and can be used by K-12 educators.

INTRODUCTION

Most U.S. students born in the 1990's are computer-savvy and have actively worked with computers for the majority of their lives. Videoconferencing is an educational technology tool that they will experience through their years in the K-12 arena, but also is one that is likely to be a part of their higher education and/or workforce lives. Current advances have not only improved the process of videoconferencing, but also have increased the quality of instruction and provided flexibility to when and where videoconferencing can take place (Motamedi, 2001). Its use not only assists in providing content-rich curricula, but it also improves students' technical knowledge skills and abilities. This information will continue to be useful as videoconferencing becomes more commonplace (Motamedi, 2001).

Why Do Videoconferencing?

Within the classroom, videoconferencing can be extremely helpful in creating student connections to authors, historians, scientists, researchers, and zoologists; through select access, these outside experts can present valuable, content-rich curriculum to students reflecting their unique field of expertise. Educators also benefit from the content providers' current research; videoconferencing can be valuable in extending the education of teachers in the field. For example, when there are breakthroughs in science, educators can access the newest information, and discuss it based on firsthand knowledge given by the external content provider. Many times, these experts are providing information to schools that may be a great distance from the provider site (Motamedi, 2001). As part of this process, these providers supply educators with informational articles, charts, graphs, videos, and materials that will enhance curriculum instruction in the classroom.

Maintaining a long-lasting relationship with an external provider also can have great educational value in the classroom. Because most videoconferencing providers are professionals and experts in their respective field, they oftentimes have cutting-edge information that teachers could not adequately present to their students. Through the use of planned instruction, students are able to see research facilities, museums, and other real-life work areas that they may not be able to access through conventional educational resources. For instance, by interacting with NASA experts, students are able to see the thought processes of real scientists and hear the scientist's feedback to their questions and work. Students also put forth more effort when they know their work is going to be looked at by an expert, and have received a glimpse of the equipment and buildings where real scientists work, and how they use labs and conduct experiments (Peterson, 2000).

Purpose of the Chapter

This chapter will present videoconferencing from the teacher's point of view. It will discuss how to contact, prepare, conduct, and follow up on a videoconference in the classroom. It also will discuss the procedures that teachers should follow to ensure that the videoconference is relevant and appropriate for their students. It will cover perceptions that many educators have about the external content providers, and will give guidelines to help create long-lasting and meaningful relationships with these experts that will not only provide camaraderie, but also will serve as an invaluable resource for information and materials that are relevant to curriculum standards. Examples will be provided so that differences can be examined and commonalities can be observed. Finally, this chapter will discuss why videoconferencing, if properly integrated into the classroom, can be an excellent, educationally-sound practice that can really engage students in activity-based lessons and involve them in their own learning process.

BACKGROUND

Some Important Terms that Teachers Should Know

This chapter will make reference to some terms that may be new to educators who have not used videoconferencing. A *videoconference* is when two parties in separate locations are able to connect to each other via computer and can interact via picture and sound. This occurs frequently in business and has expanded to the field of education. Most of the videoconferences to which this chapter refers to are between a group of students and an external expert who can provide them with learning opportunities that cannot be afforded to them in a classroom setting. This chapter will also make reference to electronic field trips. *Electronic field trips* are a specific type of videoconference where the expert is providing information to numerous students at many different locations. For example, the *Smithsonian Environmental Research Center* presented an electronic field trip from the second largest coral reef in Belize. Schools throughout the country could connect and watch as the content provider explored and examined the reef. Electronic fields trips usually provide a question-and-answer segment; but questions need to be called in, and getting through may not be possible during a ten-to-fifteen-minute question period. This is not as intimate an experience as a *point-to-point* videoconference, where the expert is speaking only to the twenty or so students in one specific classroom and can interact directly and answer questions from all students.

Other terms that will be used frequently in this chapter are: *external content provider, external provider,* and *content provider.* All of these terms refer to the presenter of the videoconference. The presenter is usually from an institution that has information which is relevant to a specific curriculum area. A provider could be from an almost endless list of institutions; specific providers that are commonly seen are museums, zoos, aquariums, research centers, NASA, institutes of art and music, and authors. This chapter will utilize these three terms interchangeably.

Research You Might Want to Reference that Supports Videoconferencing

It is important to know some of the potential outcomes of videoconferences, and how they positively impact the learning of students when you are first trying to obtain and build support for the program. Support for videoconferencing is relatively simple to find; multiple articles praise the role of the videoconference in making connections to external experts. The following are some sample studies that can be used to show potential benefits.

- **Support for general curriculum:** David Hearnshaw (2000) from the University of Westminster conducted research to determine the objective value of videoconferencing. Hearnshaw focused on a college class that was using videoconferencing for a seven-week course; he used student comments to determine if they were truly engaged and processing the information being taught during the videoconference. Data were coded to represent students' deep understanding and interpretation of the material presented, or they only had a surface-level understanding. Findings of the research showed that deep responses increased from the beginning use and more than doubled by week six of the videoconference course.

Jody Howard-Kennedy (2004) also writes about post-use outcomes of videoconferencing, noting the excitement that teachers in her middle school have for the process. She reports that videoconferencing allowed teachers to bring multiple real-life experiences in science, social studies, and foreign language classes into the classroom by connecting to places across the country and also in Mexico, South Africa, and even New Zealand.

Similarly, Howard-Kennedy (2004) discusses the cultural diversity that videoconferencing has brought to her school, noting that it encourages tolerance and understanding of foreign places and populations. She comments, "Without a doubt, videoconferencing benefits all who are involved. Most importantly, it enriches the curriculum by allowing students to connect to the whole world…from the comfort of their own classroom (Howard-Kennedy, 2004, p. 17)." Ferrer (2006) comes to parallel conclusions while writing about a teacher who was able to create a videoconferencing program that allowed his school to connect with NASA, Spain, and the Cleveland Institute of Music.

- **Support for English language art curriculum:** Uhlman (2006) shows positive outcomes of Michigan students conducting videoconferences with an author. In this program, the students read the author's work and then interviewed him through videoconferencing, helping students to better comprehend and read with purpose. Watkins (2002) writes about librarian colleagues from different areas of the country working together to successfully link their libraries to each other, and who are now conducting book groups with each other. They also have offered programs for students and parents to participate, provided the community with a ten-week interactive series from the Indianapolis Zoo, and offered a program with the Indianapolis Museum of Art that allowed students to present art and have the museum personnel interpret and comment on it.

Loveman (2004) describes a high school in Ohio that uses videoconferencing as an integral part of their English curriculum. Students in the class looked intensively at a specific writing piece and then wrote a screenplay based on the work of literature. They then participated in a videoconference with a screenwriter. After the videoconference the students conducted online discussions to further their learning and understanding of the content from the videoconference.

- **Support for at-risk students:** Videoconferences also can be used to help enrich curriculum for at-risk groups. Teachers from California have reported using videoconferencing to assist at-risk students by helping them to become active learners (EBSCO). In addition, rural schools in remote locations also get benefits for their students from videoconferences. For instance, students in the rural towns of Alabama are connecting to sites thousands of miles away not only to provide curriculum content, but also to expose students to new experiences. Located in a town where only ten adults have bachelor's degrees, the science teachers used videoconferences to expose students to what is outside the town's limits. They now have had multiple videoconferences with NASA and with other students and adults throughout the country (Dishongh, 2005).

An additional useful resource is provided by Rural Hall Elementary School, which put together a list of successful videoconferences that they have conducted in grades one through twelve. Through these providers, they have been able to give their students a variety of experiences with experts within a given year (McDermon, 2005) and are "impressed with the quality of content that is available at reasonable costs…and that high-quality, time-saving, and cost-effective, distance learning is truly elementary" (McDermon, 2005, p. 30).

Accurate and Inaccurate Perceptions of External Reviewers

Once a teacher has made a decision to become involved in the new technology of videoconferencing, there are some steps and guidelines that can make the process easier and more effective. First and foremost is how you interact with the provider. At first, you may feel as if you are an inconvenience to external providers. You may feel that the external providers do not have time to specialize a videoconference to your specific class. You may have a difficult time contacting providers, because they have limited time for videoconferences and their time is highly sought after. Though external providers are busy people, those who are good are generally efficient and can be reached, and will be an invaluable resource to your classroom. Remember, an *external content provider* is anyone that presents a videoconference to students. It can be a professional in the field, a museum affiliate, another teacher, or any other type of educator using this media to spread knowledge. Good external providers are willing to adapt; they are trying to disseminate their information and knowledge as much and as quickly as possible to as many students as possible. You should also be aware, however, that there are poor external providers who, without careful contact and arrangement, can turn a videoconference into an educational disaster. An example is a videoconference with a zoo that offered nothing more than what I could have presented in the classroom. The videoconference was from a carpeted, barren room, and made no use of the zoo at the content provider's disposal. The provider presented information that my students already knew and was clearly below their level of understanding. No efforts were made to adapt materials either before or during the process. If the external provider does not use their facilities properly, or understand the background and ability level of the students, videoconferencing can be a wasted use of educational time. Avoid these providers by reviewing their materials ahead of time and asking other teachers for references. If a provider does not ask about your class or your curriculum or about the artifacts and experience

that you want your students to receive, you may have a problem. You are the one who can ensure that this adaptation happens.

STEPS FOR SETTING UP A SUCCESSFUL VIDEOCONFERENCE

As indicated above, it is essential that a teacher research providers and make meaningful contact with them before embarking on a videoconferencing experience. The key to preparing for a videoconference is "early and frequent contact". The steps listed below are questions and actions that teachers can take to seek out information and to prepare students for a good videoconference that will result in information that is relevant to the curriculum that is being covered in the classroom. These steps will help guarantee that your students get a worthwhile experience out of the videoconference (see Table 1). Note that throughout these steps, I have used a videoconference on global warming to help explain the process.

1. **Do your homework. Research the institution with which you are looking to make**

Table 1. Checklist for steps for setting up and executing a successful videoconference

1. Do you homework. Research the institution you are looking to make a connection with. What is special that they offer or advertise that you cannot present to you students in the same detail.	
2. Initiate contact and be clear with your expectations. The external provider's time is as valuable as yours so try to be direct and clear about what you are looking for from them. Give them a few dates to choose from to limit the emails back and forth if they are already filled on your first two dates.	
3. Book a date early and be prepared. If you do not get a response from the content provider in a week, email them again or call to try to make contact with the provider. If they do not respond to your second attempt in a few days, find a different but similar provider and begin to contact them.	
4. Preparing the students for the videoconference. Seek out information from the external provider. Are there things you can prepare the kids for or give them a basic background in before the conference?	
5. Preparing the external content provider. The content provider needs to know what you have already taught the students about the topic. It is essential to plan and conduct a test run.	

a connection. What is special that they offer or advertise that you cannot present to your students in the same detail? To answer this question, you can navigate through the Web site of the location that you are considering for use, look for supporting content information Internet lists or providers (e.g., www.projectview.org), call and contact potential institutions, or seek out references of other educators that have used videoconferencing and get their responses. In researching for the Global Warming Videoconference, the Internet was used to examine the validity of the research center; it was contacted via email, and the content was discussed with the provider.

2. **When you initiate contact, be clear about your expectations; what kind of help do you really need?** The external provider's time is as valuable as yours, so try to be direct and clear about what you are looking for from them. Give them a few dates to choose from to limit the emails back and forth, in case they are already booked on your preferred date. Remember, you are paying for the videoconference, and it is a waste of your teaching time if it is not what you are seeking. Be sure that you are going to get what you want. Give the content provider a thorough background of what your students know about the topic and about what areas you would like them to know more details. Also, give them a list of state and national standards that you are looking to address with this videoconference. When contacting the Global Warming Research Center, I sent a list of state standards on the topic of ecology and a brief paragraph explaining activities and projects that were going to be completed before the videoconference. Finally, I explained that I wanted this to be a highly-intensive look into global warming, because the students would be coming in with a solid background on the topic.

3. **Book a date early, and be prepared; where does it fit into your instrumental sequence?** If you do not get a response from the content provider in a week, email them again or call to try to make contact with the provider. If they do not respond to your second attempt in a few days, find a different but similar provider and begin to contact them. Once a date is agreed upon, make sure all the equipment is available and then reconfirm the date with the content provider. A week before the conference, touch base with the external provider and again make sure that you have the same goals and that you are going to get the presentation that you want from the provider. This final confirmation can be done by phone or email. In the Global Warming Videoconference, the content provider was contacted by phone to reconfirm the date and to quickly review the content to be presented.

4. **Prepare the students for the videoconference. Seek out information from the external provider. What specific preparation and background should the students have before the conference?** Do they need to bring any materials to the videoconference? Are there charts, graphs, articles, or videos that can be provided to prepare the students for the conference? Make sure you set aside at least ten minutes at the conclusion of the videoconference for questions. You may have questions that are written before the videoconference or just questions that students may have from the presentation. Tell the students how excited you are that they get to access live experts in the field and that they are going to be able to ask questions. This is a big deal and a great opportunity for students to get excited and involved in their learning while having fun. It was important, for the Global Warming Videoconference, that the students already have an understanding of global warming and had completed

the graph on atmospheric carbon dioxide levels. Students' graphs were graded before the videoconference. As a result, students were motivated to form questions for the providers. These were reviewed, discussed, and ultimately chosen by the students before the conference.

5. **Prepare the external content provider. Did you tell the provider your pre- and post-videoconference plans? Is your equipment and connection ready?** As noted above, the content provider needs to know what you have already taught the students about the topic. In addition, it is essential to plan and conduct a test run. A good provider will want to reference things that you have already done in the classroom to trigger students' previous learning; this helps them plan an in-depth content-rich videoconference that will make it a success for all involved. Prior to the conference, test the connection and make sure that both the school and the external provider have both of the IP addresses. This will ensure that you have all the information needed to connect to the provider. I suggest doing this approximately one week ahead of time. If there is a bad connection or a problem connecting, you will have some time to contact someone for technical assistance to fix the problem. If you are going through this for the first time, it would be a good idea to have an experienced technology teacher or technical assistant there to troubleshoot anything that you may come across. If they could also run a test an hour or so before the scheduled conference, this would guarantee a good connection and not result in a loss of valuable time with the content provider. The teacher spent ample time teaching the concept of global warming with the video clips and charts/graphs provided by the content provider. On the day of the conference, it was arranged for a library media specialist to test the connection one hour before the videoconference.

6. **Check your background; make sure your classroom is set up for videoconferencing. Lights? Camera? Action?** Once the connection is made, during the test run and before the real videoconference, make sure you have the proper lighting and that there are no glares. The cameras need to be set so that the external provider can zoom in on a few students and also have a perspective to see the entire class. Make sure that you know how to use all of the equipment. Preset your camera angles and know how to transition between them during the conference. Again, ask for assistance with this if it is your first time or if you are having problems with working the equipment. Before the Global Warming Videoconference, the teacher had two preset camera positions: One was up close on a podium, from which the students could ask questions, and the second was of the entire class. A technology technician was present at the beginning of the Global Warming Videoconference for troubleshooting, but left after the videoconference started successfully.

STEPS FOR CONDUCTING A SUCCESSFUL VIDOECONFERENCE

At this point, you are now set up and your video-conference is a "go". If you are well prepared, you can be pretty sure that things will go according to plan during the videoconference, but there are some things you should do at the time of the videoconference that will help it to run smoothly. After introductions, the provider will take over, but you need to be there to monitor behavior, to move the camera angles when necessary, and to enjoy and learn from the show (see Table 2).

1. **Introduce yourself to the content provider and the content provider to your class.** Make sure you know their name(s) and the establishment from which they are

Table 2. Checklist for conducting a successful videoconference

1. Introduce yourself to the content provider and the content provider to your class.	
2. Make sure you covered the curriculum you told the external provider you were going to.	
3. Provide some assessment to ensure that the students are knowledgeable and understand the material you presented.	
4. Have the students in position and ready to go ten to fifteen minutes early. Turn the camera on and show them what it is going to look like on the screen.	
5. Explain that there is a small delay in the sound. It will appear as if the content provider did not hear what the student said because they may not receive immediate feedback.	
6. Make sure that the students have clear expectations on how to behave. They need to be silent and paying attention if the conference is not directly involving them at a given time.	
7. Watch the clock and make sure that when there are ten minutes politely bring it to the content provider's attention.	

broadcasting. If they have special titles, make sure you introduce them as such. Remember, your role will change, and you will become a spectator and classroom monitor for teh duration of the videoconference. For the Global Warming Videoconference, the speaker was introduced Mrs. Janet McNary, and she asked the students to call her Janet.

2. **Make sure that you have covered the curriculum that you told the external provider that you were going to cover.** The external provider has customized their conference based on what you told them that you were planning to do in the classroom. Make sure that you did your end of the preparation. The Global Warming Videoconference required students to make a graph of carbon dioxide levels in the atmosphere of a period of time. Without this prior work, Janet would not

have been able to give the videoconference that she had prepared.

3. **Prior to the videoconference, provide some assessment to ensure that the students are knowledgeable and understand the material that you presented.** If the students are not ready for the highly-detailed conference, which the content provider is expecting, it will limit the students' in-depth learning of the topic, and the content provider will not be able to showcase the extensive background and knowledge that they have prepared. Students were graded on their graphs on Global Warming, and a class discussion was held to begin to interpret the data.

4. **Have the students in position and ready to go ten to fifteen minutes early. Turn the camera on and show them what it is going to look like on the screen.** Have them make funny faces, wave, and point at themselves to get it out of their system.

Explain that when the conference starts, they must be serious and on their best behavior. Before the Global Warming Videoconference, cameras were turned on and students were told to wave and smile at themselves. After that, they were instructed that there should be no more "silliness", but that they should be ready to participate.

5. **Explain to students that there is a small delay in the sound; it will appear as if the content provider did not hear what the student said because they will not receive immediate feedback.** Let students know about the time delay, that the content provider will hear them and respond in a few seconds, and that they are going to need to speak and then wait a few seconds for a response; they should not start repeating themselves immediately when the content provider does not respond quickly. This will take a few minutes to get used to; once the conference is underway, however, the students will get the hang of it and adapt quickly. Students in the Global Warming Videoconference were told to speak and count to five silently, then expect to hear a response from the content provider.

6. **Make sure that the students have clear expectations on how to behave. They need to be silent and pay attention if the conference is not directly involving them at a given time.** Part of your role is to be the classroom monitor. Students need to be polite and respectful to the content provider and to complete the tasks asked of them. Make sure you monitor their behavior and remove any distractions; this conference probably cost a good amount of money and should not be limited because of the bad behavior of a few students. Background noise can be distracting to the external provider and distract other students that are engaged and listening. As the classroom teacher, you need to make sure that students have clear expectations

and that all students are following them. If this will be a problem with the students that you service, invite an administrator to the conference. It is a unique experience, and the administrator would probably be happy to see how teachers are implementing technology into their curriculum. During the Global Warming Videoconference, the teacher circulated to different areas of the room making sure that all the students knew that she was watching and monitoring their behavior.

7. **Watch the clock and when there are ten minutes left, politely bring the time to the content provider's attention.** You also will need to be the timekeeper once the content providers get started; they are usually very engaged in the conference and oftentimes lose track of the time. There are very few conferences that end early or where the content provider or the students run out of things to discuss. The students will enjoy the one-on-one interaction with the content provider about their specific questions and will want to have as much of this as possible. Oftentimes, this is what the students like and remember most about the video-conferencing experience. Make sure that there is time left for this to happen. At the Global Warming Videoconference, students prepared questions ahead of time, reviewed what questions would be good to ask. They also decided that time could not be wasted on questions that were off-topic.

FOLLOWING UP ON A SUCCESSFUL VIDEOCONFERENCE AND CREATING MEANINGFUL RELATIONSHIPS WITH CONTENT PROVIDERS

Successful completion of a videoconference can leave an educator with many options. The stu-

Table 3. Checklist for following up on a successful videoconference and creating meaningful relationships with content providers

1. Make sure you and your class thank the content provider at the conclusion of the conference.	
2. Have the students make cards or sign a card thanking the external provider. Send this out within a week of the videoconference to the content provider.	
3. In a separate mailing than the thank you card, send the content provider work that resulted from the videoconference.	
4. Contact the content provider and see if they would answer additional questions that the students may have. You can also ask them if they would answer additional questions that you may have about the topic.	
5. If you get a positive response from the email referenced above, reply with any questions you or the students may have.	
6. Express that you look forward to working with them again next year.	

dents are interested by the topic, and it will help teachers to explain more about the topic. They are excited that they worked with a real scientist and may want to continue correspondence with the content provider. Teachers may want to make arrangements to have email correspondence with the content provider to answer questions that came up after the conference. The content provider can also keep you updated to the newest discoveries and articles that are coming out in the field so that you are updated on topics that are being taught. For instance, research centers may be able to distribute information about everything that is going on at the research facility, in addition to the specific content of the videoconference. Because, as a teacher, you are busy planning and carrying out the day-to-day requirements of teaching, staying updated in your content area can be challenging. This type of ongoing connection with an active professional can have huge impacts

on your curriculum if new information is readily and easily available.

Many external content providers are busy people and they may not all be able to continue contact with students; however, many are genuinely interested and are willing to help students continue to learn in their area of expertise after the videoconference. With limited contact through email and direct questions, a relationship with external content providers can be established, and years of valuable content-rich and up-to-date information can be gathered. The following steps will help to establish these types of relationships.

1. **Make sure you and your class thank the content provider at the conclusion of the conference.** This can be quick, but should be very sincere and not appear as if the students are being forced. The teacher that conducted

the Global Warming Videoconference had arranged for the class to say "Thank You" on her count of three at the conclusion of the conference.

2. **Have the students make cards or sign a card thanking the external provider. Send this out within a week of the videoconference to the content provider.** This can be assigned as a homework assignment, or you can ask if some students could make a thank-you card during a study hall or during a lunch period. Usually students will jump at the chance to create artwork, and will be happy that you asked them to help. After the Global Warming Videoconference students were given five points of extra credit on a quiz if they made an individual thank-you card for the content provider.

3. **In a mailing separate from the thank-you card(s), send the content provider examples of work that resulted from the videoconference.** Multiple examples from those students that were really impacted by the conference are a good group from which to choose. The teacher of the Global Warming Videoconference sent a handful of essays on pollution and global warming that the students wrote as part of an assessment.

4. **Contact the content provider and see if they would answer additional questions that the students may have.** You can also ask them if they would answer additional questions that you may have about the topic. Additionally, this would be the time to see if the content provider has any additional materials that they may have that they can share with you. This can be done through email a week or even two weeks after the videoconference. After the Global Warming Videoconference, the teacher sent an email indicating that the students had more questions and asked if there were additional

resources that could be used in the classroom.

5. **If you get a positive response from the email request, reply quickly with any questions that you or the students may have.** Additionally, ask if the content provider can keep you updated on their work or send along articles and other teaching materials which you might find useful. The Global Warming Videoconference teacher indicated that this topic was very interesting and asked that if or when breakthroughs or new articles were published, the content provider could send them along. She provided her email and school addresses to facilitate the process.

6. **Express that you look forward to working with them again next year,** or again this year if there is a follow-up conference or an additional curriculum topic with which they can assist you in the current school year. At the conclusion of the email sent in step five, the Global Warming Videoconference teacher thanked the content provider for their continued help and established a month to complete the videoconference again next year.

After this initial relationship is set up, an educator can feel comfortable contacting the external provider several times a year to inquire about their current projects. Again, teachers must realize that content providers are very busy people, and it is important that they do not overload them with emails. Give them ample time to respond to the email and, if they do not, try to realize they are busy and do not get offended. Try again in a few months and see if they respond. Hopefully, these steps will lead you to a content provider that is dedicated to education and who will send articles and updates on their work throughout the year. This relationship may take some time to establish. You should plan on having a videoconference with them each year and expand the relationship.

If a content provider is not willing to develop any type of link outside of the videoconference, I would suggest researching and finding a different external provider and beginning the process over again with them. You may have to interact with a few content providers before finding ones that best fit your expectations and personality. This may be a long process, but the rewards will be long-lasting and educationally-sound, providing you with an external expert for many years to come.

As you work through this process, remember that other educators have used videoconferences, and have had mixed results. Some have encountered content providers that are not good presenters and do not use the background or graphics of their establishment to their best effect during the conference. On the other hand, many educators have good words to say about videoconferences. Videoconferencing is a teaching tool that has only recently become available to students; it has many potential benefits that you need to evaluate and incorporate into your use. According to Ba and Keisch (2004), "examples of such programs include the JASON Project, founded by scientist and oceanographer Dr. Robert Ballard; the NASA CONNECT program; and San Francisco's Exploratorium museum's live Web casts and digital library" (Ba & Keisch, 2004, p. 2). The SeaTrek series of videoconferences is a marine lab and research center that is involved in making students aware of marine life and bringing their research to school children grades four to eight. Through interviews, surveys, and data analysis, the SeaTrek program continues to grow and change to engage students in science and conservation (Ba & Keisch, 2004).

An in-depth example of outcomes resulting from a post-conference relationship is that of a middle-school social studies and English educator who participated in a videoconference on labor unions. The content provider had multiple activities that the teacher could use to prepare the students for the videoconference, and was willing to adjust the conference based on the activities which were covered in the classroom. The conference was for a group of at-risk students, and the educator was amazed at their level of interest and the students' participation with the external provider. After the conference, the external provider gave the educator more lesson plans and materials that they could use, as well as an evaluation form.

Additionally, a month or so later the content provider sent the teacher a map of the world showing at what different ages that children could work in various countries and where there were no age requirements. This was updated information that the teachers could not have created and which was very valuable. It could be used in future current events and economics discussions; it was a resource that they will be able to use for many years to come.

In another setting one teacher went through a handful of content providers before finding a content provider from an aquarium that provided the required content and enthusiasm. This content provider supplied the teacher with materials that she could use in the classroom both before and after the videoconference, and was such a great resource to the class that they intend to use the content provider every year. The teacher is extremely happy with the quality of the conference and the relationship established with the content provider. The teaching materials and videoconferences now provide the teacher with the opportunity to grow, enrich, and enhance the instruction to students (M. Leach, personal communication, March 10, 2006).

THE BENEFITS OF VIDEOCONFERENCING

Videoconferences and electronic field trips, at an average of $100 to $200 in cost, are relatively inexpensive options when compared to field trips. Rural Hall Elementary School, which offers students multiple videoconferences per year, reported that most of their videoconferences are free and that the most expensive one in which they participate is $125 an hour. This price was much less than it would have cost to take a field trip ($1,800 per grade level). The teachers in the district also note that they do not lose a day of instruction due to long bus trips (McDermon, 2005). This cost differential is important: In recent years, there have been many cuts in the ancillary aspects of education, and the funds to support field trips out of town or to an educational site are limited. In addition, there are frequent costs assigned to students who attend these trips, and some students may not be able to afford the cost. With decreasing costs, more availability of providers, and a growing number of free offerings, it is oftentimes more economical to have a videoconference and have direct contact with a provider at a specific location. In addition, this may give the class more time to directly interact with the provider and answer many more questions than may be asked from a walking tour of an establishment.

Along with travel and cost concerns, many locations are unattainable for field trips; for example, through videoconferencing, students were able to see an actual research site where studies were being done on global warming. Students would not, however, be able to go to these types of sites to visit. As another example, Vanderbilt University has a program that allows college professors and university researchers to lecture about environmental issues with students through videoconferencing (Tillett, 2005). These university officials "provide reliable, up-to-date, and cutting-edge science to classrooms" (p. A668). The scientist-student interaction is emphasized, and questions are encouraged as part of the videoconference. Scientists give virtual tours of their laboratories and enjoy taking an active role in education. This laboratory would be unattainable by students under any other circumstances. Other places may not have room to accommodate all of your students except through a Webcam. Students

can see uncommon animals and artifacts that no local establishment could provide.

Videoconferencing is a new and emerging technology that students of today will most likely have to use, as it may be the driving force behind society and education in the future. NASA believes that as the technology to videoconference becomes cheaper, they will increase the number of videoconferences that they present annually (Peterson, 2000). This has multiple benefits that can influence student outcomes. One of NASA's guidelines for its presenters is, in addition to the content, to explain the career path that they have chosen, and allow students to ask questions about employment opportunities at NASA. As a result, students in one videoconference session were very surprised to hear that students looking to work at NASA or in related fields need to be able to speak many languages in order to be effective in their work (Nkrumah, 2003). Accessing these external providers can pique students' interest, and help them to make decisions about their future careers and college choices.

CONCLUSION

Videoconferencing is an emerging technology that has had many positive impacts on education. As illustrated in this chapter, it is a technology that can be used by any discipline and has long-lasting results. It is important to find an external content provider that is vested in education and will work with you to produce the most productive and meaningful learning experience possible. It is very important to plan well and be prepared in order to conduct a successful videoconference. The steps suggested in the chapter will lead to the establishment of professional relationships that can foster amazing learning opportunities for students. This may be a long process and require the testing of many external content providers, but in the long run it will prove worthwhile.

I personally have been able to work on the development of two videoconferences and have participated with my students in approximately 20 sessions of videoconferences. I have been able to develop lasting relationships with providers that continue to supply me with charts and graphs, articles, and updates on their personal research. This information has been vital to my continuing education as a teacher and the quality of materials that I have been able to present to my students. Videoconferencing is an excellent way to engage all types of students and create long-lasting memories of curriculum topics.

REFERENCES

Ba, H., & Keisch, D. (2004). *Bridging the gap between formal and informal learning: Evaluating the SeaTrek distance learning project.* Center For Children and Technology, New York, New York: Education Development Center, Inc. Retrieved August 14, 2006, at http://www2.edc.org/CCT/Publications_report_summary.asp?numPubId=177.

California school district employs videoconferencing units for global studies. *T H E Journal,* October 1997, pg. 38. EBSCOhost. Retrieved June 11, 2007, from <http://searchepnet.com>

Dishongh, K. (2005, December 28). Ideas bubble up when students put their heads together. *USA Today,* 8d.

Ferrer, G. (2006). Videoconferencing brings world to CdA students. *The Spokesman-Review.*

Gibson, S., & Nocente, N. (1999). Computers in the schools. *Computers in social studies education: A report of teachers' perspectives and students' attitudes, 15*(2), 73-81. New York: Haworth Press.

Hearnshaw, D. (2000). Towards an objective approach to the evaluation of videoconferencing. *Innovations in Education and Training International, 37*(3), 210-217.

Howard-Kennedy, J. (2004). Benefits of videoconferencing in education. *Media and Methods, 41*(1), 17.

Loveman, S. (2004). Bartley would have enjoyed this: Explorations in online/distance learning at an independent school. *Independent School, 63*(4), 72-77.

McDermon, L. (2005). Distance learning: It's elementary! *Learning and Leading with Technology, 33*(4), 28-30.

Motamedi, V. (2001). A critical look at the use of videoconferencing in United States distance education. *Education, 122*(2), 386-395.

Nkrumah, W. (2003). Portland, Oregon, Museum puts students in touch with NASA. *The Oregonian.*

Peterson, R. (2000). "Real-world" connections through videoconferencing—we're closer than you think! *TechTrends, 44*(6), 5-11.

Tillett, T. (2005). Virtual school. *Environmental Health Perspectives, 113*(10), A668.

Ullman, E. (2006). Students in Michigan connect with authors. *District Administration, 42*(3), 106.

Watkins, C. (2002). Videoconferences can bridge the gap. *American Libraries, 33*(11), 14.

Wheeler, S. (2000). User reactions to videoconferencing: Which students cope best? *Education Media International, 37*(1), 31-38.

Chapter VIII
Designing, Assessing, and Scaffolding Student Learning in Videoconferences

Harry Grover Tuttle
Syracuse University, USA

ABSTRACT

This chapter provides a three-step framework for improving student learning in videoconferencing. Using the Understanding by Design model, educators can design videoconferencing instruction that focuses on specific student learning. As they pre-assess their curriculum and instruction goals and shape the videoconference plan, as they assess students' learning before, during, and after the videoconference, and as they scaffold the learning to meet these goals and assessment needs, they will automatically build in structured, successful learning experiences. While discussing the transfer of the understanding by design model to videoconferencing settings, the author provides specific examples of each step of this process that will help other educators use the system in their own instructional practices.

INTRODUCTION

Learning is the star or primary goal of videoconferencing (Amirian, 2003; Tuttle, 1996). Videoconferencing is when people learn interactively by hearing, seeing, and sharing over distance in real-time. Since learning is the goal of videoconferencing, it is important for educators to structure the process in a way that will support students' learning and the assessment of that learning.

When educators select videoconferencing, they are using a technology that provides for robust learning blocks of multiple interactivity (student to content, student to instructor, and student to student), audio and visual modalities, authentic connections, collaboration across distances, multicultural connections, access to primary sources, and collaboration with experts and peers (Greenberg, 2004). Educators can use these learning blocks as they design the learning experience, scaffold it, and assess the student learning.

Depending on their goals for student learning, educators may choose to incorporate videoconferencing with its learning blocks into a particular aspect of class learning, possibly serving as:

- An introduction to the unit
- An activity during the unit
- Several activities during the unit
- The main activity during the unit
- The only activity in the unit
- An end of the lesson summary
- A follow-up activity to the unit
- A special motivator

Educators can increase their students' academic growth through videoconferencing by learning how to:

1. Design the students' learning in videoconferencing around the Understanding by Design model
2. Build in assessments before, during, and after the videoconferencing learning experience
3. Scaffold the students' learning before and during the videoconference for successful learning

BACKGROUND

When educators investigate the possibility of improving student learning through videoconferencing, they find an abundance of references that focus on the students' enjoyment of the videoconferencing experience or the educators' stories of their first experiences with videoconferencing; only rarely do they find examples that focus on student learning (Anderson & Rourke, 2005). Documentation of learning via reliable

and valid assessment also is limited. In fact, the word "assessment" does not appear in many videoconferencing manuals (Classroom and Media Services Information Services and Technology of the University of Manitoba, n.d.; University of Ulster, n.d.). For example, the Bethpage Union Free School District's (n.d.) videoconferencing manual is a listing of content providers and the topics they offer; there is no mention of the assessment of learning.

Videoconferencing assessment resources that are available tend to focus primarily on the evaluation of the videoconferencing experience, not on student learning in the videoconference. For example, none of the 16 "Before I Die" videoconferencing evaluation questions assess student learning (PBSOnline, n.d.) and, although the *Digital Handbook* (2003) asserts that assessing videoconferencing requires a complex set of assessments, it focuses on measuring participation, project visuals, and on-camera presentation, and only refers to content assessment through rubrics. Other methods focus on project assessments. For instance, Bernhardt's videoconferencing evaluation form concentrates on teacher-centered activities with statements like, "How effective was the content of the videoconference? (How well was the content delivered)" rather than on learner-centered activities such as, "How well did the student learn the content?" (Knowledge Network Explorers, 2006b).

Research on content-based outcomes that is available appears to support mixed findings. The early research of Russell (1999) on student learning in videoconferencing showed a "no significant difference" while recent studies, such as Newman, Barbanell, and Falco (2005), showed the positive impact of videoconferencing on student learning. These research studies, however, used videoconferencing in ways that differ from teachers' more complex uses (Anderson & Rourke, 2005).

ISSUES, CONTROVERSIES, AND PROBLEMS

The paucity of resources on how to use a learning model in the designing of a videoconference that uses embedding assessment and structures it for learning creates a pedagogical pit. In earlier writings, Tuttle (2003) presented a potential model that included pre-analysis of the videoconferencing planning process that can be used by teachers to determine how well they are designing, assessing, and scaffolding a program so that it will promote student learning (see Figure 1). This pre-analysis will allow instructors to make necessary modifications before the actual videoconference. In this process, several weeks before the actual videoconference, teachers rate multiple constructs on a scale on 1 (very low) to 10 (very high) based on what they think will mostly likely happen during the videoconference by referring to what they have actually written into their plans; they do not rate it on what they would like to happen. Teachers tally these scores, paying particular attention to those items with ratings below five. For example, as educators analyze what will probably happen during the videoconference, they may realize that they have not built in techniques to determine if all students will have learned the concept at the evaluation level of thinking; therefore, if this is a priority, the educators can modify their videoconferencing plans to include more higher-level thinking, thereby increasing the students' learning. Likewise, through this pre-analysis process, teachers might discover that they will be assessing the class as a whole, but not each student individually. Again, if this is a priority, instructors can modify their videoconferencing plans to meet this need.

Understanding by Design Model

The effectiveness of Tuttle's pre-analysis of videoconference learning demonstrates the need for more structured designing, assessing, and scaffolding of videoconferences so that they will result in effective learning environments. One approach that meets this need is the *Understanding by Design model* (Wiggins & McTighe, 1998). In this model, educators first choose a specific learning goal, determine how they will assess the learning, select or develop activities based on the specific learning goal and the assessment, and then select the technology appropriate to support those goals, activities, and assessments.

A common question on videoconference evaluation forms is, "How well did the content of the videoconference connect to your curriculum?" (Knowledge Network Explorer, 2006b). Under the *Understanding by Design model*, educators will answer this crucial question, not after the videoconference, but before selecting the videoconference. In this approach, an educator will work with the videoconference partner to insure that both have the same learning goal established for students. If an educator wants her students to compare animals from different habitats, a videoconference on watching an elephant eat does not match that purpose. If a science educator decides that he wants his students to compare five trees from another location, having his class videoconference with a class in a distant location and discuss trees found at that geographic setting is a solid educational fit. If an educator wants his college students to be able to broaden their research skills, videoconferencing with an author who continually expands her research is an educationally-meaningful experience. There is a drastic difference between a learning activity that "somewhat" fits the teacher's chosen standard and one that specifically meets it. If the videoconference does not match with the academic levels of the specific students in the class and the specific content which is required, the instructor should not choose it. Using this approach, if a commercial partner asks the teacher to select from one of five preestablished presentations, without being willing to adapt it to the specific needs of

Figure 1. Pre-analysis of student learning in an expert videoconference (Tuttle, 2003, used with permission)

Expert Videoconferences - Categories	Scale: 1(low)-10 (high)	Comment
The videoconference focuses on a stated specific standard and specifically on a subpart of the standard.		
All activities focus on the stated learning standard.		
The videoconference is scaffolded so all students will be successful in their learning.		
Students will be pre-assessed on their learning about the topic.		
The Expert will provide unique or localized information that could not be obtained elsewhere.		
The Expert will use gestures, movement, and actions to communicate the learning.		
The Expert will use many different types of visuals and objects to illustrate or model the learning.		
The Expert will send scaffolded materials ahead for the students' use during the videoconference.		
The Expert will pause every few minutes to ask or answer questions to clarify learning.		
All students will be highly engaged in meaningful learning at least 70% of the time.		
The Expert will engage students in higher-level thinking activities at least 50% of the time.		
The Expert will engage students in multicultural and global interactivity to learn from diverse perspectives.		
The Expert or host teacher will distribute the assessment before the students do the activities.		
All students will create at least one product or demonstration by the end of the conference.		
All students will receive individual feedback during the conference.		
All students will be assessed at the end or after the videoconference and will be given feedback.		
Total	/160	

the classroom and the students' needs, it should not be used. If another class wants someone to videoconference with them on "social studies," the educator should avoid such general, nonstandard-based learning.

The process of assessment of learning detailed in *Understanding by Design* also transfers to videoconferencing. Wiggins stresses that teachers spend too much time in teaching and covering content and not enough time in assessing learning (Wilcox, 2006). Using the Understanding by Design model, once educators have defined the precise learning purpose, they would then select the assessment or a series of assessments that measure the students' progress toward the chosen subpart of a more general standard. Amirian (2003) supports this emphasis, noting that one of the most important steps in facilitating videoconferencing learning is assessment, stressing that students' learning needs to be measured, and the learning process needs to be reiterative. Kerka and Wonocott (2000) also state that assessment has to be continuous and interactive.

Pre-assessment: Good assessment starts with a pre-assessment of what students already know about the designated learning. For instance, educators might choose to assess the students' creation of materials that the students will use during the videoconference. Consequently, the educators will evaluate if the students have communicated their ideas clearly, succinctly, and visually. For example, art students might create some abstract landscapes using warm and cool colors as part of a demonstration on abstract and representational art in elementary art education. The instructor will assess them using a rubric that includes whether they have: used at least two warm colors; used at least two cool colors; and used those colors to create an abstract (not detailed) representation of the photograph that they were given. Based on this formative assessment, the art

students can improve the quality of their work before they use it in the conference.

Alternately, before the videoconference, the hosting educator might pre-assess his students' knowledge and skills and gives the partner that analysis. As an example, a teacher might give the students a quick pretest on the topic, such as their knowledge of chaos theory, analyzes the results, and shares the analysis with the partner educator at least a week before the actual videoconference. Or, another hosting educator might send a low-, a medium-, and a high-scoring student lab report on a purifying water experiment to a water purification expert prior to the videoconference. Or a third teacher might have her elementary science students play with a toy and hypothesize how it works. The teacher will then communicate a summary of the hypotheses to the virtual science expert.

The provider partner also should begin a videoconference with a pre-assessment. For example, a virtual physical education teacher might ask students to demonstrate any exercise. He watches the students to see how many can do the exercise correctly. He uses that assessment to determine what the students need to learn. All students would be assessed; a good pre-assessment involves responses from everyone, not just those who volunteer or sit nearest the videoconferencing camera.

If possible, both the host teacher and the expert or visiting class should work together on a pre-assessment at the start of the videoconference. For example, a virtual writing instructor may ask students to write a three-minute change poem in which they show the differences in the two states of something such as a green banana and a rotten banana. She will have several students read their poems to determine if they use precise descriptive terms. The host teacher quickly reads all the other students' poems and gives more feedback to the virtual poetry instructor, who decides how much structure the students need in order to be successful in writing their descriptive poetry. As another example, a teacher may prepare his students for a visit to a museum by doing a virtual museum visit. As the students see many of the exhibits that they will physically visit, they write down what they already know about the exhibits, and they write down their questions about the exhibits or the connections among a series of exhibits. The teacher will analyze their responses, and communicates that analysis to the virtual museum guide so she can construct a more meaningful educational tour.

During: When using Understanding by Design, teachers also realize that they need to carefully assess students during the learning process. When educators assess student learning during the process, they can "monitor and adjust" instruction (Hunter, 1984). The issue is not how many notes students take during a videoconference, but what they are learning during the videoconference. Educators can embed assessment during the interactive videoconferences. For instance, in an elementary science class, each student can complete a similarities-and-differences chart as the student examines the trees near the school and the trees from another location. The host teacher can walk around and observe how well the students complete the similarities-and-differences chart; the teacher may ask students for clarification on their charts or ask the other school to tell more about a certain tree so that students can understand the similarity or difference.

In another situation, college students who virtually observe primary children through videoconferencing might select a student and analyze the student's skills. Halfway through the observation, they might be asked to orally give a mini-report to the instructor who will then give them feedback. She may ask her students to observe their designated primary student for particular

behaviors to better analyze the child's skills that they did not notice the first time. Alternately, in an Assistive Technology class, a virtual expert might describe a certain student's conditions through a short video clip, and ask each student to write up a quick diagnosis and write, in big print on a sheet of paper, an appropriate assistive technology for that individual. The students can show their information to the expert, who can then provide instant feedback to the students, both individually and as a class.

Educators can plan a videoconferencing in which the learning is continually assessed. A virtual expert might assess middle-school students' learning during the videoconference through polling techniques. She can ask questions as she presents, with questioning starting at the knowledge level but quickly climbing and staying at the analysis level of thinking. The host professor's students hold up 3 x 5 response cards of "A", "B", "C", and "D" as the visiting professor asks the questions. She can look at their answers to see if they understand the concepts that she is presenting. If the hosting classroom has electronic student response devices, she asks the students to use these so that the results of their answers show up on a graph in the classroom.

Oftentimes, an in-class assessment involves a performance activity. As an example, physical education students at one university can teach students at another university how to stack cups and then ask the other students to demonstrate their new skills. The "teachers" praise and offer suggestions to improve the skill; they then teach a more advance form of stacking and critically watch as the other students do the more complex stacking, providing more feedback to the stacking students. Alternatively, in a social studies videoconference on the U.S. Civil War, students might plot out a war strategy based on the information given to them by the expert. After each group shows their strategy, the expert tells what probably would have happened if each strategy actually had been used. In a more extensive setting, various student groups from one elementary class might participate in the Read Aloud program by reading a story to students in distant elementary schools through videoconferencing. Then the hosting students assess the other students' story comprehension by: having them act out a scene; reorder a set of visuals to tell the sequence of the story; draw what they think is the most critical scene; and decide what type of music represents each major character. The hosting class gives feedback after each class does its comprehension activity.

An in-class assessment can also involve extending the students' learning on a prepared topic. When students prepare for a videoconference topic, they often learn information within a limited context; however, the other teacher or expert can pose a question that requires the students to extend their learning beyond that context. For instance, a teacher can extend a videoconference on the prepared topic of reducing pollution in the school to reducing pollution in the community by having the students "think on their feet" about the topic and come up with realistic solutions based on what they presently know about school pollution. After each school gives their suggestions, the teachers provide feedback as to the viability of their suggestions.

Peer-review or peer-assessment provides another embedded assessment strategy during a videoconference learning experience. Students in one location can write a poem, and students in another location can draw or take pictures of something that they feel represents the message or tone of the poem. The poem authors comment on whether they feel that the drawing or picture does or does not capture the message or tone of their poem and tell why or why not. As a second example of peer-assessment, students from three locations might write and perform songs about ways to reduce pollution in the school. Each school can assess the pollution songs on how specific and practical the solutions are. A third peer-to-peer assessment might involve a Spanish-to-English

language project. A student in the USA school says as many sentences in Spanish as he can about a given topic within one minute. His partner in the Spanish country class counts the sentences and gives suggestions for improvement. Then his Spanish-speaking partner is given a topic, and she says as many sentences as she can in English in a minute. Her English-speaking partner counts her sentences and gives her suggestions for improvement. These two groups meet monthly to help each other in their language learning.

Many teachers use class discussion as a way of assessing student learning during a videoconference; however, this approach may not be appropriate. When educators apply Wiggins' feedback system to videoconferencing discussions, several key assessment elements are missing such as ongoing, individual focus, tasks division, multiple opportunities for retrying, and inclusion of what learners did and did not do (Wilcox, 2006). Because videoconferencing discussions favor the multiple intelligence of the verbal learner, not all students may participate in the discussion. In addition, teachers may not be assessing the students against any given discussion rubric or content rubric. Consequently, a class discussion may not serve as an effective assessment of learning for all students in a videoconference.

Post-assessment: The final assessment of videoconferencing can take place at various times such as: immediately at the end of, but still during, the videoconference; just after the connection is terminated; within a few days; or with a purposeful time delay. For instance, during a videoconference, an elementary music teacher can show the students how to indicate if a note is a high or low by using the Kodaly system of hand signals; as he ends the videoconference, he can have them quickly show if they can do the hand signal for several notes. If the students' hand signals match the notes, then the provider knows that they have successfully learned the concept. He can "talk" with the class teacher about any student who was not successful.

Assessing student learning just after the videoconference learning experience allows more latitude in the type of testing. As an example, an elementary teacher could have her students list three things that they learned from an ocean videoconference. She might have them write one fact about each animal, while another teacher has his students compare each of the sea creatures in a detailed analysis using structured Venn diagrams.

In a "next day" or delayed assessment, a teacher can check for long-term learning and integration of material. For instance, a teacher utilizes a "within a few days" assessment technique when her students answer the essential question, "How does reality interfere with a person's dreams?" that the virtual expert presents at the start of the videoconference. During the videoconference, the expert explains the role of dreams in Don Quixote, and asks the students to compare it to Rev. Dr. Martin Luther King's, "I have a dream" speech. During the next few days, the students read Emma Lazarus' "The New Colossus" poem about the state of liberty; they write a comprehensive essay based on the essential question that includes all three perspectives. The teacher assesses how well they incorporate the three perspectives in answering the essential question.

Pre-post assessment: A combination of pre- and post-assessments allows instructors to discern the degree of students' learning, not just achievement of a benchmark. English students who have studied Macbeth and have watched a local production of it are asked to write an essay demonstrating their understanding of the play. After this task, their English instructor connects his class with a Shakespeare videoconference in which several schools act out scenes from Macbeth. His students watch these different productions, and then they rewrite their original essays. Using a different text color to indicate the changes from the original, the instructor can now assess the differences in each student's thinking due to the Macbeth videoconferencing scenes.

ASSESSMENT OF LEARNING OVER TIME

Sometimes it is beneficial for educators to assess the learning done in videoconferences on the same learning topic during a longer period of time. For instance, a teacher may arrange for her class to have an ongoing videoconferencing discussion about what freedom means with students in another country. Before doing the videoconference, each student does a KWL chart (Know, Want to know, have Learned at the end) in which they indicate what they already know about freedom, what they want to know, and what they learned. In the first session, each class presents its own view of freedom with a few examples and asks each other some general questions, and students once again do a KWL. In the second session, they delve more deeply into how freedom shows itself in each country and answer the other group's questions in more detail. Both groups ask additional questions of each other and do another KWL. During the third session, they discuss their enlarged views of freedom. They do their final KWL after the last videoconference. By comparing the information over time, the teacher can see the learning difference in each student over the course of the videoconference.

Assessment of Multicultural or Global Learning

In addition to subject area content learning, many teachers stress that an important learning goal of a videoconference is its multicultural or global attitudinal dimension (Howard-Kennedy, 2004; Tuttle, 1996). In these settings, the instructors want their students to develop different attitudes or perceptions as a result of videoconferencing. If this is a learning goal, instructors must then design or find assessment strategies to measure the changes in attitudes or perceptions. Teachers can, during pre-assessment, determine the degree of "global sharing" that will take place during the conference. If there is a limited degree, they can extend the global reach of the videoconference. As part of the process, students may develop more complex ways of viewing and explaining the other culture by acknowledging differences and similarities. For instance, students who participated in a videoconference with various sites in Spain can realize that it has a varied geography, and that variety reflects itself in the national dish of paella. Students can compare the ingredients in paella from the coast to inland as they videoconference with people from these various Spanish locations. In turn, they can do a similar lesson with food presenters within the United States.

Assessment as the Purpose of a Videoconference

Assessment can also serve as the sole purpose of the videoconference. Students at distant locations from the university can use videoconferencing to present their work to faculty. For example, they could send their portfolios to the university and go through them "live" with their advisor. The instructor could provide immediate feedback on the students' strength and areas for improvement. Alternatively, assistive technology experts could analyze a student with complex needs via videoconferencing observation. The local assistive technology educators could have the student do many different diagnostic activities according to the evaluators' prescribed order. The evaluators can then review the recorded videoconference and give their final recommendations about the student.

SCAFFOLDING THE VIDEOCONFERENCE TO MAXIMIZE LEARNING

After educators have identified the desired student learning and have determined how they will assess that learning, they need to scaffold or structure the videoconferencing learning experience (Amirian, 2003). Scaffolding organizes and supports the learner by:

- Providing clear directions
- Clarifying purpose
- Keeping students on task
- Offering assessment to clarify expectations
- Pointing students to worthy resources
- Reducing uncertainty, surprise, and disappointment
- Delivering efficiency
- Creating momentum (McKenzie, 1999)

Hunter (1984) suggests a model for structuring for student success that can be applied to videoconferencing. Her scaffolding includes these progressive steps:

- Providing an objective
- Setting a motivational hook
- Sharing the expectations or high standard of learning
- Teaching needed prerequisite skills for success
- Modeling
- Giving directions for step-by-step progression
- Checking for understanding
- Guided practice
- Providing closure to connect to bigger concepts
- Supplying independent practice

Her model incorporates a critical aspect of scaffolding, going from a state of dependence on the teacher to student independence in the task. Also, her model includes many different groupings that support the transition from whole class through small group to the individual. Identification of the zone of proximal development allows instructors to help students grow academically.

Educators can use essential questions as a scaffolding tool since these questions provide stepping-stones to comprehensive learning. Wiggins and McTighe (1998) underscore the importance of essential questions that clearly explain why the topic is important to the students and put this learning into a larger context. A teacher starts the videoconference with the general essential question of, "What does freedom mean?" and then asks a stepping-stone essential question of, "What freedom do you have as an American?"

There are several criteria that can help an educator to determine if scaffolding is being used in videoconferencing and to reinforce its use. These include: built-in mini-steps or structures that enable all students to move forward in their learning; checks for successful learning by all students; an increase in student autonomous learning; a gradual removal of teacher-given structures or rules; and the inclusion of multiple teacher feedbacks and student self-evaluation.

CONCLUSION

As the use of videoconferencing becomes more frequent, educators are becoming more concerned about the quality of the students' learning that it supports. They want evidence that it supports high cognitive levels of learning that target their specific goals.

As a result, educators want commercial partners to embed more informal and formal assessment into their programs. They want assessment to be a natural part of "real-life" videoconferencing experiences. As a result, there is a need for both educators and providers to begin addressing the following questions:

- How does the role of educators and providers change when they are host to many partners who teach parts of the class? When, how, and who controls the assessment?
- Does that assessment change transfer to the educators' face-to-face classroom instruction and assessment?
- In what ways will assessment of a school's curriculum reflect global issues as a result of videoconferencing?
- What impact will the students' ability to videoconference from another site have on assessment? Who rates these students' performance?

Academically-robust student learning from videoconference does not just happen; it needs to be constructed carefully just as building is. Builders need to know an architect's design before they can begin construction; they do not just start putting blocks together. Just as each building is designed for a specific purpose, teachers decide on the precise learning for their students. The *Understanding by Design Model* can assist in this process. Builders continually verify that what they are doing is helping to create the building that the architect envisioned; educators must continually assess students' progress toward predetermined learning. The builders construct each part of the building to support the next part; each building block is placed with the knowledge of how each level should be. Educators also scaffold learning for all students, providing the necessary background skills and content needed for each phase. When educators follow these steps, they can create rich videoconferencing learning environments in which students' learning will build up like a skyscraper.

REFERENCES

Amirian, S. (2003). Pedagogy and videoconferencing: A review of recent literature. In *Proceedings of the First NJEDge.NET Conference,* Plainsboro, NJ, October 31, 2003. Retrieved April 10, 2006, from http://www.iclassnotes.com/amirian_handout.pdf#search='NJEDge.NET%20Conference %20%20Amirian' and http://www.iclassnotes. com/amirian_megacon.pdf

Anderson, T., & Rourke, M. (2005). *Videoconferencing in kindergarten-to-grade 12 settings: A review of the literature.* Retrieved April 1, 2006, from http://www.d261.k12.id.us/VCing/curriculum/design.htm

Bethpage Union Free School District (n.d.) Videoconferencing manual: Content providers.

Bethpage Community. Retrieved April 26, 2006, from http://www.bethpagecommunity. com/Schools/technology/Videoconferencing%2 0Manual.pdf

Classroom and Media Services Information Services and Technology of the University of Manitoba (n.d.). Videoconferencing manual. *University of Manitoba.* Retrieved April 27, 2006, from http://umanitoba.ca/campus/ist/cms/video-conferencing/manual/index.shtml

Cross, K. P., & Angelo, T. A. (1988). *Classroom assessment techniques: A handbook for faculty.* Ann Arbor, MI: National Center for Research to Improve Postsecondary Teaching and Learning.

Digital Handbook (2003). *A videoconferencing guide for teachers and students.* Retrieved April 11, 2006, from http://www.d261.k12.id.us/VCing/curriculum/design.htm

Greenberg, A. (2004). Navigating the sea of research on videoconferencing-based distance-education: A platform for understanding the technology's effectiveness and value. *Wainhouse Research.* Retrieved April 2, 2006, from http://www.wainhouse.com/files/papers/wr-navseadist-edu.pdf

Howard-Kennedy, J. (2004). Middle school videoconferencing fosters global citizenship. *Center Digital.* Retrieved April 25, 2006, from http://www.centerdigitalgov.com/international/story.php?docid=90700

Hunter, M. (1984). *Mastery teaching.* El Segundo, CA: TIP Publications.

Keasley, G. (2005). Social developmental theories - L. Vygotsky. Retrieved April 22, 2006, from http://tip.psychology.org/vygotsky.html

Kerka, S., & Wonocott, M. E. (2000). Online assessment: Continuous and interactive. Retrieved April 20, 2006, from http://www.calpro-online. org/eric/docs/pfile03.htm

Knowledge Network Explorers (2006a). Videoconferencing directories. Retrieved April 6, 2006, from http://www.kn.pacbell.com/wired/vidconf/directory.cfm

Knowledge Network Explorers (2006b). Videoconferencing evaluation. Retrieved April 15, 2006, from http://www.kn.pacbell.com/wired/vidconf/eval.html

Lim, J. (2006). Ask donut. *Word Press.* Retrieved April 12, 2006, from http://bcisdvcs.wordpress. com/2006/03/23/ask-donuthead

McKenzie, J. (1999). Scaffolding for success. *From Now On: The Technology Journal, 9*(4). Retrieved April 17, 2006, from http://fno.org/dec99/scaffold.html

Newman, D., Barbanell, P., & Falco, J. (2005). Achievement of student cognitive growth: Results of integrating interactive museum video-conferencing. In J. Trant & D. Bearman (Eds.), *Museums and the Web 2005: Proceedings.* Toronto: Archives Museum Informatics. Retrieved on April 20, 2006, from http://www.archimuse. com/mw2005/papers/newman/newman.html

PBSOnline (n.d.). *Before I die.* Retrieved April 13, 2006, from http://www.thirteen.org/bid/pevalhost.html

Russell, T. L. (1999). *The no significant difference phenomenon: A comparative research annotated bibliography on technology for distance education.* North Carolina State University: IDECC.

Schrock, K. (2006). Kathy Schrock's guide for educators–Assessment and rubrics. Retrieved April 17, 2006, from http://school.discovery.com/schrockguide/assess.html

Tuttle, H. G. (1996). Learning: The star of video-conferencing. *MultiMedia Schools, 3*(4), 37-41.

Tuttle, H. G. (2003). *Maximizing student learning in a videoconference.* Paper presented at the New York State Association for Computers and Technology in Education Annual Conference. Rochester, NY.

Tuttle, H. G. (2004). *Learning and technology assessments for administrators.* Ithaca, NY: Epilog Visions.

University of Ulster (n.d.). Videoconferencing manual. Retrieved April 24, 2006, from http://www.ulster.ac.uk/isd/itus/media/vcmanual.pdf

Wiggins, G., & McTighe, J. (1998). *Understanding by design.* Alexandria, VA: Association for Supervision and Curriculum Development.

Wilcox, J. (2006). Less teaching, more assessing. *Association for Supervision and Curriculum Development Education Update, 48*(2) 1, 2, 6, 8.

Willis, B. (n.d.). *Distance education at a glance: Evaluation for distance educators.* Retrieved April 10, 2006, from http://www.uidaho.edu/eo/dist4.html

Woodruff, M., & Mosby, J. (1996). *A brief description of videoconferencing: Videoconferencing in the classroom and library.* Retrieved April 15, 2006, from http://www.kn.pacbell.com/wired/vidconf/description.html#what

Chapter IX
Designing and Implementing Collaborative Classroom Videoconferences[1]

Temi Bidjerano
University at Albany/SUNY, USA

Diane Wilkinson
Schenectady City School District, USA

ABSTRACT

The chapter introduces collaborative classroom projects implemented through videoconferencing technology as a means of enhancing and enriching classroom instruction. The various applications of collaborative classroom videoconferencing are discussed in the light of social constructivist learning theory. Special attention is devoted to teacher professional development training in designing and implementing collaborative classroom videoconference projects. Distinctive types of collaborative classroom implementation projects with supporting examples, as well as effective outcomes associated with student learning, are presented and discussed. The chapter concludes with a summary of the best practices in the utilization of collaborative classroom projects; directions and recommendations for future research are also offered.

INTRODUCTION

Telecommunications have proven to have a pervasive effect on people's everyday lives; they have been brought in the classroom because of the general belief that they would be beneficial in helping students to realize their own academic potential. Videoconferencing, as implemented for the purposes of classroom instruction, bridges physical distances and provides access to distant educational resources. Among the acknowledged advantages of videoconferencing over traditional classroom instruction are the opportunities provided to students to have authentic experiences through interaction with experts, and to acquire knowledge in a dynamic and visual fashion that is rooted in dialogue and discussion. In addition, collaborative classroom experience can result in the implementation of projects that involve two geographically-distant classrooms using videoconferencing to access, share, or transmit information to each other (Newman, Barbanell, & Falco, 2007).

Collaborative classroom projects are built on the premise that opportunities for interaction and discussion with peers across distances will nurture student interest and motivation, and will eventuate in cognitive gains. Thus, the purpose of any collaborative classroom project is to engage students in the process of instruction and assessment, and to model and support higher-level thinking and problem-solving (Jonassen, 2002).

The overarching goal of this chapter is to provide an overview of best practices in designing and implementing collaborating classroom videoconferencing. The various applications of this form of videoconferencing, from training and teacher preparation to actual implementation and post-videoconference activities, will be delineated so that the information provided here can serve as a means of modeling future collaborative classroom videoconference projects.

THEORETICAL BACKGROUND

Collaborative classroom projects are based on current understanding of how children think and learn and are rooted in the theories of cognitive and social constructivism. Unlike the transmission model of learning and instruction, in which students are assumed to be passive recipients of the existing knowledge, contemporary learning theories emphasize inquiry, critical thinking, and acquisition of the skills of abstraction, experimentation, and collaboration (Awbrey, 1996).

The constructivist approach to learning and instruction stems from Jean Piaget's pivotal theoretical work on a child's cognitive functioning. The underpinning of Piaget's theory is that children construct their own understanding of the world through interaction and free exploration. The child is metaphorically depicted as a little scientist and self-directed problem-solver, who constantly tests, accepts, or refutes hypotheses about the world (Flavell, 1992). According to Piaget, children actively construct their knowledge of the world by acting upon objects in space and time, and by being provided with ample opportunities to generate ideas on their own. The role of a teacher is to facilitate this natural course of cognitive development by exposing a child to other points of views and to conflicting ideas that may encourage a child to rethink or review his/her own conceptions of the world. If children never experience information that contradicts the erroneous ideas that they have constructed by themselves, they would never develop conceptual knowledge. Although Piaget has never articulated the instructional implications of his theory, social scientists and educators have translated their understanding of Piaget into curriculum designs, teaching approaches, and a whole new philosophy of education (Wood, 1988).

Lev Vygotsky's (1978) influential theory of social constructivism posits that children's thinking and learning are shaped by the social activities in which children participate. Learning and instruction are defined as a social construction of knowledge. A child's potential for learning is realized in his/her interactions with more knowledgeable others. Vygotsky introduced the concept of the "zone of proximal development" to refer to the gap that exists for a child between what she/he is able to do alone and what she/he can achieve with help from more knowledgeable or skilled (than her/him) adults and peers. Vygotsky's approach has helped educators and practitioners understand that specific instructional practices should not only follow but be one step ahead of a child's current level of thinking and comprehension. Students' ability to solve problems and to think critically and creatively is enhanced through discussion and interaction with peers that entails exploration of topics from another perspective. As in Piaget's theory, cognitive growth is assumed to result from exposure to different interpretations of a problem or situation; being confronted with viewpoints and opinions different from their own, students are forced to refine, enrich, and eventually change their cognitive structures and understanding of a particular problem (Bruner, 1985).

To be productive, classroom collaboration with peers should be "built upon topics that invoke discussions, and they should demand the input of several new sources and opinions" (Johnson & Johnson, 1996, p. 1028). In the process of collaboration, students receive immediate feedback from peers about their understanding of a particular topic. The groups of students who participate in the collaborative projects develop interdependence on each other, discuss and exchange information, provide and receive support, challenge each other's points of views and reflect on their own evolving understanding (Johnson & Johnson, 1996). What distinguishes collaborative learning from other forms of learning is that the learning tasks require students to mutually depend on one another. As pointed out by Johnson and Johnson, all students have an equal opportunity to interact with one another and to communicate their ideas openly; thus they become accountable for the

processes that occur and the level of learning that takes place. The nature of the task conditions the learning outcomes. Johnson and Johnson (1996) emphasize that collaboration is especially valuable and produces more positive outcomes when the tasks at hand are complex and require good problem-solving skills; learning is derived through conversations with others and is being enhanced by a learner's own intrinsic motivation to participate in learning with others.

The transfer and the application of the ideas, derived from the grand constructivist learning theories, to the traditional classroom setting has produced evidence supporting the postulated fundamental learning principles. Research has shown that collaborative learning increases the frequency of behaviors associated with improved problem-solving and critical thinking skills techniques (Beilin & Rabaw, 1981; Gabbert, Johnson, & Johnson, 1996); augments student satisfaction with learning, improves oral presentation skills, and motivates students to take a greater responsibility for their own learning (Davis, 1993; Totten, Sills, Digby, & Russ, 1991; Woolfolk, 2004); facilitates the long-term retention of knowledge and enhances self-directed learning (Norman & Schmidt, 1992); and promotes student achievement (Wulff, Nyquist, & Abbott, 1987). Meta-analytic studies, summarizing the outcomes of numerous empirical researches on cooperative and collaborative learning have established that student collaboration has positive effects on measures of student achievement and productivity, and promotes favorable attitudes to learning along with higher self-esteem (Springer, Stanne, & Donovan, 1999).

Although the potential benefits of the collaboration in school settings have been examined predominantly in the context of the traditional classroom instruction, there is no reason to believe that the important observation made in the regular classroom would not apply to technology-mediated instruction (Johnson & Johnson, 1996). For these benefits to be brought to the classroom in the context of videoconferencing, however, a great deal of initial planning and preparation has to take place. The intended productive utilization of the collaborative classroom involves an array of planning activities ranging from solving technology and equipment issues to careful development of instructional methodologies in delivery and design (McAlpine, 2000). It is incumbent upon the teacher to accumulate skills and knowledge in conducting videoconference–mediated collaborative projects in order to be able to design and to orchestrate the social context of learning by the means of these telecommunication tools. In this sense, teacher training in the implementation of the classroom project is conceived as the very first step towards creating a foundation for integrating interactive collaborative classroom projects (Falco, Barbanell, Newman, & DeWald, 2005; Newman, Barbanell, & Falco, 2005).

COLLABORATIVE CLASSROOM TRAINING[2]

The creation of the collaborative classroom training (CCT) can be a direct result of teachers inquiring about the possibility of connecting to other teachers not only within their district but also outside of their district. As teachers' technologi-

cal understanding of videoconferencing grows, the creativity within the teachers can take over. Before long, an abundance of possibilities emerge. Teachers exchange e-mails and phone numbers, knowing that as soon as they get back to their classrooms, the next step will be to exchange IP numbers. With no program fee cost or ISDN charges, collaborating classrooms can call and interact as many times as they wish without the budgetary constraints that are associated with connecting to content providers. Further, CCT can be an avenue for providing teachers with competencies for conducting videoconferences, since it focuses explicitly on building skills using two-way interactive videoconferencing in a K-12 classroom.

Training

Training is essential for gaining skills for successful collaborating classroom programs. The objectives of training are to provide teachers with an overview of the nature and the essential features of the videoconference collaborating classrooms, and guide and assist them in the process of building a successful collaborating classroom program. Training provides the necessary time for teachers of different buildings and districts to meet and plan for collaboration.

Table 1. Checklist for building interactive collaboration

	Steps
√	Determine Collaborating Partners
√	Pinpoint Curriculum
√	Review Technological Logistics and Teaching Environment
√	Brainstorm and Design Collaborative Content Based on Curriculum Goals and Objectives
√	Determine Collaboration Content Structure for Project
√	Select Strategies for Student Learning Activities
√	Develop Curriculum Materials, Lessons, Activities, Resources, and so forth
√	Develop Assessment Components

The steps that direct the teachers through the process of developing a collaborative classroom project are summarized in Table 1. The development of a collaborative project incorporates the best practices and models for traditional lesson plan development. In this process, however, an emphasis is placed not only on providing training and guidelines for formulating instructional objectives and selecting appropriate methods and strategies for implementing the lessons, but also on solving issues pertaining to the utilization of the videoconference technology.

Educators seek to assure that the application of videoconference technology improves the characteristics of the learning environment and provides the desirable learning outcomes; a clear vision about the role of this specific technology in enhancing learning needs to be present at the onset of each collaboration. In addition, each collaborative project has to be supported by all the materials necessary for students and teachers to complete the planned lesson activities.

As a result of training as well as the exchange of information that occurred among the participating teachers, a plethora of collaborative classroom projects have been generated. These projects illustrate not only these teachers' creativity, but also their pedagogical knowledge and understanding of cognitive theories which lead them into the finest exemplary applications of the concepts of cooperative and collaborative learning and instruction. Table 2 contains the synopses of five collaborative classroom projects created by teachers trained in VIT and CCT. An example of a complete collaborative classroom development plan could be found in Appendix A.

Evaluation

A content analysis was conducted on 26 collaborative classroom integration plans developed by teachers who completed CCT (Newman, Du, Bose, & Bidjerano, 2006). A number of characteristics were documented in the study. Table 3 contains information on selected features of the integration plans such as learning objectives, materials, activities, and mode of instruction. Bloom's taxonomy was utilized to evaluate the expected quality and level of student cognitive engagement. In addition, the structure of the curriculum was evaluated based on the role/purposes of the collaborative classroom videoconference in the curriculum.

As seen in Table 2, the integration plans addressed all grade levels (K-12) and represented a variety of content areas including English Language Arts, mathematics, science, technology, social studies, and career and occupational development. The integration plans tapped into multiple learning standards both at state and national levels. In addition to a clear vision and planned efforts for the classroom-to-classroom videoconference, most of the integration plans included pre-videoconference and post-videoconference lessons, designated to reinforce the concepts around which collaboration was conceived.

In-depth investigation of the characteristics of the collaborative classrooms integration plans indicated that implementation required an extended multiple-session format to provide a comprehensive coverage of the topics at hand. The analysis showed also that collaborative classroom videoconferencing was not conceived as a single, isolated activity; in contrast, it was intended to be highly relevant to the curriculum and form a cohesive whole with pre- and post-session lessons and activities. The planned pre-videoconference objectives ranged from providing basic knowledge and understanding to application of the acquired knowledge, and could be achieved by activities such as direct instruction, independent research, and creating products. The classroom-to-classroom videoconferences were planned to focus predominantly on interaction, sharing of information in the form of discussion, and presentations of created products. In most integration plans, teachers emphasized project-based learning as one of the strategies through which collaborative

Table 2. Examples of collaborative classroom projects

Program Title: **Fun and Fantasy Through Fairy Tales**
Participants: Third-grade students from two different schools
Synopsis: Children will read and share fairy tales through art and drama. They will videoconference to learn about animal habits and habitats, and use this information to identify fictional aspects of the fairy tales.
Program Title: **"Acting " with Respect**
Participants: Elementary- and middle-school students from different schools
Synopsis: Elementary-School students will brainstorm issues related to respect; this will include respect toward other students, faculty, and staff. Middle-school students will dramatize these concepts during a videoconference. All students will participate in a discussion of issues related to the concept of respect.
Program Title: **Reading Buddies**
Participants: First- and fourth-grade students from two different schools
Synopsis: Elementary-school students will introduce themselves through two videoconferences. Initially, the fourth graders will share information about themselves and their own book choices in order to model how to make literary choices. In the second videoconference, the first graders will share their interests in order to help the fourth graders choose appropriate literature for their buddy reading time.
Program Title: **Totally Turtles**
Participants: First and third graders from two different schools
Synopsis: Both first and third grades share a common science strand regarding animals. First graders will study various types of animals and the classification system. Third graders will learn about animal life cycles and endangered species, focusing on sea turtles and ways to protect them. The third graders will share their learning experiences through the medium of videoconferencing.
Program Title: **Developing Values and Character through Literary Tales**
Participants: Second, third, and fifth graders from three different schools
Synopsis: Fifth graders will perform the puppet show, Goldilocks and The Three Bears / Rizitos de Oro y Los Tres Osos, in Spanish. At the end of the performance, the second and third graders will interview the puppeteers from the first school and ask questions incorporating character education concepts.
Program Title: **Adaptations and Classification of Animals**
Participants: Six and fourth grade students
Synopsis: Sixth grade students will study classification and present a project to fourth grade students from another school. Fourth grade students will create projects on animal adaptation and present them to the sixth grade students. During videoconference presentations, students will use vocabulary learned to identify important concepts.

classroom projects' goals could be successfully achieved. The projects were infused with authentic tasks and were related not only to the curriculum goals but also to students' individual needs and everyday experiences. Also, the projects involve collaboration on multiple aspects in completing the projects: searching for sources of information, collecting data, problem-solving, negotiating roles, and generating and presenting written reports and products. The post-videoconference learning objectives tapped into the highest levels of the Bloom's taxonomy, allowing students to build cognitive skills in analyzing, synthesizing, and evaluating knowledge. Like the pre-videoconferences, the concluding post-videoconference activities consisted of extended discussions, individual writing assignments, and creating and presenting culminating projects. The analysis of the teacher-created integration plans indicates that these collaborative projects are intended to

Table 3. Characteristics that should be considered for integration in collaborative classroom plans (Adapted from Newman, Du, Bose, & Bidjerano, 2006).

	☐ *Pre-Videoconference*	☐ *Collaborative Class-room Videoconference*	☐ *Post-Videoconference*
Objec-tives	☐ Learn new information ☐ Build up vocabulary ☐ Know ☐ Understand ☐ Apply ☐ Compare ☐ Contrast	☐ Reinforce skills ☐ Understand ☐ Generalize ☐ Apply ☐ Compare ☐ Contrast	☐ Apply ☐ Analyze ☐ Evaluate ☐ Synthesize ☐ Interpret ☐ Perform
Materials	☐ Worksheets ☐ Experiment materials ☐ Textbook, books ☐ Graphic organizers ☐ Computer with Internet connection	☐ VC equipment ☐ Worksheets ☐ Qs list ☐ Displays/ Poster boards ☐ Graphic organizers	☐ Worksheets ☐ Displays/poster boards ☐ Graphic organizers
Activities	☐ Lecture ☐ Group work ☐ Reading ☐ Collecting information. ☐ Preparing questions ☐ Independent research ☐ Creating products	☐ Debate ☐ Discussion ☐ Brainstorming ☐ Interacting ☐ Presenting ☐ Dramatization ☐ Create ☐ Experimentation ☐ Exploration ☐ Role-playing ☐ Modeling	☐ Discussion ☐ Essay (fiction) writing ☐ Creating products ☐ Presenting products or performing ☐ Compose

have multiple roles and serve various purposes such as introduction to a topic, review of a topic, application of knowledge, extension on a topic, or evaluation of the learning.

THE UTILIZATION OF COLLABORATIVE CLASSROOM PROJECTS

Newman et al. (2005, 2007) analyzed the process of design and implementation of collaborative classrooms and, based on the examination of data gathered through observations, in-depth interviews, and archival records, the authors were able to differentiate various types of collaborative classroom videoconferences. The two prevail-ing forms of collaboration, documented through multiple observations of actual collaborative videoconferences, were labeled by the authors as *student-to-student* and *tutoring collaborative projects*. The grade placement and the ability level of the students were the dimensions along which the differentiation between these two types of classrooms was possible.

According to Newman et al. (2007), *student-to-student* collaborative classroom videoconferencing arises when two or more groups of students with the same grade placement and a similar ability level, located in different schools, utilize the medium of videoconferencing to achieve a common educational goal in terms of fulfilling particular curriculum requirements and mastering a specific content. This type of collaboration could be short-

Vignette 1.

A multi-stage collaborative project was implemented by the teachers of two 10th grade classrooms from two different school districts in Upstate New York. The collaboration was designed to address multiple New York State learning standards in English Language Arts, and Technology. The teachers from the two school districts created lesson plans that allowed partnership between their students. At the first stage of collaboration, the two classrooms participated in an initial student-to-student videoconference, the purpose of which was to provide students with an opportunity to introduce themselves to one another. During this videoconference, the students engaged in a free dialogue about their schools and daily routines designated to build common knowledge and understanding that, despite physical distances, daily lives of adolescents of the same age and grade levels look alike. The initial contact was then followed by a multi-point videoconference with an author, Ben Mikaelsen, whose book was the students' learning assignment and the review of which was a part of the curriculum requirements for the two school districts. During this videoconference, students communicated seamlessly with the author by asking and answering questions in an attempt to gather information about the author's life experiences and professional development. The students showed a great deal of curiosity about how the author's life experiences relate to the characters in his novel, as well as the tedious process of writing a book. The multi-stage partnership between the two classrooms was successful in achieving its goal to meet learning standards and instructional objectives, to develop technology competence, and to cultivate socio-communicative skills among the students involved.

Vignette 2.

A first-grade classroom and a third-grade classroom from two different schools within a school district participated in a collaborative classroom project. The goal of the collaboration was to increase students' communication skills by interaction with students of different age and grade levels as well as to engage in learning which meets learning standards in Social Studies, English Language Arts, and Technology. The method of collaboration consisted of both point-to-point and student-to-student videoconferencing. Each class completed a point-to-point videoconference from their location with the Indianapolis Zoo. The videoconferences shared common features: direct instruction provided by the content provider, a structured discussion, and a contextual application in the form of an experiment. Following the point-to-point videoconference, the first and third grades participated in a classroom-to-classroom videoconference. Prior to this experience, the participating classrooms read two fiction books about elephants. Additionally, after having read the books, students were to cast their vote for an elephant and nominate it for a participation in a television show. The third-grade students worked in small groups of three or four which had to campaign for the elephant of their choice by making poster presentations and writing persuasive essays. Later, in the course of the actual classroom-to-classroom videoconference with the first-grade elementary students, the third-graders shared their persuasive essays and disclosed the results from the internal elections. Both classes discussed the internal election outcomes.

lived or implemented for an extended period of time. In either setting, the classrooms involved work under the skillful guidance of the teachers at both sites to plan and implement projects, initiate contact, share and present information, investigate a topic, and do collaborative research on common themes. Vignette 1 is a representation of a typical student-to-student collaborative classroom videoconference.

The second type of collaborative classroom, tentatively termed *tutoring collaborative projects,* capitalizes on differences in ability levels and grade placement (Newman et al., 2007). In this type of collaboration, students of higher grades provide tutoring through sharing of information and knowledge with less-advanced students of lower ability level. In the process of implementation of this type of collaborative classrooms, higher-grade students take on the teachers' role by serving as lay instructors to lower-level students in geographically-distanced classrooms (Newman et al., 2007). The role of the more capable tutors are to plan instructional methods, initiate activities, discuss, scaffold, and gradually withdraw their support to allow less-advanced students to take responsibility for their own learning. An example of tutoring collaboration could be found in Vignette 2.

This type of collaborative videoconferencing exemplifies Vygotsky's theoretical approach, which stresses the role of scaffolding provided by more capable peers. The tutoring collaborative classrooms might serve as enrichment opportunities for both the tutor and the tutored student. As stated by Newman et al. (2007), the advanced students have the opportunity to review, enlarge, and enhance their knowledge base as they select and develop methods of sharing knowledge. In the process of teaching lower-grade students, the tutors achieve a much better understanding and mastery of the content themselves; they gain also socio-communicative skills as they become aware of the social aspects of the learning process and the best approaches for delivery of a particular content.

The tutored students, on the other hand, might become more motivated to learn the material and see it as more relevant because it is presented by other students. When the instruction is conducted by slightly-more-capable others, it is likely to occur in the zone of proximal development of the less-knowledgeable students, which maximizes the outcomes of learning (Vygotsky, 1978).

Two other distinctive, yet hypothetical models of collaboration have been also proposed by Newman et al. (2007). As a result of the initially-documented success in the utilization of collaborative classroom projects, the authors encouraged educators to begin to explore the application of collaborative classroom projects in the context of *after-school programs* and for the purposes of instruction and integration of *students with special needs.*

The authors maintained that collaboration for the purpose of instruction of *students with special needs* should be entertained as a new promising area of collaborative classroom utilization, and argued that this type of videoconferencing can successfully serve students with special needs for additional academic support and assistance (Newman et al., 2007). The authors based their argument on the documented growing number of students with diagnosable learning disabilities necessitating not only investment of extra school resources such as funding and availability of personnel, but requiring also instructional methods for creating environments conducive to learning with increased opportunities for knowledge and skill acquisition. In the special-need collaboration model, geographically-distanced inclusion or self-contained classrooms can work together with the assistance of special education and more academically-capable students towards accomplishing a common academic objective. The cognitive, social, and emotional needs of the special-education students could be met and the desired mastery of skills and knowledge could be achieved by drawing on the excitement that the videoconference technology could produce (Newman et al., 2007).

In addition, the possibility of applying collaborative projects in *after-school programs* has captured the attention of educational professionals (Newman et al., 2007). In response to national and state-mandated requirements for higher academic achievement and to the infusion of state and federal funding, many schools nationwide have implemented after-school programs. The functions of these programs, designated for students at various grade levels, are to serve low-income communities by providing a quality after-school care and to tutor children at risk of academic failure. These programs not only empower lower-performing students to become academically successful, but they also offer important developmental opportunities and resources for educational and cultural enrichment. In order for the new after-school organizational structures to be accommodated, new instructional delivery methods have to be designed and implemented. In this sense, collaborative classroom videoconferencing can be regarded as a promising new means of fulfilling some of the various purposes of the after-school programs. As pointed out by Newman et al. (2007), by the use of collaborative videoconferencing working virtually with peers at distant locations,

students in after-school programs can be provided with increased opportunities for exposure to curriculum areas such as mathematics, creative writing, and literature. In the context of after-school programs and activities, communication between the collaborating classrooms could be structured in task-specific ways. This collaboration can take different forms such as role-plays, debates, brainstorming, discussions, and working on common projects. Like the other three forms of collaboration, the after-school collaboration rests on reciprocal teaching; students exert positive influences one to another through the discourse (Newman et al., 2007).

As part of the evaluation efforts to assess the effectiveness of the collaborative classroom projects in meeting instructional goals, observation and information from students, teachers, and staff was gathered (Newman, 2006). Selected groups of students at elementary-, middle-, and high-school levels who were exposed to collaborative classroom videoconferencing were asked to indicate, by means of group-administered surveys, their general perceptions and attitudes towards these two different types of videoconferencing. The results of the conducted analyses on the student survey data are shown in Table 4.

Table 4. General student perceptions of collaborative classroom videoconferences (Note: The percentages are based on responses, "Sort of Agree" and "Agree")

Statement	Elementary-School Setting	Middle-School Setting	High-School Setting
	Percent Agree		
The videoconference was easy to understand.	58	79	95
The videoconference was interesting to me.	79	88	81
I learned a lot from the program.	95	84	76
The topic fit with what I am learning in school right now.	95	95	87
I would like to learn more about what I saw or learned during the program.	90	63	73
I learned more about the topic through the videoconference than I would have in an ordinary class.	95	74	84

Across grade levels, students were generally supportive of the collaborative classroom videoconferencing; they reported that the videoconference was interesting to them and that the material which had been presented was closely related with their learning needs, aligning with their curriculum. Almost all elementary-school students and approximately four-fifths of the middle- and high-school students reported that they learned a lot from the videoconference. Compared to the perceptions expressed by the middle- and high-school students, a relatively smaller number of elementary-school students indicated that the videoconference program was easy to understand. Nevertheless, the majority of the elementary-school students indicated that they would like to learn more about what they learned during the program, and that they learned more about the topic through the videoconference than they would have in an ordinary lesson. The pattern observed in the middle- and high-school students' responses was the reverse; although these students judged the programs as easy to understand, they agreed to a slightly lower rate with the last two statements in the survey. Observation of collaborative classrooms revealed that an important element of the collaborative learning is the discussion that occurs during the completion of a particular task. The success of a specific collaborative classroom project depends largely on the quality of the exchanges that occur in the collaborative environment. Documentation of greater student autonomy led to an increased quality of learning experiences; students tended to perceive more ownership of their work and be more engaged in the proposed classroom activities. Aggregated observational data also indicated that the opportunity for interactions with other students of different ethnic, socio-cultural backgrounds reinforced students' understanding of the notion of cultural diversity (Newman, 2005).

In interviews, teachers indicate that collaborative classroom videoconferencing brings tremendous benefits for enriching their teaching methods and strategies and for increasing their knowledge and competencies in both videoconferencing and curriculum design. Teachers convey their beliefs that this form of videoconferencing was another avenue for enhancing student interests and motivation to learn. Teachers note that the conducted collaborative-classroom projects excite and engage students, as the students work much more diligently to prepare for their classroom-to-classroom videoconference experience. The collaborative classroom projects are perceived as highly successful, for the designed and implemented lessons are able to meet individual grade, subject, and classroom needs.

SUMMARY AND CONCLUSION

Videoconference-supported learning is a rapidly-developing new field of the implementation of technology. Research has demonstrated that, as a distinct form of application of videoconferencing in the classroom, collaborative classrooms are learning tools which possess huge potential. Collaborative classroom videoconferencing can be used to extend the interactive (conversational/collaborative) learning beyond the classroom. The informal setting, which usually dominates collaborating classroom learning environments, facilitates discussion, interaction, and active exchange of knowledge and ideas which nurture critical-thinking skills; it also eventuates changes in student cognition. Collaborative classroom projects provide a highly-interactive, student-centered experience and create a learning environment tailored to the individual needs of the students; they encourage the exploration of different viewpoints and perspectives, and their utilization results in social empowerment. Allowing participants to converse freely, interact, and observe maximizes engagement and cognitive involvement.

Learning in the collaborative classroom setting is complex, dynamic, and multidimensional; the utilization in this form of videoconferencing rests on the understanding of how the learning process operates on both individual and group settings. In summarizing evaluation findings, Newman et al. (2005, 2007) conceptualized collaborative classroom videoconferencing as a form of interdependence. Since there is more than one classroom involved in such projects, identifying the unique needs, characteristics, and roles of the participants at each site becomes of paramount importance in the process. The outcomes of the collaboration rest not only on the evolving mutual understanding of the characteristics and the role of each community involved in the process, but also depends on mundane factors such as availability of technology resources and access to technical support.

Evidence in Newman's (2005) study of collaborative classrooms unambiguously showed that providing teachers with adequate training in the use of videoconference technology, and guiding them in the process of developing full-blown integration plans which capitalize on and integrate sound learning principles and theories, is necessary for the successful implementation of collaborative classroom projects. The experience gained throughout the implementation of the collaborating classrooms has also demonstrated that an effective and truly integrated project needs careful exploration and subsequent evaluation of the achieved outcomes. The accumulated knowledge suggests that several criteria have to be employed in judging the effectiveness of these types of videoconferences. Opportunities provided for the exchange of content-rich information, learning experiences integrated with classroom instruction, student-centered interactivity and effective use of the medium based on logistical parameters and digital content, are all essential components to be considered.

There is a paucity of literature that focuses on the multifaceted aspects of, and processes within, the collaborative classroom videoconferencing. Future research should address not only how this type of videoconferencing effects instruction, teachers' pedagogies, but also student characteristics such as motivation, ability, skills, and attitudes. Empirical studies might focus on in-depth investigations of the short- and long-term effects of this type of videoconferencing in terms of learning and instruction, or on how collaborative classrooms compare to traditional instruction or conventional point-to-point videoconferencing with a content provider. Changes in prior attitudes to videoconferencing, student and teacher expectations, learning behaviors such as persistence, effort, and time-on-task, are promising areas of research, which require further investigation.

REFERENCES

Awbrey, S. M. (1996). Successfully integrating new technologies into the higher education curriculum. *Educational Technology Review, 5*.

Beilin, R., & Rabow, J. (1981). Status value, group learning, and minority achievement in college. *Small Group Behavior, 12*, 495-508.

Bruner, J. (1985). Vygotsky: An historical and conceptual perspective. In Wertsch, J. (Ed.) *Culture, communication, and cognition: Vygotskyan perspectives* (pp. 21-34). London: Cambridge University Press.

Davis, B. G. (1993). *Tools for teaching*. San Francisco: Jossey-Bass.

Falco, J., Barbanell, P., Newman, D., & DeWald, S. (2005). In L. T. Wee Him & R. Subramaniam (Eds.), *E-learning and virtual science centers*. Hershey, PA: Idea Group, Inc.

Flavell, J. H. (1992). Cognitive development: Past, present, and future. *Developmental Psychology, 23*, 998-1005.

Gabbert, B., Johnson, D. W., & Johnson, R. (1986). Cooperative learning, group-to-individual transfer, process gain, and the acquisition of cognitive reasoning strategies. *Journal of Psychology, 120*, 265-278.

Johnson, D. W., & Johnson, R. T. (1996). Cooperation and the use of technology. In D. H. Jonassen (Ed.), *Handbook of research for educational communications and technology* (pp. 1017-1044). New York: Simon and Schuster Macmillan.

Jonassen, D. H. (2002). Engaging and supporting problem-solving in online learning. *The Quarterly Review of Distance Education, 3,* 1-13.

McAlpine, L. (2000). Collaborative learning online. *Distance Education, 21,* 66-80.

Newman, D. L. (2005, March). *Beyond the barriers: Benefits of K-12 teacher participation in collaborative classroom videoconferencing training.* Paper presented at the annual meeting of the SITE, Phoenix, AR.

Newman, D. L. (2006). *The virtual information education Web project: Summative evaluation of the Schenectady city school district technology innovation challenge grant, Schenectady component, Five year report.* SUNY Albany, NY: Evaluation Consortium.

Newman, D. L., Barbanell, P. & Falco, J. (2005). Documenting value-added learning through videoconferencing: K-12 classrooms' interactions with museums. In G. Richards (Ed.), *Proceedings of World Conference on E-Learning in Corporate, Government, Healthcare, and Higher Education 2005* (pp. 389-401). Chesapeake, VA: AACE.

Newman, D. L., Barbanell, P., & Falco, J. (2007). Videoconferencing communities: Documenting online user interactions. In N. Lambropoulos & P. Zaphiris (Eds.), *User-centered design of online learning communities* (pp. 122-140). Hershey, PA: Idea Group, Inc.

Newman, D. L., Du, Y., Bose, M., & Bidjerano, T. (2006). *A content analysis of videoconference integration plans.* Paper presented at the annual meeting of SITE , Orlando, FL.

Norman, G., & Schmidt, F. (1992). The psychological basis of problem-based learning: A review of the evidence. *Academic Medicine, 67,* 557-565.

Springer, L., Stanne, M. E., & Donovan, S. S. (1999). Effects of small-group learning on undergraduates in science, mathematics, engineering, and technology: A meta-analysis. *Review of Educational Research, 69,* 21-51.

Totten, S., Sills, T., Digby, A., & Russ, P. (1991). *Cooperative learning: A guide to research.* New York: Garland.

Vygotsky, L. (1978). *Mind in society: The development of higher psychological processes.* Cambridge, MA: Harvard University Press.

Wood, D. (1988). *How children think and learn.* New York: Basil Blackwell, Inc.

Woolfolk, A. (2004). *Educational psychology (9th ed.).* Boston, MA: Pearson Education, Inc.

Wulff, D. H., Nyquist, J. D., & Abbott, R. D. (1987). Students' perceptions of large classes. In M. G. Weimer (Ed.), *Teaching large classes well* (pp. 17-30). *New Directions for Teaching and Learning, 32,* (Winter). San Francisco: Jossey-Bass.

ENDNOTES

[1] Sections of this chapter were extensions in part of a presentation and paper (Newman, D. L., Du, Y., Bose, M., & Bidjerano, T., 2006) presented at the annual meeting of SITE , Orlando, FL.

[2] Based on experience and study of the work of Project VIEW, a U.S. Department of Education-funded Technology Grant Award Number R303A000002.

APPENDIX A: AN EXAMPLE OF COLLABORATING CLASSROOM DEVELOPMENT PLANS
Collaborating Classrooms Program Development Plan

Collaborating Teams: Four elementary-school teachers, Grades 1, 2, and 3

Learning Context: Purpose, Objective, or Focus, including:

A description of where this program fits in the school or course curriculum:
√ Communicate through writing, including friendly letter and email
√ Complete citizenship-based research and presentation
√ Access, generate, process, and transfer information using appropriate technologies, such as √ email, videoconferencing, and the use of a content provider

What students potentially need to know and/or be able to do to succeed with this learning experience:
√ Use resources to research a topic related to citizenship
√ Present the findings of that research
√ Understand and utilize the medium of videoconferencing
√ Learn how to write and send a friendly letter
√ Learn how to write and send an email
√ Listen for information and understanding

How will classes collaborate:
√ Videoconference to brainstorm a list of what they think citizenship entails
√ View PowerPoint on Symbols of Citizenship
√ Participate in a videoconference with a content provider
√ Email/snail mail second-grade pen pal on a monthly basis
√ Research a common topic with buddy, with the research being done in the home building. Their research will be presented at an evening gathering. Learn and sing a patriotic song to each other through videoconferencing
√ Make something for the other class (flags, cookies, etc.)

What is added to educational experience by collaboration:
√ Be exposed to the diversity of students between school districts
√ Benefit from the expertise of other professionals
√ Learn how to use email, snail mail, and the etiquette and procedures of videoconference
√ Broaden their view of the world outside their own communities

NYS Learning Standards

English Language Arts

Standard 1: Students will read, write, listen, and speak for information and understanding.
Standard 2: Students will read, write, listen, and speak for literary response and expression.

Standard 3: Students will read, write, listen, and speak for critical analysis and evaluation.
Standard 4: Students will read, write, listen, and speak for social interaction.

Mathematics, Science and Technology

Standard 2: Students will access, generate, process, and transfer information using appropriate technologies.

Social Studies

Standard 3: Students will use a variety of intellectual skills to demonstrate their understanding of the geography of the interdependent worlds in which we live, local, national and global, including the spatial distribution of people, places, and environments over the Earth's surface.
Standard 6: Students will use a variety of intellectual skills to demonstrate their understanding of the basic civic values of American constitutional democracy; the roles, rights, and responsibilities of citizenship; and the avenues of participation in American civic life.

Time Required: For each aspect of the learning experience, state the amount of time for:

Training: Collaborating classrooms training - 3 days / videoconferencing workshop - 3 days
Planning: 20 – 30 hours
Pre-activities and lessons: Approximately 20 - 25 hours
Program implementation: Approximately 5 hours
Post-activities and lessons: Approximately 5 hours
Assessment: 1 – 3 hours

Collaborating Classroom Program Development—Program plan:

Program title: Partners in Patriotism
Synopsis: Classes will collaborate in learning the rights, rules, and responsibilities of being an American citizen. Students view a PowerPoint on Symbols of Citizenship as well as complete a collaborative research project. In addition, students will participate in a videoconference with Paul Stillman as Ben Franklin.
Time: This particular plan is part of a year-long collaborative project.
Materials: Symbols of Citizenship PowerPoint, videoconference equipment as provided by the schools, digital video camera

Procedure

- **August**—Teachers arrange for a content provider
- **Beginning mid-September**—Teachers reserve times with librarian for research curriculum
- **Mid-September**—Teachers meet to pair up kids for pen pals and compare schedules; schedule days to reserve teleconferencing equipment; make video of the school and classroom, which will include school building from front, interesting places in the building, and classroom.

- **End-September**—The classes involved will videoconference to show each other's video; the children will introduce themselves by saying one thing about themselves and the name of their pen pals.
- **October**—Pen pals write to each other through snail mail.
- **November**—There is a videoconference at which the participating classrooms show the projects that they created for Thanksgiving; students exchange mail after the videoconference.
- **December**—There is a videoconference at which the participating children show their holiday projects; students exchange letters through snail mail.
- **January**—Participating classrooms conduct library search in preparation for the Citizenship Unit; children write to each other through email to determine what topic related to citizenship they want to research together.
- **February**—Citizenship unit:
      Videoconference—PowerPoint on Symbols of Citizenship
      Videoconference—Paul Stillman on citizenship
- **March**—Students write about St. Patrick's Day event through snail mail.
- **April**—Students write about maple sugaring through email.
- **May**—Students write about their science tree through email.
- **June**—Students write invitation to other students to come to their school for a final meeting picnic. The students on the other side send a class response. A videoconference is conducted featuring patriotic songs for Flag Day; students present pen pals with a class-made gift.

Supporting Curriculum

Pre-lessons and activities to be conducted prior to the videoconference program:
Children in both schools will:
√   Participate in research classes with the librarian
√   Learn how to write and send a friendly letter
√   Learn how to write and send an email
√   Learn the etiquette of videoconferencing
√   Make a video introducing themselves and their school to their buddies
√   Correspond regularly by letter or email to buddy

Post- lessons and activities to be conducted after to the videoconference program:
Students will:
√   Continue pen pal correspondence
√   Videoconference with patriotic songs
√   Attend a picnic at Stevens Elementary School and display good citizenship

Assessment Plan:
√   Short answer reflection
√   Essay evaluation
√   A rubric will be used to assess each student's performance individually; part of this assessment will include how well each student contributed to the group's project and overall presentation

Section IV
Building and Supporting
a System of Videoconferencing

Chapter X
Leading the Art of the Conference:
Revolutionizing Schooling through Interactive Videoconferencing

John Falco
The College of St. Rose, USA

ABSTRACT

The purpose of this chapter is to examine the role of leadership in interactive videoconferencing. Interactive videoconferencing provides the opportunity for schools to bring content-area experts from anywhere in the world into the classroom to engage students in real-time learning. The effective integration of interactive videoconferencing into classroom practice requires leadership. This leadership is rooted in a belief in providing world-class, student-centered learning through interactive videoconferencing. It is a vision that is results-driven in terms of measuring student learning, and realized through instructional leadership that is committed to collaboration, professional development, appropriate technical support and infrastructure, and the use of research to support practice.

INTRODUCTION

Under-challenged students and over-challenged staff can render both American and global school organizations aspirants for minimal standards. The bar set for most standardized testing scenarios is a narrow level of competency, whether it is in mathematics, science, history, or language literacy (Rothstein, Jacobsen, & Wilder, 2006). It is, therefore, no surprise that if school organizations strive for mediocrity, they fall short of the mark for many or at least some of their students.

Advancing curriculum, enriching content, and accelerating learning are viable outcomes through the appropriate use of technology, interactive videoconferencing in particular, in the classroom.

Broadening what is learned with measurements, rather than narrowing what is learned to meet immediate objectives, is the more appropriate vision for schooling. Engaging students in content is a key element in approaching the realization of such a vision. Engaging the learner, in light of technology advancements, should not be confined to the four walls of the classroom.

Real-life, content-area experts in all fields of endeavor practice their craft daily and are seldom sought by schools. In the near and certainly distant past, it would not have been feasible, practical, or possible to bring experts from distant locations into classrooms with any regularity. Both the technology and models for instructional delivery, however, now exist to bring content-area experts into the classroom, in order to engage students in real-time learning.

Organizations do not advance based on what exists but rather on its application. It is a fact that students can engage in real-time learning, through interactive videoconferencing, because the technology and models for instruction now exist; yet this fact remains a concept until it is practically applied. Introducing and sustaining any new application within an organization is a function of leadership.

Advancing the goals of any organization requires leadership and often requires change. Effective change within an organization requires leadership that is capable of building consensus and/or managing conflict (Heifitz, 1994). Introducing, supporting, and sustaining a learner-centered culture (Senge, 1990) in schools must include a responsibility to explore non-traditional methods of content delivery. The concept of imbedding learner-centered, content-delivered technology can be bottom-up or top-down (Senge, 1990), but ultimately requires the formal leadership of the organization in order to be effective.

Leading the art of interactive videoconferencing emanates from a passionate belief in a vision for world-class, student-centered learning. It is a vision that is results-driven in terms of measuring student learning and realized through collaboration, professional development, technical support and infrastructure, and a commitment to research to support practice. It is a vision that has evidenced success in theory, practice, and outcomes.

Leading the art of interactive videoconferencing is a function of instructional leadership, (i.e., the principal). Instructional leadership is central to the successful integration of technology into a school's curriculum (Granger, Morbey, Lotherington, Owston, & Wideman, 2002; Staples, Pugach, & Himes, 2005; Wetzel, Zambo, Buss, & Padgett, 2001). To ensure that a tool such as interactive videoconferencing is not merely an "add-on", the principal must take on the role of leading faculty and staff in a collaboration that focuses on integrating technology-delivered curriculum. It is also the role of the principal to provide professional development opportunities and support so that teachers can develop their capacity for leadership and collaboration as well. Staples et al. (2005) identified teacher leadership as a vital component of successful technology integration into a school. Teachers acquire an understanding of the use of technology that surpasses that of principals because they apply it in their classroom practice. Collaborative leadership can support and sustain the use of technology in education long after its introduction.

The interactive videoconference is a powerful learning and teaching tool. It is a lesson that is the culmination of a series of planning activities. The interactive videoconference is a lesson, facilitated by a teacher, which engages learners with a content-area expert from a distant location via a technological connection between the two organizations. It is visible and audible to all parties via a monitor or screen or projection device. The content-area educator may provide a demonstration or present artifacts or documents as a part of the lesson. Through preplanning, learners physically may have items in their home environment which are germane to the lesson. Museums are natural partners for schools since, as institutions, they are rich in content and, in general, have informal educators within the organization. Museum content and delivery methodology have an authentic ability to engage students (Gardner, 1983). The content provider may engage students through the presentation of information (i.e., lecture, and through questioning) and by engaging learners through individual or group activities. Learners have the opportunity to engage the informal educator, that is, content provider, through questions and discussion. The lessons, as are most "schoolhouse" lessons, are interactive and in real-time.

Curriculum content delivered with the assistance of technology has been a part of schooling, to varying degrees, from the use of the chalkboard to the use of the smartboard. Most uses of technology are, however, passive in nature. The interactive videoconference is unique among other uses of technology for education. Most uses of educational technology represent a scale that ranges from passive to interactive computer software to asynchronous courseware. Within a continuum of technological learning and teaching strategies, all the aforementioned have a place in the educator's toolbox, but none have the degree of authenticity of instructional delivery and the power of synchronistic conversation as the interactive videoconference.

Video technology (i.e., television) has been used in the classroom to supplement and/or enrich curriculum. Regardless of the quality or appropriateness of the program, it represents a passive activity for the learner (Cronk, 1996). Teachers have used television shows and films to enhance curriculum for many years. Whether the film was shown on a 16-millimeter projector forty years ago or a DVD player in the present, it was archival in nature. The purpose of the viewing may have been to reinforce or to illuminate curriculum material, but the interactivity remained between the learner and the teacher in the classroom.

Electronic field trips, through technology, take learners on a journey through a museum or zoo-

logical park. The field trip may be accomplished through the Web, DVD, or even video-on-demand (Tuthill & Klemm, 2002). They may be interactive to the degree that there are more choices for the order in which areas are viewed or sections in which artifacts may be visually examined in detail. Field trips may be Web-cast at times. The size of the broadcast audience, however, precludes more than one or two class locations from authentic engagement with the informal educators. Although electronic field trips provide some interactivity, they are, by and large, a passive activity for learners.

The use of software programs (i.e., computer-assisted instruction) provides a degree of a one-to-one experience for the learner. Software programs in numerous subject areas provide, in most instances, individual interaction with the learner. The interaction may be in the form of activities and/or monitoring and leveling the learners' skills and progress. In some instances, software is designed for "teams" of learners. This use of technology is interactive for individual and, at times, for small-group instruction (Lou, 2004).

The use of technology for online course delivery and online discussion groups has increased at both the secondary and higher education levels. Both mediums provide, for the most part, asynchronous interaction.

Distance learning models generally involve a teacher providing instruction to students at a home base simultaneously with students at a distant location. It is real-time learning and teaching that generally provides sharing of teacher expertise that is not available in the distant location, or is more cost-effective, or both. This use of technology is both synchronistic and interactive as it uses video to replicate the traditional classroom teaching model (Rice, 2006).

Video materials, Web-based materials, virtual field trips, software programs, online course delivery and discussion groups, and distance learning are all effective instructional uses of technology depending on the instructor's purpose. The interactive videoconference lesson remains the most pro-active for learners in terms of engaging content-area experts in real-time.

The interactive videoconference provides an opportunity for the learner to experience primary sources, enriching materials, and content-area experts far beyond the classroom walls. Content-rich museums have traditionally been natural partners for schools through both the traditional and virtual field trip. Museums are also natural partners for schools for content delivered through interactive videoconferencing. Museums are rich in content in areas too numerous to list. Museums generally provide content to schools through educational programs and have a full- or part-time museum educator in service. In the past, distance has been the obstacle to museums in providing content through their rich and varied collections to schools. Museums have, prior to today's technology, been limited to those school organizations that are either local or those who choose a, perhaps, costly field trip. Museums, no matter how large a city they are housed in, have not been accessible to the majority of schools, both nationally and globally, as they are today through technology (Tuthill & Klemm, 2002). However, the interactive videoconference collaborative planning process can add to the dynamics of both the content and the delivery. In the past, the school field trip, particularly for larger museums, generally involved a tour. A school visit to the larger museum, including travel time and lunch, generally made for a "short" content day. The virtual field trip can now accomplish this in less time.

A second trip to a larger museum or a trip to a smaller museum might provide time to focus on a particular exhibit, artifact, or theme. This event takes the form of a lesson. The lesson delivered to one class in real-time is the interactive videoconference. The collaboration between the formal and informal educator now becomes a component critical to the success of the conference. The interactive videoconference is specific

and individual in nature, and requires planning as such. It is a one- to one-and-one-half-hour experience for one class, and must be planned accordingly.

COLLABORATION

The currency of leadership in introducing, developing, and sustaining the use of interactive videoconferencing for enriched curriculum delivery is collaboration. Collaborative leadership is fundamental in moving toward a technology-assisted, learner-centered culture. It is the process of sharing and shaping the vision. To a certain extent, it is "getting people on board". Leading the art of the conference must be both top-down and bottom-up to be successful. The plan for the content of the interactive videoconference comes from the classroom-based teacher and the distance-based content provider. The formal organizational leadership provides the infrastructure and technical support. The inquisitive intellect of the learner provides individual, constructivist-in-nature meaning to the conference (Sprague & Dede, 1999). The combined will of all parties is the underpinning of an effective interactive videoconferencing program.

The creation of an interactive videoconferencing lesson requires input from both the teacher and the content provider. This collaboration allows for the development of a lesson that is in alignment with the teacher's curriculum and is also compatible with the resources that the content provider can offer (Barbanell, Falco, & Newman, 2003). Such collaboration benefits all parties. The classroom teacher currently practices in an environment where instruction is driven by testing. Content must be in alignment with standards for schools to achieve competencies on standardized assessments. It is not an environment in which the concept of enrichment, particularly in urban settings, is part of the teacher's content delivery strategy. In an age when school visits were the only option, the museum lesson, although good, was generally prepackaged. Although the lesson may have gone into depth in a particular area, its general purpose was enrichment. The teacher generally viewed the school trip as enrichment as well. The physical school visit to the museum was and is dependent on transportation, schedules, and cost. It was and remains nearly impossible to schedule this visit in alignment with the teacher's curriculum calendar. The content presented was, therefore, generally out of "alignment". In addition, the content of the prepackaged lesson might not be on-point with specific learning objectives and therefore was collateral in nature, hence, the enrichment experience. In the absence of existing technology, most teachers, especially those who face a rigorous testing structure, would not "give up a day of instruction" for a museum visit. The virtual field trip can now accomplish such a visit. The interactive videoconference, however, provides the teacher with the opportunity to collaboratively plan the lesson content delivery (Tuthill & Klemm, 2002). The experience is on-point for the teacher, fits synchronistically with the curriculum, and is experienced in the school building as part of the instructional day.

The planning of videoconference lessons need not be limited to the collaboration of one teacher and one content provider. Barbanell, Falco, and Newman (2003) found that teams of three or four teachers working together were effective. Team members can provide one another with assistance during the development of a lesson. Teachers who use interactive videoconferencing generally understand that the lesson, through collaborative planning, will be in alignment with local and national standards. Teachers from fields closely associated with a content provider's focus ensure that the videoconferencing lesson will meet curriculum standards (Newman, 2005). It is a lesson which is collaboratively planned as an integral part of the curriculum calendar and not viewed as an "add-on" to be reconciled. It minimizes or eliminates the "risk" of not staying on course with the

external standards-driven systems environment in which schools currently function. It provides an alternative enriching, learning and teaching tool that students, particularly in poor schools, might not experience. Interactive videoconferences can also cross disciplines. A team of teachers and the content provider may collaboratively plan a multipurpose conference. Newman (2005) found that interactive videoconferencing led teachers to "integrate multiple content areas" into their lessons (p.35). A multidisciplinary collaboration can develop videoconferencing lessons that have greater relevance and can be used more frequently than a lesson focused on a single discipline (Barbanell, Falco, & Newman, 2003).

Newman (2005) also found that the collaborative process allowed content providers to create programming for schools that was more in alignment with the teacher's lesson plans and local and national curriculum standards; the collaborative process made the content providers aware of these needs. Through the collaborative process, content providers who use interactive videoconferencing generally understand that their content materials, information, and expertise will motivate and engage learners. The engagement of learners is fundamental to better student achievement (Newmann, 1992). Content providers in this process can be flexible and individualize the lesson through planning with the teacher or team. Content providers understand that through the use of videoconferencing their collections are accessible to the universe of schools.

The interactive videoconferencing process also increases the likelihood that teachers will offer their students more opportunities for collaborative learning (Newman, 2005). Wetzel et al. (2001) observed that teachers who integrated technology into the curriculum moved away from a lecture format in their classes and toward greater opportunities for student collaboration.

Collaboration is an essential element in realizing a vision for world-class, student-centered learning through the use of interactive videoconferencing. Collaboration among teachers and with content providers requires mutual understanding of desired outcomes and a commitment of time, energy, and creativity.

PROFESSIONAL DEVELOPMENT

Professional development for the use of interactive videoconferencing should not be focused on learning "how to" use the technology. It is the educator's responsibility to focus on the "what." It is an opportunity for teachers, school leaders, and content providers to learn how this medium can be integrated into the schoolhouse day for the purpose of improving student learning. Professional development for the use of interactive videoconferencing is the formal learning process by which opportunities for collaboration are codified. Collaboration for both teachers and school leaders is relatively new. Educators have traditionally practiced in isolation (Abdal-Haqq, 1989). Leading the art of the conference requires a commitment to professional development and the collaborative process.

Professional development can range from understanding the availability of content to facilitated interactive videoconference planning. Initial professional development may include exposure to a wide variety of museums and the content specifics offered therein. It involves an initial understanding of content offered and probing as to how that content may be integrated into a specific curriculum schedule. Initial professional development should also include a basic understanding of the equipment and connectivity utilized to conduct the conference.

Extended professional development involves the facilitated planning for the conference. The planning process may be between the teacher and the content provider that customizes the information, materials, and delivery. It may also involve very practical aspects of a co-teaching or semi-co-teaching model of instructional delivery.

Who does what, when, is important in presenting a "seamless" lesson to the learners.

As previously noted, the concept of collaboration among practitioners is relatively new to the field of education. Traditionally, teachers have practiced in isolation from one another regardless of grade or school-wide goals. The process of working together, sharing curriculum expertise, and exposing content-area strengths and weaknesses is part of the professional development experience (Abdal-Haqq, 1989). Principals, in their roles as instructional leaders, can encourage technologically-motivated teachers to take on leadership roles and serve as mentors to other teachers as schools integrate technology-delivered curriculum (Glazer, Hannafin, & Song, 2005). Functioning as a team working toward mutually-agreeable learner outcomes is also part of the process. The codeterminant in the process is planning with the content provider, either initial or subsequent to formal teacher-to-teacher team planning.

As with all fields of endeavor, the frequency of planning and use of the interactive videoconference develops practitioner expertise. The advanced practitioner(s) may collaboratively plan, develop, and operationalize interactive videoconferencing with greater frequency and efficiency.

TECHNICAL INFRASTRUCTURE AND SUPPORT

Leading the art of the conference should include a fundamental belief in the two-way transmittal of content that ultimately benefits the learner and, therefore, is far more a function of instructional leadership, not necessarily technology leadership. The technology is the medium, not the content.

The use of technology has greatly increased positive results in all fields of endeavor, yet in comparison to medicine, engineering, science, and industry, education has remained somewhat technology-proof, or resilient at best (Satterlee,

2002). By and large, technology progress in the field of education has evolved from cave etchings on slate to the chalkboard. Chalkboard technology, be it in the form of whiteboard, overhead projector, smartboard, or PowerPoint are variations on a technology theme, and not an advancement. Technology for most school organizations is used for administrative purposes (i.e., grades, attendance, etc.) and email communications. Although these uses are time-saving, they are not applications that improve learning and teaching. School organizations have taken only basic steps in the use of technology in improving learning as compared to the vast promise that such use may hold.

The instructional leadership that school administrators can provide in this area is important. In a rapidly-moving, competitive global economy, educators have a moral imperative to expand the tools necessary to provide students with world-class learning opportunities (CEO Forum, 2001; Fullan, 2003; Sergiovanni, 2001). The investment in the equipment, tools, and connectivity for a school organization is directly related to how technology-enabled content is valued. Briefly, where there is a will to provide world-class, student-centered learning through technology, there is a way to connectivity. However, the lack of such will may be a lack of information. Several factors may help school organizations make informed decisions regarding technology-enabled learning and teaching, including:

- Continued and expanded research, particularly effects on learner outcomes
- Greater emphasis on technology-enabled learning and teaching, especially in preservice teacher development
- Continued decrease in the cost of equipment and connectivity over time
- Increased support for teacher creativity and "risk-taking" in their practice

Technical support is also critical to the success of interactive videoconferencing. The teacher's role in this process is teaching. Aside from a rudimentary understanding of the basics of the technology, the teacher's focus is on content. If the assumption is that there can be a quality education for every student, then the educator must be a teaching practitioner. In the field of medicine, for example, there is an expectation that the operating room is prepared, functioning, and ready for the use of the medical practitioner. There is not an expectation in the medical field that the practitioner fully understands and is able to operate and "trouble-shoot" the technology and equipment that is utilized. The educational practitioner must be able to concentrate on teaching, that for which they have been trained, and that which they continuously strive to improve in similar fashion.

LEARNER OUTCOMES

Data regarding learner outcomes is sparse in relationship to participation in content lessons delivered through interactive videoconferencing. However, initial studies indicate improved learning for students engaged in content delivered through interactive videoconferencing when compared to students engaged in content through traditional classroom delivery.

Schools have effectively utilized interactive videoconferencing to develop, with content-area experts, instructional resources that are in alignment with curriculum standards and are designed to improve student academic achievement (Barbanell, Falco, & Newman, 2003). In addition, interactive videoconferencing engages students and increases their motivation (Newman, 2005), which is linked to student achievement (Newmann, 1992). Newman (2005) found that 92% of students participating in videoconferences thought the videoconference "was interesting to me" (p.72). In addition, 88% of students said they "learned a lot," and 81% understood the connection between material presented during the videoconference and current topics of study in their class. Also, most students (79%) expressed interest in knowing more about the subject of the videoconference. Evaluator observations and teacher perceptions agreed with this student feedback. Other researchers have noted the link between videoconferencing and increased student interest in learning (Gage, Nickson, & Beardon, 2002), as well as an increase in student achievement (Green, 1999).

While the early research on interactive videoconferencing and improved learner outcomes seems positive, it is not yet sufficient enough to warrant wholesale, universal adoption by today's educational standards. Further studies should yield greater tangible results directly related to what has been taught and learned. There are variables in the teaching and learning process that we are only beginning to understand. There are elements with the delivery of curriculum that ignite the learner's thought process. It is not necessarily a wholesale element. This is to say that there is no one element that, like a vaccine, promotes the thought process for all learners. Therefore, we know that the cognitive process is ignited for learners in different ways and at different times. The greater that the level of individual student engagement is, the greater will be the opportunity for learning. For example, most students engaged in interactive videoconferencing wanted to know more about the subject of the videoconference (Newman, 2005).

Engaging students through varied, content-rich, and enriching learning experiences may increase immediate measurable student outcomes as well as future motivation for increased learning. Future motivation for increased learning is a variable in the continuum of learning and teaching that is not fully measured. The museum experience may, for example, have the potential to "stimulate understanding" and to help students "assume responsibility for their own future learn-

ing" (Gardner, 1983, p. 194). It is not necessarily tangible or direct. In simple terms, it appears that the student who learns what is taught tests better than the student who has not learned what is taught. A student who learns what is taught through an alternative strategy, in this case interactive videoconferencing, tests better than a student taught through a traditional strategy which is also tangible and direct. In these instances, there appears to be a relationship between what is taught and what is learned.

Engendering motivation to increase learning may not always be immediately measurable. It is a variable that can remain dormant. As a latent variable, it (i.e., cognitive ignition) is difficult to measure because it may not necessarily be traced back to root events or causes. It is a variable that is and may remain intangible for some time to come. It is difficult to speak to an intangible, seemingly non-quantifiable variable in an age of scientific educational practices, yet subjectively, it is a variable that exists.

Teachers have subjectively and anecdotally experienced the effect of engendering motivation for increased learning in students well after they leave the classroom. Teachers throughout time have experienced, although not necessarily with any frequency, appreciation from returning adult students. It is generally in the form of something that the teacher did, said, or provided that remained with the student and, at some point in time, positively changed that student's attitude toward schooling. It was an impact that motivated a student well beyond the teacher's reach. It is something that the teacher happily recognizes but does not necessarily understand (Pace & Tesi, 2004).

Aspiring teachers are generally interviewed by school organizations as part of the application process. A common question asked is whether or not a specific teacher or teachers made a significant difference in the aspirant's life, and, if so, how (Lesley University, 2005). Responses vary, but generally point to something that the teacher did, said, or provided. Responses seldom point to a specific test score or measurement. It is rather something that is intangible, yet far-reaching.

The challenge is to begin to measure what have been, heretofore, intuitive educational practices in providing enriching and various methods of curriculum content to engage and motivate the individual learner. As an educational tool, interactive videoconferencing has the potential to increase learning, not only in the present, but potentially in ensuring educational experiences for the student.

The art of leading the interactive videoconferencing requires a commitment to further understanding the nature of learning. It requires a commitment to research to support practice. And it requires the courage to take risks.

CONCLUSION AND TRENDS

Introducing, sustaining, and assessing interactive videoconferencing as a means of providing students with content-rich, real-time learning is a function of leadership. Leading the art of the interactive videoconference requires collaboration, professional development, technology infrastructure and support, and a commitment to research to support practice for a vision of world-class, student-centered learning that improves achievement. Leading the art of the conference is the window through which the future of schooling can be viewed. Educational leadership pioneers will come forward now or in the not-so-distant future to pave the way.

The technology that exists today can provide real-time learning for students from distant locations to any setting. The use of this technology for the delivery of content will change school organizations as they exist today. Schools, or better said, learners, will not be bound by walls or geographic location to access curriculum content, information, or expert delivery. The use of technology to provide world-class learning for individual

and groups of students, in particular the real-time interactive videoconference, is the most significant educational breakthrough since the printing press. The printing press, in time, has provided access to information for the masses unheard of prior to its invention. In time, today's technology will provide information, expertise, values, and opinion to a universe of learners unheard of prior to its arrival. School organizations have a moral imperative in leading the revolutionizing of education, both nationally and globally.

The courage to meet this imperative is greatly challenged by the narrow environment in which learning and teaching currently exists. Effective teaching requires educators to take informed and creative risks in order to advance learning for every student. Revolutionizing schooling means exploring and discovering what schools can be, not fixing the status quo. Reforms, such as charter schools and vouchers, are a triage approach that attempts to reaffirm that traditional school pedagogy is sufficient for all learners. Reform efforts focusing on reinventing that which met the societal needs of an age past contradicts the challenges of reconciling the delivery of education in post-industrial America.

Learner access to museums, as a natural starting point, is only a prelude to access to expertise in corporations, research facilities, government agencies, and higher education globally. The interactive videoconference will not only remain synchronistic, but will also simulate environment at all points of connection to create a real-time, real-place presence for the learner. In the not-so-distant future, schools without walls will be the rule rather than the exception. Principals will continue to lead in visioning and supporting a learner-centered culture. Teachers will continue to be the primary source of content transmittal, facilitating and coordinating learning. Content-area expertise provided by informal educators will engage learners through the use of primary sources. Real-time problem-solving and project-based education will engage learners and collaborative teams of learners. High school will not be boring. Spending will focus on virtual learning environments that require periodic in-person meetings and not rely solely on brick and mortar. The educational focus will be on the individual learner, who in the tradition of the work of Piaget, Dewey, and Wordsworth will evidence that it takes a "whole child to raise a village."

REFERENCES

Abdal-Haqq, I. (1989). The influence of reform on inservice teacher education. *Eric Digest*. Retrieved November 30, 2006, from http://www.thememoryhole.org/edu/eric/ed322147.html

Barbanell, P., Falco, J., & Newman, D.L. (2003). *New vision, new realities: Methodology and mission in developing interactive videoconferencing programming.* Paper presented at the annual meeting of the Museum and the Web, 2003. Retrieved November 14, 2006, from http://www.archimuse.com/ mw2003/papers/barbanell.barbanell.html

CEO Forum on Education and Technology (2001). *Educational technology must be included in comprehensive education legislation.* Retrieved November 14, 2006, from http://www.ceoforum.org

Cronk, R. (1996). *The television mystique: Electronic synchrony and the television totem.* Retrieved November 30, 2006, from http://www.westland.net/venice/art/cronk/tv.htm

Fullan, M. (2003). *The moral imperative of school leadership.* Thousand Oaks, CA: Corwin Press.

Gage, J., Nickson, M., & Beardon, T. (2002). *Can videoconferencing contribute to teaching and learning? The experience of the motivate project.* Paper presented at the Annual Conference of the British Educational Research Association. Retrieved November 14, 2006, from http://www.leeds.ac.uk/educol/ documents/00002264.htm

Gardner, H. (1983). *Frames of mind: The theory of multiple intelligences.* New York: Basic Books.

Glazer, E., Hannafin, M. J., & Song, L. (2005). Promoting technology integration through collaborative apprenticeship. *Educational Technology Research and Development, 53*(4), 57-68.

Granger, C. A., Morbey, M. L., Lotherington, H., Owston, R. D., & Wideman, H. H. (2002). Factors contributing to teachers' successful implementation of IT. *Journal of Computer Assisted Learning, 18*, 480-488.

Green, J. N. (1999). Interactive videoconferencing improves performance of limited English proficient students. *T.H.E. (Technological Horizons in Education) Journal, 26*(4), 69-70. Retrieved November 14, 2006, from http://thejournal.com/articles/14095

Heifetz, R. A. (1994). *Leadership without easy answers.* Cambridge, MA: The Belknap Press of Harvard University Press.

Lesley University (2005). Interview questions for teachers. Retrieved December 4, 2006, from http://www.lesley.edu/services/crc/interview-forteachers.html

Lou, Y. (2004). Understanding process and affective factors in small group versus individual learning with technology. *Journal of Educational Computing Research, 31*(4), 337-369.

Newman, D. L. (2005). *The virtual information education Web project: Summative evaluation of the technology innovation challenge grant end of the grant report 2000-2005.* SUNY Albany, NY: Evaluation Consortium. Retrieved November 14, 2006, from http://www.projectview.org/ProjectVIEW.Endof GrantReport.2000-2006.pdf

Newmann, F. M. (1992). *Student engagement and achievement in American secondary schools.* New York: Teachers College Press. Retrieved November 14, 2006, from http://eric.ed.gov/ERICDocs/data/ericdocs2/content_storage_01/0000000b/80/26/c2/ 2b.pdf

Pace, S. & Tesi, R. (2004). Adult's perceptions of field trips taken within grades K-12: Eight case studies in the New York metropolitan area. *Education, 125*(1), 30. Retrieved November 29, 2006, from http://web.ebscohost.com/ehost/deli very?vid=7&sid=46751b8

Rice, K. (2006). A comprehensive look at distance education in the K-12 context. *Journal of Research on Technology in Education, 38*(4), 425-448.

Rothstein, R., Jacobsen, R., & Wilder, T. (2006). 'Proficiency for all' is an oxymoron: Accountability should begin with realistic goals that recognize human variability. *Education Week, 26*(13), 42.

Satterlee, B. (2002). *Applications of technology, currently being used in business and industry, to education.* Retrieved November 7, 2006, from http://eric.ed.gov/sitemap/ html_ 0900000b8017a8a8.html

Senge, P. (1990). *The fifth discipline.* New York: Doubleday.

Sergiovanni, T. J. (2001). *The principalship: A reflective practice perspective.* Boston: Allyn & Bacon.

Sprague, D., & Dede, C. (1999). If I teach this way, am I doing my job? Constructivism in the classroom. *Learning and Leading with Technology, 27*(1), 6-9.

Staples, A., Pugach, M. C., & Himes, D. (2005). Rethinking the technology integration challenge: Cases from three urban elementary schools. *Journal of Research on Technology in Education, 37*(3), 285-311.

Tuthill, G., & Klemm, E. B. (2002). Virtual field trips: Alternatives to actual field trips. *International Journal of Instructional Media, 29*(4), 453-468.

Wetzel, K., Zambo, R., Buss, R., & Padgett, H. (2001, June). *A picture of change in technology rich K-8 classrooms.* Paper presented at National Educational Computing Conference, "Building on the Future". Retrieved November 8, 2006, from http://www.eric.ed.gov/ ERICDocs/data/ ericdocs2/content-storage-01/0000000b/80/0d/ d0/48.pdf

Chapter XI
Infrastructure for Videoconferencing

Mohua Bose
University at Albany / SUNY, USA

Sal DeAngelo
Schenectady City School District, USA

ABSTRACT

Due to the increases in connectivity capacities prevalent in our nation's schools, educational administrators are utilizing a variety of resources in their classrooms, including interactive videoconferencing. For videoconferencing to be successful, however, planning for technological infrastructure must occur prior to program implementation. It is important for both schools and providers to be aware of the infrastructure requirements needed in order to provide students with knowledge and learning via videoconference experiences. The purpose of this chapter is to identify the key components of the technological infrastructure needed to support videoconferencing within K-12 in the schools, such as connectivity needs and essential hardware requirements including computers, cameras, audio essentials, and operating controls; in addition, the chapter provides, in easy-to-read language, an overview of many of the key technical terms used in the videoconferencing literature, and provides teachers with a graphical display of use.

INTRODUCTION

Educational technology has advanced greatly in the recent years with the advent of the Internet. Born in the 1970's, the Internet gained momentum in the early 1990's with the dawn of the World Wide Web (WWW). As reported by the National Center for Education Statistics, there has been a marked increase in school connectivity and access from 1994 to 2001 (Kleiner & Farris, 2002). In 1994, only 35% of the public schools had access to the Internet, whereas in 2001, access had increased to 99%. Similar statistical increases were noted by the National Center for Education Statistics on instructional room or classroom access to the Internet (Kleiner & Farris, 2002). While in 1994, only 3% had instructional room access, in 2001, 87% of the public schools had instructional room access to the Internet.

Changes also have occurred in the types of Internet connections. In 1996, dial-up connection was the most frequently-used mode in three-fourths of the public schools (Heaviside, Riggins, & Farris, 1997); but by the turn of the twenty first century, T1/DS1/Cable and broadband lines were used in the majority of the schools (Kleiner & Farris, 2002). These lines provided for significantly-faster Internet connections than the dial-up connections.

Due to these increases in connectivity capacities, school administrators are supporting utilization of a variety of medium in their school classrooms, especially since both financial and safety constraints in schools have led administrators to seek alternative solutions to field trips. Administrators also know that that when external resources are used in the classroom, they tend to trigger student interest and curiosity in the content area. As a result, teachers and administrators have been attempting to use different multimedia resources within their classroom instruction to be able to keep the students cognitively engaged (Jonassen, 2002), yet provide them with access to external resources.

One of the more promising multimedia modes utilized by educators in schools is the use of videoconferencing. According to Penn (1998), videoconferencing entails two or more groups of individuals located at different locations, who are able to connect via telephone or Internet to transmit video and audio data. This media allows educators to bring content into the classroom, directly from an expert in the field who is located at a distant setting. Schools that have connections available can link to content providers who provide educational resources via videoconferencing. This provides students not only rich content in a non-traditional format, but according to research, creates authentic and interactive learning opportunities and leads students to think at a higher cognitive level (Gerstein, 2000; Jonassen, 2002; Newman, Barbanell, & Falco, 2004; Silverman & Silverman, 1999). In addition, there are several other advantages to using videoconferencing, such as having access to an expert without having to leave the school building, as well as eliminating student travel time and costs (Pachnowski, 2002).

Videoconferencing allows the schools to connect to various professionals in the real world without actually having to go out of the classrooms; however, it requires considerable preparatory arrangements in infrastructure to enable a teacher to actually conduct videoconferences. The importance of infrastructure cannot be overlooked. Infrastructure requirements can be both the enablers and limiters to a school's ability to videoconference. If a district/school's infrastructure is robust and properly configured, videoconferences can be delivered to any classroom with predictable scheduling systems and quality. A district that does not have a robust backbone, or has an infrastructure which is constrained, will be limited significantly in its the ability to deploy videoconferencing as part of an integrated curricula approach to teaching and learning. The objective of this chapter is to discuss the infrastructure requirements needed to be able to conduct successful videoconferencing.

Types of Systems

The different types of systems that are used today in the market can be classified under three categories: desktop or personal videoconferencing systems, set-top videoconferencing systems, and integrated videoconferencing systems. These systems can be used to videoconference between a combination of individuals and groups.

- **Desktop or personal videoconferencing systems:** At the very basic level, there could be *one-to-one* videoconferencing conducted between two individuals across two sites. Such systems allow for videoconferencing between individuals at a low cost, with easy installation and no sizeable hardware to be placed on the desk. *Desktop systems* are often used for personal videoconferencing where two participants can collaborate using their own PC's that are equipped with videoconferencing facilities that enable them to connect using video and audio at a much higher quality than a Webcam connection. Desktop systems are, however, unsuitable for groups of people. *Personal systems* are like videophones that allow two people to see, hear, and talk to each other, but are limited to a single or two people at each end. Access to desktop or personal videoconferencing systems in an educational setting could help foster discussions and interactions between the two parties; enhance individuals' knowledge; or serve as a precursor to an actual videoconference between a content provider and a classroom teacher. It is, however, inadequate when used to support two classrooms' endeavors to videoconference with each other.
- **Set-top videoconferencing systems:** Set-top systems may be used when groups of people are involved and are frequently used in a school setting to conduct videoconferences with collaborating sites. In this sys-

tem, the videoconferencing equipment is placed on top of the television, and, in the case of some set-top systems, an option is available to wheel the system to any room, as needed. Set-top systems allow for connection between *one small group to another small group,* such as between classrooms collaborating with each other; *medium-sized group to medium-sized group,* such as a slightly larger classroom groups, by combining students from two classrooms at each end; or a *large group to large group* in an auditorium encompassing multiple classrooms between the location sites.

The type of connections in videoconferencing is numerous and may include not just two sites, but variations that include multiple sites (three or more), with the group sizes ranging from one to large at each of these sites. Many of these systems allow for videoconferencing only to and from two locations, but the higher end set-top models allow videoconferencing between four or five locations. Many set-top systems are equipped with a camera that has a pan, tilt, and zoom facility that allows for flexibility in capturing speakers, or helps to focus on specific objects/artifacts used during the videoconference.

- **Integrated videoconference systems:** Integrated multimedia systems, as the name suggests, are equipped with a variety of media that can be used at the same time (e.g., telephone, slide and data projector, VCR, DVD, plasma screens, etc.), and can be used to conduct videoconferencing with a large number of remote locations. Collaborative systems are further advanced models that allow file-sharing facilities that enhance discussions involving spreadsheets, technical drawings, and so forth. Individuals from remote locations can work on the same file at the same time; this system has the capacity to provide the same experience as a meet-

Figure 1. Desktop videoconferencing collaboration: Small group collaboration between groups of one to three students (Used with permission from Project VIEW training manual)

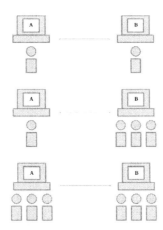

Figure 2. Desktop to large group collaboration: Collaboration between groups of one to three students and a large group of students (Used with permission from Project VIEW training manual)

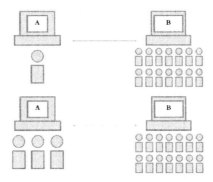

Figure 3. Collaboration between large groups (Used with permission from Project VIEW training manual)

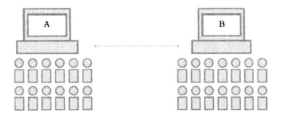

Figure 4. Content provider integration: Collaboration occurs prior to connecting to a common content provider and then continues after the connection (Used with permission from Project VIEW training manual)

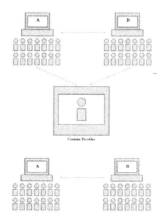

Figure 5. Content provider integration: Collaboration occurs after connecting to two different content providers and then disseminating the learned information in post collaboration (Used with permission from Project VIEW training manual)

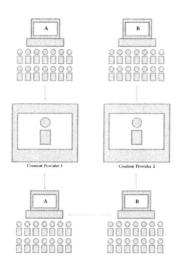

Figure 6. Content provider integration: Small group collaboration occurs with the content provider in a unique expert mini-session; post-dissemination collaboration can occur to a small or large group (Used with permission from Project VIEW training manual)

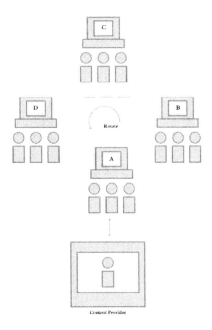

ing held inside a room. Collaborative and integrated multimedia systems frequently are used by businesses, agencies, and organizations.

All of these above-mentioned types of systems can be used to support learning and instruction with the caveat that the participants in the videoconference are prepared and have focused on a specific content matter. Most schools are now moving toward the set-top videoconferencing equipment, which allows them to use videoconferencing with groups of people, accessing multiple locations at the same time, and that are equipped with presentation tools such as Microsoft's PowerPoint.

Basic Equipment Components

- **CODEC:** One of the basic components required to conduct a videoconference include

the compressor/decompressor (CODEC), which can be considered to be the loci of videoconferencing system. The CODEC is the equipment that is used to input or feed the video from the camera, and the audio from the microphone at the source point. At the destination point, it is the equipment responsible to translate the digitized signals back to regular audio and video data. In simple terms, the CODEC is the equipment for compressing/coding the analog video signal by digitizing, and also for decompressing/decoding the signal at the receiving station. This is an important equipment for processing data, as a slow codec could lead to an audio time delay or shaky pictures. The videoconferencing industry is beginning to increase the options available, and they now include both hardware- and software-only CODECs. This increase in options is also significantly reducing the entry-level costs, with prices as low as $400. On the upscale side, the videoconferencing industry has just begun to introduce CODECs capable of broadcasting and receiving high-definition video and supporting higher fidelity audio. The range of CODEC options comes with varying sets of capabilities, ease of use, and cost factors. A school or content provider needs to determine the type of CODEC that is appropriate for their needs.

- **Display:** To be able to see what is happening at each end of communication, a display system such as a television, projector, or plasma screen is required. Typically in a school setting, a television monitor is used to view the image. The size of the monitor would depend upon the size of the classroom. A 27" to 32" television monitor would work for standard-sized classrooms. In place of a television monitor, a LCD data projector with a minimum brightness of 1,400 lumens could also be used (Wilkinson & DeAngelo, 2001). If a district were to deploy high-definition videoconferencing equipment, they would be required to update all their monitors and projectors that are used for videoconferencing to accommodate the higher-quality video images.

- **Camera:** Cameras play an important role in enhancing the quality of the videoconference. The better quality the camera, the more enhanced the image is at the receiving end, triggering interest and sustaining motivation. Most videoconferencing equipment comes with a built-in camera; in other cases, there may be a need to purchase one. The cameras used can range from a tiny desktop camera to a higher-end pan, tilt, and zoom camera. It is essential to have a camera that will reproduce good quality images to the remote site, as good quality pictures would serve to maintain the interest of the participants. A camera with a pan, tilt, and zoom (PTZ) feature is helpful to focus more closely on participants during a videoconference, especially while engaging in question-and-answer sessions. Most hardware videoconferencing equipment

Figure 7. Overview of videoconferencing materials (Used with permission from Project VIEW training manual)

Feature	Software codecs	Desktop systems	Set-top devices	PC-based integrated
Camera	Webcam	Webcam	PTZ CCD camera	PTZ CCD camera
Display	Computer screen	Computer screen	TV, projector or flat display	TV, projector or flat display
Microphone	Headset	Headset/ Handset	Table-top microphone	Table-top microphone
Speakers	Headset	Headset/ mini-speakers	TV speakers or external	External speakers
Encoding/ Decoding	Software/ Software	Hardware/ Software	Hardware/ Hardware	Hardware/ Hardware
User interface	Computer application	Computer application	On screen menu	On screen menu plus computer application
Control device	Mouse/keyboard	Mouse/keyboard	Remote control	Remote control plus wireless mouse/keyboard
Portability	High	High for USB Low for PCI	Medium	Medium
Audio/Video input/output connectivity	Low	Low	Medium/High	Medium/High
Audio/Video quality	Decent	Fairly good	Very good	Very good
Ease of use	Medium	Medium	High	Medium
Collaboration capabilities	High	High	Medium	High
Reliability/ease of maintenance	Medium	Medium	High	High
Price	Very low	Low	Medium	High

allows for multiple camera inputs and allows the end user to switch cameras during the session to maximize the visual impact and to insure that the best images are being projected. In addition to traditional cameras, it is possible to add document cameras and video microscopes to the camera inputs on the CODECS. This allows for a large range of content to be presented.

- **Audio:** Videoconferencing involves conversation between two or more parties, and therefore, audio transmission is a very important part of the process which is involved. Based on the kind of system that is available, the audio unit might include some combination of microphone, headset, handset, and speakers. Microphones often are used to capture the audio, and most high-quality systems come with a microphone that could be used with a small group of people. If the videoconference involves a large group of participants, it is advisable to have additional microphones. Speakers are required to be able to hear the audio from the remote site. For a classroom or a library, the speakers in a TV monitor would be sufficient, but for larger venues such as in a cafeteria or an auditorium it may require separate speaker systems to be connected. While using a combination of microphone and speaker, care must be taken to handle the echo that might arise from the sound waves emitted from the speaker that feeds back into the microphone. There are some systems that provide an echo cancellation speaker/microphone combination; in other cases, care must be taken to place the microphone as far away as possible from the speakers. Headsets and handsets can also be used as an input device to transmit and receive audio from participating sites.

Controls: To be able to operate the equipment, there is a need to have user controls. This could include a remote control, or a mouse, keyboard or, in advanced systems, touch-panel controls. These controls allow the user to make the calls to the connection site, make volume and picture clarity adjustments, switch to document or other cameras and to control a PTZ camera.

Supplementary Infrastructure Resources

In addition to the basic infrastructure mentioned above, there are certain supplemental multimedia resources that could serve to enhance the videoconferencing experience. These include peripherals that allow presenters and participants to increase the range of material that they present and to enhance the ability to create more interactive environments. The most common peripheral is the document camera. These devices, which are essentially a video camera on a stand, allow the user to easily display pictures and objects. They allow the user to zoom in on fine detail and to change contrast and color balance to accurately display the objects. Handheld and stand-based microscopes allow the presenters and participants to move from static images of very small objects to live interactions at the microscopic level. Combined with annotation devices, they allow the presenter to focus the viewer's attention to fine details and structures.

Additionally, more commonly-found peripherals, like audio cassette/CD player, electronic whiteboard, VCR/DVD, and a wireless microphone can increase the content density that can be transmitted. Audio cassette/CD players help teachers to make use of additional audio material that the on-site teacher could present for the classroom or for participants at the remote site. Electronic whiteboards can be used to draw diagrams like a regular whiteboard so that all participants can view the creation of information. A VCR/DVD serves the function of showing video footage, while a wireless microphone allows one to move around the room.

At the network host level (often at the district or organization level like NYIT's EEZ (www.nyiteez. org), the capacity to stream the videoconference and to record both sides of the presentations so they can be accessed simply via the Internet are beneficial. This streaming capability allows other locations to view the live session and, while not able to directly participate, they can experience the interaction between the two sites. As noted by Barnett, Truesdell, Kenyon, and Mike (see Chapter XIII, in this volume) and Mountain (see Chapter XVI, in this volume), this also could be useful for training of preservice teachers and for professional development.

Connecting Between Sites

Connection refers to the way in which data are transmitted between the sites and is a primary determinant of the audio and video quality which is transmitted. Without a way to connect locations, there is no way to have a videoconference, and the type and configuration of these connections significantly impacts what a school, district, or provider is capable of doing. The sending and receiving of information is commonly made through two types of connections: either Integrated Services Digital Network (ISDN) phone lines, or through Internet using Internet protocol (IP) connections. Depending on the type of CODEC which has been purchased, the equipment will be able to handle one or both types of connections. One of the factors to consider is the bandwidth of the available communicating system. Bandwidth refers to the amount of information (bits) that can be transmitted every second, and its requirement depends on the type of data which is being transmitted (Coventry, 1995). Textual data can be transmitted slowly using a narrow bandwidth, while speech sound needs a wider bandwidth to be able to be transmitted at the normal conversational speed. If transmitting picture images along with sound, a very high bandwidth is required to send the information quickly. A connection with a high

bandwidth indicates that the process of receiving information will be quick, and also the picture and sound will be clear.

The most popular IP network uses T-1, T-3, DSL, or broadband cable, whereas the ISDN connections use digital telephone lines. The advantages of ISDN connections are that they work over regular digital phone lines and, therefore, no special wiring is required; the connections are available worldwide, and a dedicated bandwidth with high-quality transmission and reliable technology is provided. The disadvantages, however, include the higher per-minute long-distance cost and in the equipment installation, setup, and maintenance. The IP connections, on the other hand, have the advantages of no per-minute long-distance calling charges, but the quality of the service is not guaranteed and there can be challenges to configuring a school or district's network to accommodate the videoconference. These challenges include sharing bandwidth with other instructional and administrative applications, providing Internet access into locations which best serve the videoconference, and opening firewalls to allow the video and audio to come in and out of the school. Some schools have used the availability of broadband cable Internet access to provide separate Internet connections to be used for their videoconferencing applications. In these cases, they have essentially created a separate network to handle their videoconferencing needs. In the next few years, we will see the deployment of broadband wireless Internet by wireless phone providers and by various local governments. These networks hold the promise to provide the ability to increase the locations and in the deployment of videoconferencing units.

Another popular connection used for videoconferencing in recent years is Internet 2. This system is a connection that is approximately 1,000 times faster than the regular commercial Internet. For example, if it takes 168 hours to download a 2-hour lecture DVD with a 56 kbps, it would take 74 hours on ISDN lines, 25 hours on DSL/

Cable, and 6.4 hours on a T1 line, whereas the Internet2 is even faster with land-speed record (Seifert, 2006). The need for the Internet began with initial talks about a faster system in the mid-1990's. A need was expressed for a way to overcome the problems associated with masses using the Internet at the same time, checking emails, engaging in Internet chat, coupled with a congestion of homepages (Seifert, 2006). As a result, Internet 2, which initially started with 30 universities, has now expanded to 207 universities, and today also includes 53 corporations, as well as connections with U.S. government and internationally (Seifert, 2006). In addition, the Internet2 has a special initiative for educational institutions called Internet2 K20 for primary and secondary schools, higher institutions, libraries, and museums. A recent survey conducted on the use of Internet2 reported that in 2006, over 46,000 K-20 institutions in 35 U.S. states have made connections using this network mode (Rotman, 2006). More specifically, 37% of U.S. K-12 schools, 54% of community colleges in the U.S., 57% of all U.S. four-year colleges, 20% of all U.S. libraries, 35% of museums, historical and cultural centers, 79% of performing arts centers, 16% of science centers, planetariums, and observatories, and 6% of zoos and aquariums are connected to the Internet2 (Rotman, 2006). However, while these numbers look promising, there are still significant issues for schools in terms of costs and access to Internet2 in underserved rural communities.

Planning a Videoconference

- **Program planning and confirmation:** There are several key procedural steps that will help facilitate a videoconference. The teacher would have to book or schedule a videoconference with content providers. Many popular content providers are booked early during the school year, and thus it requires planning to book key experts. If the arrangement has been done ahead of

time, it is wise to confirm the booking and all other details, as the date of the actual videoconference approaches nearer. At this time, the teachers or tech support staff should have all the information, such as the ISDN and phone numbers, which will be needed for making the connection.

- **Preparedness: Learning the videoconferencing system:** Prior to an actual videoconference session, it is important to feel comfortable using the system. "Practice" is the key word. The staff needs time to practice making connections and starting the equipment in informal sessions with colleagues at other institutions. Practice may be required with other equipment such as the camera so users are able to move the camera into a variety of positions as required during the class session. One way to do it is to have "presets" for the camera that would make the movement and positioning of the camera easier. Practice also may be needed with using the keyboard and the mouse. All of this preparation leads to the teacher having a control over the equipment, thereby focusing on the content material during the actual videoconference, rather than the technology aspect taking over the learning situation.

Logistics in the Environment

- **Background:** A solid-colored background seems to be the best in transmitting images to the remote site. Among solid colors, a gray or a slate blue works best; green, yellow, and red are poor choices (SBC Knowledge Network Explorer, 1995). A background that is patterned makes it difficult to distinguish students from the other end. The room which serves as the background for the videoconference needs to be fairly clutter-free, to project a clearer and neater image to the other end.

Camera: The camera should be positioned such that it can capture a clear image of the person talking. If it is a group, a pan, tilt, zoom camera could be focused on the person talking. An important aspect in a successful videoconference is eye contact with participants in the remote site. One technique that can be done is to position the camera as close as possible to the display area that would allow the speaker to look at the remote participants, while at the same time looking into the camera. If the camera cannot be placed near the display area, practice may be needed to concentrate on looking into the camera and not the person's image on the monitor.

Lighting: With regard to lighting, there are two problems that can arise: one, with the position of the camera, and two, with fluorescent lighting. First, pertaining to the position of the camera, if there are windows behind the students, and the camera is facing the window, the video image transmitted will not be clear. The light from the windows will dominate, and the participant's images will shadow out. This can be avoided by placing the back of the camera facing the window, which will ensure light on the participant's face, and will not lead to a blackening of the image. Second, florescent lights sometimes create a glare on the videoconference monitor and may create problems during videoconferencing.

Dress and movement: Similar principles related to background also apply to clothing; solid-colored clothing is transmitted best. If students wear stripes, polka dots, or other complex patterns, it tends to vibrate on the screen. Also, there is a loss of picture quality during rapid gesturing or movements. It is a good idea to mark out the section that is within the camera range, so that any movement to show something or make a presentation is within the camera's range.

Audio-voice: The placement of the microphone is an important decision to make prior to videoconferencing. If there are a large number of participants in the room, it is helpful to have more than one microphone placed at strategic locations. Microphones should never be placed near speakers or equipment. While speaking into a microphone, some of the sound waves are fed into the microphone, whereas other waves bounce off walls and ceilings, creating an echo. To handle this problem, many systems include a near-end echo canceller. Good audio communication occurs also with the use of a headset or handset, which helps to minimize the distance between the equipment and the mouth, and thereby, reduces the echo. If the room where the videoconference is going to be conducted has a lot of glass windows, it may be a good idea to hang curtains as glass is a bad audio reflector.

While communicating during a videoconference, there is sometimes a time lag between the sites. It would be essential to prepare the students to practice waiting until the other person stops speaking. Care should be taken to also ensure that there are not multiple speakers at the same time; thus, a system to facilitate multiple speakers needs to be preplanned with the students. In addition, it is important to reduce or possibly eliminate as much of the background noise as possible during a videoconference.

Building Infrastructure within the Building

The next question that arises is, after conquering the basics in videoconferencing, how does one develop videoconferencing capabilities or infrastructure within a school building? Data indicate that this requires an organized approach to bringing about systems change within the school building. In documenting successful long-term support of videoconferencing, Newman (2005) found that the process typically involves three phases: initiation, implementation, and impact. At the initiation phase, it is important to conduct an initial needs assessment of personnel, equipment, and infrastructure. In an effort to building videoconference capacity within the school building/district, this requires the creation of awareness of the value of employing videoconferencing as an educational tool, apart from assessing the hardware and software availability and the number of educators who will be able to confidently utilize the videoconferencing medium. Specific steps include cultivating a common vision among educators, analyzing the organization's environment and resources, identifying the strengths and weaknesses within these institutions, and developing and implementing key strategies for the funding of equipment and personnel during the planning process. This initiation process involves multiple stakeholders engaging in collaborative planning to develop concrete plans regarding acquiring, piloting, and implementing necessary technologies, and establishing training for the educators and technical support resources.

During the implementation phase, once the support of the educators in the building is obtained, training needs to be provided to administrators and to educators to utilize the videoconferencing medium. The training would help to understand the basics of videoconferencing equipment, along with how this medium can be incorporated into their regular curriculum plans. During the videoconference trainings provided to the teachers, it is beneficial to involve a few content providers to share ideas about the possibility of videoconferencing on various topics. It would also allow the content providers to showcase their programs to the teachers; whereas for the teachers, it would be beneficial to identify content providers that could be easily integrated into their curriculum.

Gaining a deeper understanding of videoconferencing and reflecting on how it can be adapted to the curriculum is essential during the implementation process. In addition during this phase, teachers need to feel extremely comfortable in using the videoconference equipment. This might require supportive practice with a technology specialist beyond the initial videoconference training, to give teachers the needed confidence to implement the technology in their classrooms. To bring about systemic change within the school building, one needs to ensure that coupled with teacher and support staff training, the school has the technology available and functional. A school building can be said to be in the impact phase of infrastructure building when the teachers in the building regularly implement videoconferencing, and it has become a regular basis of instruction. Educators in the school building continue to utilize videoconferencing materials designed by content providers to enhance their own teacher and their students' learning experience.

CONCLUSION AND TRENDS

Videoconferencing will be used widely in the future as the costs go down, and the technology becomes easier to install and operate. Schools are already looking for ways to: utilize the technology to connect teachers and students to mentors; reach students who are homebound because of physical or school suspension issues; open up their board of education meetings to a wider group of participants; interview perspective employees; set up college interviews for their students; and work with other schools, locally, nationally, and internationally. Overall, videoconferencing is a technology that has the capacity to transcend geographical boundaries. It is being used widely by large corporate organizations as part of their regular business operations across the globe. With increased capacity in technological communication, there is an increasing trend towards globalization, leading to a greater interaction and communication between countries for businesses. Students in the schools today will find themselves in a future world where global business and economy are key features; thus, it is essential to sensitize and equip them with skills needed to function in the world. One way to do so is to introduce videoconferencing into educational settings. Not only will videoconferencing help students to have access to international expertise, but it will also help foster cultural understanding. Involving students in schools with worldwide friendships can help build a global community that links and unites the world. This would help to develop students who will grow to become "citizens of the world", who can appreciate and respect the diversity of people from around the globe.

REFERENCES

Coventry, L. (1995). Video conferencing and learning in higher education. A report to the advisory group on computer graphics. SIMA Report Series ISSN 1356-5370. Retrieved March 15, 2006, from http://www.agocg.ac.uk/mmedia.htm

Gerstein, R. B. (2000). Videoconferencing in the classroom: Special projects toward cultural understanding. *Integration of Technology in the Classroom, 16*(3-4), 177-186.

Heaviside, S., Riggins, T., & Farris, E. (1997). Advance telecommunications in U.S. public elementary and secondary schools. *Fall, 1996 (NCES 97-854), U.S. Department of Education, Washington, DC: National Center for Education Statistics.* Retrieved March 16, 2006, from http://www.anchoragepress.com/archives-2006/news-2vol15ed13.shtml

Jonassen, D. H. (2002). Engaging and supporting problem-solving in online learning. *The Quarterly Review of Distance Education, 3,* 1-13.

Kleiner, A., & Farris, E. (2002). Internet access in U.S. public schools and classrooms, 1994-2001. *U.S. Department of Education, Fall, 2002 (NCES 2002-018), Washington, DC: National Center for Education Statistics.* Retrieved March 23, 2006, from http://nces.ed.gov/pubs2002/2002018.pdf

Newman, D. L. (2005). *Beyond the barriers: Benefits of K-12 teacher participation in collaborative classroom videoconferencing training.* Paper presented at the Annual Conference of the Society for Technology in Teacher Education (SITE), Phoenix, Arizona.

Newman, D., Barbanell, P., & Falco, J. (2004). *Documenting value-added learning through videoconferencing: K-12 classrooms' interactions with museums.* Paper presented at the annual meeting of E-Learn Conference, Washington.

Pachnowski, L. (2002). Virtual field trips through videoconferencing. *Learning and Leading with Technology, 29*(6), 10-13.

Penn, M. (1998). Videoconferencing one to one but far from home. *Technology Source, 5,* 22-23.

Rotman, L. (2006). Internet2 survey finds over 46,000 K20 institutions connected to its next-generation network. *Internet2.* Retrieved April 21, 2006, from https://mail.internet2.edu/wws/arc/i2-news/2006-03/msg00004.html

SBC Knowledge Network Explorer (1995). *Videoconferencing: Introduction.* Retrieved March 16, 2006, from http://www.kn.pacbell.com/wired/vidconf/intro.html

Seifert, B. (2006, March). The Internet just got a lot faster. *Anchorage Press, 15*(13). Retrieved April 21, 2006, from http://www.anchoragepress.com/archives-2006/news2vol15ed13.shtml

Silverman, S., & Silverman, G. (1999). The educational enterprise zone: Where knowledge comes from. *T H E Journal, 26,* 56-57.

Wilkinson, D., & DeAngelo, S. (2001). *Project VIEW videoconference integration training.* Project VIEW, Schenectady City School District.

Chapter XII
Policy Issues Regarding the Instructional and Educational Use of Videoconferencing

Joseph Bowman
University at Albany/SUNY, USA

Felix Fernandez
ICF International, USA

Sharon Miller-Vice
University at Albany/SUNY, USA

ABSTRACT

The purpose of this chapter is to identify policy issues for videoconferencing at the elementary through college levels. As videoconferencing becomes a part of our educational landscape in schools across the country, it is important to understand what policy implications need to be addressed in regards to this educational resource. Issues such as ownership, content, and access are some of the areas that suggest policy discussion. Federal, state, and international policies that guide the use of videoconferencing will be discussed. In sum, this chapter attempts to investigate policy issues and trends related to videoconferencing that informs the educational (PreK-12), business (training), and academic (higher education) communities that use this resource.

INTRODUCTION

The use of the Web/Internet in classrooms has quickly evolved from an occasional resource to a mainstay in education. The trend is clearly evident in New York State's mandate that all public schools be equipped with Internet access. It also can be argued that all major universities in the United States now use and rely on Web resources for many of their educational needs (Bruce, Dowd, Eastburn, & D'Arcy, 2005). Web and Internet resources have revitalized interest in distance education in that they provide a cost-effective and rapid way in which to deliver quality education to a broad spectrum of students. In this respect, online education is quickly becoming a central component of higher education; more colleges and universities are now offering courses using this resource (Lewis, Snow, Farris, & Levin, 1999). The recent explosion of distance learning technologies clearly demands greater attention from educational researchers and policy-makers if we are to develop a complete understanding of the limitations and possibilities of this innovation. If distance learning is to be viewed as a new venue for learning, rather than as a technology or tool, it is important to examine the new and exciting possibilities made available by new communications and computing technologies.

These possibilities include advancements in videoconferencing that allow classrooms to obtain real-time answers to their questions, to have close-up views of marine life hundreds of miles away, to interview authors of their favorite books, and to exchange ideas for a project with students from another country. Unlike other distance learning tools that have been known to lack interpersonal instructional support crucial for reflective learning (Nobel, 1998), videoconferencing allows for face-to-face interactive experiences that are not possible with e-mail, chats, or threaded discussions. Furthermore, current Internet-based connections have given schools a much more cost-efficient method for establishing

videoconferencing, while expanding the possibilities for intellectual growth. Schools are able to take advantage of their pre-existing Internet connections, rather than having to purchase and maintain an ISDN telephone line, which can be prohibitively expensive for schools.

As videoconferencing becomes a part of our educational landscape in schools across the country, it is important to understand what policy implications need to be addressed in the implementation of this educational resource. Issues of ownership, content, presentation, and access are some of the areas that suggest policy discussion. Questions arise such as: Are there federal and international policies that guide the use of videoconferencing? Are there state regulations and policies that focus on videoconferencing? What do school district administrators, board members, and teachers need to be aware of when they create videoconferencing environments? This chapter proposes to identify policy issues of videoconferencing instruction at the Pre-K through college levels.

BACKGROUND

Before our discussion of policy implications, in regards to videoconferencing, it is important to describe what we mean by videoconferencing, what the origins of videoconferencing are, and the history of videoconferencing. The term "videoconferencing" can be traced back to two Latin words, "videre" which means "I see" and "confere" which means to "bring together."

Videoconferencing, which is a collection of technologies that form the foundation for a wide variety of applications, can be defined as being an exchange of digitized video images and sounds between conference participants at two or more separate sites (Wilcox, 2000). Videoconferencing allows people at two or more locations to see and hear each other at the same time, using a compressed video system to transmit information from one location to another (Packard Bell, 1995).

In the 1930's, Bell Laboratories gave the first public demonstration of two-way videoconferencing, which involved picture and sound between locations in New York City (Montagna & Carlton, 1998; Wilcox, 2000). In the 1930's as well, Europe began experimenting with the technology, but due to World War II, the technology was not further developed for almost two decades. In 1964, Bell Laboratories introduced the first picture phone at the World's Fair in New York City. The first videoconferencing systems developed by Bell Laboratories failed in part because of poor picture quality and the lack of efficient video compression techniques. In 1970, videoconferencing capabilities were offered to consumers for the cost of $160.00 a month, but the new innovation proved to be too costly for most consumers. Improvement of the technology needed to take place, along with affordability. This led other companies to improve upon the technology in the 1970's (Wilkerson, 2004). After many setbacks of videoconferencing, mainly due to the lack of quality in the technology, the medium finally arrived in the 1980's as a learning tool, particularly in medicine in the form of tele-lectures (Cannavina, Stokes, & Cannavina, 2004).

In general, videoconferencing has three distinct characteristics that separate it from other types of instruction: its capacity to reach large numbers of distant and dispersed learners, the ability for learners and presenters to interact, and its emphasis on the visual components of learning. In common practice, participants on either end need only a camera, a monitor, a microphone, and speakers, equipment to which most schools already have access. Additional requirements may include access to an information technology specialist to troubleshoot any problems that may occur. In addition to the organizational concerns of a normal classroom (such as the topic to be covered, instructional goals, and assessment), videoconferencing requires a specific amount of planning. For example, although it may seem obvious, it is important to schedule when and for how long the videoconference will be, a process that must be confirmed at both ends. If at all possible, test runs should be performed prior to use to ensure a connection, thereby limiting frustration and difficulties during the videoconference.

Overall, videoconferences can have a broad range of benefits. First of all, it is the closest thing to actually being there without leaving the classroom. Videoconferencing allows interaction to occur between students and instructors, and this enhances understanding not capable through e-mail, telephone, or online chats. Other noted benefits include heightened motivation, improved communication and presentation skills, increased connections to the outside world, and an increase in the depth of content knowledge. Clearly, videoconferencing provides a novel approach to instruction that excites students, thereby allowing them to form meaningful relationships with others, while encouraging them to ask questions and demonstrate more depth of understanding.

Policy-Makers

As policy-makers define issues for videoconferencing and distance learning, it is essential that they understand the elements that are involved in this environment. A key element is the role of the teacher and the impact that they play on policy decisions. Policy-makers must understand the process, pedagogy, and classroom management expectations of teachers (in videoconferencing environments) to insure that they have the breadth of knowledge to make an informed policy decision. Board members will be asked to make decisions about technology, distance learning, or video distance learning, and base their conclusions on old and outdated concepts of instruction, teaching, learning, and integration of technology. Policy-makers must be reeducated to the new standards of teaching and learning in the technological classroom. Our goal in this discussion is to raise the concern and offer suggestions to policy-makers as they prepare to meet the challenge of policy determination for videoconferencing.

Teachers' Roles in Videoconferencing

Teachers also need to understand the person, the spirit of every child, and find a way to nurture that spirit. And they need the skills to construct and manage classroom activities effectively, communicate well, use technology, and reflect on their practice to learn from and improve it continually. The importance of powerful teaching is increasingly important in contemporary society. Standards for learning are now higher than they have ever been before, as citizens and workers need greater knowledge and skill to survive and succeed. Teachers need not only to be able to keep order and provide useful information to students, but also to be increasingly effective in enabling a diverse group of students to learn ever more complex material (Darling-Hammond, 2006).

For teachers to reach these goals, we need to insure that policies are in place to support the appropriate deployment of videoconferencing in our schools, while recognizing that these policies are shaped at the local, state, national, and global level. The use of this rich media in classrooms is on the edge of a broad-based discussion of who creates, controls, and distributes the content. Educators would be mistaken not to understand the political forces and why it is important to participate in the dialogue on the policies that are being framed as this process evolves.

Policy Trends Facing Videoconferencing

Videoconferencing has been used in the educational arena since the mid 1980's (Smith, 2003). Because of the capabilities of this ever-expanding technology, some educational institutions have implemented policies that govern its use. Most K-12 schools, as well as colleges and universities, have developed policies that are not stand-alone policies, but have been included in computer technology use regulations or guidelines. The policies that most schools have adopted are generic. They usually include information such as: services offered; acceptable/unacceptable use; the person to contact for scheduling; hours of operation; available equipment; set up and technical support for the equipment; rates; terms of use; ramifications for violating the use of the technology; and responsibility of the user.

Specific information regarding videoconferencing policies can be garnered from policies such as the Child Internet Protection Act (CIPA), which was signed into law in 2000. This law required schools and libraries to operate "a technology protection measure with respect to any of its computers with Internet access that protects against access through such computers, visual depictions that are obscene, child pornography, or any material that is harmful to minors," and that such a technology protection measure be employed "during any use of such computers by minors" (Wikipedia, 2006). CIPA requires filtering on computers that are used by minors. Because some videoconferencing systems use a broadband connection, it is important to make sure that videoconferencing systems are used for connectivity only and are not used for accessing the Internet (North Dakota State Government, 2005).

Whereas some policies specify use and tacit agreements among and between users, most regarding videoconferencing are merely informal agreements regarding the responsibility of those who use the technology (DeFord & Dimock, 2002). Policies are needed in many states and institutions that address the variety of legal and other responsibilities borne by states, regions, districts, and schools when offering videoconferencing opportunities to students. Because most educational institutions have generic and often limited information regarding the use of videoconferencing in the school setting, a national policy or template that schools can follow will be needed, which governs the use of videoconferencing in the educational setting. Additionally, most institutional policies were developed many years ago and need to be revised to reflect the changing conditions (United States Senate, 1999). Whereas videoconferencing is a technology, its uses are much more complex; hence, it requires stand-alone policies. Because this technology is being used in K-12 schools, and colleges and universities at an increasing rate, it is important to develop separate policies that will help to define how the technology is and should be used in the classroom setting.

In an attempt to facilitate this process, we have identified a group of current policy issues that must be addressed by developers, end users, teachers, college faculty, researchers, and content creators. These issues range from very personal concerns to international implications that will impact Internet visions and usage in the future. In this section, we will move from the personal to the global issues that face videoconferencing.

Intellectual Property: Personal

The World Intellectual Property Organization (WIPO) defines intellectual property as the creations of the mind: inventions, literary and artistic works, and symbols, names, images, and designs used in commerce.

Intellectual property is divided into two categories: industrial property, which includes inventions (patents), trademarks, industrial designs, and geographic indications of source; and copyrights, which includes literary and artistic works such as novels, poems, and plays, films, musical works, artistic works such as drawings, paintings, photographs, and sculptures, and architectural designs. Rights related to copyrights include those of performing artists in their performances, producers of phonograms in their recordings, and those of broadcasters in their radio and television programs (World Intellectual Property Organization, 2006)

Intellectual property and ownership of content material concerns are probably the main issues that must be addressed in developing content for

videoconferencing. Issues of intellectual property and ownership will grow in importance, as teachers and educators create more content material with videoconferencing and other resources (Web sites, books, novels, video production, pod-casting, and lesson plans). When teachers create curricula, lesson plans, and content material for videoconferencing courses, workshops, or seminars, intellectual property and ownership have to be taken into consideration. Does a content developer have exclusive rights or ownership over the teacher's material? Does ownership have to be shared with the district, company, or other entities that owns, leases, or represents ownership of the videoconferencing equipment or network that the content is sent or delivered over? What type of contract has to be developed, and how long should it last? Can the developer take their content and use it with another videoconference network, school, or business situation?

Many educational institutions have developed policies that were designed to recognize a faculty member's intellectual property rights in the courses that they develop and teach. But these institutions have not kept pace with the changing technologies or laws that govern their use. General terms of these agreements typically specify whether or not the university may continue to offer the course if the faculty member who wrote it no longer wishes to teach it, retires, or resigns; the agreement specifies how the net income resulting from sale or license of the course materials will be divided among the owners (United States Senate, 1999).

Copyright ownership is a very complex issue when it comes to videoconferencing and because of this, the educational community believes that a change in the law is required to optimize the quality and forms of distance education that take full advantage of today's technological capabilities (United States Senate, 1999). Discussions with videoconference service providers, schools, businesses, and colleges should be established to identify their policy on these issues. A written agreement that is satisfactory to all parties involved should be developed and signed. Individual knowledge of intellectual property and ownership protects an individual, an individual's work, and the time spent developing content material for videoconferencing.

Accountability: Building/Local Level

The teacher's role in the classroom, as technology is integrated into the classroom setting, is changing from the "sage on the stage" to a "guide on the side." This constructivist notion follows in the development of the "student-centered learning classroom environment" where the focus is on student learning. As the teacher in a videoconferencing classroom or environment starts to plan their instruction, there are many aspects that have to be considered before actual course implementation can begin.

Teachers are expected to be "content-knowledgeable" and ready to provide information resources that support classroom instruction in their content area. But what content-level knowledge is needed to integrate videoconferencing? Is an information technology specialist degree required? It is suggested that teachers and/or instructors who teach in videoconferencing environments must be knowledgeable and comfortable with their subject area (English, math, science, history, and other content areas). A strong case can be made that teachers should be certified in the subject area that they are videoconferencing. Content material, lesson plans, Web sites, and resource material all exist on the Internet that can supplement and support classroom instruction. Many times, students can locate electronic or digital content quickly, but they do not have the skills to determine if the information is authentic. The teacher provides that support and instructs the student on how to evaluate the information that they gather from the Internet. The teacher must become a "facilitator of information" that can recommend, evaluate, and create content resources for students and other teachers.

Once content issues are defined, accountability concerns on the part of the instructors can be addressed. How do we address accountability concerns when implementing videoconferencing in the classroom? Numerous state education departments have established educational standards, by content areas, for their K-12 students and mandate that teachers incorporate these standards into their curriculum materials and lesson plans. As such, the performance indicators that are associated with each standard should also be integrated with videoconferencing activities to insure that the content supports student learning and achievement.

Educators also should consider student diversity, including ethnicity and gender, when developing curriculum or lesson plans for a course. In an electronic videoconference environment, it can be a real challenge to get to know the history and culture of the students who may be in your courses. When using constructivist learning techniques, knowledge of your students is an important factor in the developmental process of supporting instruction of all students in your course. Requesting biographic information about students can assist in learning about the background of each student. Learning about a student's culture also may provide information that will help in adapting course material.

E-Rate: National

The Telecommunications Act of 1996 required that elementary and secondary schools and libraries be offered discounted access to telecommunications for educational purposes (Federal Communications Commission, 1996).

The Schools and Libraries Program of the Universal Service Fund, commonly known as "E-Rate," is administered by the Universal Service Administrative Company (USAC) under the direction of the Federal Communications Commission (FCC), and provides discounts to assist most schools and libraries in the United States to obtain affordable telecommunications and Internet access. It is one of four support programs funded through a universal service fee charged to companies that provide interstate and/or international telecommunications services (Federal Communications Commission, 2004).

The Schools and Libraries Program supports connectivity, the conduit or pipeline for communications using telecommunications services and/or the Internet. Funding is requested under four categories of service: telecommunications services, Internet access, internal connections, and basic maintenance of internal connections. Discounts for support depend on the level of poverty and the urban/rural status of the population which is served, and range from 20% to 90% of the costs of eligible services. Eligible schools, school districts, and libraries may apply individually or as part of a consortium. Each year funding is capped at $2.25 billion and unused fund balances can be rolled over to the following years. Annual requests for E-rate funding far exceed the monies available (Federal Communications Commission, 2004; Federal Legislation and Education in New York State, 2006).

The FCC, in 2004, determined that the E-rate program should be subject to the Anti-Deficiency Act. The Anti-Deficiency Act prohibits committing funds not actually accrued, so E-rate could not make funding commitments to school districts and libraries for the upcoming fiscal year. Late in 2005, Congress temporarily exempted E-rate from the Anti-Deficiency Act until December 31, 2007. Without continued, uninterrupted E-rate funding, schools and libraries, especially in rural and low-income areas, would not be able to install the technology that students, educators, and library users need to access critical information. Without this exemption, the program could once again be unnecessarily disrupted, causing schools and libraries to delay or eliminate education technology needs (The New York State Education Department, 2006). As educators who utilize these funds to support our work in videoconferencing,

we must contact district and legislative officials and share our concerns about E-rate.

Universal Service: National

In the Communications Act of 1934, Congress established a national policy of universal service that went beyond merely laying the wires and infrastructure to connect each to all. It included a commitment to making service economically accessible to all Americans.

The Federal Communications Commission (FCC) was created at this time for the purpose of regulating interstate and foreign commerce in communication by wire and radio, so as to make available, so far as possible, to all of the people of the United States, a rapid, efficient, nationwide, and worldwide wire and radio communications service with adequate facilities at reasonable charges (Thomson/West, 1997). Today, Congress has not only reaffirmed the central importance of universal service in telecommunications, but it has vastly expanded the concept.

Section 254 of the Telecommunications Act of 1996 significantly expands the concept of universal service (Federal Communications Commission, 1996):

1. The FCC is charged with assuring that all rates for universal service are just, reasonable, and affordable, not just the rates for interstate services.
2. The word "affordable" had not been used before this legislation, but the 1996 Act introduces the concept of affordability directly and explicitly into national policy.
3. The 1996 Act expands the services to which the universal service concept applies and institutes a formal process for expanding the definition of universal service over time.
4. Although access to the network for high-cost areas and low-income consumers has been supported for years, the 1996 Act explicitly requires this policy and requires that it be

implemented with specific and predictable mechanisms, in the form of contributions from all providers of telecommunications services, to support universal service.

5. A whole new range of institutions has been identified as having a role in universal service policy.
6. Section 255 also adds a commitment to consumers with disabilities.

Cooper (1996) and Mueller (1993) provided the resources for this section, and their work supports the importance of this area. This is important because of the focus on the "last mile" of connectivity, where the homes of the users are reached. We are requesting a move from telephone access and service to the provision of broadband services to the communities that need services. Regular telephone service that is supported by universal service at this time does not support the new forms of information (digital text, digital audio, digital images, videoconferencing, and interactive video) that is being passed across the present networks and telecommunications infrastructure. Universal service must keep pace with the information resources that are provided to all people presently in the United States and around the world. Currently, universal service continues the digital divide by not providing broadband capability to all users.

Cyber Security: International

We must determine how videoconferencing will impact national issues of cyber security. Are our networks secure, and do we provide information that may put our nation and end users (students and teachers) at risk? How do we protect our K-12 population and teachers from growing concerns about child pornography, identify theft, and plagiarism? The potential uses of videoconferencing can offer other opportunities where cyber security issues become equally important. These issues include: the use of e-mail and instant messaging

to communicate off-line when courses or seminars are not in session, and using Web resources (e.g., Web sites, Web quests, wikis, and blogs) to support instruction. The point here is that as content developers use videoconferencing resources, we have to address cyber security issues because we are using one of the most powerful education media tools: interactive television.

Two legislative acts, the Deleting Online Predators Act (DOPA) and the SAFER NET Act have been introduced in the U.S. House of Representatives in 2007.

Deleting the Online Predators Act of 2/16/07 amends the Communications Act of 1934 to require schools and libraries that receive universal service support to enforce a policy that:

*   Prohibits access to a commercial social networking website or chat room unless used for an educational purpose with adult supervision
*   Protects against access to visual depictions that are obscene, child pornography, or harmful to minors
*   Allows an administrator, supervisor, or other authorized person to disable such a technology protection measure during use by an adult, or by minors with adult supervision, to enable access for educational purposes
*   Directs the Federal Communications Commission (FCC) to issue a consumer alert regarding the use of the Internet by child predators and potential dangers to children because of such use, including the potential dangers of commercial social networking websites and chat rooms
*   Establishes a website resource of information for parents, teachers, school administrators, and others regarding potential dangers posed by the use of the Internet by children.

There is no companion Senate bill at the present time. (Representative Kirk Mark Stevens, [IL-10] 2007).

The Safeguarding America's Families by Enhancing and Reorganizing New and Efficient Technologies Act of 2/13/07 (SAFER NET) requires the Federal Trade Commission (FTC) to establish an office of Internet safety and public awareness, headed by a director. The office will carry out a nationwide program to increase public awareness and education regarding Internet safety, that utilizes existing resources and efforts of all levels of government and other appropriate entities and that includes:

- Evaluating and improving the efficiency of Internet safety efforts provided by such entities
- Identifying and promoting best practices
- Establishing and carrying out a national outreach and education campaign
- Serving as the primary contact in the federal government and as a national clearinghouse for Internet safety information
- Facilitating access to, and the exchange of, such information
- Providing expert advice to the FTC
- Providing technical, financial, and other appropriate assistance to such entities

There is no companion bill in the Senate (Representative Melissa L. Bean, [IL-8] 2007).

Reauthorization of the Telecommunications Act of 1996

Our greatest concern at this point is net neutrality. Ben Worthen's (2006) article, *The Net Neutrality Debate: You Pay, You Play?*, provides an excellent backdrop for this discussion. Worthen (2006) provides a scenario and definition that informs the reader about this situation:

Last April, Cisco Systems published a white paper explaining how the companies that own the phone lines and cables that connect homes and businesses to the Internet, the proverbial last mile, could use new routing technology to boost revenue. The technology would allow telephone and cable companies to establish priority lanes for high-bandwidth traffic like video, games, or voice-over-IP (VoIP) calls and then charge the Googles, Yahoos, and Amazons of the world for access to these highway toll roads. Cisco's paper predicted that this new strategy would allow broadband service providers to create new revenue-sharing business models with any company that sells content online. The plan had only one problem: It was illegal.

Worthen continues the discussion by providing background and definition about net neutrality. He states that the telecommunications laws that have governed the Internet since its inception require network owners to treat all traffic the same. The laws date back to the 1930's, and were put in place to force telephone companies to prevent a scenario where one company could refuse to carry calls placed by a rival's customer. The Internet was designed with the same principle in mind. Routers are programmed to direct each packet of data on a best-effort basis, regardless of file type, video, voice, e-mail, or who the sender and recipient are. The bill was not finalized in the summer of 2006 and is still under review and discussion in both houses of the United States Congress.

Since then, a Supreme Court ruling and a series of Federal Communications Commission (FCC) decisions have eliminated this barrier, prompting Congress to rewrite the nation's telecommunications laws. The result is that the entire Internet is now essentially outside the law. The new bill, which could be finalized as early as the summer of 2006, will in all likelihood officially eliminate net neutrality as the legal principle that governs the Internet. "If net neutrality goes away, it will fundamentally change everything about the Internet," says James Hilton, associate provost for Academic IT Works of the University of Michigan. More bluntly, Steve Effros, former president of the Cable Television Association, says, "This is about who pays." Worthen (2006) observes, "the competition that emerged in the telecommunications industry is between cable and telephone companies, and the service they are vying to provide is not just phone, but high-speed Internet access and television as well—the so-called triple play." This is the most serious event and challenge that we as educators, content providers, and end users are facing today, and will have a direct impact on how our educational information will be used in the future. In the past, our videoconference information was available to everyone who had access to the equipment and enough bandwidth to receive the conference. The potential exists that the telephone and cable companies will regulate the freedom of access that we currently have and the amount that we will pay to use their networks.

REAUTHIRIZATION OF THE NO CHILD LEFT BEHIND ACT OF 2001 (NCLB)

The No Child Left Behind Act of 2001 is being re-authorized and the Achievement through Technology and Innovation (ATTAIN) Act was introduced by a group of bipartisan legislators in the U.S. House of Representatives on May 23, 2007. The ATTAIN Act is designed to make improvements to the Enhancing Education through Technology (EETT) (Title II-D) program. The ATTAIN Act focuses on priority funding for schools in need of improvement, state assessment of technology literacy of students by eighth grade, systemic reform programs with strong technology components, and professional development (Roybal-Allard, 2007). The Act has the support of several education organizations including: Consortium for School Networking (CoSN), International Society for Technology in Education (ITE), State Educational Technology Directors Association (SETDA), National Education Association (NEA), National School Boards Association, American

Association of School Administrators, and the Nation Council of La Raza (Jones, 2007). There is hope that similar legislation will be sent to the Senate in the near future. Advocates for the AT-TAIN Act are working diligently to have this Act included in the larger NCLB reauthorization bill the House Education and Labor Committee will present later. Overall reauthorization of NLCB is not clear at this time.

FUTURE TRENDS

Videoconferencing has recently gained much wider acceptance as an instructional tool in the academic community (Fels & Weiss, 2001). Because of its increased use for instruction in the classroom setting, the ways in which to use this technology is increasing as well. The world of videoconferencing is continuously changing everyday to reflect the ever-changing educational landscape in the United States schools, colleges, and universities.

One reason for the change in educational institutions is the increase of students in class-rooms, specifically in schools that serve students in grades 9-12. It is expected by 2009 that the United States will graduate its largest high school class, and college enrollment will increase by 16 percent over the next ten years as well (Howell et al., 2003). As the enrollment of students in high schools and colleges expands, the need for video conferencing will increase. As the size of enrollment changes in colleges and universities, the needs of students will change as well. Students today are seeking educational institutions that meet their needs in regards to schedules and circumstances. Videoconferencing and distance learning are helping to meet the needs of those students who need flexibility when it comes to receiving an education.

The future uses of videoconferencing in the educational setting are many. For example, videoconferencing today in the educational arena involves the educator delivering a lecture or presentation to an audience. Videoconferencing in the future will become a full interactive experience, where the audience can play a role in the discussion, be seen, heard, and even share their own documents (Good, 2003). As such, visual and audio cues will help the instructor and students with developing a rapport (Galloway, Boland, & Benesova, 2002).

Furthermore, educational organizations and institutions can, and commonly do, limit access of materials to students enrolled in a particular class or institution. Additional technology and software will be required to address the multitude of intellectual property, ownership, and copyright concerns. The most effective means now available are secure container/proprietary viewer technologies that allow copyright owners to set rules for the use of their works, which are then attached to all digital copies, and prevent anyone from making a copy that is not in accordance with the rules. For example, students could be allowed to view the work or print a single copy, but not save it to disk or distribute it to others electronically. Streaming formats also will be used because they do not facilitate the making of copies as does the use of low-resolution digital copies (United States Senate, 1999).

The tools for videoconferencing will change as well in the future. Videoconferencing will no longer be stand-alone tools. A person will be able to go to a computer, select who to invite to a meeting, and then start a meeting. There will not be a need to upload materials ahead of time or convert them. Loading the materials onto your screen and sharing them with one click will be all that is needed (Good, 2003).

Another way in which this technology will be used in the future is to support students who will not be able to attend school. For example, students who may be in the hospital for an extended period of time or home convalescing from an illness will be able to participate in a lesson at their school from the hospital or their home. This will enable the student to keep their schoolwork current and not fall behind in their studies (Arnold, Cayley, & Griffith, 2003).

Videoconferencing and other technologies help to enrich distance media and provide many benefits of face-to-face instruction. Technology fluency is becoming a graduation requirement. Many colleges and universities are requiring students to complete at least one online course before graduation. More and more colleges and universities are offering coursework through distance learning (Howell et. al., 2003).

The integration of videoconferencing with other technologies such as video streaming and chat will be used as more schools move to Internet protocol (IP) environment for videoconferencing. The use of IP-based conferencing will increase the number of systems available in the school setting. Futuristically, every computer will have conferencing capability (Arnold et al., 2003). Videoconferencing also will have the capability to be integrated with content management tools, such as: presentation software, video and audio editing, and interactive white boards. The simultaneous use of these technologies will enable more people to take part in a conference by watching it live and feeding back responses via other media such as e-mail (Arnold et al., 2003; JKC, 2006). New ways in which to use videoconferencing for educational purposes are being developed. A recent development is to incorporate videoconferencing into Web-based systems. Web-based systems using streaming video multicasting are now reaching the educational arena. With these systems, educators can sit in their own office or other location and present a live lecture in front of a camera attached to a Web server. With the use of a simple switching device, the educator can provide remote participants with graphics, whiteboard, flipcharts, and other visual aids as well as alternative views of the classroom or lecture room. Video streaming in this manner also will be used to archive recordings of videoconferences and make these available via the Internet, possibly packaged with other teaching resources (Arnold et al., 2003; JKC, 2006; Plymouth, 2006).

Mobile videoconferencing, which is still in its infancy, will enable a user to conference while on the move using portable devices. Mobile videoconferencing also will help to increase the awareness of and interest in desktop-based videoconferencing. Mobile conferencing has the ability to change the entire landscape of the videoconferencing market, and the prospects for growth is tremendous (JKC, 2006; National Informatics Centre, 2006).

Lastly, technological advances will allow the user to manipulate video images, such as moving one image with another and overlapping different images to provide a continuous picture appearance. Frame-by-frame manipulation also will be available, and will enable the user to print still pictures, rewind to a particular frame, interleave frames, and synchronize frames. Because videoconferencing systems are becoming less expensive, multiple participants will be able to videoconference with other participants in the conference simultaneously (National Informatics Centre, 2006). The use of videoconferencing in the academic community will soon become a regular part of teaching. This technology will be useful for a variety of activities by teachers and students alike. Videoconferencing is changing the way in which we communicate with each other, much like the telephone did when it was first invented. Videoconferencing is continuously growing and changing the educational arena and, more importantly, videoconferencing is here to stay (JKC, 2006).

CONCLUSION

Our research on policy issues regarding videoconferencing has led us to several issues that we have identified and discussed. The conversation is not over, however; there is a need for more sharing of thoughts on the development and deployment of policy decisions about videoconferencing. The major limitation of the above discussion is the lack of informed data and research focusing specifically on videoconferencing. In most areas, policy research has focused on technology integration in general and is not specifically focused or targeted at videoconferencing. It is our hope that we have provided a strong case to document the importance of further research into videoconferencing-based learning policy issues. There is a need for research regarding policies for videoconferencing that can be shared to inform policy-makers about important issues around this topic. Should our research interest focus on higher education, cultural education (libraries and museums), and pre-K-12 uses of videoconferencing individually? And what collaborations may evolve that relate to policy issues?

The goal of our discussion was to provide policy guidance and leadership for users of videoconferencing. Our findings promote the use of videoconferencing across the Pre-K-16 spectrum to support program development and create a larger research base. This larger base expands the concerns about policy issues for videoconferencing and the discussion about new policies that need to be addressed in the future. Concerns such as cyber security issues, protection of access, and content are critical points that policy-makers must address. Is there a need to monitor, assess, and regulate content? These questions will certainly raise concerns about intellectual property issues for faculty and others that produce videoconferencing course material and teach classes. More importantly, could policy-makers develop policy that protects content development?

Videoconferencing provides great instructional opportunities to students and teachers in urban and rural communities, because it provides access to instructional material that may not be available. Many school districts use videoconferencing to enhance instruction and provide additional shared resources to classes, library, and administrative activities. Having an understanding of the policy issues and concerns associated with videoconferencing strengthens the opportunities and reduces the challenges to provide the best instruction possible in this environment. Whether there is a need for policy or just regulatory statutes to be in place for videoconferencing is an area for further research and discussion. We believe that both should be in place and that policy issues should be discussed, planned, and developed. State education boards, business council organizations, and state offices of technology should be working together at the state level. At the federal level, we should look for collaborative support from the Department of Education, Department of Commerce, and the Federal Communication Commission to manage and monitor videoconferencing policies. Furthermore, we support the call for a national clearinghouse on videoconferencing that provides information, best practices, and policy decisions.

DEDICATION

The authors of this chapter would like to dedicate it to Mrs. Violetta Bowman, Mr. Joseph Bowman, and Mia Felice Fernandez.

REFERENCES

Arnold, T., Cayley, S. & Griffith, M. (2003). *Videoconferencing in the classroom: Communications technology in the classroom.* Retrieved May 16, 2006, from http://www.becta.org

Bean, M. L. [IL-8] (2007). SAFER NET (Safeguarding America's Families by Enhancing and Reorganizing New and Efficient Technologies) Act (HR 1008) U.S. House of Representatives, Washington D.C. Retrieved June 14, 2007, from http://www.house.gov/apps/list/press/il08_bean/2132007_SAFER_NET_Act.html

Bruce, B. C., Dowd, H., Eastburn, D. M., & D'Arcy, C. J. (2005). Plants, pathogens, and people: Extending the classroom to the Web. *Teachers College Record, 107*(8), 1730-1753.

Burgstahler, S. (2001). Use of telecommunications products by people with disabilities. *Do-It. University of Washington.* Retrieved April 11, 2006, from http://www.washington.edu/doit/brochures/pdf/telcom.pdf

Cannavina, G., Stokes, C. W., & Cannavina, C. (2004). Evaluation of video-conferencing as a means to facilitate outreach and work-based learning. *Work-Based Learning in Primary Care, 2,* 136-47.

Cooper, M. (1996). *Universal service: A historical perspective and policies for the twenty-first century.* Benton Foundation. Retrieved June 12, 2007, from http://www.benton.org

Darling-Hammond, L. (2006). Constructing 21st-century teacher education. *Journal of Teacher Education, 57*(3).

DeFord, K., & Dimock, V. (2002). *Interactive video conferencing: A policy issues review.* Retrieved February 6, 2006, from: http://neirtec.terc.edu/k12vc/resources/ivc%20policy%review%june%2002.pdf

Federal Communications Commission (1996). Telecommunications act of 1996. Public law 104-104. 110 statute 56 (hereafter, 1996 Act, or the conference report). *Washington, DC.* Retrieved April 17, 2006, from http://www.fs.fed.us/recreation/permits/commsites/pl-104-104.pdf

Federal Communications Commission (1999). Section 504: Programs and activities accessibility handbook. *Washington, DC.* Retrieved April 11, 2006, from: http://www.fcc.gov/cgb/dro/section_504.html

Federal Communications Commission (2004). E-rate. *Washington, DC.* Retrieved April 11, 2006, from: http://www.fcc.gov/learnnet/

Federal Legislation and Education in New York State (2006). University of the State of New York (pp. 22-23). The State Education Department.

Fels, D. I., & Weiss, P. L. (2001). *Video-mediated communication in the classroom to support sick children: A case study.* Retrieved May 16, 2006, from www.ryerson.ca/pebbles/publications/ijie-pebblesfinal.pdf

Galloway, W., Boland, S., & Benesova, A. (2002). *Virtual learning environments.* Retrieved May 16, 2006, from http://www.dcs.napier.ac.uk/~mm/socbytes/feb2002_i/3.html

Good, R. (2003). *The future of Web conferencing: Good interviews with Keith Teare.* Retrieved May 18, 2006, from http://www.masternewmedia.org/2003/11/24/ the_future_of_web_conferencing.htm

Holznagel, D. (2003). *Access and opportunity policy. Options for interactive video in K-12 education* (pp. 25-46). Northwest Regional Educational Laboratory, Portland OR.

Jerome School District (2003). Strategies for using video conferencing technology in the K-12 classroom: A teacher's digital handbook. Retrieved April 11, 2006, from http://www.d26/k12.id.us/vcing/index.htm

JKC (2006). *Video conferencing and video conferencing systems–Video conferencing trends and the future?* Retrieved May 16, 2006, from http://www.jkcit.co.uk/video-conferencing-future-trends.htm

Jones, K. C. (2007). *No Child Left Behind could get boost for tech: New legislation would invest in classroom technology to prepare U.S. students for work in the information economy.* Retrieved from, http://www.informationweek.com/industries/showArticle.jhtml?articleID=199701868&subSection= p.1

Lewis, L., Snow, K., Farris, L., & Levin, D. (1999). *Distance education at postsecondary education institutions: 1997-98.* Washington, DC: U.S. Department of Education, National Center for Educational Statistics.

Library of Congress (2002). *Copyright law.* Retrieved April 11, 2006 from: http://www.copyright.gov

Motagna, M., & Carlton, M. (1998). *Bell labs helps Clinton students make a video call to Russia.* Retrieved April 15, 2006 from: http://www.bell-labs/news/1998/june14/1.html

Mueller, M., (1993). Universal service in telephone history: A reconstruction. *Telecommun. Policy, 17*(5), 352-369.

National Informatics Centre (2006). Faqs. Retrieved May 16, 2006, from http://vidcon.nic.in/faq.htm

Nobel, D. F. (1998). *Digital diploma mills: The automation of higher education.* Retrieved April 4, 2006, from http://www.firstmaonday.dk/issues/issue3_1/noble/index.html

North Dakota State Government (2006). Internet filtering policy. Education Technology Services. Retrieved June 11, 2007, from http://www.edutech.nodak.edu/support/policies/filtering/

Packard Bell (1995). *Video conferencing for learning.* Retrieved April 17, 2006, from www.kn.pacbell.com/wired/vidconf/vidconf.html

Plymouth (2006). The future of video conferencing. Retrieved May 16, 2006, from http://www.2.plymouth.ac.uk/distancelearning/vidconf.html#future

Roybal-Allard, L. (2007). Congresswoman Lucille Roybal-Allard (CA-34) testifies about her legislation to improve student academic achievement through technology. U.S. House of Representatives, Washington D.C. Retrieved June 14, 2007, from http://www.house.gov/list/press/ca34_roybal-allard/pr070516.html p.1

Smith, S. (2003). Online video conferencing: An application to teacher education. *Journal of Special Education Technology, 18*(3), 62-64.

Stevens, K. M., [IL-10] (2007). Deleting Online Predators Act (H.R.1120) U.S. House of Representatives, Washington D.C. Retrieved June 14, 2007, from http://www.house.gov/list/hearing/il10_kirk/Bill_targets_online_predators.html

Thomson/West (1997). United States code annotated title 47. Telegraphs, telephones, and radiotelegraphs. Communications act of 1934, 47 U.S.C.A. 151. Retrieved April 11, 2006, from www.fcc.gov/omd/pra/docs/3060-1-41-07.doc

U.S. House of Representatives (1996). Committee on the judiciary. Subcommittee on courts and intellectual property. Fair use guidelines for educational multimedia. Retrieved April 11, 2006, from http://www.ccumc.org/copyright/cguides.html

Wikipedia (2006). Children's Internet protection act. Retrieved April 21, 2006, from: thttp://en.wikipedia.org/wiki/children's_internet_protection_ac

Wilcox, J. R. (2000). *Video conferencing and interactive multimedia: The whole picture.* New York: Telecom Books.

Wilkerson, L. (2004). *The history of video conferences—Moving ahead at the speed of video.* Retrieved April 15, 2006, from www.ezinearticles.com

World Intellectual Property Organization (2006). *Copyright and related rights.* Retrieved April 17, 2006, from http://www.wipo.org

Worthen, B. (2006, April 15). *The net neutrality debate: You pay, you play? CIO.* Retrieved April 24, 2006, from http://www.cio.com

Section V
Videoconferencing and Teacher Preparation

Chapter XIII
The Real World Buffalo[*]:
Reality TV Comes to a Charter School

Marion Barnett
Buffalo State College, USA

Kim Truesdell
Buffalo State College, USA

Melaine Kenyon
Buffalo State College, USA

Dennis Mike
Buffalo State College, USA

ABSTRACT

Videoconferencing is one form of distance learning that can enhance teacher-education programs by linking students in higher education with Pre-K–12 schools. As part of a Preparing Tomorrow's Teachers to use Technology grant (PT3), a teacher-education program utilized distance learning to link college classes with an urban school. Mediated observations of specific literacy practices were integrated into a traditional introductory literacy course. Preservice teachers observed urban teachers teaching literacy. Immediately following these observations, the preservice teachers were granted the opportunity to reflect on the lesson by conversing with the teachers via distance learning. Initial findings suggest that students acquired positive attitudes toward teaching in urban classrooms and preferred this virtual field experience to a traditional in-school placement.

INTRODUCTION

Two children collide and tussle over some props in the dramatic play area of a kindergarten classroom. Tempers flare and arms begin to flail. Twenty teacher-education students are sitting in a campus distance learning room miles away from the classroom. Their eyes are fixed on TV monitors watching for the teacher's response to the children's struggle. The teacher calmly intervenes and mediates the struggle. The college instructor "voices over" the ongoing scene, describing to the students the importance of body position and eye contact, and explains the conflict resolution strategy of active listening and validating feelings, which the students are observing. She prompts them to listen to the teacher's language and to watch the children's faces for signs of what they might be thinking and feeling. The college instructor briefly connects what the teacher is doing with points made in the chapter on guidance and discipline from the course textbook. Ten minutes later, the kindergarten teacher, on site at the school, enters a distance learning room (the collaboratory) and spends fifteen minutes answering questions and commenting on the 30-minute lesson. Students question the teacher about the conflict, and the teacher provides answers interspersed with her own reflections, a critical component in understanding teacher behavior. She returns to her classroom, and the live video session concludes. The college instructor urges the students to think more about the conflict scenario. She queries them: "In your experiences, what are some of the ways you have seen teachers resolve conflicts among children? What did this teacher do that worked? What did she say? What else might she have done? How do you think the children felt at the end? What will you need to know and be able to do to resolve a conflict with children?"

The setting above describes an ongoing transformation in teacher preparation programs. Research suggests that the more classroom experi- ence that preservice teachers have, the better it is for their expanded repertoire of teaching strategies, by providing for more thoughtful decision-making when responding to children (Darling-Hammond, 1998). Experiences over time are needed for pre- service teachers to acquire teaching confidence, make connections from theory to practice, and engage in reflection on teaching; however, time constraints, lack of access to classrooms, school safety issues, and liability concerns are some of the issues prompting teacher-education programs to find alternative ways to design and structure early field experiences (Adcock & Austin, 2002). Though the nature and frequency of early field experiences is changing and expanding, the diver- sity, quality, and consistency of the experiences can be greatly enhanced (from what existed in the past) by using the technology available to students and faculty in teacher-preparation programs. The videoconferencing technology described in the opening scenario is just one means of using tele- communications. The range of technologies and their use in teacher-education programs is growing and expanding to include both videoconferencing and Internet protocol videoconferencing.

This chapter describes the collaboration be- tween a teacher-education program and a unique urban charter school equipped with the technol- ogy to broadcast live teaching episodes from four primary classrooms. The project began using videoconferencing technology with preservice teachers to conduct guided observations of chil- dren and teachers working and learning in an inner-city charter school. Encouraged by positive feedback from students and faculty who used the technology, a pilot program was implemented ex- amining the potential of the technology to mediate reflection with preservice teachers. Two different Preparing Tomorrows Teachers to Use Technology grants (PT3) from the U.S. Department of Educa- tion funded the work. The first grant, Project Ac- cess[1], enabled the development of the consortium between higher education and a high-need urban school, and provided the technology for real-time video linkages with four primary classrooms. The second PT3 grant, Reflective Mediation Through the Use of Technology[2], continued the work of the first with the development of a research-based set of best practices for supporting reflection with technology.

CHANGING FIELD EXPERIENCES AND THE ROLE OF TECHNOLOGY

Teacher-preparation programs in the sixties and seventies often had the luxury of a laboratory school on campus (usually attended by the children of faculty and staff). Eager, inexperienced preservice teachers were able to observe and occasionally participate at the lab school for short field experiences, testing their "teaching wings" prior to the student teaching year. Many of these schools had rooms equipped with one-way mirrors and microphones allowing guided observations to occur for a whole college class. The sixties version of "high-tech" classrooms enabled students to unobtrusively see and hear the culture of a classroom under the interpretation and mediation of an instructor. If time permitted, the teacher might join the college class to talk about their teaching and answer any questions. This provided a less intrusive way for an entire class to watch teaching in action.

Evidence suggests that labs schools have been in a steady decline since the 1970's. In 1964, a survey had responses from 186 schools, while in 1980 there were around 100 lab school respondents (Levin, 1990). As college budgets tightened, lab schools became financial burdens and less of a priority. Faculty began seeking natural settings for fieldwork more representative of the increasing diversity of modern classrooms. Laboratory schools were converted into child development centers, office, and classroom space, and teacher educators turned to the schools in the community to provide classrooms and teachers for early field experiences in addition to the capstone semester of student teaching.

MacNaughton and Johns (1993) suggest that the professional development schools (PDS) movement was the next step in the evolution to improve connections between university-based and field-based teacher-preparation components. College faculty began negotiating with schools interested in forming collaborations for the purpose of mentoring preservice teachers by providing early field experiences, methods classes, and student teaching on-site in school buildings.

Professional development schools made sense because they involved multiple players (college instructors, preservice and in-service teachers, and the students and their families) in helping to reduce disconnect between theory and practice. Darling-Hammond (1992) identified professional development schools as positioned to provide accountability "by ensuring that they (preservice teachers) have the tools to apply theory in practice and by socializing them to professional norms and ethics" (p. 91). Others (Levine, 1992) argued that typical schools are ill-suited to provide the right environment and support for professionalization, and that the cooperating teacher/student clinical practice model implemented in most teacher-education programs does not support the "reflection in action" necessary for the preparation of quality teachers.

In the movement for professionalization of teaching, teacher-education programs seek accreditation to improve outcomes for teacher-education candidates and to distinguish their programs. In the past, teacher-education programs could become accredited if they could demonstrate their curriculums provided the appropriate experiences for candidates to become knowledgeable in both content and pedagogy. There was little emphasis on early field experiences before the student teaching year. Current standards from accreditation organizations like the National Council for Accreditation of Teacher Education (NCATE) call for field experiences that are clearly defined by individual teacher-education programs. Candidates should have "diverse, well-planned, and sequenced experiences in P-12 Schools" (NCATE, 2002, p. 4). The PDS Standards Project of NCATE has identified 28 highly-developed PDS sites, which in a survey described their practices, goals, and funding sources. These data, along with a literature review and other commissioned papers, were used to develop a set of standards for PDS endorsed by the Unit Accreditation Board Standards Committee in March, 2001 (Teitel, 1999). Work of the PDS movement, along with more clearly-defined statements from accreditation councils and state boards of education, seems to suggest that preservice field experiences are equally as important for preservice teachers as the student teaching year and should be given careful attention. Teacher education programs are encouraged to give consideration to the quality of the setting, number of hours, and how the placements are supervised.

With the challenge to meet high standards, teacher-education programs have been pushed to improve in many areas simultaneously. Technology, diversity, and quality field experiences are three areas that have been targeted as needing improvement (Cochran-Smith, 1995; Irving, 2000; NCATE, 1997). Research has documented the value of using technology in teacher-education programs, and teacher educators are asked to model the integration of technology to ensure that future teachers will include technology in their own classrooms (Strudler & Wetzel, 1999). Many have documented the effectiveness of early, ample, and well-supported field experiences and focused observations in urban schools in order to facilitate confidence, commitment, and readiness to succeed in teaching in urban schools (Groulx, 2001). Classroom observations are enhanced when preservice teachers are able to engage in collaborative reflection with urban teachers and college faculty (Fountain, 1994).

With increased emphasis on enriching the number, quality, and diversity of preservice school experiences, and preparing preservice teachers to utilize technology, the following questions could be posed to assess the effectiveness of any changes as to how teacher education programs implement and structure field experiences:

1. How have technology innovations been able to reproduce and improve the experience of the guided observation (allowing students to observe a common teaching episode) as it unfolds live and unedited?
2. Can the quality of students' reflections be changed and enhanced by the opportunity to watch a common teaching episode while an instructor mediates what is being observed?
3. Can students be encouraged to use a higher level of reflection if the field experience is technologically-mediated instead of actively participating in a randomly-assigned classroom?
4. How have technology-mediated observations reduced students' stereotypes of working in an urban classroom?

These are some of the questions under investigation in a project using technology to mediate reflection involving teacher-education students and the teachers and children at one charter school.

A UNIQUE URBAN SCHOOL: THE KING CENTER CHARTER SCHOOL

In the mid 1980's, a 100-year-old church scheduled for demolition in inner-city Buffalo was given "historic landmark" status, thus saving it from destruction. A committee was commissioned to study possible adaptive reuses for the building. It was agreed, since the hope for reviving this community would reside in ensuring the education and well-being of its children, that the facility would be used to provide the highest quality of education for this predominantly African-American community's youngest children. Support from local colleges and universities would be essential to the project.

After years of fund raising and planning, a Pre-K through Grade 2 program, designed to model a high-quality, research-based, holistic education opened as the King Center, and was housed in an early childhood center in a public school until the church was renovated and ready for occupancy.

In 1993, Yale University's Bush Center in Child Development and Social Policy designated the King Center as New York State's first "School of the 21st Century" (Hoot, Massey, Barnett, Henry, & Ernest, 2001). As New York State joined other states in passing a charter school law, the King Center submitted a proposal to the SUNY board of trustees for a charter. The King Center School's application to begin a K–3 school for 80 children was approved, and the school opened in August, 2000. Grade 4 was added in 2002.

Phase I: Videoconferencing Technology and Guided Observations at the King Center Charter School

The school's virtual learning collaboratory (distance learning room) has the capability to bring professors from area colleges/universities and their students together with teachers and children for the purpose of observing "real-time teaching" using a distance learning environment. Four classrooms (K-3) are equipped with corner-mounted cameras. The teacher is provided with a microphone and camera remote pack. A laser-tracking device follows the teacher's movements in a limited range within the classroom. The microphone picks up conversations between the teacher and children. Typically the children know when the camera is on for an observation, but within minutes they are usually absorbed in their work, easily ignoring the presence of the camera.

The school utilizes the technology for many projects. For example, the director of the school has asked each teacher to videotape several lessons and decide on one to use for performance evaluation and assessment of teaching skills. From the initial installation of the cameras, however, the school was primarily interested in linking with higher-education institutions for consultation and to serve as a virtual urban lab school. Buffalo State College responded to the invitation to partner and subsequently included King Center Charter School in two PT3 grants acquired in 2001 and 2003.

Teacher Participation

The PT3 grant project relied on teachers from the school to volunteer. In the beginning, all classrooms were equipped with cameras, but only two teachers agreed to participate. After several guided observations, the two teachers shared their enthusiasm with the rest of the staff at the school. All were continually encouraged and invited to join *when they felt ready*. Within two years, all teachers were hosting guided observations for students in teacher-education programs.

The four participating teachers have two to fourteen years of teaching experience. One was designated as a "master" teacher when she was employed in the public school system. Two of the teachers have been with the school since it opened in 2000. The school enrolls 100 children in five classrooms, with the same building leader since inception. There is cohesiveness in the philosophy, teaching strategies, and behavior management that preservice students see during each virtual observation.

Participating teachers comment that they get nervous before each session begins and are constantly aware that twenty to twenty-five preservice teachers are watching every move and hanging on their words. Every teacher expressed the realistic worry that a child might have a "meltdown" while the camera was on. On the positive side, teachers state that participating in the guided observations makes them conscious of teacher language, lesson materials, and student feedback.

I try to model appropriate and logical consequences for students' misbehavior. I try to make sure that I model various strategies for motivating and engaging students in a lesson.

I find that I try to stress positive teacher language and consistency when the college students are watching me teach. I try to be explicit with logical consequences.

I try to model using a quiet voice and redirecting in a neutral tone. I try not to become emotionally charged when students make poor choices regarding behavior/conduct. I try to model a deep sense of respect and reverence for the individual humanness of each student. I model my relationship as a nurturer/caretaker.

In spite of the pressures and responsibilities of normal classroom teaching, the added complications of scheduling videoconferencing sessions, and the need to leave the classroom and their children to talk with the college students, the teachers continued to volunteer because they believed in professional development and giving back to teacher-education programs by sharing their experiences and expertise, even at a beginning or emerging level. Their continued willing participation highlights the critical importance of trust in relationships between partners. This seemed key to sustaining the work. For the teachers in this project, knowing that a person who knew both their work and them professionally and personally was stationed in the college distance learning room, interpreting and moderating the videoconference for the college students, kept them volunteering and participating in the program.

Technologically-Mediated Guided Observations

Buffalo State College education faculty were invited to schedule a session (during their regular class time) in the distance learning room on campus and participate in a "guided observation" of an unedited, live teaching episode. Initially there was concern that the project might be overwhelmed with requests. If so, it would not be possible to burden the four participating teachers and the children at the charter school with too many interruptions in one week. However, as Boccia, Fontaine, and Lucas (2002) found in their "Looking into Classrooms Project", the college faculty seemed reluctant to take time out of scheduled class meetings to have students participate in this unique new format for guided observations. After a campus-wide mailing, posting flyers, scheduling a demonstration seminar, describing the project, and inviting people to sign up, the project has sustained a small group of regular participants who typically requested one observation each semester. Once instructors had a direct experience using the technology, they were eager to repeat the process with students each semester.

The teacher education classes that participated came from several departments, including Elementary Education, Early Childhood, and Art Education. The students enrolled in the classes were in the first three years of their teacher-education program. For most students, the guided observation experience represented only one piece in a collage of early clinical field experiences prior to student teaching. The college instructor of the class and the project liaison mediated every distance learning session. As is the case with all college/school collaborations, the project was possible because a level of trust had been established between the teachers at the charter school, their director, and the higher education project director, prior to the implementation of the first grant. Teachers were more comfortable being observed knowing that a person that they knew and trusted (the project director) was on-site and available to clarify for students what they were observing.

The guided observations were structured for different purposes, depending on the request of the college professor. For example, an Introduction to Education class asked to observe 15 minutes in each of the kindergarten through third-grade rooms. The instructor wanted students to look at room arrangement, transition techniques, activity level across grade levels, and behavior management techniques. A reading methods instructor requested an observation of a guided reading lesson. A literacy methods professor wanted to observe the kindergarten teacher model interactive writing or sharing the pen (something which had been difficult for students to observe in their live field placements). With prior planning, requests were easily accommodated in the classroom teacher's normal daily schedule. Teachers e-mailed the lesson plan prior to the scheduled observation. Students were encouraged to follow the plan and match what they observed with what had been planned. Detours taken from the original lesson plan were frequently a source of questions and reflection in the debriefing talks following each observation.

Immediately following the 20- to 30-minute observation, the classroom teacher moved to the school's collaboratory and held an interactive session with the college students, including questions and answers. Initially, students seemed quiet during the question-and-answer period. In spite of this generation's increased use of technology, seeing themselves on TV and being asked to speak into a microphone as the camera focused on them was novel and unsettling for them. Almost all students who participated reported that they had never been in the distance learning room prior to the guided observation. The students seemed to need encouragement and prompts for asking questions. It appeared that they felt uncomfortable voicing a question to the classroom teacher in front of peers while the camera focused on them. Students were encouraged to write down a question or thoughts that occurred during the observation, with the intent of asking the teacher during the debriefing. Additionally, the project leader and the instructor would pose questions (during the observation) about what the teacher appeared to be doing and saying, and suggested

that students should ask the teacher to clarify these points during the debriefing. Questions commonly asked by the students centered around specific aspects of a lesson plan, the reaction of the children to the lesson, and what the teacher planned to do in a follow-up lesson. Students asked about teaching strategies, the children's behavior, curriculum requirements, discipline, family involvement, and differences between charter and public schools. Students frequently queried the teacher about a specific child's behavior and the teacher's use of different behavior management strategies. Another common question was how the teacher acquired ideas for a particular lesson, and how long it took to prepare and plan the entire lesson.

Students' Reactions

From surveys collected during the initial phase of the guided observations, students reported a positive reaction to this virtual field experience and an increased understanding of the realities of teaching and urban schools. It was revealing to read some of their misunderstandings and sobering to realize the work still needing to be done in teacher-education programs to uncover and discuss misperceptions and biases.

The obvious strength of this experience is being able to look over the shoulder of a skilled professional as she demonstrates the concepts we have read and talked about. Nothing (short of actually doing it) makes a concept clearer than seeing it actively and accurately portrayed in real-world settings.

This experience gave us an unedited picture of a teacher and students in action. It was great to see what we've learned about in every education class in an actual setting, not just words in some text.

I have gained more confidence. It is easy to read information in a textbook or watch videos, but to actually see everything implemented live by a teacher who is unable to go back and redo or erase mistakes...This was so inspiring and gave me a realistic view that everything is not always going to be perfect and that it does not have to be either.

I expected a bunch of wild, out of control children. What I saw was a group of bright, well-behaved children with just as much potential as other children.

I was much more afraid of urban schools before this experience. There are a lot more similarities to suburban schools than I previously thought.

REFLECTIVE MEDIATION-IN-ACTION

Mediated reflection using a virtual field experience evolved and changed over several semesters. After three semesters of scheduling guided observations and receiving positive student feedback, the project added additional open observation times and invited all students enrolled in any section (usually six or seven) of Introduction to Literacy, an early course in the teacher-education program, to take advantage of the opportunity to watch good teachers teach literacy.

A graduate student was hired to monitor the open sessions, but the teachers at the school were unable to leave their classrooms for the question-and-answer period due to the frequency of the open observation times (three mornings a week for one-and-a-half hours).

The open observation model proved problematic for many reasons. Few students were able to come to the distance learning room in the mornings because of other course commitments. Instructors had other teaching responsibilities and could not be there to observe alongside the students. The classroom teachers at the school felt burdened by having to "go live" so many hours in one week.

Reflecting on the data collected, we found that the students reported experiences of using video-conferencing to conduct the guided observations as valuable. The guided observations, though valuable and positive, were still disconnected and needed to be included in the content of individual courses if faculty were to become convinced to use class time to fulfill the field experience requirement. Following one semester of combining some scheduled guided observations including student/teacher debriefing sessions, and adding open observation times which proved ineffective, we decided to develop a model using a class-embedded virtual field experience. One course section of the Introduction to Literacy class served as the pilot for the project.

After assessing feedback from preservice teachers, instructors, and the classroom teachers, it seemed that the true value of observation for preservice teachers lay in the opportunity to hear classroom teachers reflect on their teaching immediately after a lesson, to have their instructor mediate discussion, and to integrate the virtual observation into college classroom conversations and activities. This led to reconceptualizing and implementing phase two of the virtual field experiences.

Phase II: Using Technology to Meditate Reflection in a Course-Linked Virtual Field Experience

Reflection is a complex, abstract concept. Though most educators state that it is an important trait for teachers to possess, it has become a difficult term to concretely define and even more difficult to determine how to prepare teachers to be reflective practitioners, especially in unfamiliar cultural contexts. The preservice teachers quoted in the Instructor's Vignette show how traditional field experience conditions perpetuate limited opportunity for reflection. Frequently, instructors send class participants to different schools

Figure 1. Instructor's vignette

Instructor's Reflection

The first semester, I taught the Introduction to Literacy class using a traditional field experience model. Throughout the fifteen-week semester, students went to various schools to observe in the classroom for a total of ten hours. The students kept observation logs and wrote a culminating paper describing their experience. This field experience was problematic in a number of ways. Because many of the preservice teachers were non-traditional students and local schools are at capacity with teacher education students (there are nine institutions preparing teachers within a fifty mile radius), placing students for observations was always difficult.

A second difficulty with traditional observations was students were watching one 45 minute to one hour lesson with no context of what happened prior to or what would happen in the future. There was no way to control for good, bad or indifferent teaching, and I was unsure whether the students would even recognize the quality of the teaching they observed. The students were very quick to judge the teachers and the children's behaviors without reflecting on what they were seeing. They just reacted. Compounding that, students all observed different classes at different times, so it was impossible to have class conversations regarding the observations. Often what they observed in their separate schools was disconnected to the conversations, readings and activities taking place in class.

These issues led to a discussion with the project director about other possible formats for observation. The following semester we decided to have students utilize an open observation plan at the distance-learning laboratory. The teachers agreed to take turns being observed for three mornings a week for one and a half hours at a time. After the observations occurred, the preservice teachers were excited to talk about what they observed. Again though, only two to three students of a class of twenty-four observed the same lesson, and I, as the instructor, was unable to observe any of the lessons. A major complaint of the preservice teachers was that the open observation times were not convenient for them since the school taught literacy in the morning and most college students had a full schedule of classes in the morning. There were issues with the technology not working on several occasions further frustrating the preservice teachers.

Once again, with the help of the project liaison, we re-conceptualized the field experience. This time, we decided to utilize class time to facilitate and mediate the field experience observations. Because this is a critical course, prior to the field-based literacy methods classes held in professional development schools, agreeing to give up class time were very difficult. One stipulation was that the observations had to be integrated with the content of our college course. The project liaison and I met with the teachers from the school. The teachers were each given a copy of the syllabus with topics, assignments, and dates (Appendix A). We discussed which topics would be best for observation and which teacher's style was best suited to that topic. We determined that, after the lesson, the teacher would go into the collaboratory and reflect on her teaching and answer the preservice teachers' questions.We agreed on six observations and determined the dates to correspond with course content. After each observation, I posted one question on a collaborative Web-based discussion

Continued on following page

Vignette continued

group site (Appendix B). All students were required to respond. They were encouraged to respond to others' postings.

My misgivings about relinquishing precious class time for the observations were eliminated about ten minutes into the first observation. The students (and I) were mesmerized by the classroom teaching. The discussions on Blackboard and in class were far richer than the old "field experience paper" that was required during previous semesters. Because we all had a common observation experience connected to our classroom readings and discussions, we could dialogue based on our personal interpretations. This allowed us to debate, break down stereotypes, and change some of our notions of teaching. After the final observation, I posed the following questions:

On a scale of 1 (poor) to 10 (great), how would you rate the usefulness and the relevance of our observations in the distance-learning lab? How did these observations enhance your learning? What did you get in the observations that would not have been possible by observing in person? Do you feel you missed out on anything by not observing in person? What might it have been?

Every student rated the experience an 8, 9 or 10. Comments from students included:

...one of the great things about observing in the lab was that you were able to communicate with the teachers and have them do plans on what we were learning about in class...

We didn't have to get into a car and drive somewhere and only spend 30 minutes in the classroom. Then the students are not going to behave normally because someone is new and they will act up for the time that I am there.

We did not interrupt their learning process and got to see how the kids really do act during a typical day.
...we could talk about the events from the observation as a class and we had the opportunity to observe the things that we were learning about.

I did like that we did this as a class, so that all of us were on the same page and could discuss some of the effective as well as ineffective practices that some of the teachers were taking. If we would have all went to different schools, and seen different exercises being implemented in the classroom, our discussions would not have gone very far as none of our classmates would have known what we were talking about. Also, we cannot be guaranteed that what we would have observed would have reinforced the concepts that we were learning about in the classroom.

In my opinion, one of the best things that came out of these observations is the knowledge that we gained as a result of talking with the cooperating teachers. When doing observations in classrooms, it is rare that we are able to talk with the teacher after we have seen her in action. Talking with the teachers after observing them allowed us to grasp a true understanding of what they did and why, and allowed us to ask them questions if we were unclear about any of the exercises that they did with their students.

Continued on following page

Vignette continued

It seems clear the mediated field experiences were more meaningful to the preservice teachers and enhanced the classroom readings, discussions and activities. Final evidence of the success of the virtual field experience came from the department evaluation which all students are required to fill out at the end of the semester. In response to the question "What aspects of the course were most beneficial to you?" eleven students out of twenty, unprompted, mentioned the distance learning lab observations. Clearly I'm encouraged to continue to use this model. The evolution of planning for and thinking about this integrated field experience has enabled me to reflect on my own teaching. I find myself more intentional about including what we see in the observations into class activities and conversations. On one occasion we observed a vocabulary lesson. Following this, the students were required to present, with a group, a vocabulary mini-lesson. The students incorporated several strategies they observed the teacher from the charter school model during her vocabulary lesson into their mini-lessons. Rather than feeling students missed out on instructional time, I think the students have been enriched and their professional development supported by the video- conferencing experience.

for short periods of time with no opportunity to integrate what they observe in schools to course content or class conversations. In essence, students are left to observe and participate in individual field placements with limited opportunities for any meaningful discussion or reflection with an instructor or mentor.

To complicate matters further, reflection is not generally associated with teachers. Teaching is seen as immediate action, whereas reflection is perceived as a more academic action (Hatton & Smith, 1995). Additionally, it has been suggested that preservice teachers tend to revert to traditional notions of teaching and learning during student teaching. These assumptions may be further reinforced in a traditional teaching environment. If these beliefs are firmly held, teacher candidates are resistant to reflection and change (Yost, Sentner, & Forlenza-Bailey, 2000). Furthermore, it is often difficult for teacher candidates to even know what to reflect about (Dieker & Monda-Amaya, 1997). It is important, then, for teacher educators to facilitate this reflection before the teacher candidate reaches the point of student teaching. In the course-embedded vir-

tual field experience, preservice teachers were engaged in mediated reflection on teaching from three different viewpoints. Preservice teachers were watching and reflecting on the classroom teacher's teaching. Simultaneously, the college instructor was watching, reflecting, and talking with them about the classroom teacher's teaching, and finally they were hearing the classroom teacher reflect on their own teaching during the question-and-answer period. Contrasted to the traditional field experience, where the preservice teacher is alone in a classroom watching and observing and returns to campus without time for debriefing with a classroom teacher, the virtual field experience can simultaneously provide four two-way communication opportunities: students and classroom teacher, instructor and students, instructor and classroom teacher, and student to student.

The teacher educator must "induce disequilibrium and cognitive conflict" in the learner to prepare him/her for critical reflection (Yost et al., 2000, p. 42). As the instructor's reflections in the vignette suggests, the instructor can mediate reflection through a common virtual field experience. The instructor can facilitate reflection by posing questions before, during, and after the observation (Appendix B). Preservice teachers can observe the classroom teacher's thought processes while she/he responds to questions posed following each observation.

Reflective teachers and teacher candidates develop a *habit* of continually learning from experience. According to Whipp (2003), reflective teacher candidates have the ability to stand back from their own assumptions and biases to notice problems in their practice. They can then reframe problems in light of multiple perspectives and take action that is informed by reframing. As shown in the students' comments, preservice teachers were forced to confront their biases and assumptions of urban schools and children by having the opportunity to observe, reflect on what they were seeing, and then speak directly with the classroom teachers following each observation.

Reflectivity appears to develop in stages. Researchers have found that teachers who are reflective move from a singular focus on technical issues surrounding the delivery of lessons when they first enter the teaching field, to critical reflection, where master teachers regularly examine the technical, practical, social, and moral issues inher-

ent in their design of the learning environment in their classroom from multiple perspectives. Master teachers are also able to make changes to their teaching that improve student learning based on a variety of sometimes competing factors. These teachers take responsibility for their own learning and that of their students (Giovannelli, 2003; Hatton & Smith, 1995; Truesdell, 2004; Yost, Sentner, & Forlenza-Bailey, 2000).

Videoconferencing, as described in this project, provides a unique forum for preservice teachers to be in a field experience environment where reflection dominated the conversations with the college instructor and the classroom teachers. For example, they might (and did) question teachers about the details of their lesson plans by asking how long something took to plan or prepare (singular focus), yet have the opportunity to hear a response from the teacher who would speak with them about how that lesson looked in the first year that she taught it and the changes that had been made based on her own reflection on practice.

Our attempt in both phases of this project was to move preservice teachers from reporting what they observed, which is evidenced in early iterations of the traditional field experience, to more

Figure 2. Opportunities for mediated reflection in traditional and virtual field experiences

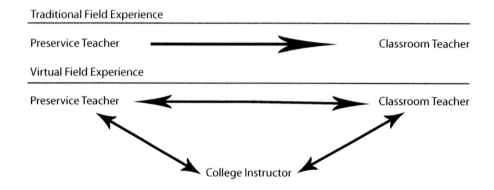

critical reflection based on a common mediated experience.

NEW TECHNOLOGIES BRING BOTH CHALLENGES AND PROMISE

Distance learning via interactive television (programmable two-way audio and video signals for communication using television monitors as a display) began at Buffalo State College in 1995 when the campus was granted funds to purchase equipment to create two distance learning classrooms and join the Western New York Fiber Network. At its peak, the network included over 100 classrooms in K-12 schools throughout the western eight counties in New York State. Buffalo State College built two of the original distance learning classrooms for two consortia within the network, Buffalo CityNet and Project Connect.

Over the past 11 years, the network was quietly phased out by nearly all of the original schools. The initial contracts with Verizon for access to the network were for ten years; for many school districts in Western New York, this contract period has ended. Using E-Rate funds, the original local BOCES centers have entered contract discussions with local cable companies to create a Gigabit Ether Network (Gig-E), which will continue to provide high-speed connections not only into specially-equipped classrooms but, via videoconferencing technologies, having the potential to make any classroom, any laboratory, or any media center into a distance learning facility.

The distance learning classrooms at Buffalo State College were built with a diffusion fund and grants via Buffalo's local telephone company, Verizon (formerly Nynex). Each classroom in the network contained the same equipment: eight 32-inch SONY television monitors; one teacher station that included a touch panel to control the equipment; a computer with Internet access; an Elmo document camera to display items; a telephone/fax machine; and two VCRs, one to play videotapes and the other to record class sessions to tape. Each classroom had a multifaceted sound system, student area and teacher station microphones, and separate student view and teacher cameras. Students and teachers in each classroom were able to see and hear each other at television broadcast quality audio and video.

Despite the successes, there have been challenges which discouraged the use of the present model for more preservice field experiences in teacher education. Access to high-quality schools with distance-learning facilities is unique and not commonly found. The consortia fees enabling the college to connect to King Center Charter School and belong to both Project Connect network the CityNet were $40,000 annually. Scheduled sessions are sometimes abruptly cancelled (due to unforeseen occurrences at the charter school), or the technology at one of the sites fails.

Many factors contributed to the decline in use of the original distance learning classrooms. Maintenance and repair of the equipment was costly and required trained technicians. All of the classrooms were built with grant or diffusion funds and, at the conclusion of the grant, there were districts that could not continue with the expensive consortia fees (approximately $16,000 yearly).

Given all of the changes to the original Fiber Network, the college and the charter school have continued their involvement due in part to the successful relationship of this project involving the education department and the charter school. The college will leave CityNet consortium this year, having recently purchased a videoconferencing unit that will allow expanding virtual field observations and offering college courses to other locations in Western New York and around the world.

The new videoconferencing unit, a Tandberg 6000 codec, costing $19,000, will be integrated into the old Fiber Network classroom. The classroom will be redesigned with upgrades to accommodate the change from fiber to Internet protocol (IP) video conferencing. The eight SONY television monitors will be removed and replaced with two movie-sized projection screens. Two projectors will be mounted to the ceiling of the classroom, one to display the teacher view and one to display the student's view of the other distance sites. A new teacher station will be incorporated, one that is consistent with other teacher stations in smart classrooms on campus, in order to facilitate faculty use. New furniture will be added along with wireless microphones, new cameras, and, with an eye to the future, an expandable option that will allow the college to add on video capture software and other emerging technologies.

Transferring from the current system will be expensive for both partners, but, in the long run, will potentially save thousands of dollars each year. The old system relied on a local phone company with fees and a network manager with additional fees. The new system will allow for an organization to manage the site internally. While even more cost-effective solutions (such as using the Internet with cameras positioned at both locations) are a possibility, closely monitoring these less-expensive solutions for quality of the virtual field experience is important.

While the use of interactive videoconferencing continues at educational institutions worldwide, there are other emerging technologies that will impact teaching and learning. As the cost of videoconferencing equipment and broadband connections continue to decline, and the quality of the audio and video increases, more schools may have the opportunity to become involved in virtual field experiences and other technology-supported preservice-education activities.

FUTURE TRENDS

This model suggests potential for addressing key issues in teacher preparation. Since the literature states that students tend to default to the model that they experience in student teaching, it seems

important for teacher-education programs to search for ways to increase the quality, diversity, and number of early field experiences which preservice teachers encounter. Observing and reflecting on many different teaching behaviors in a mediated environment prior to student teaching, preservice teachers have the opportunity to internalize multiple responses and, rather than defaulting to what they experienced as children in school or to their one student-teaching model, are prepared to respond more appropriately to individual children.

Feedback from the guided observations conducted in phase one of the project suggested the power of a single virtual observation in helping students alter their perceptions and attitudes about urban classrooms and teaching. With repeated mediated observations, students saw numerous respectful student/teacher interactions, more examples of positive behavior management and culturally-responsive teaching, and many targeted literacy strategies. Students could begin to rethink their notion of teaching and learning and move further along the continuum of internalizing reflective teaching rather than relying on a singular reactive response applied uniformly for all children. This leads us to speculate that repeated selective observations in different classroom settings (rural, exceptional education, culturally-responsive, and linguistically-diverse classrooms) would enable preservice teachers to have a repertoire of responses, strategies, and behaviors to bring to the first years of teaching in any setting.

Additional work by Garrett and Dudt (1998) suggests that videoconferencing can be effectively used to supervise student teachers. In a project using three wired sites and 24 student teachers, preliminary findings suggest that videoconferencing for student teaching supervision works across settings and disciplines with minimal preparation. Students, cooperating teachers, and supervisors can effectively collaborate in the supervisory process. Similar to the participants of the charter school project described in this chapter, Garrett and Dudt (1998) found that the human aspects of the planning, scheduling, and conferencing were more important to the quality of using distant supervision than the technical aspects (problems and quality) of using videoconferencing equipment.

Initial findings from the project described in this chapter suggest some benefits for all stakeholders (see Figure 3). Unique to this project is the opportunity for preservice teachers, college instructors, and classroom teachers to engage in observations and conversations simultaneously reflecting on the process of teaching and learning.

CONCLUSION

While the use of interactive videoconferencing continues at educational institutions worldwide, there are other emerging technologies that will impact teaching and learning. As the cost of videoconferencing equipment and broadband connections continue to decline, and the quality of the audio and video improves, more schools may have the opportunity to become involved in virtual field experiences and other technology-supported preservice-education activities. While we cannot prepare preservice teachers for every situation that they will encounter, we can do a better job of diversifying their teacher-preparation experiences by using opportunities like technology-mediated virtual field experiences.

REFERENCES

Adcock, P., & Austin, W. (2002, March). *Alternative classroom observation through two-way audio/video conferencing systems.* Paper presented at the Society for Information Technology and Teacher Education Conference.

Figure 3. Benefits for stakeholders

Preservice teachers can…
- Observe one teacher and classroom at the same time
- Eliminate travel time and transportation issues
- Concentrate without being distracted by being inside the classroom environment
- Gain more opportunities for mediated reflection with an instructor
- Ask questions about what is happening immediately and in later class sessions

Talk simultaneously with college instructors and classroom teachers about teaching and learning

College faculty can….
- Request and plan specific lessons related to course readings and assignments
- Supervise all students in their virtual field placement simultaneously
- Have the opportunity for "in-the-moment" reflection on teaching practice and refer back to scenarios that the whole class observed
- Ask questions of the classroom teacher in the presence of the preservice teachers to raise teachable moments, thus intentionally connecting theory to practice

Talk simultaneously with classroom teachers and preservice teachers about teaching and learning

Classroom teachers can…
- Eliminate the distraction of too many adults in the classroom
- Model good practices and think more intentionally about their teaching and student learning
- Influence the curriculum of teacher-education preparation
- Participate in research influencing teaching and learning
- Learn more about current theory and practice in teacher-education programs
- Share "practical experiences" gained from classroom teaching
- Talk simultaneously with college instructors and preservice teachers about teaching and learning

Boccia, J., Fontain, P., Lucas, F. Michael. (2002, March). *Looking into classrooms: A technology mediated observation program for preservice teachers.* Paper presented at Society for Information Technology and Teacher Education Conference.

Cochran-Smith, M. (1995). Uncertain allies: Understanding the boundaries of race and teaching. *Harvard Education Review, 56,* 541-570.

Darling-Hammond, L. (1992). Accountability for professional practice. In M. Levine (Ed.), *Professional practice schools: Linking teacher education and school reform* (pp. 81-104). New York: Teachers College Press.

Darling-Hammond, L. (1994). *Professional development schools: Schools for developing a profession.* New York: Teachers College Press.

Dieker, L.A., & Monda-Amaya, L. E. (1997). Using problem solving and effective teaching frameworks to promote reflective thinking in preservice special educators. *Teacher Education and Special Education, 20*(1), 22-36.

Fountain, C., & Evans, D. (1994). Beyond shared rhetoric: A collaborative change model for integrating preservice and in-service urban education delivery systems. *Journal of Teacher Education, 45,* 218-227.

Garrett, J., & Dudt, K. (1998). Using video conferencing to supervise student teachers. In *Proceedings of the SITE 98: Society for Information Technology & Teacher Education International Conference,* Washington, DC: Vol. 9 (pp. 142-150).

Groulx, J. (2001). Changing preservice teacher perceptions of minority schools. *Urban Education, 36,* 60-92.

Hatton, N., & Smith, D. (1995). Reflection in teacher education towards definition and implementation. *Teaching and Teacher Education, 11*(1), 33-49.

Hoot, J., Massey, C., Barnett, M., Henry, J., & Ernest, J. (2001). A former church as a center of excellence for children. *Childhood Education, 77*(6), 386-392.

Irving, K. (2001). Innovations in observing children: Use of new technologies. In Yelland, N. (Ed.) *Promoting meaningful learning: Innovations in educating early childhood professionals* (pp. 77-83). Washington, DC: National Association for the Education of Young Children.

Levin, R. (1990, November). *An unfulfilled alliance. The lab school in teacher education: Two case students, 1910-1980.* Paper presented at the Annual Meeting of the History of Education Society, Atlanta, GA.

Levine, M. (1992). *Professional practice schools: Linking teacher education and school reform.* New York: Teachers College Press.

MacNaughton, R., & Johns, F. (1993). The professional development school: An emerging concept. *Contemporary Education, 64*(4), 215-218.

National Council for Accreditation of Teacher Education (NCATE) (2002). Professional standards for the accreditation of schools, departments, and colleges of education (p. 4). Retrieved March 19, 2006, from http://ncate.org/documents/unit_stnds_2002.pdf

Strudler, N., & Wetzel, K. (1999). Lessons from exemplary colleges of education: Factors affecting technology integration in preservice programs. *Educational Technology Research and Development, 47,* 63-81.

Teitel, L. (1999). Looking toward the future by understanding the past: The historical context of professional development schools. *Peabody Journal of Education, 74*(3/4), 6-15.

Truesdell, K. S. (1998). Broadening professional development through school-university collaboration. Thesis (Ed.)—State University of New York at Buffalo.

Whipp, J. L. (2003). Scaffolding critical reflection in online discussions. *Journal of Teacher Education, 54*(4), 321-333.

Yost, D. S., Sentner, S. M., & Forlenza-Bailey, A. (2000). An examination of the construct of critical reflection: Implications for teacher education programming in the 21st century. *Journal of Teacher Education, 51*(1), 39-49.

ENDNOTES

*   The name "The Real World" is copyrighted by MTV.

[1]   Preparing Tomorrow's Teachers to Use Technology (2001-2004). Title: Technology = Access: Teaching Future Urban Teachers Project, U.S. Department of Education, P342A010061

[2]   Preparing Tomorrow's Teachers to Use Technology (2004-2007). Title: Reflective Mediation Through the Use of Technology, U.S. Department of Education, P342A030088

APPENDIX A

Sample Schedule of Mediated Observations in Literacy Instruction

September 13: Community building—Kindergarten
September 22: Emergent reading/writing—1st Grade

September 29: Phonics Lesson—1st Grade
October 27: Vocabulary—2nd Grade
November 10: Poetry—2nd Grade
November 17: Reader's workshop—3rd Grade
December 1: Assessment—Reading support instructor

APPENDIX B

Discussion Board Questions Posted Following Classroom Observations

Observation 1: How did Ms. Lockhart model reading, writing, listening, and speaking? How did it enhance the children's learning?

Observation 2: What dispositions did Miss Ortiz display that are important for teachers of young children? Why are these important? How do these dispositions enhance learning?

Observation 3: So far in our observations, we observed lessons in kindergarten and first grade. This week, we observed a 3rd grade classroom. What did you notice about the comparison in pacing and length of activity, conversations between teacher and child, and behavior management strategies? Thinking about the text reading, activities/discussions in class, and the observation, were the teacher's vocabulary strategies effective? Explain. What was one strength? What would you have done differently?

Observation 4: What were your thoughts and feelings about the content of today's lesson (poetry in 2nd grade), what the children brought to the lesson (and how they responded), how the teacher handled the interactions, and anything else you reflect on what you observed.

Observation 5: Ms. Schwartz discussed early on that she was going to do assessment rather than testing with the students. How does this correlate to our discussion in class on assessment versus evaluation? How can this type of assessment be useful to you as a teacher?

Chapter XIV
Virtual Field Trips:
Advantages and Disadvantages for Educators and Recommendations for Professional Development

Dean T. Spaulding
The College of Saint Rose, USA

Patricia A. Ranney
The College of Saint Rose, USA

ABSTRACT

The purpose of this chapter is to provide a brief history of videoconferencing when used as virtual field trips in educational settings, and to discuss some of the various aspects in which they can be implemented. In addition, this chapter focuses on the unique benefits to students and teachers as noted in the literature that videoconferencing field trips can bring to the learning community, and some of the challenges that many educators, eager to use this technology, have experienced. Speculation as to what the future will hold for virtual field trips and where the technology will possibly take us is also discussed.

INTRODUCTION

The purpose of this chapter is to provide an overview of the history of virtual field trips and a discussion about their recent increase in use in America's classrooms. In addition, this chapter clarifies some of the many operational definitions and terms that currently exist in the literature regarding videoconferencing field trips, to document ways in which educators have integrated this technology into their classrooms to provide richer learning experiences for their students.

Despite the large volume of literature depicting positive experiences in using virtual field trips, there are certainly challenges and disadvantages to their use. One noted disadvantage is the wide range of definitions and descriptions used by proponents. Although this range of definitions is certainly helpful in bringing multiple perspectives to the arena, Clark, Hosticka, Schriver, and Bedell (2002) and others report that such a wide array might actually be confusing for educators who are new to the concept. In fact, Clark et al. believe that the enormous amount of varying descriptions and definitions may actually have adverse effects and, in turn, discourage, rather than encourage, educators from implementing aspects of a virtual field trip into their classrooms. Professional development groups and those that provide such enrichment opportunities to teachers interested in implementing VFT should be aware of these benefits and challenges and address them during training.

Another aspect that appears to be consistent in the literature on virtual field trips is the lack of sufficient evaluation and empirical research to support their use. It appears that the majority of literature is comprised primarily of testimonials and first-hand accounts of teacher/developer perspectives rather than empirical research. In fact, rigorous evaluation methodologies and research studies appear to be limited, particularly those empirical studies that are cause-effect in nature. In addition to overviewing aspects of research on virtual field trips and their impact on students' achievement per se, this chapter will discuss the challenges often faced by educators in their delivery of virtual field trips and the utilization of information gained from these field trips. Additionally, we will proffer recommendations that address these issues for the novice, as well as the expert field trip "traveler."

BACKGROUND

The traditional school field trip as described above, but within much shorter distances and with far greater limitations, has, without a doubt, been the main staple of enrichment for K-12 education.

Long before there were thoughts of technology integration, the traditional field trip to a museum, local farm, or factory was one method in which educators could provide their students with an alternative forum for learning. A review of literature on the traditional school field trip reveals that while much of the scientific documentation supporting its use has focused on student recall and memory of events, there has been little evidence to support this recall in terms of classroom curriculum and overall learning (Hudson & Fivush, 1991).

In the 21st century, the traditional school field trip has changed. No more do teachers have to spend their days organizing chaperones, loading students onto crowded buses, taking periodic head counts, and monitoring the bus ride home, all for the purpose of visiting a local museum or historical battle site a few miles from school. Virtual fields trips (VFTs) are providing "virtually" thousands of educators and their students the opportunity to visit many exciting attractions without ever leaving their seats (Ashton, 2002; Hayne, 2002; Roush, 2004; Sullivan & Smith, 2001). This technology integration has allowed many educators in America's schools to exceed time and physical distance (Klemm & Tuthill, 2003) during a morning field trip to the Great Wall of China, the Grand Canyon, and the Statue of Liberty, and be back in time for lunch.

Born out of early videoconferencing, virtual field trips have increased dramatically in the last decade in both their development by providers (e.g., museums) and the frequency of their use by consumers (e.g., school classrooms) (Klemm & Tuthill, 2003). Although many still hold the notion of a typical VFT as being a visit to the Museum of Modern Art (MOMA) in New York City or the Smithsonian in Washington D.C., the fact is that, in their rise to popularity, VFTs have taken on many new forms. In reality, educators are engaging in many different types of field trips: visiting the desk of a best-selling children's author for an in-depth discussion of a book that the class is currently reading or visiting the inside of a bluebird housing box to monitor and observe young fledglings as they are being fed by their attentive parents. The places and interactions are "virtually" endless.

DEFINITIONS OF VIDEOCONFERENCING

As many educators are discovering, virtual field trips (VFTs), also known as virtual field trips (VFTs) can be extraordinarily simple or intensely complex in content, presentation, production, and interaction. Regardless of how narrow or how elaborate, VFTs share common characteristics that are critical in formalizing an operational definition. An equally crucial component of conceptualizing an operational definition of a VFT is recognizing what does not always qualify, nor disqualify, a learning tool that can be characterized as a VFT.

Woerner (as cited in Cox & Su, 2004) defines a VFT as "a journey taken without actually making a trip to the site" (p. 113); however, a VFT does not necessarily attempt to recreate reality through what has come to be known as *virtual reality*; rather, note Cox and Su (2004), "It simply attempts to place further independence in the user's hands by allowing observations to be made without being on the actual site or having a lecturer at hand to explain" (p. 113). Cox and Su's opinion that VFTs are not to be replacements of "the real thing" is widely held and written about among most of the VFT community.

For our purposes, however, Woerner's as well as Cox's and Su's definitions are too restrictive and confining. They fail to recognize that there are interactive VFTs that *do* have a virtual or live lecturer who *is* "at hand to explain." Their definitions ignore VFT methods that enable the student to interact either immediately or in a delayed manner. Within the literature, these live components are referred to as *point-to-point field trips,* and contain characteristics much more in-

dicative of active videoconferencing, whereby the technology brings together one or more groups of people for a live, interactive discussion or learning exchange.

A virtual field trip, simply stated, brings to the student what the student might not ordinarily be exposed to outside of a standard classroom setting. More technically stated, our definition of a VFT includes the following: A VFT utilizes communication technology (e.g., videoconferencing, teletraining, online classes, the Internet, DVDs/videotapes, etc.) to enhance the learning experience. (For the purposes of this chapter, we shall not define "to enhance the learning experience," as the type and purpose of a researcher's study will determine this.) A VFT allows one to travel virtually to:

1. Real sites (e.g., Grand Canyon, zoos, White House, rain forests, Titanic wreckage, museums, other countries, etc.)
2. Imaginary/unreachable sites (e.g., other planets; the Earth's core)
3. Time periods (Dark Ages, Jurassic Period, the future)
4. Experiences/events (Civil War, being inside a tornado, Colonial living)

A VFT also includes virtual classes, thus encompassing virtual schools and distance learning. Our discussion will focus on virtual field trips involving sites, time periods, and experiences/events.

All of the above have the ability to be presented live or recorded, with synchronous (immediate) interaction, asynchronous (delayed) interaction, or no visible interaction on the part of student and educator. Our concern is interaction from the perspective of the student.

Immediate interaction allows students to communicate synchronously with the instructor/educator, other students, and/or technical system, thus allowing the student to become a highly-active participant in the learning process. This particular approach is often referred to in the literature as point-to-point. The ability to interact in real-time depends on the type of technology and the time of participation in the VFT. For example, if 8th graders in a California school district were visiting the White House through a live, interactive VFT, two-way audio capability throughout that tour would allow the students to ask questions to the educator conducting that tour. Although a student who missed the live VFT would not reap the advantages of synchronous interaction, he could still benefit greatly from a tape of that trip, wherein he could hear the questions and comments of his peers, questions and comments he might have put forth himself. Interaction would not be visible, but the learning experience itself would not be completely passive, as it would have been if a classroom teacher had merely lectured about the White House.

The VFT as an experience could also provide immediate interaction for students. For example, educators could play characters during a specific time period, responding to student questions as people living in that time period would respond, that is, they would role-play, never coming out of character. In this manner, the students would be actively participating in and learning through conversation, which lends itself to the increased questioning so critical in constructivist theory.

The scope of virtual field trips is limited only by the creativity and knowledge of those who are technically capable of developing them and their success by those who are able to incorporate an appropriate pedagogical methodology. As cited in Newman (2006), authors such as Greenberg (2004) and Omatseye (1999) note that the interactivity, a key characteristic of VFTs, combined with a student-centered instructional approach can make for an incredibly rich learning situation.

Through the use of VFT, students have the opportunity to interact with educators who will have far more expertise, interest, knowledge, and teaching ability than ever possible in the standard classroom.

Paradigm

The flow of communication between and among communicators is central to a meaningful VFT paradigm and can best be discussed by building on Farrell's (1999) model entitled "The Four Conversations," which details four specific dialogues that contribute to learning. These include:

1. The "conversations" a learner has with an instructor
2. The "conversations" among groups of learners
3. The "conversations" a learner has with instructional resources
4. The "conversations" a learner has with himself or herself (i.e., reflection)

When examining this model in terms of learning, we found it to be somewhat

closed and vague, and, more importantly, ignoring the critical element of time. Clarification of the roles of stakeholders or participants is needed, and the concept of time needs to be incorporated in order to provide a more functional paradigm. (As a caveat, it should be noted that no single paradigm could address every VFT, because not every VFT is live, instructional resources are not available to all students, and educators and their availability vary).

In the paradigm, dialogue #1, *the conversations a learner has with an instructor,* is unclear as to the identification of the "instructor." The instructor may include a number of people, including the individual(s) guiding the VFT, playing characters/performing during the VFT, conducting experiments/teaching during the VFT, and/or the regular classroom instructor.

Dialogue #2, *the conversations among groups of learners,* has a similar problem in its lack of explanation as to the identification of "learners." Virtual field trips are not necessarily restricted to a single classroom; learners could include other students in the same school, home-schooled students, and students from other geographic regions and/or cultures, just to name a few.

"Instructional resources" are also unclear as presented in the above. We clarify this by stating that there needs to be not only "conversations with," but "access *and instruction or instructions to*" the hardware, software, and any print materials used during or in conjunction with the actual VFT, and *after* the VFT.

In addition, we add a fifth and sixth group of individuals to whom the learner would communicate as a result of VFTs (see Figure 1). We include (1) non-academic individuals who did not participate with the VFTs (e.g., parents, siblings, friends, other adults, other students, etc.) and (2) other non-participating instructors with whom the student interacts. Having identified all the communicants, we also employ the concept of time in our paradigm and refer to "interaction" rather than "conversation." Conversation implies vocalization, which is certainly not a necessary function of communication. We have identified two types of interaction: synchronous interaction (e.g., real-time discussion, instant messaging,

immediate "game-playing") and asynchronous interaction (e.g., e-mail, chat boards, additional readings, self-tests).

From the perspective of a single student, the ideal VFT paradigm appears with the following:

VFTs AND RESEARCH STUDIES

As noted in examining the literature on VFTs, it is quite clear that the majority of work is not in the nature of educational research. In fact, it is fair to say that the majority of information and writing on the topic of VFTs tends to be considerably limited to non-research materials, which consist primarily of narrative descriptions. For the most part, these descriptions are first-hand teacher accounts of actual field trip experiences and practices. In some cases, universities or school districts have reported overview and descriptions of larger federally-funded projects, although, in some cases, evaluation documenting both formative and summative findings is present. The

Figure 1. Ideal VFT paradigm

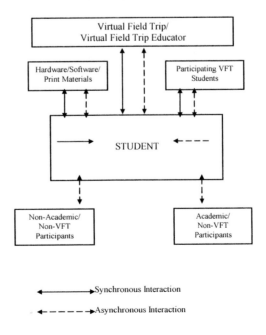

limited empirical evidence on VFTs tends to be focused on methodologies that employ self-report-type measures on behalf of participants or staff involved in the project. These studies have taken place across a wide range of K-12 settings and content areas where video field trips have occurred. While we are certainly not attempting here to devalue the importance of any one methodology, such self-reporting perceptional studies of VTFs do not answer the question on many educators' and school administrators' minds: What are the academic gains made by students whose instructors incorporate VFTs into the curriculum and classroom?

As noted earlier, there appears to be a limited number of rigorous studies that truly examine the impact of VFTs on its relationship to student learning and academic achievement. Cavanaugh, Gillian, Kromrey, Hess, and Blomeyer conducted one example of such a study in 2004. This meta-analysis examined the effect of 14 Web-based distance education experiences on K-12 student outcomes. Overall, Cavanaugh et al. found that there were no significant differences in performance between students who participated in online programs and those who were taught in face-to-face classrooms. Advocates of VFTs, however, are quick to point out that results of such investigations are insignificant, because outcomes of a teacher implementing a virtual field trip may not be measurable in the way that they have been measured traditionally (e.g., standardized accountability assessments).

Perhaps the most interesting studies are a series of short, quasi-experimental studies conducted by Newman (2006). The overall purpose of these studies is to examine the impact of using VFTs on students' affective and cognitive education outcomes when compared to non-users of VFTs. While affective measures focused on gathering student interest in content and material being delivered, cognitive gains were measured using student general and content-area specific grade point averages (GPAs). Baseline GPA data also

were used to control for variation among and across groups. Findings concluded that students who participated in VFTs reported more and greater interest in the content that was being provided. In addition, these students also reported a greater desire to learn more about a topic or content area than those students who participated in the traditional classroom didactic setting (Newman, 2006). As for students' cognitive outcomes, Newman reported that for six of the nine studies conducted, students exposed to VFTs had significantly higher outcome scores than students who did not receive the treatment. Without a doubt, this work is a definite asset to the literature on VFTs, and one that is desperately needed by advocates and supporters of VFTs at a time when federal and state funding for technology is being cut for lack of such quasi-experimental evidence required under NCLB. We, the authors, encourage other researchers and program developers in VFTs to continue working in all areas of research and to replicate and expand on such work as described above, thus providing further support that links VFTs with improvement in student outcomes and achievement.

ISSUES, CONTROVERSIES, AND PROBLEMS

Advantages of VFT

The literature on VFTs is "overflowing" with narratives and discussion pieces that support the use of this technology in classrooms, noting many advantages. As we described earlier in this chapter, one obvious advantage for a teacher using a VFT is the time factor in bringing an entire class or multiple classes to a place that might not otherwise be possible. In some cases, particularly for those educators working in more urban areas, a field trip to an internally-recognized museum might be physically possible, and, in fact, it might be something that has been traditionally conducted by the district. In this particular situation, a certain advantage of the VFT is that it can be used as a precursor to the actual field trip. Through a VFT, educators can introduce students to specific aspects about the museum or exhibit, thus focusing students' attention and alerting them to be cognizant of certain things that they might not remember to look at otherwise (Clark et al., 2002). Professional development for teachers interested in VFTs should provide such educators with both a sufficient background in delivering VFTs, but also provide enough support for teachers to expand on the possibilities that VFTs can offer to creative educators.

Clark et al. (2002), and others point out that VFTs may hold advantages for educators working in districts or buildings with unusually-high absenteeism rates. Unlike a traditional field trip whereby students who were absent on a particular day would not be able to take part in any aspect of the trip other than to "hear about it" later from other students or from the teacher as it was integrated into future lessons, VFTs allow even absent students to experience some piece of the field trip. While these students would miss the actual "live" VFT, aspects of the trip can be saved and recorded virtually, including links to both support and extend the learning experiences for students. VFTs also provide students with the opportunity for longitudinal or extended study through multiple visits to the site over a period of time.

One distinct advantage to VFTs is that there are so many possibilities, particularly alternative approaches to using them. VFTs do not necessarily require the use of group settings to be deemed successful. In fact, one of the interesting aspects of VFTs is that they can be conducted on an individual basis, as well. One example of this practice would be a high-school student working in an open-ended, inquiry-based course. This student could set up weekly one-on-one sessions with a mentor, an expert in the content that the student is investigating, to further refine a research

question, examine research and literature on the topic, discuss data collection tools and efforts, and so forth. In the mid-1990's, we evaluated a science program with a mentor component very similar to this one, with students using e-mail to communicate with mentors (Newman & Spaulding, 2001) rather than a VFT, which was still in its infancy, and found the communication to be highly productive.

Although some authors do note both logistical and content limitations of VFTs, surprisingly, a review of literature on VFTs turned up very few articles that noted harsh criticisms of VFTs or even questioned their usefulness. One interesting aspect of VFTs is that even the strongest of proponents recognize the importance of the traditional field trip. In fact, even those who actively support VFTs note that they are not a replacement for "the real thing," but that the two should be, whenever possible, used collaboratively for the richest learning experience.

Spicer and Stratford (2001) examined the perception of students in a higher-education setting to determine if they preferred the VFT or the actual field trip. While students reported that they enjoyed the VFT, they also noted that they would not want to give up or abandon the experiences that they had with the actual field trip. This is similar to studies and literature in this area that note that virtual field trips are not meant to be, nor probably will ever be, a complete replacement to actually traveling to the location and engaging in this experience with all of one's senses.

Disadvantages and Limitations

Even the most enthusiastic proponents of videoconferencing cannot help but note some of its disadvantages. Those providing professional development to teachers on VFTs should be aware of these disadvantages. One such disadvantage commonly identified in the literature is the issue surrounding expense. Aside from the initial expense of building videoconferencing capacity,

Motamedi (2001) also notes that another expense which needs to be carefully considered by school districts interested in videoconferencing is the cost of transmission. Motamedi notes that these costs can vastly differ depending on the type of transmission, the time of day that the transmission occurs, and its method (e.g., high-speed). For school districts entertaining the idea of implementing videoconferencing, both the initial start-up costs and the expense of delivering and maintaining videoconferences are key elements to consider. Unfortunately, for many districts, particularly those that already have limited technology capabilities in the building (e.g., being wired), these expenses become major challenges when working to implement videoconferencing in their K-12 settings. This may be particularly so for rural schools, who have traditionally been challenged institutionally by the physical distance in delivering new and innovative learning environments to students (Barker & Taylor, 1993).

An additional issue preempting many schools and teachers from participating in the virtual field trip experience may be time. Professional development for teachers using VFTs in their classrooms also must address this issue and provide teachers with a series of strategies to better use VFTs to address multiple learning experiences for students and use classroom, on-task time to its fullest. In today's classroom, time is perhaps one of the most endangered resources, particularly with the majority of emphasis now being placed on student outcomes and academic achievement for school accountability purposes. Even the most organized educator discovers that at the end of the school day, there is not enough time to cover everything. Although proponents are quick to point out that one of the advantages of video field trips is their ability to address multiple modalities and reach multiple learning standards and objectives in an integrated fashion, time to plan and coordinate such activities continues to be an issue in reaction to their increased use. Stainfield, Fisher, Ford, and Solem (2000), have examined the disadvantages of virtual classrooms in higher education settings for both national and international VFTs. Gender issues, difficulties for students with special needs, language barriers, and cultural differences have all been noted to be challenges for faculty conducting international field trips. There is no reason to believe that these same challenges, although we did not find specific mention of them in the K-12 literature, would not also apply to educators working in these settings.

FUTURE TRENDS AND CONCLUSION

While some believe that VFTs are merely buzzwords of the day for integrating technology (Clark et al., 2002), the demand for and use of virtual field trips will no doubt increase dramatically as school districts address a number of issues, from budget constraints to teacher shortages to new learning initiatives. While schools struggle with limited budgets, on-site field trips are often among the expendable programs. At the same time, many schools are increasing their technology funding and looking for ways to use their current technology. Virtual field trips will still provide students with a field trip experience, albeit not as sense-filled as an on-site trip, while potentially keeping costs down and employing technology that a school may already have available.

Futurists in the area of VFTs believe that VFTs will not only increase in use in the next five years, but will take on many new forms to address both individual learning needs, as well as dynamic teacher instruction. For example, in 1993, Halal and Liebowitz predicted that VFTs would be used by students to receive individual training "when and where they needed it" (p. 21), with students basically selecting the instructional times to meet both their learning needs and personal schedules.

Virtual Field Trips

REFERENCES

Ashton, T. (2002). New virtual field trips (Book). *Roeper Review, 24*(4), 236-238.

Barker, B. O., & Taylor, D. R. (1993). *An overview of distance learning and telecommunications in rural schools.* Paper presented at the 58th Annual Conference of the National Association of Counties, Chicago.

Cavanaugh, C., Gillian, J. K., Kromrey, J., Hess, M., & Blomeyer, R. (2004). *The effects of distance education on K-12 student outcomes: A meta-analysis.* Naperville, IL: Learning Point Associates.

Clark, K., Hosticka, A., Schriver, M., & Bedell, J. (2002). Computer-based virtual field trips. *ERIC Document.* Retrieved April 1, 2006, from EBSCOHost

Cox, S. E., & Su, T. (2004). Integrating student learning with practitioner experiences via virtual field trips. *Journal of Educational Media, 29*(2), 113-123.

Farrell, G. M. (1999). *The development of virtual education: A global perspective.* Vancouver, British Columbia: The Commonwealth of Learning.

Greenberg, A. (2004). Navigating the sea of research on videoconferencing-based distance education: A platform for understanding research into the technology's effectiveness and value. *Wainhouse Research.* Retrieved December 28, 2006, from http://www.wainhouse.com/files/papers/wrnavseadistedu.pdf

Halal, W. E., & Liebowitz, J. (1994). Telelearning: The multimedia revolution in Education. *The Futurist, 28*(6), 21-26.

Hayne, P. (2001). New virtual field trips (Book Review). *Media and Methods, 37*(7), 30-36.

Hudson, J. A., & Fivush, R. (1991). As time goes by: Sixth graders remember a kindergarten experience. *Applied Cognitive Psychology, 5,* 347-360.

Klemm, B. E., & Tuthill, G. (2003). Virtual field trips: Best practices. *International Journal of Institutional Media, 30*(2), 177-193.

Motamedi, V. (2001). A critical look at the use of videoconferencing in United States distance education. *Education, 122*(2), 386-394.

Newman, D. (2006). *The impact of multi-media videoconferencing on children's learning: Positive outcomes of use.* Paper presented at the Annual Meeting of the American Educational Research Association. San Francisco.

Newman, D. L., & Spaulding, D. T. (2001). *Evaluation of the science research in the high-school program: 2000-2001 program implementation* (Evaluation Report). State University of New York at Albany: The Evaluation Consortium.

Omatseye, J. N. (1999). Teaching through teleconferencing. *Learning and Leaning with Technology, 29*(6), 10-13.

Roush, N. (2004). Colonial Williamsburg virtual field trips. *Social Studies and the Young Learner, 16*(4), 29-32.

Spicer, J. I., & Stratford, J. (2001). Student perceptions of a virtual field trip to replace a real field trip. *Journal of Computer Assisted Learning, 17,* 345-354.

Stainfield, J., Fisher, P., Ford, B., & Solem, M. (2000). International virtual field trips: A new direction? *Journal of Geography in Higher Education, 24*(2), 255-262.

Sullivan, L., & Smith, S. A. (2001). Charting your journey to distance learning. *Multimedia Schools, 8*(5), 12. Retrieved December 28, 2006, from http://www.infotoday.com/mmschools/oct01/sullivan&smith.htm

199

Chapter XV
Enhancing Teacher Preparation through Videoconferencing Types

Harry Grover Tuttle
Syracuse University, USA

ABSTRACT

This chapter focuses on the enhancement of teacher preparation through various types of videoconferences and through various types of engagement within a videoconference. These can include: expert; university to school; peer-to-peer and meetings; multiple sessions; mentoring/observation; learning about videoconferencing; and interviewing/job searching. Both preservice students and their professors can benefit from involvement in videoconferencing. Teacher-preparation students become more engaged in the content through interactive activities, streaming video, blogs, discussion areas of programs, Webinars, shared applications, tele-education aspects of videoconferencing, and follow-up discussion boards. Instructors can improve the quality of their instruction to maximize learning by transforming their teacher-preparation classes into ones in which students have more in-depth and comprehensive experiences to prepare them for future teaching.

INTRODUCTION

The purpose of educational videoconferencing, people learning interactively by seeing, hearing, and sharing over distance in real-time, has remained constant over the years of videoconferencing. In 1995, a small group of teacher-preparation educators began to use Cornell University's CUSeeMe, the first commonly-used videoconferencing desktop program, to videoconference with classes from other universities, experts from other universities, and experts from outside the university (Wilkerson, 2006). Today, teacher-preparation instructors use videoconferencing to address many potential barriers to instruction such as student placements in distant locations, students living far away from the university, a growing number of critical topics to be covered in-depth for which the instructor may not be an expert, and the need to model global collaboration. Overall, educators can use the tool of videoconferencing to help better prepare their students for future employment as teachers and for future professional development.

Videoconferencing use is on the rise at universities. Northwestern University (2004) reported that in 2004 they conducted twenty-five videoconferences a week, and there was a growing increase in the request for this service; also, George Mason University increased its videoconferencing by 350% from 2002 to 2003 (DoIt Support Services of George Mason University, 2004). Teacher-preparation instructors are using it to communicate with colleagues about teacher-preparation issues, as well as with their students as an instructional tool in a multitude of ways that range from accessing virtual experts to observing student teachers in remote locations (Lehman & Richardson, 2004). Setups also vary; education instructors use formal videoconferencing room systems with multiple cameras and microphones as well as desktop/laptop videoconferencing systems with a portable microphone and camera to connect to students and colleagues. With the right support, university educators can videoconference with many students or colleagues (multi-point) just as easily as one-to-one (point-to-point).

The versatility of videoconferencing in education has led to a multitude of descriptive terms such as distance education, interactive videoconferencing, transmissive pedagogy, tele-teaching, visual collaboration, digital communication, computer-mediated learning, online learning, e-learning, Internet-based learning, or virtual learning. Teacher-preparation videoconferencing can range from a one-time educational use to a series of videoconferences within the class to a complete course conducted through this media. This chapter will not address videoconferencing as total course delivery, but as a component embedded within a class.

BACKGROUND

Before instructors in the field of P-12 teacher preparation utilize videoconferencing, they need to learn the advantages and disadvantages of its use. Frequently-cited advantages indicate that the use of videoconferencing:

- Lessens or eliminates travel time
- Is cost effective since a "visiting" expert or class has no travel costs
- Enables the participants to see and hear each other
- Allows for diverse perspectives from an audience outside of the classroom
- Provides a vehicle for global collaboration
- Allows for materials and presentations to be shared
- Provides access to experts and equipment that is unavailable in certain locations
- Permits a high level of interactivity
- Incorporates many multiple intelligences
- Requires little skill to run a videoconferencing session

On the other hand, educators acknowledge potential disadvantages of videoconferencing:

- It is synchronous so all participants have to be at the conference at the same time, regardless if one person is from Australia and one is from New York
- It may present a language issue if all participants do not speak the same language
- It requires an fast Internet connection
- It necessitates faculty and student preparation for an effective videoconference
- It depends on technology assistance if there is a major connectivity problem
- The quality of videoconferencing varies not only with the equipment, but also with the speed and quality of the Internet connection

- There may be a delay between the picture of a people speaking and their actual speaking
- A projection device is required for a class to see the other class
- Students may want to be passive as if they are watching TV
- Some students may feel that they do not have eye-to-eye contact with the instructor
- Students will need instruction in videoconferencing etiquette
- Use may be prohibited by firewall connectivity issues when working with P-12 schools
- They may have to verify that the connection is secure and safe (Tuttle, 1998)

When higher-education instructors search the literature and online resources for ideas on how to use videoconference in their teacher-preparation classes, they will encounter a preponderance of resources focused on the noninstructional aspects of videoconferencing, such as the equipment (Northwestern University Information Technology, 2005a; University of Ulster, 2002), instructor's perceptions about videoconferencing (Woods, 2005), instructors' perceptions about training (*Kosak,* Manning, Dobson, Rogerson, Cotnam, Colaric, & McFadden, *2004), videoconferencing etiquette (Instructional Services of Penn State, 2003), and the cost effectiveness of videoconferencing (Adams, 2002).* These reflect knowledge of or information on videoconferencing systems or perceptions about technology, but not how videoconferencing can help students learn and promote professional growth (Lai, Pratt, & Grant, 2003).

In addition, much of the higher-education videoconferencing resources focus on using videoconferencing as the course delivery for a whole class (Northwestern University Information Technology, 2005b). The University of Virginia Information Communication and Technology (2006), however, lists four categories of videoconferencing that should be considered in supportive ways: coauthor, interviews, programming, and staff meetings. Overall, available resources do not appear to provide university educators with a robust, practical description of these types of videoconferences, nor ways in which they can be adapted for use in teacher preparation, nor how educators can engage students in this media. Consequently, educators need more information on how to utilize interactive videoconferencing for learning excellence in professional development, especially within the K-12 teacher-preparation arena.

TYPES OF VIDEOCONFERENCES

As in any other form of instruction, the higher-education faculty member must first select the precise learning goal and the assessments to be served by videoconferencing. They can then explore the various types of videoconferences to discover which will most benefit the students in this particular learning. Options from which they may select include: expert, university to school, peer-to-peer collaboration and meetings, multiple-session learning, mentoring/observation, interviewing/job searching, learning about videoconferencing, and social aspect. The following sections describe these types and provide examples that indicate potential uses.

Access to Experts

Many teacher-preparation educators use experts in their classroom to assist in knowledge transfers; methods of content include journal articles, Web sites, DVDs, TV documentaries, and phone conferences. Through videoconferencing, they can virtually bring the experts into the classroom or can be the expert for another class through videoconferencing. Examples of potential uses include the following:

- An instructor in an undergraduate Social Studies methods class has her students learn how to use archives and develop document-based questions (DBQs) from an expert at the U.S. National Archives and Records Administration (NARA) via videoconferencing. This expert carefully takes the preservice teachers through the steps in identifying the historical context of a letter to a president and of a postcard. Then she has the preservice students analyze some documents downloaded from the NARA Web site. The NARA person alternates between having students do document-based activities, talking, showing mini-PowerPoints, and going to the NARA Web site.

- In a science education graduate research class, the instructor asks an outside expert via videoconferencing to talk to his students about how a researcher constantly expands his topics for research. The author-researcher quickly demonstrates through the endings of several of his articles how one research topic opens the doors to many other research topics within the same field. The expert asks students to describe their present research topic, and to brainstorm several connected research areas. He gives them detailed feedback on their ideas by suggesting additional ways to widen their topic.

- A graduate class uses videoconferencing to interview the author of an article about improving learning to obtain more in-depth information on the process and outcomes. The class asks the author detailed questions about the techniques described in the provided material. The author answers their questions and asks them how they would create a similar setting in their subject area and with their students.

- Spanish-education majors study a play and then watch that play being performed in Madrid, Spain, using videoconferencing. Each student analyzes the performed play's interpretation. Then their class uses video-conferencing to explore their analysis with the expertise of the Spanish actors, director, stage manager, and costume manager.

These examples show how the ability to bring "outside" experts into the classroom increases the learning environment of the teacher-preparation students; the students go far beyond reading an expert's written thoughts to interacting with that expert, expanding and creating new information. In turn, the teacher-preparation students learn that they, along with their professors, can share expertise with other educators, regardless of distance; they realize that the community of learners can be seen and heard over far-away distances.

University-to-Schools

Another type of videoconference is when the university collaborates with public schools to use videoconferencing as a means of teaching and supporting practices. Examples of potential uses include the following:

- The State Education Department works with major universities to host a statewide videoconference on assessment. After a formal presentation, various university experts give short presentations, and educators from around the state react to this information. A series of follow-up videoconferences occur, each sponsored by a different university. Preservice and P-12 teachers watch these videoconferencing and gain insights into policy formation.

- One university sponsors statewide videoconferencing presentations for P-12 school administrators and faculty on current developments in technology. The instructors demonstrate technology applications for the P-12 schools, highlight some implementation issues, and encourage questions from the P-12 audience who are from all areas of the state. As the teachers ask their questions about the mechanics of using a particular technology, a university person shows how to use that particular technology through a step-by-step process. Teacher-preparation students benefit from learning about any of these technology applications that they do not know; if they already know the technology and have used it in their classes, they may be asked to be the virtual instructors on a particular technology application.

- An English methods professor teaches an English Language Arts P-12 professional development course via videoconferencing. She has teachers do a frieze of a scene from Shakespeare's *A Midsummer Night's Dream* in which a group of teachers position their bodies to convey the message and emotion of the scene. Then she has another group analyze which teacher is what character in the scene and what emotion the body language of each person portrays. Afterwards, she asks the teachers to select a passage from the literature that they are doing in their own classroom, plan out how to do the friezes in their own classrooms, and actually do some of those friezes with their students to improve students' comprehension of the literature.

- A science professor demonstrates, to a high-school science class, the many different experiments that the university is doing on very complex and expensive equipment. As she does an actual experiment with the equipment in the college laboratory, she asks the high school students what they think the results will be and why. Then she shows them the results and helps them to comprehend those results.

- A university hosts a "visit with the expert" videoconferencing program where students in local high schools indicate the type of expert to whom they want to talk. A student who is doing a senior project on aquatic ani-

mals has a videoconference with the head of the veterinary school, while another student who is interested in working conditions is linked up with a labor relations professor.

These university-to-school videoconference experiences can provide the teachers, students, parents, and other educational stakeholders with access to many experts inside and outside the university setting, and can provide learning experiences that they may not encounter in a physical classroom. They also help to establish networks for future in-person, electronic, and videoconferencing communications as addressed in the following sections.

Peer-to-Peer Student Collaboration

The university-to-school type of videoconferencing can be expanded to become a peer-to-peer student collaboration or meeting type of videoconference. These types of videoconferencing are highly supportive of construction-based activities. What follow are examples of potential uses.

- A university with a strong multicultural program sponsors a "24 hours around the globe" videoconference in which they "visit" with people from a different country every hour. They focus on the theme of "daily life" so that each hour people explain what their life is like and hear about daily life from people from the hosting university. Teacher-preparation students virtually attend the videoconferencing and ask additional questions of the speaker. Future teachers are not studying another culture through texts or outdated Web sites; they are directly interacting with people from other countries and gaining real insights and examples that they can transfer to their own classrooms and students in the years to come.

- In a graduate education class, a virtual professor has his students explain how they prepare their educational e-portfolios, and they show their actual e-portfolios. Then students at the receiving end tell how they prepare their e-portfolios, and they show their e-portfolios. Both groups examine and discuss variations and similarities in their universities' proficiencies, and how they are being prepared to be future leaders.

- Students in an English methods course who live geographically-distant from one another conduct their study group or Literature Circle through videoconferencing. They rotate through their roles, such as leaders of important events, special quotations, themes, and literary devices. The students see each other's reactions to their information and share charts and diagrams through the medium of their videoconference.

- An instructor arranges for a three-college videoconference discussion about classroom management. She involves a university who has rural placements, one with suburban placements, and one with urban placements. Each university group shares specific classroom management problems that they have had, and how they attempted to solve the problems. All students come to have a better view of classroom management issues in various settings.

These peer-to-peer collaborations work well since they are based on the idea that learning is social. The students engage in constructivist learning activities where they create their own knowledge. This videoconferencing collaboration moves far from the simple text messaging which has been the usual media of peer-to-peer collaboration of students who work together on a project when they live in distant locations. Preservice teachers learn that their learning community can be worldwide.

Peer-to-Peer Faculty Collaborations

Videoconferencing also can be used to support peer-to-peer faculty/researcher interactions that support preservice-teacher preparation. The potential for use is only limited by the creativity of those involved; some examples of potential uses include:

- One education professor cowrites articles with a colleague who works in a university in another country; they have periodic "face-to-face" videoconferences to talk through the articles after they have exchanged e-mail drafts of the articles. They finalize details and identify future areas for research in these short, one-hour videoconferencing meetings.

- A university professor attends a virtual conference from the comforts of his office, delivers a paper, and listens to the responses of other professors from their distant locations. He selects which virtual sessions he wants to attend, visits the virtual poster gallery, and joins in a videoconference research discussion.

- Faculties from two universities who collaborate on the same grant have bimonthly meetings to assess their progress on the grant. During the videoconference meeting, they share findings and progress, evaluate what they have done since the last meeting on the grant's goals, and determine what activities are left to be done.

Instructors and other education people realize that they can work closer with far-away colleagues for their professional development and for the benefits of their students. They can share knowledge and new information quickly and effectively, improving not only their own practice but also that of their students.

Multiple Sessions

Regardless of whether the videoconference type is expert, university-to-school, or collaborative, educators know that students often need multiple exposures to a concept before mastery can occur; as a result, many instructors feel that a series of interconnected videoconferences are beneficial. For example:

- A methods professor has a series of videoconferences on the same topic with several different partners so that her students explore the same issue from multiple viewpoints. One week, she has different experts express their perspectives on how to help young children to read. Since each videoconference lasts about thirty minutes, the students interact with three to four visitors during the same three-hour class. They use the last hour to discuss and analyze the strengths and weaknesses of each perspective.
- An art education professor has a series of videoconferences on discrete photography skills. This professor sponsors photography experts for the topics of symmetry, light and dark, and closure. The experts for each topic show pictures that demonstrate each of the skills, explain various factors in the developing of that skill, and ask the students to take pictures showing that concept. That virtual expert returns the next week to comment on the students' photographs that used the requested skill.

Preservice students learn more in-depth when they have repeated videoconferencing exposure to new concepts from an expert. Each time they increase their skills to higher levels, since they can interact verbally and visually with the expert.

Mentoring and Observing Students at a Distance

Just as the use of multiple sessions is a valuable type of videoconference for in-depth learning, so is the videoconference type that allows students to be mentored or to be observed remotely. Following are possible uses of videoconferencing that facilitate these roles.

- A student-teaching supervisor has several students in a placement that is about three hundred miles away from the university. The students e-mail him their lessons and their reflections on the lessons. He meets with them biweekly via videoconferencing to discuss their lessons and their experiences. He talks with their supervising teachers via videoconferencing. He maintains constant communication with these students between his physical visits to their schools.
- Supervisors virtually observe student teachers in their placement through videoconferencing. The student teachers have set up a desktop videoconferencing system in their classrooms. Since the supervisors do not have to drive to distant locations, they do more observations; the supervisor does not have to drive to the location, but can simply turns on the videoconferencing unit located in his or her classroom or the building's technology center.
- A university has real-time observations of a pre-K class through a videoconference system in a campus lab school. The early childhood methods classes observe the students in a pre-K class without interrupting the class. The methods class students talk to their professor or other students about what is happening without disrupting the actual class. They use the camera to zoom in on a particular student. They clearly hear what the student is saying, and how the teacher reacts and supports learning.

When teacher-preparation supervisors can observe more students more often due to videoconferencing, the quality of the teacher-preparation program increases. Likewise, when teacher-preparation students are mentored by an expert via videoconferencing, either on an as-needed basis or on a regular schedule, these students improve in their content and pedagogical skills.

Learning about Videoconferencing

An increasing number of teacher-preparation faculty want their students to experience videoconferencing before they begin their careers as teachers in P-12 schools. The purpose of this videoconferencing experience is to ensure that the next generation of teachers has the technology knowledge and skills that will allow them to participate in future use.

- In an educational communications class, the instructor arranges a videoconference with a colleague on an educational topic. The students learn how to mute, move the camera, and how to ask questions. After the videoconference, they talk about how to improve the mechanics of videoconferencing. The emphasis in this use is the tool and its potential.
- An instructor has the students participate in a videoconference, then analyze the engagement and learning in the videoconference. Her students then plan and do a short five-minute videoconference in which they create their own visuals, plan the interactions, and create a learning assessment. They analyze that conference to determine how they can increase the learning.

When teacher-preparation students learn about videoconferencing before they start teaching, they have an additional educational tool to use to promote student learning. They can better understand the concept of "virtual" P-12 schools that are increasing in number.

Interviewing and Job Searching

Students who have experience in videoconferencing will feel at ease as they use it to find future employment as a teacher. In the future, students may be interviewed with perspective employers through the use of videoconferencing.

- After a general "job fair" on the campus, the potential school employers set up a series of videoconferences with those candidates that seemed most appropriate to their school. The students have a half-hour interview. They can show their portfolios and talk about how they will contribute to the school.

New teachers and potential employers can use videoconferencing to reach many more prospects, and can do preliminary reviews of candidates, positions, and environments.

Networking and Social Aspects

Instructors frequently want to continue relationships with their students who have obtained jobs, and they want to continue relationships with colleagues who are not at their location. This content promotes continual learning, helps maintain a professional support system, and adds the "personal" touch to educational settings.

- Science faculty members videoconference about every three months with recent graduates to hear about their lives as science teachers; they discuss common issues, joys, and share.
- When a faculty member retires, his department sponsors a virtual retirement party. Many of his colleagues who have collaborated with him on articles, books, grants, and presentations join the party through videoconferencing.

These examples show that videoconferencing is not just for work; as it becomes part of educators' lives, its use will expand into the social and political areas that are common with educational settings. Indeed, it is possible that educators will learn from their students in this domain.

ENGAGEMENT/INTERACTIVITY

Once teacher-preparation educators have selected their precise learning, designed their assessments, and selected the type of videoconference, they will want to design the videoconference to maximize student engagement or interactivity for successful learning. Lecturing or being a "talking head" is an ineffective use of videoconferencing; interactivity is critical to the success of a virtual class. Teacher-preservice educators need to modify not only their content, but also their pedagogy for the very interactive nature of videoconferencing (Greenberg, 2004). With proper design and support, student engagement can be at a high level throughout videoconferences. The students do not have to sit placidly in their chairs; students can move, act, sing, and dance during a videoconference. Additional non-lecture interactive ways of engaging students include brainstorming, simulations, skits, roundtable discussions, points of view, debates, group presentations, jigsaw information, language and culture examples, models, demonstrations, mysteries, games, and interviews (Tuttle, 1996). To support this interactivity, teacher-preparation educators can employ multiple technologies during a videoconference. Some examples include:

- An instructor may use numerous one-to-two minute video streaming clips that students can watch during the videoconference if they want more examples or to see precise examples of what the instructor is explaining or, students may post a list of Web sites that deal with the same topic with different

approaches; students can visit these sites during a quick four-minute break in the videoconference and then talk more analytically about the topic when they return to videoconferencing, or students may share materials through an Elmo image-capturing device connected to the videoconferencing system.

- The "visiting" instructor or the host instructor uses a blog as part of the videoconferencing experience, posting the essential questions of the videoconference and posing examples for reaction. The students who are reticent about responding orally offer ideas in the blog. The expert or discussion leader from the host class frequently checks the blog to see what questions are being raised, and how the students are responding to the blog's questions or examples.

- Educators may also use multiple technologies in a Webinar (Web-seminar) that combines various technologies such as online presentation, online chat, and telephone. For example, the Access Center (2006) has sponsored professional development Webinars on differentiated instruction, supervising coteaching teams, science as inquiry, and making math meaningful. Since students use multiple technologies, they can select the medium in which they best prefer to communicate, in real-time, about the topic.

Teacher-preparation instructors also have found that they can increase student interactivity in videoconferences through the wide variety of shared applications. This process is especially helpful in peer-to-peer videoconferencing. For example:

- An art education student can upload his art images through a shared virtual whiteboard, and students from distant universities can make annotations on the images. Or, business students in one school share their findings on business data with students in other universities through a common spreadsheet; the other students can add their data to the common spreadsheet or suggest another analysis of the business data.

- Several classes from around the globe write a common document on the role on constructivism in the math classroom through the shared whiteboard. Students take turns controlling the scientific instrumentation at a remote site as they learn about astronomy. Or, English students from many colleges enter a shared virtual reality where they become characters in a novel; chemistry students from various colleges enter the world of atoms.

In general, teacher-preparation students become even more engaged in videoconferencing content through interactive activities, streaming video, blogs, discussion areas of programs, Webinars, shared applications, and tele-education aspects; they become active, not passive, learners in virtual worlds and see education as engaging and not lecture-centered.

ANALYZING THE QUALITY OF LEARNING

If educators want to improve on the quality of student learning in videoconferences, they need to reflect on the process both during and after use. This formable feedback will strengthen both current and future learning. Potential methods of analysis are reflected in the following examples:

- A professor reflects on his own teaching through a recorded videoconference. The instructor notices that he frequently says "um". He analyzes how much "teacher-talk" there is compared to "student-talk". He analyzes what percentages of his questions

are open-ended as opposed to close-ended. He decides on what changes he will make. After the next videoconference, he reviews the recorded session to see if he has implemented the desired changes.

- A professor examines the words and actions of the students in a recorded videoconference. She analyzes the students' statements to a greater degree that she can during a face-to-face session. The professor analyzes the complexity of their answers. She gives students feedback not only on the quality of their comments, but also on their ability to communicate effectively during the videoconferencing. She can do research, either action or formal, on her students' interaction during a videoconference.

- To improve on the educational quality of the videoconference, an instructor has his students write down what they thought helped them to learn during the videoconference, and what they think will help them to learn more. He uses those assessments to improve on the quality of learning during the next videoconference.

All of these improvement strategies can lead to better learning experiences for teacher-preparation students through videoconferences. In addition, when education instructors engage in these assessment and improvement strategies, their own students have a role model for their future teaching.

RESOURCES TO HELP CONNECT TO OTHER SITES

After teacher-preparation educators know the advantages of videoconferencing, become aware of the various types of videoconferencing, and learn how to help their students become engaged, they will want to find educational partners for their videoconferencing. AT&T's Knowledge Adventures (2006) has a very comprehensive listing of both expert and peer-to-peer videoconferencing so the preservice educators can select the most appropriate videoconferencing partner for the particular learning experience.

FUTURE TRENDS

The increasing use of videoconferencing in preservice and in-service teacher edcuation is resulting in ongoing changes to expectations, processes, and use. The following are some trends that make the use of videoconferencing more effective:

- Many universities have switched to Internet2 which gives greater speed and bandwidth and, therefore, provides drastically-improved audio and video quality. It now feels like the virtual expert or peer is actually in the room; shared presentations can be done smoothly across thousands of miles.
- Many universities are installing more videoconferencing systems, and instructors are purchasing their own laptop or desktop videoconferencing systems. Physical office hours are being replaced by virtual ones, and a far drive to visit teacher-preparation students teaching is being replaced by a videoconference visit. Students have more frequent visual and sound access to their instructors.
- Desktop videoconferencing can now be done from any location where there is an Internet connection, so more on-site videoconferencing can be done from locations such as a science lab, a field station, a factory, or an archaeological dig. Students can do more than study about a location; they can virtually visit it.
- More teacher-preparation faculty are realizing that culture is not confined within the walls of buildings; videoconferencing is being used to take students to other cul-

tures, regardless of the distance from the university.
- More instructors are changing videoconference from instructor-centered to student-centered, and include more interactivity. The instructors will come to realize that the interactive nature of videoconference can be made even more interactive through other technologies. The use will require more exposure with multiple tools.

FUTURE QUESTIONS

In addition to trends, there are several potential, overarching changes, as reflected by the following questions that might impact the future of videoconferencing:

- Will there be worldwide universities where students from any location can take workshops or mini-courses from the experts in any field, even if those experts are located around the world? Will a university give credit for such "expert" learning?
- How will universities connect students to appropriate people in the working world to see how their new knowledge is applied in authentic situations? How can university educators use videoconferencing to provide authentic learning experiences for their students?

FUTURE RESEARCH

The solutions and answers to these questions and trends may be based on research. Some areas for which immediate answers are needed include the following:

- What percentage of teacher-preparation instructors presently videoconference for their classes?

- What percentage of each type of videoconferencing is presently being done, and what is its impact on student learning?
- How do communication-rich environments impact on student learning in videoconferencing?
- Does multitasking during a videoconference positively influence student learning?

CONCLUSION

The role of a teacher-preparation educator in a teacher-preparation videoconference is "mentoring like Merlin", in which the educator has the students virtually experience situations that foster growth (Sherron & Boettcher, 1997). Science students go from being with a doctor as she operates to being with a forensic scientist as he uses complex technology to create three-dimensional images from a bone fragment; preservice instructors dialog with the students regardless of their locations; teacher-preparation learners are transported instantly to far-away global and cultural locations to learn from people and things in those highly-interactive environments. The more that teacher-preparation instructors know about the various types of videoconferences, the more Merlin-like virtual worlds they will have for their students. Likewise, as preservice-teacher educators discover the more diverse ways to engage the students in videoconferences, they will have the students interact in virtual worlds in ways that cannot even now be imagined. They will be able to transform parts of their "class" into a Merlin-like magical place where teacher-preparation students learn not only in-depth content, but also new pedagogy, all through interactive videoconferencing.

REFERENCES

Access Center (2006). Webinars. Retrieved August 1, 2006, from http://www.k8accesscenter.org/online_community_area/Webinar.asp

Adams, S. (2002). Cost effective real-time video conferencing for instruction and collaborative learning in music and the performing arts via next generation Internet powered virtual laboratory environment. In G. Richards (Ed.), In *Proceedings of World Conference on E-Learning in Corporate, Government, Healthcare, and Higher Education, 2002* (pp. 2531-2532). Chesapeake, VA: AACE.

Amirian, S. (2003). Pedagogy and videoconferencing: A review of recent literature. In *Proceedings of the First NJEDge.NET Conference, Plainsboro, NJ.* Retrieved April 10, 2006, from http://www.iclassnotes.com/amirian_megacon.pdf

AT&T Knowledge Explorers (2006). Videoconferencing directories. Retrieved April 6, 1946, from http://www.kn.pacbell.com/wired/vidconf/directory.cfm

Dolt Support Services of George Mason University (n.d.). Videoconferencing. Retrieved April 25, 2006, from http://www.doit.gmu.edu/portfolio/2004/CT/VTC04.htm

Greenberg, A. (2004). Navigating the sea of research on videoconferencing-based distance education: A platform for understanding the technology's effectiveness and value. *Wainhouse Research.* Retrieved April 2, 2006, from http://www.wainhouse.com/files/papers/wr-navseadist-edu.pdf

Instructional Services of Penn State (2003). *Etiquette and tips for a successful videoconference.* Retrieved April 23, 2006, from http://www.hbg.psu.edu/iit/mw2/etiquette.htm

Kosak, L., Manning, L., Dobson, E., Rogerson, L., Cotnam, S., Colaric, S., & McFadden, C. (2004). Prepared to teach online? Perspectives of faculty in the University of North Carolina system. *Online Journal of Distance Learning Administration, VII-III*. Retrieved April 10, 2006, from http://www.westga.edu/~distance/ojdla/fall73/kosak73.html

Lai, W., Pratt, K., & Grant, A. (2003). *State of the art and trends in distance, flexible, and open learning.* Retrieved April 10, 2006, from http://hedc2.otago.ac.nz/TLI/distance_learning_pdf/distance_lit_review.pdf#search='review%20of%20the%20literature%20videoconference%20learning

Lehman, J. D., & Richardson, J. (2004). *Making connections in teacher education: Electronic portfolios, videoconferencing, and distance field experiences.* Paper presented at Association for Educational Communications and Technology. Retrieved August 1, 2006, from http://p3t3.soe.purdue.edu/AECT%202004.pdf

Northwestern University Information Technology (2004). *Videoconferencing at Northwestern.* Retrieved April 2, 2006, from http://www.it.northwestern.edu/bin/news/vidconf_pr2.pdf

Northwestern University Information Technology (2005a). *Understanding videoconferencing.* Retrieved April 6, 2006, from http://www.it.northwestern.edu/videoconferencing/understand/index.html

Northwestern University Information Technology (2005b). *Videoconferencing examples.* Retrieved April 22, 2006, from http://www.it.northwestern.edu/videoconferencing/understand/examples.htm

Sherron, G. T., & Boettcher, J. V. (1997). Distance learning: The shift to interactivity. *EDUCAUSE* (pp. 23-24). Retrieved April 9, 2006, from http://www.educause.edu/LibraryDetailPage/666?ID=PUB3017

Telemedicine Information Exchange (2006). Telemedicine and tele-health articles. Retrieved August 1, 2006, from http://tie.telemed.org/articles.asp

Tuttle, H. G. (1996). Learning: The star of video-conferencing. *Multimedia Schools, 3*(4), 37-41.

Tuttle, H. G. (1998). *Improving student learning in videoconferences.* Paper presented at National Educational Computer Conference, San Diego, CA.

Tuttle, H. G. (2004). *Learning and technology assessments for administrators.* Ithaca, NY: Epilog Visions.

University of Ulster (n.d.). Videoconferencing manual. Retrieved April 24, 2006, from http://www.ulster.ac.uk/isd/itus/media/vcmanual.pdf

University of Virginia Information Communication and Technology (2006). Videoconferencing examples. Retrieved April 22, 2006, from http://www.itc.virginia.edu/videoconf/video-info/vr-sec8.html

Wilkerson, L. (2006). *The history of video conferencing.* Retrieved April 25, 2006, from http://www.video-conferencing-guide.com/history-of-video-conferencing.htm

Woods, T. J. (2005). *Instructor and student perceptions of a videoconference course.* Retrieved April 11, 2006, from http://www.uleth.ca/edu/grad/pdf/thesis_woods.pdf

Chapter XVI
Videoconferencing:
An Alternative to Traditional Professional Development in the K–12 Setting

Leigh A. Mountain
University at Albany/SUNY, USA

ABSTRACT

This chapter introduces ways in which videoconferencing can be used to support professional development which is being provided to educators. It looks at the ways in which adults learn, the need for quality professional development in education, and the different types of professional development which are being provided. It then goes on to discuss ways in which videoconferencing can be used to make the transfer of knowledge more effective. After reading this chapter, educators will be able to identify ways in which they can utilize videoconferencing to make professional development more beneficial and cost-efficient. It also shows educators how they can break away from ineffective traditional modes of providing in-service training and move toward more high-quality, comprehensive, and embedded professional development, which addresses the individual needs of teachers and buildings.

INTRODUCTION

As professional development continues to transmit practices to educators working in the field, it is necessary to consider what the most effective methods and modes are for assisting in the transfer of new skills, abilities, and knowledge. When planning a professional development session, many variables need to be considered including: who is the audience for the professional development; what is the audience's preferred method of learning; and what is the most effective way to teach this topic so that people will learn the information. A more current area of interest to those providing assistance in improving the transfer of knowledge into practice is the role that technology can play as a support to professional development. More specifically, what role can videoconferencing play in supporting professional development for teachers and administrators who are in the field?

Adult Learners

Professional development is generally provided to adults who are working in real-time settings. When planning a professional development session one must, therefore, consider how adults learn. Adult learning theory indicates that characteristics of adult learners that need to be considered include autonomy, self-directed, goal-oriented, relevancy-oriented, and practical (Speck, 1996). Adults also have accumulated life experiences and knowledge that need to be acknowledged and respected during the learning experiences so that they do not fear being criticized (Speck, 1996).

Merriam (2001) discussed the concepts of andragogy and self-directed learning as two ways to define adult learning as a unique field of practice. Merriam noted that, in addition to bringing the concept of andragogy to light in 1968, Malcolm Knowles developed five assumptions underlying the concept. These assumptions were that an adult learner: is someone who has an independent self-concept and who can direct his or her own learning; has accumulated a wealth of life experience that is a rich resource for learning; has learning needs closely related to changing social roles; is problem-centered and interested in immediate application of knowledge; and is motivated to learn by internal rather than external factors (Merriam, 2001). These are very similar and somewhat overlapping to what Speck identified as adult learning characteristics.

Tweedell (2000) pointed out that adults require learning programs which are specific to their learning style, and that adults learn best when

Table 1. Adult learning characteristics (Adapted from Speck, 1996)

Autonomous
Self-directed
Goal-oriented
Relevancy-oriented
Practical

knowledge is presented in an interactive format with emphasis on how they can apply their learning to practical applications. Tweedell also noted that adults desire learning situations that do not require them to compromise their family and professional obligations.

Since adults are self-directed, instruction should allow them to discover and construct knowledge for themselves, while providing guidance and help when mistakes are made (Chadwick & Shrago, 2001). They go on to note that one way to provide this is the use of just-in-time access to professional development via the Web and other methods of support, in which mentors or other knowledgeable personnel are available to answer questions and guide the adult learner. These last few points indicate that we are beginning to see researchers making the connection between adult learning style characteristics and the ways in which technology can help support knowledge development.

Professional Development and Education

Education is one particular field in which adults are provided professional development on a regular basis as a means of keeping them up-to-date on the latest practices and research. "Never before in the history of education has greater importance been attached to the professional development of educators" (Guskey, 2000, p. 3). Many educators view professional development not as an opportunity, but as something that they are required to do (Guskey, 2000). Educators have argued that providing professional development to all teachers is critical to ensure that teachers are highly skilled (Darling-Hammond, 1999). No Child Left Behind legislation is currently mandating a stepped-up program of high-quality job-embedded professional development (Carter, 2004). It is very important that teachers, like other professionals, keep up-to-date on the most cur-

rent concepts, thinking, and research in the field (Guskey, 2000; Mouza, 2003). Consequently, it is necessary to build a culture of lifelong learners and change negative attitudes towards professional development. Resulting from this shift has been increased time devoted to providing teachers with professional development (Doherty & Skinner, 2003; Spillane, 2000).

Over the past decades, views of professional development in K-12 education have shifted. In the 1970's, the major model was that of training (Filby, 1995); preservice or in-service professional development was designed to enhance the knowledge and skills which teachers needed. Current research however, supports more sophisticated modes of training (Filby, 1995). Business, government, and education groups have all acknowledged the need for high-quality professional development (Sparks & Hirsch, 1997).

Nancy Kraft (1997) discussed nine components of effective professional development as a means of providing a new way of thinking about modes and methods of training, which should help people break away from the more traditional means of providing professional development. The nine components that she presented were:

- Teacher involvement
- Content in context
- A sense of continuity
- A sense of collegiality
- Reflective practice
- Conceptual approach
- Team-building emphasis
- Based on principals of adult learning
- Includes an evaluation component (Kraft, 1997)

A review of research literature conducted by The Institute for the Advancement of Research in Education at AEL (2004) uncovered nine components of effective professional development as well. These included:

Videoconferencing

- Student-learning needs
- The incorporation of hands-on technology use
- Whether or not it is job-embedded
- Does it have applications to specific curricula, knowledge, skills, and beliefs
- Does it occur over time
- Does it occur with colleagues
- The provision of technical assistant and support to teachers
- The incorporation of evaluative measures

Research has indicated that professional development methods are frequently ineffective in providing increased knowledge on a topic (Gutsky, 2000; Richardson, 2003); in many K-12 settings, professional development still consists of three or four special days per year, with teachers having very little input on the topics for these sessions. These events generally are short-term workshops, with little to no follow-up or guidance for implementation and with no attention paid to what is already going on in the particular classroom, school, or district. Alternately, teachers sometimes select to take college courses to obtain

their required hours of professional development; this process presents similar problems in that the material may have little connection with what the teachers are focused on in their classrooms (Guskey, 2000).

Despite its failures, many schools and districts continue to use these models because other more effective models require more extensive resources, more extensive time, and more extensive follow-up (Richardson, 2003). Many school districts today are trying to move away from district-wide designs of providing professional development to a more site-based design that are more relevant to that school's content, procedures, and topics, and reflect the specific needs of that school's teachers (Guskey, 2000).

These alternative methods are justified by Joyce and Showers (1995) and Bradshaw (2002), who stated that it is more likely that a teacher will transfer knowledge learned in professional development when it includes presentations of theory and information, demonstration, practice with feedback, and coaching and follow-up over time. More specifically, Wade (1984) noted that observation of actual classroom practices, micro-

Table 2. Effective professional development (Adapted from Kraft, 1997)

Teacher Involvement
Content in Context
A Sense of Continuity
A Sense of Collegiality
Reflective Practice
Conceptual Approach
Team Building
Adult Learning
Evaluation Component

216

teaching, video/audio feedback, and practice were the most effective instructional techniques for real-time teachers.

Professional Development via Videoconferencing

When one considers adult learning styles, the constant need for educators to be kept up-to-date on best practices and the demand for more effective professional development technology and, more specifically videoconferencing, appear to have the potential to provide effective professional development suitable for K-12 educators.

Distance education is now considered an effective mode of providing education or training. Distance education refers to transfer of knowledge between an instructor and a learner who are separated during the learning process by physical distance and time (Motamedi, 2001). Overall, distance learning, especially when supported by technology, is on the rise. One form of distance education, which has grown greatly in the U.S. since the early 1990's, is videoconferencing (Motamedi, 2001).

By 1969, distance teaching had developed into an important part of higher education and today plays a vital role in transferring knowledge, skills, and abilities (Matthews, 1999; Tucker, 2001). According to Witherspoon (1996), there are various means of providing distance education that range from mail correspondence, radio, television, telephones, Internet communication, to various video options. Over the years, however, the predominate modes of distance learning have moved from correspondence mail toward a mixed media approach which included audio and video material, followed by the use of television, radio, and telephone, and now generally includes the use of interactive multimedia including hardware, software, and peripheral equipment that provide a mixture of text, graphics, sound, animation, and full-motion video. This now includes satellite broadcasts and teleconferencing (Halal & Liebowitz, 1994; Mat-

thews, 1999). The technology has increased the numbers of distance education courses (Dubois, 1996), with online instruction quickly becoming the more popular delivery method.

One emerging technology that is being seen as an effective instrument for active learning is videoconferencing (Norman & Hayden, 2002). The availability of the interactive real-time audio and visual approach to learning is causing people to think differently about how learners can connect to experts, peers, and instructors and provide instructional opportunities not otherwise available (Cradler, 1994; Norman & Hayden, 2002). Multimedia and videoconferencing methods vary from the more traditional disciplinary-based knowledge centers and are likely to be the key technology in future education and lifelong learning (Halal & Liebowitz, 1994; Yorks, 2005).

This supports the findings of Carter (2004) who noted a problem with the use of asynchronous (participants and the trainer do not have to be online at the same time) modes of providing professional development. He noted that asynchronous communication, while a highly-flexible model, makes it harder to maintain learner interest and motivation. Instead, he proposed the use of synchronous activities, such as real-time interaction with an instructor through the use of videoconferencing.

While asynchronous and synchronous technology both can provide learners with new opportunities to access information, experience new things, and connect to different places, people, and things all over the world (Marshall, 2002), videoconferencing offers learners real-time access and real-world problem-solving (CEO Forum, 2001; Silverman & Silverman, 1999). Several researchers (e.g., Cavanaugh, 2001) have noted that the use of videoconferencing in the K-12 classroom environment is a valuable resource for bringing external educational programs and individualized instruction methods to a local academic setting. Among the advantages of videoconferencing is its ability to provide access to instruction and training by eliminating travel (Motamedi, 2001). It also offers flexibility in time, place, and pace of instruction (Belcheir & Cucek, 2001; U.S. Department of Education, 2004). This flexibility is important because it addresses the need for just-in-time and just-enough professional development. Due to the flexibility in time, meaning that videoconferencing can take place at anytime as long as both parties are available, educators are able to have access to both expert and peer support when they need it. The flexibility in time and pace also means that educators can get just-enough support to improve practices, whether it is one short session to refresh their understanding of something or several sessions to learn about a new topic. The flexibility in place allows for varying sizes of learner groups. Narrow bands are indicative of professional development where one teacher or a team of teachers from one school can receive professional development via videoconferencing to match their specific needs. On the other hand broad bands occur where a whole district, even several districts, with educators at multiple sites, participate in a videoconference providing professional development.

Videoconferencing has several other advantages such as being able to provide visual presences of participants, as well as the ability to bring external experts and resources into the classroom such as guest speakers, virtual experiences, and collaboration between classes; it also supports the integration of different medias, such as photos, videos, graphics, text, and so forth. (Motamedi, 2001).

Major barriers to videoconferencing in its current format include the cost of equipment at startup and maintenance, the need for technical support and training on use, and the authenticity of submissions (Matthews, 1999; Motamedi, 2001). These barriers are quickly being eliminated with advances in equipment, decreased costs, and the inclusion of technical support staff in instructional line budgets.

In fact, these barriers may even now be outweighed by the ability of videoconferencing to reach and service all types of K-12 educators, including preservice and in-service personnel and professionals in high need/high risk settings (Rodes, Knapczyk, Chapman, & Chung, 2000). Equally important, this mode of professional development allows teachers to discuss, document share, and to work collaboratively on common issues (Rodes et al., 2000). It encourages, in fact requires, learners to be active rather than passively involved in the learning process (O'Connor, 2003; Rodes et al., 2000).

In addition to fostering educational collaboration, this process enhances the experience of learning communities (Martin, 2005). O'Connor (2003) noted that the most effective experiences require interactions that are student-to-student, student-to-instructor, and student-to-resources. All of these methods allow for scaffolding during the learning process and interaction with the environment, both of which are theorized to lead to greater success of learning (Schunk, 1999). All of these advantages are important, since they are related to the components of effective professional development which were noted earlier.

While there are numerous case study examples of success stories when videoconferencing is used to support professional development, scientifically-based evidence is still unavailable. Several studies on the effectiveness of distance education, however, have found no significant difference between learners in face-to-face and distance education classes in the areas of learner success (Davis, 1996; Tucker, 2001). Mixed results have been found for online learning versus face-to-face classrooms; studies found either no significant difference between the two methods related to learners performance (Johnson, Arragon, Shaik, & Palma-Rivas, 2000; LaRose, Gregg, & Eastin, 1998; Smeaton & Keogh, 1999), or that learners in online learning situations out-performed the face-to-face learning group (Dutton, Dutton, & Perry, 2001; Hiltz, 1997; Schutte, 1997; Souder,

1993). Similarly, studies on the use of interactive television to deliver courses to learners found that satisfaction levels were similar to that of learners enrolled in the same course delivered in the traditional face-to-face manner (Haga & Heitkamp, 2000; Heitkamp, 1995; Petracchi & Patchner, 2000).

On the other hand, Carter (2004) discusses how Southern California's Imperial County Office of Education has discovered economic benefits of online professional development via videoconferencing, reporting that the estimation of savings for a single meeting being held via videoconferencing instead of on-site was $18,000 (Carter, 2004). This was money saved on travel, time, hotel, and food (Carter, 2004).

In addition, there is evidence to support the use of videoconferencing in preservice-teacher preparation programs. The use of synchronous or real-time digital video is being used in many teacher-education programs at universities as a means of providing preservice teachers with the opportunity to observe classroom teaching or to be observed, and allows for feedback and assessment of the teaching practices used (Barnett, Truesdell, Kenyon, & Mike; see Chapter XIII in this volume). One program in the UK that is using this method finds it a viable model for providing training to students in higher-education settings who are studying to become teachers (Dyke, Harding, & Lajeunesse, 2006).

Videoconferencing Supporting the Major Models of Professional Development

Guskey (2000) noted eight major models of professional development offered to K-12 educators; these include: trainings, observation/assessment, involvement in a development/improvement process, study groups, inquiry/action research, individually guided activities, and mentoring. These models include some of the more high-quality, job-embedded models, which are being

called for to meet the needs of providing effective professional development. The models of professional development discussed in more detail below are ones which videoconferencing can help to support.

- Training is described as having a presenter or team of presenters that share their ideas and expertise through a variety of group-based activities. The format includes large-group presentations and discussions, workshops, seminars, colloquia, demonstrations, role-playing, simulation, and micro-teaching (Guskey, 2000). In training settings, videoconferencing can bring people together who have similar needs and interests but are separated by distance. Real-time videoconferencing would allow educators to view demonstrations and presentations provided by an expert, and engage in group discussions and activities.

- Observation/assessment uses collegial observation to provide educators with feedback on their performance. Peer coaching and clinical supervisions are examples of this method (Guskey, 2000). Peer coaching, similarly noted by Bradshaw (2002), allows teachers to observe and help each other with implementation. Videoconferencing is one way in which observations can be carried out without a stranger needing to be present in the room. This mode would allow for real-time peer-to-peer or expert-to-novice observations of teaching practices from a distance. Videoconferencing also allows a means of discussing what was observed in real-time after the observation is over.

- Study groups are when educators work together to increase their knowledge base. Collegial study groups, as noted by Bradshaw (2002), are generally organized by grade level, departments, or special-interest groups with ongoing support and dialogue, and provide opportunities for collabora-

Vignette 1.

A school district has just decided to switch to a new math curriculum. The district now needs to decide how it will provide training to all of its teachers on this new curriculum. They want to be able to bring in an expert from the company who developed the curriculum to provide the training. This will ensure that the teachers in the district get the best information on how to use the curriculum appropriately. It is clear that they will not be able to train all the teachers at the same time in one place, due to the fact that the district does not have a space that is large enough to allow teachers to work comfortably while learning. Due to budget limitations, they also would not be able to afford to pay enough trainers to teach multiple smaller groups of teachers at different locations. To provide consistent curriculum and instruction, the district needs to begin implementing this curriculum in all schools in the district during the coming school year, so only training some of the teachers now is not an option.

The option of videoconferencing is brought up during a meeting on how to solve this problem. It is pointed out that videoconferencing would allow teachers to stay in their own building for the training. The district would just need to move the videoconferencing equipment, which is already available in each school to a central location, such as the library. This would solve the space problem by spreading out the teachers across various buildings, allowing them to have room to learn comfortably. The trainers would be able to teach the new curriculum to all the teachers in the district from one central location, either from one of the schools or even from the trainers' own office. This would solve the budget problem of not being able to afford multiple sessions of the training. If the curriculum company has videoconferencing equipment, the trainers may choose to do the training from their office rather than travel to the district. If this is the case, more money could be saved.

The technology coordinators for the district shares with everyone that videoconferencing would allow for interaction among teachers and trainer due to its real-time connection, meaning that teachers could ask questions and get feedback immediately from the trainer or other teachers located at different schools in the district. Due to its video capabilities, teachers also would be able to see the trainer, the resources, and other teachers' use of the resources. In addition, the district could use videoconferencing and provide follow-up sessions between the expert and small groups, and between grade-level teachers at different buildings.

tion on planning and problem-solving. In this case, videoconferencing can be used to bring educators together in real-time to discuss and work together to increase their knowledge on a particular topic. Groups can be expanded to serve teachers across buildings and districts which may not otherwise have a common group interaction.

• Individually-guided activities are when individuals determine their own professional development goals and select activities that will assist them in achieving their goal. In this case, it is important that an individual know their needs and are capable of self-direction and initiation (Guskey, 2000). Videoconferencing supports these activities by

Vignette 2

A teacher who had just started using a new reading curriculum package to support her current curriculum had some questions on how to use it in conjunction with her current materials. She knew that other teachers currently used it, and wanted the opportunity to see how one of them used it to support instruction. She decided to contact the company that developed the curriculum package to see if they could put her in touch with any teachers who currently use it. As it turned out, all the districts using it were located out-of-state from her district. She decided to e-mail one of the teachers to at least ask a few questions. The other teacher mentions the option of watching him teach a class via videoconferencing, if she had the capabilities. This would allow her to see firsthand how he incorporates the reading curriculum package. She had not thought of this; however, she felt that it was a great idea. Both of the teachers set up a date and time for the one to watch the other conduct a lesson via videoconferencing. The first teacher had her building technology coordinator help her set up the equipment on the day of the lesson. After watching the other teacher use the reading package during his lesson, she was able to ask him questions, via videoconferencing, about certain strategies that he used and why he chose to use them, as well as to see up close what materials he used, as a means to gain further understanding.

After having done this, she decided to coordinate with teachers in her school and district, as well as some teachers out of the district who taught the same grade and curriculum, to set up videoconferencing once a month as a means of getting together as a group to discuss strategies that they use which might be helpful to others or to ask questions of each other. This also was an opportunity to set up times when one teacher could observe another via videoconferencing to see a certain lesson being taught in order to help them in planning their own.

connecting an educator who has a particular question or topic on which they need more information with an expert located anywhere in the world. This unique, individually-guided approach, which otherwise would not be economically or time-wise possible, now can be a frequent occurrence.

- Mentoring is the pairing of an experienced educator with a less-experienced colleague. They engage in the sharing of ideas and strategies regarding effective practice, reflections on current methods, and observations (Guskey, 2000). With the use of videoconferencing, mentors and mentees do not need to be located in close proximity to achieve a goal of working together to learn from each other. The mentor can observer the mentee in action, as well as the mentee observing the mentor. The mentor and mentee can meet as often as they want via videoconferencing to discuss and reflect on each other's teaching practices.

Issues and Solutions

One of the issues often noted with regards to distance education is the lack of learner-instructor interaction. Peters (1993) claimed that most distance education courses lacked the ability for group interaction, and did not allow for instructor-learner interaction. Videoconferencing is one solution to this problem, in that it allows for interaction. When providing professional development using real-time videoconferencing, the learners can see the instructor, ask questions, and get immediate response.

One barrier associated with providing professional development to educators via videoconferencing is the need for users to have technology skills. When providing professional development via videoconferencing, the learners need to know how to: make a connection to the provider of the professional development; work and maneuver the remote camera; adjust microphone sound if needed; and troubleshoot if they lose a connection. The same is true for the provider of the professional development. This barrier can be remedied if there is a person in the building where the educators will be using the videoconferencing equipment that can support the technology and assist with setup and making the connection. Having a technology support person on staff and available is a resource already available to many school buildings and districts. In addition, the technology skill levels of teachers are increasing from beginner levels to intermediate, and teachers are continually receiving training to move them to higher levels yet (Ezarik, 2001).

FUTURE TRENDS AND CONCLUSION

Bradshaw (2002) found evidence in the technology plans of 27 school districts that indicate that they are moving away from one-shot professional development sessions towards providing more long-term opportunities, which include follow-up support. As a result, in the future we will see teachers receiving higher-quality professional development that supports them in integrating what they are learning into their classroom practices. This initiative also will become part of school districts' technology plans, both as support of professional development and as part of teacher training in technology.

As teachers obtain more professional development that increases their technology skills in the classroom, they will be more willing to explore new methods of receiving professional development that expand beyond the traditional on-site means. Educators will come to realize that by using videoconferencing as a means to receive professional development, they have the opportunity to connect with instructors all over the country and the world. When educators are no longer limited by distance, time, or place for their professional development, their attitudes on professional development will be a more positive one where they are seeking out knowledge and experience in areas of specific interest to them and their practice.

This shift will lead to larger numbers of experts who will be offering professional development, via videoconferencing, to an even broader audience. For companies producing educational resources and tools to be used in K-12 education, traveling to various schools to provide the professional development on their products will take place via videoconferencing. This mode also will allow for experts to provide and districts to obtain relatively cost-effective follow-up, which is one of the hallmark components of effective professional development. Only in the last decade has technology in K-12 settings advanced to the point where it allows for synchronous and interactive teaching events. Now that this technology is available, it is time to use it to support K-12 teachers as well as K-12 students.

REFERENCES

Belcheir, M. J. & Cucek, M. (2001). *Student perceptions of their distance education courses.* Boise State University, Office of Institutional Assessment. ED 480 923.

Bradshaw, L. (2002). Technology for teaching and learning: Strategies for staff development and follow-up support. *Journal of Technology and Teacher Education, 10*(1), 131-150.

Carter, K. (2004). Online training: What's really working? *Technology & Learning, 24*(10), 32-37.

Cavanaugh, C. (2001). The effectiveness of interactive distance education technologies in K-12 learning: A meta-analysis. *International Journal of Educational Telecommunications, 7*(1), 73-88.

CEO Forum on Education and Technology (2001). Key building blocks for student achievement in the 21st century: Assessment, alignment, accountability, access, and analysis. *The CEO Forum Schools Technology and Readiness Report Year 4.* Washington, DC: CEO Forum.

Chadwick, K., & Shrago, J. (2001). How Tennessee successfully motivated and supported teachers' skill development in meaningful classroom Internet use. In D. Grisham (Ed.), *Teacher professional development and technology.* Multi-paper presentation conducted at the Annual Meeting of the American Educational Research Association, Seattle, WA.

Cradler, J. (1994). *Summary of current research and evaluation findings on technology in education.* Retrieved November 17, 2005, from http://www.wested.org/techpolicy/refind.html

Darling-Hammond, L. (1999). Target time toward teachers. *Journal of Staff Development, 20*(2), 35-42.

Davis, J. (1996). Computer-assisted distance learning, part II: Examination performance of students on and off campus. *Journal of Engineering, 85*(1), 77-82.

Doherty, K., & Skinner, R. (2003, January 9). States of the states. Quality count 2003: "If I can't learn from you..." *Education Week, 22*(17), 75-78.

Dubois, J. R. (1996). Going the distance: A national distance learning initiative. *Adult Learning, 8*(1), 19-21.

Dutton, J., Dutton, M., & Perry, J. (2001). Do online students perform as well as lecture students? *Journal of Engineering Education, 90*(1), 131-136.

Dyke, M., Harding, A., & Lajeunesse, S. (2006, April). *Digital observation of teaching practice.* Paper presented at the Annual Conference of the American Educational Research Association, San Francisco.

Ezarik, M. (2001). Charting the technology explosion. *Curriculum Administrator, 37*(7), 36-41.

Filby, N. (1995). Analysis of reflective professional development models. ED 393 057.

Guskey, T. (2000). *Evaluating professional development.* Thousand Oaks, CA: Corwin Press, Inc.

Haga, M., & Heitkamp, T. (2000). Bringing social work education to the prairie. *Journal of Social Work Education, 36*(2), 309-324.

Halal, W., & Liebowitz, J. (1994). Telelearning: The multimedia revolution in education. *Futurist, 28*(6), 21-26.

Heitkamp, T. (1995). *Social work education at a distance: An innovative approach.* A paper presented at the Annual Program Meeting of the Council on Social Work Education, San Diego, CA.

Hiltz, S. (1997). Impacts of college-level courses via asynchronous learning networks: Some preliminary results. *Journal of Asynchronous Learning Networks, 1*(2), 1-19.

Johnson, S., Aragon, S., Shaik, N., & Palma-Rivas, N. (2000). Comparative analysis of learner satisfaction and learning outcomes in online and face-to-face learning environments. *Journal of Interactive Learning Research, 11*(1), 29-49.

Joyce, B., & Showers, B. (1995). *Student achievement through staff development: Fundamentals of school renewal* (2nd ed.). New York: Longman.

Kraft, N. P. (1997). Components for effective professional development. *RMC Research Corporation.* Retrieved April 8, 2006, from http://www.starcenter.org/articles/effectivepd.html

LaRose, R., Gregg, J., & Eastin, M. (1998). Audio graphic telecourses for the Web: An experiment. *Journal of Computer-Mediated Communication [On-line], 4*(2). Retrieved March 18, from http://www.ascusc.org/jcmc/vol4/issue2/larose.html

Marshall, J. M. (2002). *Learning with technology: Evidence that technology can and does, support learning.* White paper prepared for Cable in the Classroom.

Martin, M. (2005). Seeing is believing: The role of videoconferencing in distance learning. *British Journal of Educational Technology, 36*(3), 397-405.

Matthews, D. (1999). The origins of distance education and its use in the United States. *THE Journal, 27(2),* 54-60.

Merriam, S. B. (2001). Andragogy and self-directed learning: Pillars of adult learning theory. *New Directions for Adult and Continuing Education, 89,* 3-13.

Motamedi, V. (2001). A critical look at the use of videoconferencing in the United States distance education. *Education, 122*(2), 386-394.

Mouza, C. (2003). Learning to teach with new technology: Implications for professional development. *Journal of Research on Technology in Education, 35*(2), 272-289.

Norman, K. I., & Hayden, K. L. (2002). K-12 instruction in the United States: Integrating na-

tional standards for science and writing through emerging technologies. In *Proceedings of the 10th International Organization for Science and Technology Education Symposium, Foz do Iguacu, Parana, Brazil: Vol: 1 & 2* (pp. 323-333).

O'Connor, D. (2003). Application sharing in K-12 education: Teaching and learning with Rube Goldberg. *TechTrends, 47*(5), 6-13.

Peters, O. (1993). *Understanding distance education.* In K. Harry, M. Hohn, & D. Keegan (Eds.). *Distance education: New perspectives.* London: Routledge.

Petracchi, H., & Patchner, M. (2000). Social work students and their learning environment: A comparison of interactive television. *Journal of Social Work Education, 36*(2), 335-347.

Richardson, V. (2003). The dilemmas of professional development. *Phi Delta Kappan, 84*(5), 401-406.

Rodes, P., Knapczyk, D., Chapman, C., & Chung, H. (2000). Involving teachers in Web-based professional development. *T.H.E. Journal, 27*(10), 95-102.

Schunk, D. H. (1999). Social self interaction and achievement behavior. *Educational Psychologist, 34*(4), 219-227.

Schutte, J. G. (1997). *Virtual teaching in higher education: The new intellectual superhighway or just another traffic jam?* Retrieved February 13, 2006, from http://www.csun.edu/sociology/virexp.htm

Silverman, S., & Silverman, G. (1999). The educational enterprise zone: Where knowledge comes from! *T.H.E. Journal, 26*(7), 56.

Smeaton, A., & Keogh, G. (1999). An analysis of the use of virtual delivery of undergraduate lectures. *Computers and Education, 32*(1), 83-94.

Souder, W. E. (1993). The effectiveness of traditional vs. satellite delivery in three management of technology master's degree programs. *The American Journal of Distance Education, 7*(1), 37-53.

Sparks, D., & Hirsh, S. (1997). *A new vision for staff development.* Alexandria, VA: Association for Supervision and Curriculum Development.

Speck, M. (1996). Best practice in professional development for sustained educational change. *ERS Spectrum, 14*(2), 33-41.

Spillane, J. P. (2000). *District leader's perceptions of teacher learning* (Rep. No. OP-05). University of Pennsylvania, Consortium for Policy Research in Education.

The Institute for the Advancement of Research in Education at AEL (2004, April). *Review of research: Nine components of effective professional development.* Prepared for Texas Instrument Educational and Productivity Solutions Division.

Tucker, S. (2001). Distance education: Better, worse, or as good as traditional education? *Online Journal of Distance Learning Administration, 4*(4). Retrieved February 23, 2006, from http://www/westga.edu/~distance/ojdla/winter44/tucker44.html

Tweedell, C. B. (2000, October). *A theory of adult learning and implications for practice.* Paper presented at the Annual Meeting of the Midwest Educational Research Association, Chicago. ED 446 702.

U.S. Department of Education (2004). *National education technology plan. Tear down those walls: The revolution is underway.* Retrieved November 23, 2005, from http://nationaledtechplan.org/the-plan/TearDownThoseWalls.asp

Wade, R. (1984). What makes a difference in in-service teacher education? A meta-analysis of research. *Educational Leadership, 42*(4), 48-54.

Witherspoon, J. P. (1996). *Distance education: A planner's casebook.* Boulder, CO: Western Interstate Commission for Higher Education.

Yorks, L. (2005). Adult learning and the generation of new knowledge and meaning: Creating liberating spaces for fostering adult learning through practitioner-based collaborative action inquiry. *Teacher College Record, 107*(6), 1217-1244.

Section VI
The Impact of Videoconferencing:
Does it Help?

Chapter XVII
The Impact of Multimedia Videoconferencing on Children's Learning:
Positive Outcomes of Use

Dianna L. Newman
University at Albany/SUNY, USA

ABSTRACT

The use of videoconferencing as a means of bringing external informal educators into the K-12 classroom is an area of increasing interest in the field of education. To date, however, few studies have documented the impact of the process on students' cognitive and affective outcomes. This chapter presents findings from a series of studies that compared student outcomes for those who received technology-supported videoconferencing with those who did not receive videoconferencing. Findings indicate that students who participated in videoconferencing had higher scores on cognitive indicators, were more motivated to learn the material, and were more interested in learning about related topics.

INTRODUCTION

Weiss (1998) found that 88% of museums already have resources available that could provide K-12 educational settings with programming that was directly related to school-based needs. Several studies (Greenwood, 1998; Sembor, 1997; Speltz & Shaugnessy, 1990) have found that coordinating provider materials with state and national learning standards allows external educators to offer even more information and resources to K-12 users. Jonassen (2002) noted that teachers could become more effective in breaking down the barriers of learning associated with traditional classroom instruction if they would incorporate these resources into their teaching. Many districts, however, are not able to take advantage of these opportunities if their students must be transported to the provider; this is especially true for districts that are economically disadvantaged or where security is an issue. As a result, both content providers and educators have begun to look for alternate means of bridging the gap between the K-12 classroom and external expert providers (Cavanaugh, 2001). One method that appears to have potential is the use of videoconferencing.

Videoconferencing has been defined as "a live connection between people in separate locations for the purpose of communication, usually involving audio and often text as well as video" (Tufts University: Educational Media Center, n.d., Glossary). Unlike many other forms of online communication, videoconferencing requires the participants' real-time physical presence to communicate with learners at distant sites. Proponents of the medium believe that using videoconferencing in the classroom community has many advantages. One of the benefits of videoconferencing rests in its capacity to import external resources to the classroom via advanced technology (Motamedi, 2001). In addition, it is believed that videoconferencing can better accommodate communities of diverse learning styles than do other online tools in which instructional strategies may be asynchronously mismatched with learners' needs. In fact, many state that it is the interactive element of videoconferencing that is the real key to its success when combined with well-planned, student-centered instruction (Greenberg, 2004; Omatseye, 1999).

A great deal of research has been conducted on how students react to online computer or Web-supported learning (Bennet, 2002; Windschitl & Sahl, 2002), but very little scientifically-based information is available to support the impact of videoconferencing between K-12 learners and external experts. Early research on videoconferencing and student learning yielded mixed results, at best. According to Speltz and Shaugnessy (1990), a clear understanding of student needs with a direct tie to classroom objectives was needed by providers for a successful "visit" to be achieved.

Similar results were found by Furst-Bowe (1997), who reported no differences in student reactions when piloting videoconferencing, unless instructors received training in appropriate use and materials were integrated into and supported current instruction. Gernstein (2000) also found that if videoconferencing was tied to the curriculum, it would increase student motivation. Additionally, Gernstein noted that higher levels of discussion were yielded when videoconferencing was supported by inquiry-based activities. In the majority of these studies, however, major limitations can be noted; first and foremost, because the studies were conducted independently, sample sizes were either small or limited to a particular setting, provider, or grade level. Consistent variables, which would allow for aggregation, also were not used across studies. In addition, in most cases, multiple methods of assessing impact were not used, nor were follow-up studies conducted to assess long-term outcomes.

A similar lack of clarity can be found when examining early research on the impact of videoconferencing and support for educational reform. Although Cochrane (1996) and Badenhorst and Axmann (2002) indicate that videoconferencing between geographically-distanced sites eliminated travel time and reduced costs affiliated with physical field trips, they offer no scientifically-based evidence of how the process can assist schools in meeting state and national learning standards, mandated testing, or support programs that have advanced learning and problem-solving as part of their objectives. Freeman (1998), Knipe and Lee (2002), Pachnowski (2002), and Peterson (1998) provided limited evidence of support for inquiry-based learning and enrichment of resources, but again methodological independence does not allow for generalization to alternate settings, providers, and programs, nor are long-term perceptions assessed.

PURPOSE OF THE CHAPTER

The purpose of this chapter is to present the findings of a series of studies investigating the impact of technology-supported videoconferencing with external content providers on K-12 students' cognitive outcomes. Eleven quasi-experimental comparative studies were conducted as part of a large federally-funded program[1] that focused on developing standards-based, external provider-supported curriculum. The primary independent variable was type of instruction (technology-supported videoconferencing with external providers vs. traditional classroom coverage); the primary dependent variable was student score on a teacher-developed standards-based assessment scale. Additional dependent variables were evaluator observations of student interactions, student self-reports of self-directed learning, and evaluator ratings of student-generated learning reports. Two major questions are being asked in these studies:

1. Does videoconference-supported instruction impact students' affective and cognitive educational outcomes when compared to non-videoconferencing instruction?
2. Does level or type of student participation in videoconferencing impact students' affective and cognitive educational outcomes?

RESULTS OF STUDIES

Question One: The Impact of Videoconferencing

- **Purpose:** The purpose of this series of studies was to document the impact of use of videoconferencing with external providers when compared to non-use across multiple grade levels with multiple providers across different school districts. The emphasis was on immediate learning specific to standards-based curriculum that would normally be used in a classroom. Nine quasi-experimental studies were designed and implemented that allowed teachers to use videoconferencing to access external providers, while a comparison classroom presented the same information in a traditional teacher-led approach. For each study, the independent variable was mode of instruction (with and without videoconferencing); the key dependent variable was impact on teacher-developed cognitive assessment.

- **Participants:** Eight schools, 14 teachers and over 300 students participated in these studies. The schools were located primarily within urban and suburban districts. Teachers represented elementary-, middle-, and high-school disciplines; students represented all levels of ability. Eight content providers, representing zoos, art museums, historical sites, and national parks served as the external educators.

- **Instrumentation:** Both qualitative and quantitative assessment measures were employed across the studies. To document cognitive impact, the experimental and comparison teachers in each study jointly developed a post-unit assessment with the assistance of the researchers. The form of this assessment varied across the studies but was consistent within each study. In some cases, assessment consisted of multiple-choice, forced-choice, and short-answer questions. In other situations, projects, presentations, and group work were used to assess impact. In all cases, teachers were urged to use the type of assessment that would be typical of their normal student evaluation process. Each score was standardized to represent a 14-point scale (ranging from F=0 to A+=13). In addition, a sample of products was collected and scored off-site by the researchers to provide evidence of reliability and validity. Cognitive archival data that would serve as covariates to control for individual student differences were gathered as well. These consisted of students' prior year's general grade-point average and prior year's specific-content end-of-year grade in the subject that was the focus of the videoconference. Student and teacher perceptions of the process, content, and outcomes of instruction were collected for both experimental and comparison classrooms using post-affective paper-pencil surveys and interviews. Researchers also observed each classroom to validate similarity of content between experimental and comparison classrooms.

- **Results:** Multivariate analysis of variance was used to analyze the affective data; multivariate analysis of covariance was used to analyze the cognitive data. The independent variable was type of instruction (e.g., videoconference-supported and traditional). The dependent variables were student cognitive scores and perceptions of outcomes. Both prior grade-point average and prior year's content grade served as significant covariates for the cognitive dependent variables. Results of the nine studies are summarized in Table 1.

Examination of the data indicates that students who were in the videoconferencing sections consistently found the material that was covered to be more interesting and also reported greater interest in learning more about the topic in the future than did students who were in comparison classrooms. Students who received the videoconference version also self-reported higher levels of learning and indicated greater desire to learn more than did students in the comparison classroom.

Findings for cognitive outcomes also support the positive impact of videoconferencing on students' cognitive outcomes. In six of the nine studies, students who received the videoconference version of instruction scored higher on cognitive measures than did students who

received comparative instruction. In two settings (studies three and eight), instructional outcomes were equivalent for both methods. The comparison group outperformed the videoconference group in only one study (study number five). A review of the instructional process for this group identified confounding variables that might have influenced this outcome. First, the videoconference technology failed for 10 minutes of the experimental situation, causing an interruption in the instructional process, and second, the teacher provided more coverage of key concepts during the comparison hands-on exercises than did the external provider.

Overall, findings indicated that in the majority of studies, inclusion of videoconferencing in instruction did make a significant positive difference in students' cognitive scores. Students who were involved in videoconferencing tended to score higher on more complex items and were able to present more examples of applied knowledge than did students who received the traditional methods.

In addition, both teachers and students had more positive perceptions of the instructional process when videoconferencing was involved. Students indicated higher levels of interest, motivation, and long-term transfer. Observations indicated that when videoconferencing occurred, students tended to be more focused on materials, were better prepared to discuss content and application, and had more collaborative experiences than in the non-videoconference classrooms. Results of student-generated learning examples indicated that the more interactive that the videoconferencing experience was, the greater was the students' retention of knowledge.

Question Two: The Degree of Student Participation

Based on observations of the nine studies reported above, the researchers determined a need for further study of the role of student participation

Table 1. Impact of videoconferencing in elementary, middle-school, and secondary-education settings: Summary of nine quasi-experimental studies (Note: CC= comparison classroom; VC= videoconference classroom)

Study 1: Grade 9					
Content		**Affective**		**Cognitive**	
Class	Videoconference	Variables	Results	Variable	Results
English	Greek Mythology	Interesting	VC>CC	One multiple choice and 11 short answer	VC>CC
		Learned a lot	VC>CC		
		Like to learn more	VC>CC		
		More interested	VC>CC		

Study 2: Grade 8					
Content		**Affective**		**Cognitive**	
Class	Videoconference	Variables	Results	Variable	Results
Music	Commercials	Interesting	VC=CC	Five short answer items	VC>CC
		Leaned a lot	VC>CC		
		Like to learn more	VC>CC		
		More interested	VC>CC		

Study 3: Grade 6					
Content		**Affective**		**Cognitive**	
Class	Videoconference	Variables	Results	Variable	Results
Science	Moon landing	Interesting	VC>CC	Multiple choice, short answer, and essays	Equiva-lent
		Leaned a lot	VC>CC		
		Like to learn more	VC>CC		
		More interested	VC>CC		

Study 4: Grade 6					
Content		**Affective**		**Cognitive**	
Class	Videoconference	Variables	Results	Variable	Results
Social Studies	Egypt	Interesting	CC>VC	15 multiple choice and 15 short answer	VC>CC
		Leaned a lot	VC=CC		

Continued on following page

Table 1. continued

Study 1: Grade 9					
Content		Affective		Cognitive	
Class	Videoconference	Variables	Results	Variable	Results
English	Greek Mythology	Interesting	VC>CC	One multiple choice and 11 short answer	VC>CC
		Like to learn more	CC>VC		
		More interested	CC>VC		
Study 5: Grade 7					
Content		Affective		Cognitive	
Class	Videoconference	Variables	Results	Variable	Results
Technology (Bridges)	Physics of Mass & Force (Technical problems)	Interesting	VC>CC	Bridge Building Project (scored by a rubric)	CC>VC
		Learned a lot	VC>CC		
		Like to learn more	VC>CC		
		More interested	VC>CC		
Study 6: Grade 7					
Content		Affective		Cognitive	
Class	Videoconference	Variables	Results	Variable	Results
Health	Infectious disease Food-born illness	Interesting	CC>VC	Multiple choice, short answer, and essays	VC>CC
		Learned a lot	VC>CC		
		Like to learn more	CC>VC		
		More interested	CC>VC		
Study 7: Grade 10					
Content		Affective		Cognitive	
Class	Videoconference	Variables	Results	Variable	Results
Social Studies	WWII/Holocaust (VC over 2 periods)	Interesting	VC>CC	Written assignment Midterm question; DBQ	VC>CC
		Learned a lot	CC>VC		
		Like to learn more	VC=CC		
		More interested	VC>CC		

Continued on following page

Table 1. continued

Study 1: Grade 9					
Content		Affective		Cognitive	
Class	Videoconference	Variables	Results	Variable	Results
English	Greek Mythology	Interesting	VC>CC	One multiple choice and 11 short answer	VC>CC
Study 8: Grade 4					
Content		Affective		Cognitive	
Class	Videoconference	Variables	Results	Variable	Results
Science	Animal adaption: Physical and behavioral adaption	Interesting	VC=CC	Multiple choice, short answer, and an essay	Equivalent
		Learned a lot	VC=CC		
		Like to learn more	VC>CC		
		More interested	CC>VC		
Study 9: Grade 5					
Content		Affective		Cognitive	
Class	Videoconference	Variables	Results	Variable	Results
Science	Ecosystems: fresh and saltwater aquatic ecosytems	Interesting	CC>VC	Five short answer test	VC>CC
		Learned a lot	VC=CC		
		Like to learn more	CC>VC		
		More interested	VC=CC		

in videoconferencing. Initial findings, reported by Newman and Goodwin-Segal (2003) utilized systematic observations of 33 videoconferences. The data from these observations resulted in a delineation of three major types of student-provider interactions. The first of these, labeled as *provider-centered*, utilized an external educator to bring materials into the classroom. In this setting, the provider took on the role of an expert and provided information to students who observed the videoconference in a passive manner; that is,

the majority of student time was spent watching the videoconference with only limited time for question-and-answer feedback. The role of the teacher in these settings was that of classroom manager. The second type of interaction, *provider-led guided inquiry*, also had the external provider leading the instruction, but students were provided with handouts or used preplanned questions or presentations as part of the videoconference. Students generally listened to a presentation by the provider, carried out a preplanned task such as filling out a worksheet while the provider covered material, and then asked questions based on the material. In some settings the questions were pre-planned by the students and teachers; in others, the provider and/or teacher limited question content to the specific tasks or materials. The teacher in this setting served as classroom manager, but also assisted in distribution of materials, and helped call on students for questions. In the third setting, termed *student-centered*, students were actively engaged in hands-on design, implementation, and product development while the provider and teacher served as co-teachers. The provider frequently began with a problem-solving exercise, reviewed materials, and allowed students the opportunity to work on the problem during the videoconference. The teacher co-facilitated the problem-solving, working with some students while the provider worked with others. Students were actively engaged in questioning and answering with the provider, other students, and the teacher during the videoconference. Analysis of affective and cognitive data indicated that students who engaged in the more active process utilized higher levels of questioning as coded by Blooms' taxonomy and expressed greater interest in follow-up activities once the videoconference was completed.

Parallel to this data collection, the researchers also were conducting observations of a series of large participant videoconferences called virtual field trips (Newman, Catapano, & Spaulding, 2002). In these settings, a provider broadcast to over 100 sites at a preset time on a preselected topic with a semi-structured script. Students could observe these videoconferences in their individual classrooms or in large assemblies; questions could be e-mailed or phoned in to the provider, but were generally not answered during the videoconference. Direct student involvement was limited in these settings, and data indicated limited residual interest in the material.

As a result of these findings, we have begun a series of quasi-experimental studies that are examining the impact of purposely-manipulated levels of student involvement. Two of these studies are presented studies as ten and eleven.

Study Ten: Assembly versus Classroom Delivery and Student Participation

- **Purpose:** The purpose of this study was to investigate potential differences between videoconferencing to a large group of

Table 2. A comparison of students' perceptions of the effect of videoconferences' level of interactivity

Statement	% Agree Interactive Classroom (n=23)	% Agree Passive Assembly (n=80)	% Difference
I learned a lot from the videoconference	98	60	38*
I found the videoconference to be interesting	95	56	39*
I was able to partcipate by asking questions, giving answers, or working on actvities	90	42	48*
I would like to learn more about what I saw during the videoconference	54	32	22*

students in an assembly-style setting and delivery to a classroom setting. In this study, the same provider delivered the same curriculum to two different elementary-school settings; the length of the videoconference was the same as was the basic content.

- **Participants:** Participants consisted of 103 students in a suburban school system. One class received the videoconference in the students' regular classroom with the teacher in the room. The presentation reflected a *provider-guided inquiry approach*; it featured questions, answers, and guided worksheets, with students allowed to ask additional questions at the end. In the assembly setting, four classes of students were gathered in a theatre-style setting and watched the videoconference on a large screen monitor. The videoconference was *provider-centered*; it featured direct instruction followed by time for some questions at the end.

- **Instrumentation:** Evaluator observations, paper-pencil assessment of student interest, and interviews with teachers and a selective sample of students were used to assess differences in outcomes. Observations were conducted both during the videoconferences and in immediate post reviews in the classrooms; inventories of student interest were conducted immediately following the videoconferences; interviews were conducted after follow-up classroom discussions.

- **Results:** A quasi-experimental nonequivalent control group design was used for this study. Qualitative and quantitative data were analyzed descriptively and inferentially to determine if there were differences between the two groups. A summary of student perceptions is presented in Table 2. Examination of these data indicates that students who received the videoconference in an interactive manner in their regular setting reported a more positive experience. There was also a relationship between interest and self-reported learning. During follow-up interviews with students, those who reported gains in learning also reported the program to be interesting and perceived the videoconference to foster participation, while students who participated in the program that featured less active involvement reported only low level, if any, learning outcomes.

Table 3. Cognitive test score results for two types of videoconferences

Plants Videoconference				
Role	n	Pre-test score	Post-test score	Net gain
Observer	43	3.58	4.26	0.68
Participant	41	4.32	5.29	0.97
Total	84	3.94	4.76	0.82
Adaptations Videoconference				
Role	n	Pre-test score	Post-test score	Net gain
Observer	41	2.02	2.76	0.74
Participant	37	3.65	4.60	0.95
Total	78	2.80	3.63	0.83

Study Eleven: Regular Classrooms Engaged versus Passive Interaction

- **Purpose:** The purpose of this study was to investigate potential differences in learning outcomes that resulted from engaged versus passive interaction in classroom-based videoconferencing. A quasi-experimental pretest-posttest reverse-order replication design was used; the independent variable was type of student interaction with the provider (passive and engaged); the dependent variable was score on a teacher-developed instrument.

- **Participants:** The study incorporated four first-grade classrooms (n=84) in an elementary school setting; the videoconferences were embedded within their science unit on plants and animals. All students were actively engaged in one videoconference, but only observed another videoconference. Engaged participation involved interacting with the content provider throughout the broadcast by using props and asking or answering questions (*provider-led guided inquiry*). Observer students were seated in chairs around the participating group of students where they could see the videoconference but were not engaged in direct interaction with the content provider. During the second videoconference, roles were reversed, with participating students becoming the passive observing students, and those who had observed becoming engaged participants.

- **Instrumentation:** Prior to the videoconference broadcasts, the four first-grade classroom teachers adapted a published assessment instrument to evaluate students' prior knowledge of plant and animal adaptations. The final classroom exams consisted of six short-answer questions; items were scored as either correct or incorrect. The exams were administered to all students prior to the videoconference, and before students

knew what role they would take. After participating in or observing the videoconference, students were again administered the same assessment instrument. The same process was used for both videoconference opportunities.

- **Results:** A pretest-posttest reverse-order replication design was used to analyze the data. Two questions were addressed: First, was there a significant gain over time in students' cognitive test scores, no matter in what role they were? Second, did mode of participation (engaged or observer) interact with the amount of knowledge gained? Table 3 summarizes the findings of the study.

Examination of the data for the plants videoconference indicated that students in the four participating classes scored higher on an examination designed to test their knowledge of plants after either type of participatory role; variations in growth were noted, however, by the level of participation. Students that observed the videoconference on plants scored an average of 3.58 on the test prior to the videoconference and 4.26 post-conference, a gain of 0.68. The students that participated in the videoconference on plants scored an average of 4.32 on the test prior to participation and 5.29 post-conference, a gain of 0.97. Overall, participating students averaged a gain of .31 more than did those who only observed ($p<.01$).

Similar results were found for the adaptation videoconference. The data indicate that no matter what their participant role, students scored higher after a videoconference on that subject matter. Students that observed the videoconference scored an average of 2.02 on the adaptations test prior to the videoconference and 2.76 post-conference, a gain of 0.74. The students that participated in the videoconference scored an average of 3.65 on the adaptations test prior to participation and 4.60 post-conference, a gain of 0.95. Overall, participating students had an average gain that was .21 higher than that of observing students (p<.01).

The results from this study support the prior studies that found that students who receive videoconferencing learn and retain information presented during the program. Results also suggest that students learn and retain more information by actively participating in a videoconference (e.g., working with materials, directly asking and answering questions with the provider) rather than sitting passively and listening to the content provider lecture or interact with other students.

SUMMARY AND CONCLUSION

The combined results of these studies add to scientific evidence that supports the use of multimedia methods in K-12 classrooms. More specifically, they provide initial support for the use of videoconferencing between external providers such as museums, zoos, and historical sites, and students who are geographically-distanced. The findings support the following conclusions:

The Impact of Videoconferencing

Combined findings based on the nine quasi-experimental studies that tested outcomes associated with videoconferencing indicate that in general, videoconferencing had positive effects on student attitude and student achievement; students who received videoconferencing had higher scores on classroom achievement post-tests than did students who received comparable instruction without videoconferencing. Students who received videoconferencing also generally had greater interest in the material and wanted to learn more about that topic than did students who did not receive videoconferencing. These findings were consistent across students at elementary-, middle-, and high-school levels and across providers and content.

The Impact of Level of Participation

Further research suggests that student outcomes of videoconferencing are dependent on the opportunities for participants to interact with the facilitator, and on the instructional style and approaches of the videoconference host. Two quasi-experimental studies reinforced earlier descriptive studies that reported three distinct types of provider-student interactions and potential differences in learning that might result from these variations in interactions. The two comparative studies found that active participation had a positive impact on both student affect and achievement. Students exposed to active sessions of videoconferencing showed greater gains in interest and subsequent learning than did those who were passively involved.

Continued research is needed in this field. For instance, it was noted by the researchers that the instructional role or placement of the videoconference within the curriculum unit may impact student outcomes. Over the course of 100-plus observations, the researchers have noted several variations in timing and placement that should be studied further. For instance, in some settings, the videoconference was used as an advanced organizer; in others, it was embedded within the curriculum; and in others, it was used as a summative program or served to help students review material. Another area that should be examined is the use of additional digital or multimedial resources within or around the videoconferencing process (e.g., Web-based or interactive technology resources). In a preliminary study, Newman and Goodwin-Segal (2004) found that the combined use of videoconferences and online resources had a cumulative impact on student knowledge retention. Additional studies also should investigate the role of videoconferencing in providing differentiated instruction; analysis of qualitative observational data suggests that the student-centered approach may meet many of the needs associated with working with diverse learners.

Alternate forms of providers and videoconferences also should be examined. These studies only addressed videoconferencing that used external expert providers; many schools now have the ability to support collaborative classroom through the process. Case studies of this approach indicate a variety of outcomes associated with students presenting to students.

Overall, the findings of the studies presented in this chapter suggest that videoconferencing is a valuable tool that can be used to break down some of the invisible walls of the K-12 classroom. Videoconferencing can help bring external resources to geographically- and economically-distanced learners and can support standards-based curriculum in a way that improves learning. As the equipment and processes become more available, and as more providers develop their repertoire of standards-based resources, continued validation of the process and its outcomes are needed. This information is not only informative to the future development of multimedia theory and practice, but is also essential to administrators and teachers in making decisions about allocation of their resources and their students' use.

REFERENCES

Baldenhorst, Z., & Axmann, M. (2002). The educational use of videoconferencing in the arts faculty: Shedding a new light on puppetry. *British Journal of Educational Technology, 33*(3), 291-299.

Bennet, F. (2002). The future of computer technology in K-12 education. *Phi Delta Kappan, 2*(8), 621-625.

Cavanaugh, C. (2001). The effectiveness of interactive distance education technologies in K-12 learning: A meta-analysis. *International Journal of Educational Telecommunications, 7*(1), 73-88.

Cochrane, C. (1996). The use of videoconferencing to support learning: An overview of issues relevant to the library and information profession. *Education for Information, 14*(4), 317-330.

Freeman, M. (1998). Videoconferencing: A solution to the multi-campus large classes problem? *British Journal of Educational Technology, 29*(3), 197-210.

Furst-Bowe, J. A. (1997). Comparison of students in traditional and videoconferencing courses in training and development. *International Journal of Instructional Media, 24*(3), 197-206.

Gernstein, R. B. (2000). Videoconferencing in the classroom: Special projects toward cultural understanding. *Integration of Technology in the Classroom, 16*(3-4), 177-186.

Greenberg, A. (2004, February). Navigating the sea of research on videoconferencing-based distance education: A platform for understanding research into the technology's effectiveness and value. *Wainhouse Research*. Retrieved September 9, 2005, from http://www.wainhouse.com/files/papers/wr-navseadistedu.pdf

Greenwood, A. (1998). Learning science at a distance: Using interactive television to work with schools. *Education, 118*(3), 349-352.

Jonassen, D. H. (2002). Engaging and supporting problem-solving in online learning. *The Quarterly Review of Distance Education, 3*, 1-13.

Knipe, D., & Lee, M. (2002). The quality of teaching and learning via videoconferencing. *British Journal of Educational Technology, 33*(2), 301-311.

Motamedi, V. (2001). A critical look at the use of videoconferencing in United States distance education. *HighBeam Research*. Retrieved September 15, 2005, from http://www.highbeam.com

Newman, D. L., Catapano, N., & Spaulding, D. T. (2002). *The virtual informal education Web* project: *Formative evaluation of the Schenectady city school district technology innovation challenge grant* (Ball State Report - March, 2002). Albany, NY: University at Albany/SUNY, Evaluation Consortium.

Newman, D. L., & Goodwin-Segal, T. (2003, April). *Evaluating a technology integration challenge grant program: Using technology to connect museums and classrooms.* Paper presented at the American Educational Research Associaton (AERA) Annual Meeting, Chicago.

Newman, D. L., & Goodwin-Segal, T. (2004). *Civics mosaic: Cooperative civic education and economic education exchange program evaluation report* (October 2003-June 2004). Albany, NY: University at Albany/SUNY, Evaluation Consortium.

Omatseye, J. N. (1999). Teaching through tele-conferencing: Some curriculum challenges. *College Student Journal, 33*(3), 346-353.

Pachnowski, L. (2002). Virtual field trips through videoconferencing. *Learning and Leading with Technology, 29*(6), 10-13.

Peterson, R. (1998). The NASA Lewis Research Center's learning technologies project. *T.H.E. Journal, 26*(4), 63-66.

Sembor, E. C. (1997). Citizenship, diversity, and distance learning: Videoconferencing in Connecticut. *Social Education, 61*(3), 154-159.

Speltz, C. A., & Shaugnessy, M. F. (1990). Human interactions in education: The museum as an experimental learning center. (ERIC Document Reproduction No.ED328493).

Tufts University, Educational Media Center (n.d.). Glossary. Retrieved September 15, 2005, from http://www.tufts.edu/orgs/edmedia/gloss.shtml

Weiss, N. E. (1998). *True needs true partner: 1998 survey highlights.* Washington, DC: Institute of Museum and Library Services. (ERIC Document Reproduction Service No. ED434 848).

Windschitl, M., & Sahl, K. (2002). Tracing teachers' use of technology in a laptop computer school: The interplay of teacher beliefs, social dynamics, and institutional culture. *American Educational Research Journal, 39*(1), 165-205.

ENDNOTE

[1] Project VIEW is a U.S. Department of Education Technology Innovation Challenge Grant; further information on the project may be found at www.projectview.org.

Chapter XVIII
Point-to-Point Videoconferencing:
Impact of Content Providers on the K-12 Classroom[1]

Patricia Barbanell
Schenectady City School District, USA

ABSTRACT

This chapter examines evidence that there is significant value added to K-12 educational outcomes that emerge as a result of provider use of interactive videoconferencing and supporting resources in their content delivery. It includes discussion of the outcomes of several presentation approaches that have been analyzed with regard to effectiveness and impact on student understanding. The aim of the chapter is to offer a solid foundation for understanding the impact of interactive videoconferencing on student learning, and to present an overview of approaches to structuring interactive programs to enable comprehensive, systemic change in student encounters with and understanding of curriculum content.

INTRODUCTION

Throughout the world, the growing availability of broadband technologies in education is creating an exciting transformation in school classrooms by enabling teachers to prepare students with the high degree of literacy needed to succeed in the 21st century information age. At the same time, the enhanced access to academic content through digital connectivity is providing an infrastructure for new approaches to teaching and learning, including unprecedented access to academic content through real-time interactive videoconferencing with geographically-distant content providers.

As part of efforts to improve student learning and raise student performance, K-12 schools are using interactive video communications, point-to-point videoconferencing to create new curriculum delivery models. The result is the emergence of new methods and infrastructures for content delivery that both facilitate dynamic, self-constructed learning, and enable students to follow a more effective path to learning.

The underpinning of the exciting emergence of cutting-edge interactive communications in the schools is the creation and implementation of innovative approaches and organizational structures for curriculum and instruction. The key to that innovation is the fluid ability of point-to-point videoconferencing to expand the traditional constructs of academic content by facilitating the integration of programs delivered by external providers into standards-based classroom curriculum.

The use of point-to-point videoconferencing provides digital tools that make it possible for K-12 students to communicate directly with external content providers (e.g., educational staff members, content experts or other knowledgeable individuals from museums, zoos, historical sites, scientific organizations, etc.). In this twenty-first century interactive environment, the expansion of teaching and learning structures reaches beyond schoolhouse walls to create a foundation for dynamic educational change and growth.

BACKGROUND

Why Use Point-to-Point Interactive Videoconferencing in K-12 Settings?

Educational professionals are enthusiastically supportive of videoconference opportunities for the classroom, and, in anecdotal statements contained in evaluation studies, they offer praise for the efficacy and relevance of point-to-point, interactive videoconferencing (Newman & King, 2004b). This documentation of supportive responses to point-to-point, interactive videoconferencing is of high interest to educators, administrators, and content providers who are hoping to dis-

cover whether point-to-point videoconferencing provides substantive *value added*, measurable improvement, to student learning and to student academic performance. In other words, they want to know whether there is external formal validation of the positive impact of K-12 videoconferencing on student learning (i.e., on what students know and understand).

The widening support for interactive videoconferencing in the classroom is emerging from programs that provide opportunities for teachers to partner with content providers collaboratively to create educational experiences designed to raise academic performance using structured integration of standards-based videoconference lessons into curriculum. By designing educational delivery that involves students in interactive point-to-point videoconferencing, a classroom learning environment is created, enabling providers to communicate with students in real-time while they share collection objects and content, and engage students in dialog requiring higher levels of information gathering, synthesis, and analysis.

Educators express positive perceptions and observations of student performance during and after videoconferencing experiences. K-12 teachers who use point-to-point, interactive technologies in their classrooms agree that videoconferencing is an exciting tool that can address diverse educational issues and offer solutions to many common problems and unmet needs in the schools.

To begin, interactive videoconferencing can counteract barriers to achievement of equity in education by offering cost-effective, open access to external content providers (e.g., museums, zoos, libraries, etc.) and their collections. Point-to-point videoconference technologies can facilitate equitable integration of provider resources into curriculum, regardless of the disadvantaging finances and demographics of some schools, and it can also increase the quality of educational opportunity for learners in geographically-remote and access-challenged communities.

Point-to-point videoconferencing can also provide a forum for student contact with presenters, such as subject-matter experts and career role-models, who represent a broad spectrum of racial, ethnic, and gender groupings. It can also provide low-cost options for effective access to high-level resources in schools that are dealing with travel safety concerns and escalating costs of field trip travel to content provider institutions.

VALUE ADDED

There is a growing need to look beyond anecdotal evidence to establish research-based confirmation of the benefits *(value added)* to student academic progress resulting from instructional innovation, including point-to-point videoconferencing. This phenomenon arises from state and federal (No Child Left Behind, 2001) regulations that increasingly require both validation of the effect of educational strategies on student performance, and school accountability for student learning. As a result, there is widespread interest in research-based substantiation that the inclusion of point-to-point interactive videoconference programs in K-12 curriculum provides *value-added* outcomes to classroom instruction.

When teachers use interactive videoconferencing to integrate external resources into their instructional delivery, there are often *value-added* outcomes in student performance and learning. *Value-added* outcomes also may include enhanced capacity for teachers to use differentiation of instruction when appropriate (Newman & King, 2004b).

Videoconferencing provides *value added* for content providers as they take advantage of the opportunity to become involved in student educational needs. Videoconferencing can enable content providers to offer better support for K-12 education, and can provide enhanced contexts in which to develop content reflecting the learning standards, and awareness of student and teacher academic needs (Newman & King, 2004a).

Of particular interest to school administrators and teachers is reliable, emerging evidence that new digital technologies and instructional techniques (such as interactive point-to-point videoconferencing) provide a learning environment that provides tools for students to raise their academic achievement (Newman, King, Gligora, Guckemus, & Pruden, 2004). This evidence is also of importance to content providers who are working to demonstrate the value of their offerings to meet educational needs.

In assessing interactive videoconferencing in K-12 educational environments, research-based documentation of *value added* to the educational process is of increasing significance. To begin, when examining methods of sustaining educational change, the *value-added* outcomes can be of significant importance (Fullan, 2000). Integrating videoconferencing into teaching methodology can, when skillfully utilized, contribute measurable *value added* to educational effectiveness (Motamedi, 2001). "The fundamental issue is not whether new instructional tools are more efficient at accomplishing current goals with conventional methods, but instead, how emerging media [such as point-to-point videoconferencing] can provide an effective means of reaching essential education objectives in the technology-driven, knowledge-based economy of this new century" (Dede, 2001, p. 174).

Point-to-point videoconferencing creates challenges in K-12 student learning that are akin to Johanssen's (1996) *Mindtools*, i.e., learning applications that engage students in critical thinking about curriculum content. Integrating interactive videoconferencing into K-12 curriculum provides *value-added* outcomes, including enhanced student academic growth that is observable through demonstrations of positive changes in intellectual cognition, subject content interest, and motivations to learn (Newman et al., 2004). For example, the research notes that teachers observe that students, when engaging with videoconference programming, are more actively involved in their own learning than their peers (Newman et al., 2004).

In Newman's (2005) research, teachers report that students who are involved with interactive point-to-point videoconferencing demonstrate a greater perspective and understanding of curriculum content. Increased access to videoconferencing provides expanded interactive communication opportunities among participants (e.g., students, providers, and teachers). This access broadens the learning context of curriculum and results in an expanded interactive educational context that enables students to encounter a highly-enriched selection of curriculum-related information and experiences, and thereby to achieve a higher level of academic performance.

Further, research suggests that the inquiry-based discourse of point-to-point videoconferencing in K-12 classrooms raises the quality of student inquiry and increases the levels of student critical thinking skills (Andrews & Marshall, 2000). Interactive videoconferencing also provides a teaching environment that increases the ability of students to work at higher cognitive levels than they achieve in traditional educational settings with teachers who use more conventional teaching methods (Gernstein, 2000).

Value Added: Interactivity

The importance of interactivity to the success or failure of the use of interactive videoconferencing in instruction has been recognized for several years. Most notably, it has been recognized that success rests strongly on the ability of the content provider to maximize the amount of interaction with students during a videoconference (Abrahamson, 1998).

Table 1. K-12 videoconference interactivity approaches (Based on Newman & Goodwin-Segal, 2003)

Approach	Mode	Description
Provider-Centered	Passive	Students passively watch the videoconference. They ask and answer only a few questions. The role of the teacher is limited to that of classroom manager or technology monitor.
Provider-Guided	Combination: Passive and Interactive Response	Students are receivers of information from the provider for the first part of the videoconference. Then, in the second part of the videoconference, students participate in activities led by the provider. During this latter stage of the videoconference, students actively ask and answer questions, and discuss the content of the videoconference. The role of the teacher expands to that of a discussion facilitator.
Student-Centered	Combination: Passive, Interactive Response and Self-directed Interaction	Throughout the videoconference, students work in groups, ask and answer questions, and discuss the content with the provider, with other students, and with the teacher. Additionally, students often solve problems as part of videoconference activities and/or participate actively with the presenter, with the teacher, and/or under teacher leadership with other students. Both the teacher and the content provider collaboratively guide learning.

Classroom videoconferencing broadens the availability of provider and educator-generated instructional resources for K-12 classrooms (Omatseye, 1999), and expands opportunities for in-depth interactions among videoconference participants of diverse backgrounds (Wilson, 2000).

The most successful videoconferences are designed to be highly interactive (Greenberg, 2004). Teacher-assessed cognitive outcome levels are more successful for students who are most interactively engaged in learning through point-to-point videoconferencing, as compared to those whose experience is restricted to online or teacher-centered approaches. When interactivity levels are highest, the videoconferences yield the highest measures of positive impact on student learning, and the increase in the quality of *value added* to education is greatest.

Students who experience highly-interactive videoconferencing integrated into regular instruction consistently achieve higher scores on cognitive assessment than students who receive only the traditional instructional format (Newman, 2005). Nonetheless, there are many benefits to each of the approaches. The variations of interactions during K-12 videoconferences and the roles of the videoconference participants can be classified using a menu of three patterns that contain increasing levels of provider-student interactions: *provider-centered, provider-guided,* and *student-centered* (Newman & Goodwin-Segal, 2003). See Table 1 for this distinction.

- **Provider-centered approach:** This approach offers access to the exciting content of an external provider using a lecture-demonstration presentation mode. For example, a well-known museum of art may present a combination of slides, DVDs, and videos to show students how to examine artwork and to provide information about the artist who created the work. Question-and-answer experiences with students are limited to direct inquiry about specific observations and facts. The videoconferencing technology allows the museum educator to conduct a specialized kind of "gallery tour", allowing students from distant locations to have a direct encounter with the rich curriculum-related resources of the museum collection.

- **Provider-guided approach:** In this approach, the content provider uses both a lecture-demonstration presentation and an extended interaction with student participants. For example, a cultural museum could begin its videoconference by narrating a collection-related story to young elementary students while sharing story-related museum artifacts with them. Students could then participate in a question-and-answer session based on the narrative of the story and information about the artifacts. The Q&A process is partly directed by the facts and observations presented to the students, and partly open-ended, allowing students to expand their learning with their own questions about the program. This process is designed to enable students not only to absorb the information provided to them, but also to analytically think about that information and respond to it.

- **Student-centered approach:** Levels of student interactions during a videoconference, in terms of the quantity and scope of student inquiry, have the highest assessed rating during interactive *student-centered* videoconferences. With this approach, the focus of the videoconference shifts from the presenter to the students as they take ownership of their own learning. For example, a historic battlefield might provide a program that is delivered by a ranger who appears in the role of a historical reenactor. The reenactor enters into dialog with students, engaging them in discussion regarding choices and facts based on the actual history of the battle, including troop movements and geographical factors that impacted the historic event. Students are prompted to create their own solutions and choices and articulate their own reasoning based on the information that they have learned. This mode of presentation allows the students to be the center of learning, exercising higher levels of cognitive abilities, including analysis and synthesis of information.

Value Added: Collaborative Learning Communities

In point-to-point videoconferences, teachers, students, and external providers collaboratively use real-time communication to share resources that emerge from the collections and expertise of the provider institutions, and from the curriculum content being studied in the schools. This sharing of information and resources creates an active learning community that allows students to benefit from an expanded educational environment.

Another aspect of *value added* to learning context (Menlove, Hansford, & Lignugaris-Kraft, 2000), educational processes, and outcomes by interactive point-to-point videoconferencing is the increased educational impact on teaching and learning which results from the increased development of collaborative structures and their inherent interactivity. The mutual interactivity designed by collaborating teachers and content providers in videoconferencing activities requires students to demonstrate skills in problem-solving and complex thinking. The result leads to changes in both the ways that students access information, and the means by which they demonstrate understanding of lessons which have been learned.

Value Added: Knowledge Communities

One of the most important *value-added* aspects of videoconferencing is that K-12 videoconference collaborators create a *knowledge community*, a network of practitioners who encompass,

acknowledge, and respect each other's multiple skills, synergistic competencies, and specific needs (Sallis & Jones, 2002). The emergence of the *knowledge community* as a new configuration for participating in the instructional setting leads to changes in the focus and roles of the participants. These changes enhance the *value added* to K-12 education by interactive videoconferences as the needs and the responsibilities of the collaborating participants are intertwined.

Historically, content-provider institutions have pursued their core goals, and when their goals do not align with those of the schools, they have been ambivalent in aspects of their support of K-12 classroom education. Similarly, in the past, the schools have had little commitment to help in accomplishing the educational goals of content providers. In the new *knowledge communities*, however, interactive videoconferencing requires creation of content integration that changes the dynamics of these roles. The structure of interactive videoconferencing creates an environment in which participants must become collaborating mediators as they search for and find common ground. In so doing, their individual talents are articulated, and special abilities are identified. These become the foundation of innovative program plans that utilize the best of all participants' potential contributions, while ensuring that the project aligns with the institutional missions of all.

In creating collaborations and their accompanying *knowledge communities*, as noted in Table 2, there are a variety of roles assumed by the participants. The overarching role of all of the collaborating partners in interactive videoconference collaborations is to work with the other participants to find common ground in the various institutional obligations and commitments which they each have, and to find points of intersection where provider collections and content expertise can be merged with academic curriculum.

This common role (i.e., the quest for instructional common ground and content synergy) may manifest itself in many ways. For example, while one role of content provider professionals may be to serve the educational needs of students, a more primary role always supersedes that, the role of promoter and protector of their institutions' primary curatorial missions and interpretive goals. The roles of the school professionals, on the other hand, are focused primarily on addressing pupil needs and academic progress while seeking to ensure that students both achieve the learning standards and are enabled to perform at their highest abilities. The *knowledge communities* bridge these divergent agendas through a process of constructivist discussion and collaborative innovation. The result is the creation of dynamic learning opportunities for students that align with both provider and school goals (Newman & King, 2004b).

In addition, the creation of videoconference *knowledge communities* enable schools and content providers to mutually establish a trust in which they all value and respect each participant's contribution. These *knowledge communities* provide a structural context in which participating groups emerge as information hubs that join together to grow from each others' abilities and knowledge, and to create new levels of collaborative competencies and expertise. As information hubs, they interact in various ways: They exchange shared visions, identify and create common goals, develop aligned viewpoints, and participate in reflective debate.

Table 2. Videoconference knowledge communities: Roles of partners

Community	Domain	Role
Teachers	Classroom Instruction	Teachers take the lead in determining how videoconferences connect with curriculum and improve student learning. The primary task is to create new ways of structuring courses to accommodate the expansion education from the classroom to the world.
Administrators	Sustainability Support and Project Oversight	Administrators align institutional plans and priorities to provide the essential technological environment for videoconferencing, and the leadership to sustain instructional change.
Content Professionals (Museum and Zoo Educators, Curators, etc.)	Museum Interpretation and Instruction	Content professionals design and facilitate access to the interpretive uses of the provider's collection. They also develop classroom-ready programs to present materials in a manner that enhances students' learning.
Technology Support Staff	Infrastructure Support	Technology support staff provide transparent connectivity and offer support to ensure that technology creates both an environment for learning and a seamless tool for exploring content.
Curriculum Specialists and/or Development Facilitators	Collaboration Facilitation	Curriculum specialists and/or development facilitators guide the collaborative process by encouraging a partnership that allows input from all members and helps to bridge the gap between the diverse missions of the collaborators

Figure 1. Knowledge communities' interaction

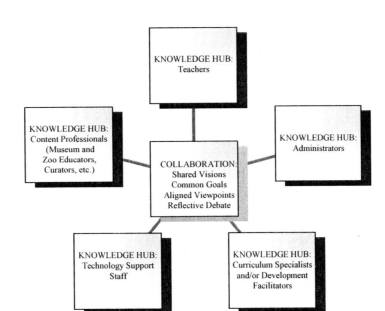

Videoconference *knowledge communities* offer school communities (teachers and students) opportunities to engage in learning. Collaborative videoconferencing measurably enhances the engagement of students with their own learning compared to their peers who do not participate in videoconferencing (Newman, 2005). The measurable enhancements go beyond the interactive videoconference structures. Students acquire a broader perception of diverse points of view in academic content and are able to engage in study and research using external (non-school) print and electronic resources. Furthermore, the expanded context for academic inquiry provided by interactive videoconferencing offers an enhanced sense of community.

Value Added: Alignment of Teaching Modalities and Content

The collaborative process and consequent creation of *knowledge communities* provides an additional and highly important *value-added* outcome: the alignment of the presentation modes of instruction (used by the teacher and/or content provider) with both the curriculum content and the learning needs of the students. This alignment allows providers to adapt their content and methods of instruction to the nature and characteristics of their collections as well as the academic and age-related needs of the K-12 students. It also allows teachers to make choices and engage in activities that ensure that the material and presentations that are brought into the classroom excite and interest students, align with the standards-based curriculum, and provide the most effective level of instruction. This alignment facilitates the selection of modes of instruction that work most effectively to teach aspects of the content that are included in the videoconference.

For example, a videoconference focusing on the science of flight is more effective for students when the content provider can provide a real-time demonstration of what occurs when air hits the shape of an airplane wing by having students simultaneously perform a simple experiment in the classroom that shows the effect of wind on an airfoil. Similarly, when presenting a program about gorillas, students are more likely to learn with greater understanding and higher information retention if a real-time observation of a gorilla is part of the program presentation. Furthermore, videoconference programs have a greater potential to have a larger and more long-lasting effect on student learning if content providers and teachers collaborate to make choices and design appropriate modes for instruction.

Outcomes

There is a diversity of outcomes that result from interactive videoconferencing in the classroom that impact student involvement, organizational systems, standards delivery, and student performance.

Student outcomes

Effective videoconferences are designed to enhance student interest in academic content, to broaden student engagement with their own learning, and to raise student academic performance. As the development and strengthening of a shared vision and common goals among stakeholders occurs, the collaborative environment serves as a foundation for the delivery of successful, content-rich learning experiences.

Cumulatively, these interactive videoconferences provide a foundation for improved educational outcomes that are changing the face of classrooms structures, teaching methodologies and learning resources. As schools and content providers are documenting the value of interactive videoconferencing technology, they are changing their primary focus of "value-added" outcomes to the student-centered benefits that will serve as the future benchmarks of educational practice.

With expanding use of videoconference programming delivered to K-12 schools by external providers (e.g., museums, zoos, etc.), validation of student achievement that is reached through videoconference experiences is growing. That validation is increasingly being used in the construction of evidence supporting the inclusion of interactive videoconferencing in K-12 curriculum delivery. In addition, as a result of the validation, provider institutions are increasingly improving and expanding their videoconferencing program offerings as they revisit their education structures and begin to infuse point-to-point videoconferencing into their missions (Newman & Goodwin-Segal, 2003).

In interactive videoconferencing, the cooperative approach of instruction and learning is resulting in multiple outcomes that are changing students' views of the learning process. For example, students are building their knowledge and appreciation of external, expert resources; and increasing their desire for and valuing of alternative sources of knowledge. Furthermore, teachers in schools who are involved with videoconferencing document higher expectations of student learning, observe greater use of problem-solving across all grades, and report a higher positive benefit ratio in terms of student learning and instructional time.

Using interactive videoconference programs and supporting Web-based resources results in a new, emerging reality of classroom pedagogy and a new, exciting extension of interpretive activities. Participants in interactive point-to-point videoconferencing observe that interactive educational technologies (such as point-to-point videoconferencing and digital archives) benefit schools by increasing their access to authentic and exceptional resources from academically-unique sources. (Newman, 2005)

Systemic Changes

As access to and usage of videoconferencing technologies increases, trends in systemic change are emerging. Content provider personnel are learning to appreciate videoconferencing not as an obstacle that exists in competition with the provider, but rather as a tool that supports ongoing institutional education efforts. Similarly, schools are changing their perception of videoconferencing from an enriching activity to an integral tool for learning.

Increased presence of videoconferencing in the schools has served as a foundation for initiating comprehensive, systemic change in educational technology integration. In general, stakeholders perceive that educational videoconferencing benefits students by increasing access to authentic, exceptional resources at museums and other institutions. Providers, on the other hand, are learning that videoconferencing benefits them by linking their institutions with new audiences for their programming. It also helps them to better align their content with the needs of those audiences.

The potentials of interactive videoconferencing transcend curriculum and grade level. Teachers from urban, suburban, and rural school districts report positive experiences with point-to-point videoconferences. The teachers find that the videoconferencing is a dynamic teaching opportunity, and they indicate a desire to utilize museums to link students more frequently with primary source materials.

Content providers also report that their understanding of effective instructional methods for K-12 students is positively impacted by the point-to-point, interactive videoconferencing experience. They indicate that the direct contact with students and the collaborative planning with teachers serve both to motivate them to retool their programs and to better align with K-12 curriculum and grade-related needs.

Standards

Videoconferencing facilitates development of interdisciplinary educational "products" that incorporate, as appropriate, various core standards areas, including mathematics, science, and technology (MST), social studies, fine arts, and English language arts. Thus, along with the development of high-quality videoconference programs has come the creation of standards-based resources that are designed to extend and expand the interactive experience into classroom lessons. The materials which are created (most of which can be found on videoconference program-related Web sites), are designed to be useful and relevant within multiple classroom settings, and are created to be useable with little teacher content research, minimal curriculum planning, and reduced lesson preparation. Videoconference materials are usually structured to be reflective of content guidelines of learning standards, and are adaptable to different levels of prior student knowledge, age, and grade level.

Similarly, as levels of videoconference programming increase, participating K-12 schools are finding that interactive, point-to-point videoconferencing provides tools for higher student achievement of the learning standards. Videoconferencing increases access to authentic and exceptional resources (i.e., rich content including historic and scientifically-unique locales, authentic museum collections, and direct content with providers who are sharing their expertise).

Videoconferencing also expands student opportunities to engage in higher-level interactions that includes analytic thinking and creative learning. As teachers engage with external providers as part of the videoconferencing collaboration process, they expose students to expanded standards-based resources at museums, zoos, and research sites. They also facilitate direct interaction with content experts with whom students would not have interaction in their normal classroom setting.

Interactive videoconferencing is easily adapted for use in specific subject (standards) areas and can provide improved delivery of instruction. The collaborative model can support character education and cultural diversity goals as well as the core curricula of math, science, social studies, and English language arts. It can also offer learning experiences in standards areas such as art, music, physical education, and career development.

Higher Student Performance

Delivery of instruction through interactive videoconferencing technologies produces evidence of higher-level student learning and academic performance. Preliminary research evidence confirms that instructional models using digital technology in a collaborative inquiry-based environment transforms educational practice and leads to higher-level learning (Newman, 2005).

As students engage providers in point-to-point videoconferencing, they hone their higher-level learning skills. The new classroom configuration results in a transformation and restructuring of teaching pedagogy from a *teacher-as-information-provider* model to a *teacher-as-learning-facilitator* model. These changes create a new approach to teaching and learning, and chart the way to a more productive and effective educational environment in which students learn better and achieve more.

Evaluator observations of students and interviews with teachers have shown that the use of videoconferencing raises the levels of cognitive experiences of students in several ways (Newman, 2005). The introduction of the use of resources from external content providers through videoconferencing creates a path for students to have access to more information than is available at their local sites (classrooms). In addition, the nature of videoconferencing forces students to work more on verbal and visual presentations of ideas. These efforts result in increased self-reflection, higher

levels of questioning of others, more prolific writing, and greater participation in speaking.

Technology literacy improves in the majority of students as they become experienced in the use of multimedia techniques beyond those offered only on a computer. In addition, the etiquette and ethics of technology use are increased. Teachers also note that the use of videoconferencing in support of collaborative classrooms allows students the opportunity to experience cultural/diversity/ability differences and to identify and discuss similarities across hidden boundaries.

A review of curriculum products created for videoconference programs verifies that students are engaged in critical thinking and complex problem-solving during videoconference programs. They are able to access levels of content beyond that which is normally available in their classrooms. Thus, access to external resources, whether peer-to-peer collaboration or expert-to-peer collaboration, allows students to break down the invisible walls of education that are normally found in the classroom.

The use of videoconferencing allows students to share knowledge with peers in both oral and visual formats that encourage growth in communication and organizational skills. Overall, the use of videoconferencing enhances collaboration and is effective in impacting classroom and student outcomes.

CONCLUSION

Inclusion of interactive videoconferencing in K-12 classrooms can fulfill a variety of instructional goals; it can serve as a source for primary and secondary research, provide interpretive resources, and offer preparatory and summative endnotes for curriculum units. The most successful videoconferences occur in classroom settings where videoconference interaction between students and external experts occurs, and where, prior to the videoconferences, teachers communicate with the external expert to explain the curriculum/instructional needs and the role of the videoconference in supporting the learning process.

As evidence confirms that there are significant *"value-added"* outcomes that emerge within the educational process as a result of the use of interactive videoconferencing and supporting resources. Additionally, it supports the increasing interest in and expansion of school access to videoconferencing as an educational tool. Furthermore, the increasing use of videoconferencing serves as a foundation for initiating comprehensive change in educational technology integration in the schools. As providers realign their content presentations to utilize interactive digital resources and interactive communication tools, a new reality is developing in education in which innovative models of videoconference technology are requiring a reallocation of instructional time.

As a result of the introduction of interactive videoconferencing into K-12 classrooms, the constraints of schoolhouse walls are fading away to allow students the experience of interacting with diverse providers as they share content. Museums are realigning their content presentations to interface with and enhance classroom curriculum. The results are new, exciting models for classroom pedagogy and interpretive activities of museums, zoos, and other professional presenters.

REFERENCES

Abrahamson, C. (1998). Issues in interactive communications in distance education. *College Student Journal, 32,* 33-43.

Andrews, K., & Marshall, K. (2000). Making learning connections through telelearning. *Educational Leadership,* 53-56.

Dede, C. (2001). A new century demands new ways of learning. In D. T. Gordon (Ed.), *The digital classroom* (pp.171-174). Cambridge, MA: Harvard Education Letter.

Fullan, M. (2000). The return of large-scale reform. *Journal of Educational Change, 1,* 1-23.

Gernstein, R. B. (2000). Videoconferencing in the classroom: Special projects toward cultural understanding. *Integration of Technology in the Classroom, 16,* 177-186.

Greenberg, A. (2004, February). Navigating the sea of research on videoconferencing-based distance education: A platform for understanding research into the technology's effectiveness and value. *Wainhouse Research.* Retrieved September 9, 2005, from http://www.wainhouse.com/files/papers/wr-navseadistedu.pdf

Jonassen, D. H., Carr, C., & Yueh, H. (1998). Computers as mindtools for engaging learners in critical thinking. *Tech Trends, 43,* 24-32.

Menlove, R., Hansford, D., & Lignugaris-Kraft, B. (2000). Creating a community of distance learners: Putting technology to work. In *Proceedings of the American Council on Rural Special Education (ACRES) Annual Conference March, 2000, Alexandria, VA. Capitalizing on leadership in rural special education: Making a difference for children and families* (pp. 247-253).

Motamedi, V. (2001). A critical look at the use of videoconferencing in United States distance learning. *Education, 122*(2), 386-394.

Newman, D. L. (2005). *Beyond the barriers: Benefits of K-12 teacher participation in collaborative classroom videoconferencing training.* Presentation at the SITE Conference, Phoenix, AZ.

Newman, D., Barbanell, P., & Falco, J. (2005). Documenting value-added learning through videoconferencing: K-12 classrooms' interactions with museums. In G. Richards (Ed.), *Proceedings of World Conference on E-Learning in Corporate, Government, Healthcare, and Higher Education, 2005,* Chesapeake, VA (pp. 389-401).

Newman, D. L., & Goodwin-Segal, T. (2003). *Evaluation of a technology integration challenge grant program: Using technology to connect museums and classrooms.* A paper presented at the Annual Meeting of the American Educational Research Association, Chicago.

Newman, D. L., & King, J. (2004a). *The virtual information education Web project: Formative evaluation of the Schenectady city school district technology innovation challenge grant* (New York Institute of Technology Component, Year Four 2003-2004 Report). Albany, NY: University at Albany/SUNY, Evaluation Consortium.

Newman, D. L., & King, J. (2004b). *The virtual information education Web project: Formative evaluation of the Schenectady city school district technology innovation challenge grant* (Schenectady Component, Year Four 2003-2004 Report). Albany, NY: University at Albany/SUNY, Evaluation Consortium.

Newman, D. L., King, J. A., Gligora, M. A., Guckemus, S. M., & Pruden, J. M. (2004). *Evaluating the impact of videoconferencing: Documenting teacher outcomes and changes in instructional strategies.* Paper presented at the Annual Meeting of the American Evaluation Association, Atlanta, GA.

No Child Left Behind Act of 2001. Public Law, 107-110. U.S. Department of Education. Retrieved from http://www.ed.gov/policy/elsec/lealesea.org/index.htm

Omatseye, J. N. (1999). Teaching through teleconferencing: Some curriculum challenges. *College Student Journal, 33,* 346-364.

Sallis, E., & Jones, G. (2002). *Knowledge management in education: Enhancing learning and education.* London: Kogan Page Ltd.

Wilson, K. (2000). Virtual seminars in European studies: A model for collaborative learning. *Computer and the Humanities, 34,* 345-347.

ENDNOTE

[1] Sections of this chapter were extensions in part of a presentation and paper (Newman, Barbanell, & Falco, 2005) presented at the World Conference on E-Learning in Corporate, Government, Healthcare, and Higher Education (ELEARN) Vancouver, Canada.

Chapter XIX
Integrating Videoconferencing into the Classroom:
A Perspective from Northern Ireland

Maire Martin
Duquesne University, USA

ABSTRACT

This chapter will focus largely on the author's experiences in promoting the creative use of video-conferencing in schools in Northern Ireland (NI) over the past ten years. It will also describe certain groundbreaking projects that educators in other parts of the United Kingdom (UK) and Ireland have undertaken in this field. Although until recently there has been little in the way of a systemic approach in Northern Ireland to the introduction and integration of videoconferencing into K-12 classrooms, there have been some striking examples of good practice. The examples chosen demonstrate the potential of videoconferencing to be inclusive of different needs and learning styles, and to extend and enrich the learning experiences available in the classroom. They are intended to show how videoconferencing can have a powerful effect on learning and teaching, and to give more educators the motivation and confidence to explore and develop this user-friendly valuable education resource.

BACKGROUND

In the mid-nineties in Northern Ireland (NI), new education technologies were emerging as potentially powerful educational tools, and were beginning to make their way into the K-12 classroom. The focus was almost exclusively on computers and computer networking. In 1997, the Northern Ireland Department of Education (DE), which is responsible for education policy in Northern Ireland and which provides 100% funding for both capital and recurrent expenditure in all schools, drew up an Education Technology strategy in which it committed to a ten-year technology development program in schools and to providing the funding necessary for implementation. This strategy was revised and updated in 2004 (Department of Education Northern Ireland, 2004). A body, known as Classroom 2000 (C2k), was established and funded by the Department of Education to deliver to schools a high-quality, sustainable infrastructure, connectivity, and resources which meet strategic targets. C2k works with a wide range of partners from both private and public sectors to deliver an integrated and supported service, which is installed, maintained and upgraded by specialist providers. As a result of a massive investment by government, all 1,200 schools in NI had, by 2004, and at no cost to themselves, a common infrastructure of networked computers connected to the Internet and linked to legacy systems; a computer-to-student ratio of close to 1:5; a local area network (LAN), bringing curriculum and administration systems together, with a fast-filtered Internet access at every workstation; broadband connectivity; connection to a NI Data Center, providing always-on, protected access to an online learning environment containing content and assessment services for the school curriculum, professional development, administration, and management needs; 200 nationally-licensed curriculum titles, greatly enhancing the digital resource available for teaching and learning; an individual password,

mailbox, and protected area for all 400,000 NI school service users, including all pupils; and a fast, direct link to the People's Network in all public libraries (where free broadband access is also provided). As a result, historic issues of equity of access and opportunity, affordability, sustainability, and the central provision of reliable systems have been addressed and resolved; however, videoconferencing technology was not included in the initial rollout of the technology infrastructure.

In addition to infrastructure provision, a major training program has taken place, following a funding initiative throughout the United Kingdom, beginning in 1998, when Lottery funds were made available to support teachers and school librarians in the use of information and communications technology (ICT). As a result, more than 20,000 teachers (almost the entire teaching force) and school librarians in NI took part in the training program aimed at improving their expertise in using technology for pedagogical purposes. This program did not include any training related to videoconferencing.

The use of videoconferencing at that time was limited, and was generally confined to higher education. This was true of the United Kingdom in general; videoconferencing had little impact in the K-12 classroom. In Ireland, its use was confined mainly to schools involved in the European Studies Project. This project was established in 1986 and funded by the Department of Education in Northern Ireland and the Department of Education and Science in the Republic of Ireland. Its aim was to use technology, including videoconferencing, to increase mutual understanding, awareness, and tolerance among students and teachers on the island of Ireland and across Europe. It was through my involvement in this project that I first experienced videoconferencing and became aware of its potential to offer authentic, beyond-the-classroom learning experiences to K-12 students and teachers. I began to explore this technology through a wide range of pilot projects, some of which are described in the case studies that follow.

CASE STUDIES

Many of the case studies arising from that exploration that I offer in this paper relate to my role as international officer from 1996 until 2002 in the Western Education and Library Board, a very large school district in NI with 60,000 students. Some are current and relate to my present work as adviser on videoconferencing to C2k. In my role as international officer, I had responsibility for developing links and collaborative work between local schools and schools in other countries. I saw the emerging technologies, especially videoconferencing, as vehicles for promoting and sustaining this work, in particular for facilitating access to experts and promoting meaningful collaborative learning experiences in real-time. I also saw this technology as a potentially effective medium for professional development. Though the case studies that I present in this chapter have not been the subject of academic research, my hope is that my storytelling will help to "ignite action" (Denning, 2001). Taken together, these "stories" will illustrate how videoconferencing can support the constructivist approach to teaching and learning (Hayden, 1999); Dewey's four categories of learning: inquiry, communication, construction, and expression (Dewey, 1943, cited in Bruce and Levin, 1997); and how it can foster the process of learning to learn. They will demonstrate how, through offering a form of distance education, videoconferencing can extend and enrich the classroom experience, adding value across a wide range of curricular areas, ability levels, and age groups, and promoting personal and professional development. They will show how videoconferencing can facilitate the three types of interaction, teacher/expert-students, students-students, and students-material, advocated by Moore (1989) to bridge the psychological gap,

which he sees as inherent in any form of distance learning. Moreover, they will illustrate that, through bringing the learning community virtually face-to-face in real-time, videoconferencing can bridge the psychological distance "in ways that cannot easily be achieved by other means" (Arnold, Cayley, & Griffith, 2002, p. 6). Finally, the stories will show how videoconferencing can cater to a range of intelligences and learning styles. The importance of this cannot be overestimated, as it is now accepted that learners learn best when different learning styles are addressed (Gardner, 1983). Specifically, the examples will cover the use of videoconferencing for access to experts, virtual field trips, collaborative learning, and professional development.

Access to Experts

Case Study 1: Politics (Grade 12)

In 1999, with the help of an American colleague, I organized a videoconference from Capitol Hill, in which congressman Jim Walsh held a three-way virtual "town meeting" with 70 Northern Irish advanced-level (grade 12) politics students from four schools, and with grade 12 students from a New Jersey high school. At the Northern Ireland site, an expert on British politics and the Northern Ireland political situation, Dr. Arthur Aughey from the University of Ulster, dealt with questions from the American students. This virtual encounter with experts involved students of high-level ability. It was part of an ambitious and very successful series of virtual visits and field trips (Martin, 2000). The aims of this videoconference were twofold: to enrich the taught curriculum by putting students and teachers in virtual face-to-face contact in real-time with remote experts, and to foster collaborative learning at an international level by connecting students simultaneously with their peers on the other side of the Atlantic. For visual and interpersonal learners, this was a rich learning experience. Feedback from the students indicated that this virtual meeting increased their motivation and enjoyment of learning by "[bringing] politics to life" (Martin, 2000). This allowed them to experience inquiry-based learning (Dewey's first category). They had taken the option of the American Constitution in their advanced-level politics course. Congressman Walsh responded to their questions in this area. The U.S. students engaged in a similar fashion with the Irish academic. For the benefit of the students, the two experts then discussed the similarities and differences between the two systems. The students also were able to express their views to the experts and to interact with one another at appropriate stages in the videoconference. This encounter revealed the value of synchronous, face-to-face discussion in distance learning, and the potential of videoconferencing to facilitate the process of learning to learn. As the videoconference, which lasted 90 minutes, progressed, the students grew in self-confidence. They shared their understanding of the issues which were raised, seeking clarification where necessary either from the experts or their peers, challenging erroneous perceptions, analyzing and evaluating responses. Dewey's four categories as well as Moore's three types of interaction were amply exemplified in this learning event, described by a New Jersey teacher as "a mind expanding experience," and by an Irish teacher as being "the best thing that had happened to Politics in his twenty years of teaching the subject" (Martin, 2000, pp. 81-82). A copy of the videotape of the virtual meeting was given to each participating school and proved a valuable learning resource. Subsequently, two other schools studying the Irish Constitution requested a videoconference link with a member of Dáil Éireann (the Dublin Parliament). The minister for health (formerly minister for education), Mr. Micheál Martin, graciously acceded to this request, and an equally productive virtual meeting took place a short time later.

Case Study 2: Special Needs (Grade 3)

By way of contrast, to illustrate the flexibility of videoconferencing as a means of accessing experts and its capability to mitigate both geographical and psychological distances, my second case study involves a grade 3 pupil with special needs in an island school of 19 students off the southwest coast of Ireland. I had been invited to advise a network of teachers who were exploring the new technology of videoconferencing and its possible integration into classroom practices. One of the applications that they piloted was the use of videoconferencing to enable a learning-support teacher to work on a regular weekly basis with a student with severe learning difficulties in the remote school, frequently rendered inaccessible by the vagaries of the weather. Before embarking on the videoconferencing lessons, the teacher-expert first visited the school to meet the student face-to-face, a strategy which I strongly advise where possible, to assess the student's needs and to draw up a program tailored to meet them. I monitored several of the ensuing videoconferences. The support teacher found the technology to be very user-friendly and mastered it quickly. She also understood the need to adapt her teaching strategies to the new medium in order to use it to maximum effect for the benefit of her student. The school principal, who was also the class teacher, sat with the child during the videoconferences to ensure continuation of the work between each session. The child responded well to the technology, developed a good rapport with the distance teacher, and gradually began to interact with her. The real-time, visible, one-on-one virtual contact seemed to give him the security necessary to reveal that natural impulse to inquire and to learn, of which Dewey speaks. It also reveals the capability of videoconferencing to facilitate interaction between the teacher and the student, and between the student and the material (Moore, 1989). In the latter instance, a document camera was used to focus on the material, which the teacher had prepared and sent in advance to the school. The teacher was therefore able to support the student's efforts to interact with the letter names and sounds, to read a five-line story, and to answer simple questions to test his understanding. She could also introduce new material in a supportive and motivating way. An important affective outcome of this process was the increase in his self-esteem. He loved videoconferencing, felt "special" because of using it, and was relaxed, happy, and hard-working throughout the lesson. An unexpected pedagogical outcome was the learning-support teacher's estimation that sections of the lessons were delivered more effectively by videoconference than they would be in a traditional classroom. An example of this was the facility of a camera close-up of her mouth when she was teaching the relation of letters and sounds (Martin, 2000). She also reported that she was more focused during a distance lesson by videoconference than in an actual class, and that her student had fewer distractions. The result was that the child made significant progress. This was noted in a later inspection (quality assurance) report. The success factors in this case study were undoubtedly careful preparation, ensuring a good fit between the technology and the pedagogy, and the support of the school principal. The success of this venture prompted the principal to use videoconferencing for some collaborative work with schools on the mainland and for contact with her professional peers. In a written communication with the author, she stated, "videoconferencing has transformed my life and that of my pupils … Videoconferencing means we are no longer isolated. We are now part of a bigger community" (Martin, 2000, p. 63).

Case Study 3: History and Culture (Grade 8)

As part of a drive to improve literacy and provide students with authentic beyond-the-classroom learning experiences, I worked with teachers and teacher-trainers to design a technology-facilitated storytelling project for Grade 8 students of moderate-to-low ability in an urban school. These students were studying Native American history and culture. We linked with a school in New Jersey which was also doing a unit on different cultures. This school invited the deputy chief of the Cherokee nation to visit them to talk about his culture and to tell them some Cherokee stories, and they willingly shared their guest with the Irish school. The project was extended to include Irish stories, with an accomplished Irish storyteller sharing some of our ancient lore with the American school. A multimedia approach was used to plan and prepare this videoconference. E-mail contact was established between the schools and with the deputy chief. The latter entered into the process with great enthusiasm, and whetted his young audience's appetite for Cherokee tales by giving them insights into his culture and traditions, and supplying them with Cherokee Web sites that they had to research before their virtual meeting with him. The videoconference was highly interactive, as the well-prepared students on both sides responded to the stories and told some simple ones of their own. These included stories from African culture, as many of the U.S. students were African-American. This resulted in a very rich "real-world" learning experience, from which, according to feedback from teachers and students, the students gained a greater understanding of, and respect for, cultural diversity, increased self-esteem, improved presentation and communication skills, and enhanced motivation for learning. They also gained a positive experience of using technology to learn how to learn, and to become part of a global learning community. Comments like: "it was just like being in their school library with Yona (the deputy chief) and the American students" (Martin, 2000), indicate a strong sense of social presence, and the ability of videoconferencing to bridge the geographical and psychological gap between expert and students, and between students and students (Moore, 1989).

Case Study 4: The Affective Domain (Grades 9-12)

Perhaps the most poignant of all the "access to expert" videoconferences were the two held in the aftermath of the terrible events that took place in the U.S. on September 11, 2001 (9/11). In the spring semester of the following year, I had a request from an American colleague to do a number of videoconferences with schools in New Jersey and New York. The idea was to allow young Americans to access the sort of "experts" who could speak most meaningfully to them, young people who had experienced comparable, unspeakable tragedies. In 1998, during the time of the IRA ceasefire in Northern Ireland, when it seemed that our thirty years of "troubles" had at last come to an end, my small hometown of Omagh (population: 25,000) had been bombed by a dissident republican group. Thirty-one people, including unborn twins, were killed and hundreds were injured, some horrifically. The atrocity of 9/11 evoked an immediate response of empathy and a desire to do whatever we could to help. Consequently, I had no lack of volunteers among young people, keen to help young Americans talk through their experience. "Talking through" was one of the strategies that our young people had found most effective when dealing with their own post-traumatic situation.

The first of the videoconferences was with grade 9 students in a school in New Jersey. These students had not directly experienced the events of 9/11, but were still shocked and disoriented by what had happened. My "experts" on this occasion were young people in a similar situation. During the videoconference, the Irish students encouraged the U.S. students to tell their story, and easily entered into the experiences that were narrated. They then recounted their own experiences and shared some of their coping strategies.

Congressman Payne, who was visiting the New Jersey school, commented on the effectiveness of videoconferencing in making virtual face-to-face peer mediation available in real-time to students in real need. In a letter of appreciation to me, the principal of the school spoke of how the virtual contact had helped his students "begin the process of mending their spirits." He explained that the videoconference was broadcast to most of the classrooms in the school, thus extending its beneficial effect. He also said that an indication of the effectiveness of the technology in this particular instance could be measured by the fact that "based upon the videoconference," teachers had designed assignments requiring students to further examine their thoughts and emotions, as well as to "explore ways in which they can contribute to the world."

The second videoconference was with grade 12 students in two schools situated only two blocks away from what became known as Ground Zero in New York. One of the schools was badly damaged. Both had just reopened, and the school administration, through my American colleague, requested a videoconference with Omagh students. It was to take place on Global Youth Services Day, April 26, 2002. This time, I invited young people who had been injured in the Omagh bomb to take on the role of "experts". The students from the Ground Zero schools had witnessed the atrocity as it was happening. In the magazine of one of the schools, students wrote of the need to tell the story of their experience to the world. "We witnessed everything: people jumping from buildings, people covered in debris, and things too gruesome to mention." They wanted their "young voice" to be heard. The videoconference gave them that opportunity. It also allowed them to listen to other young voices telling of very similar experiences. The conference opened with a letter of support from Senator Hillary Clinton. She expressed her hope that, by coming together through videoconferencing to share their painful experiences, the young people of New York and of

Omagh would be stronger as a result, and would soon be able to point the way to a "bright and shining future." That process had already begun in Omagh. A nineteen-year-old girl, who had been blinded in the explosion, spoke of her appreciation of the gift of life, and her determination to make a difference by "moving on" and creating a better future. At the time of the videoconference in April, 2002, she had become the first blind student of music at Queen's University, Belfast. Her testimony made a tremendous impact on the New York students. Other young people outlined their project "Who Cares?" which they had devised and were introducing to schools in the area in order to help their peers deal with depression or other emotional illness which can manifest itself at any stage following a traumatic experience. The idea of young people playing a part in the healing process appealed to the U.S. students. I was aware of the strong sense of social presence apparent throughout the videoconference. This was corroborated by statements from the young participants at the Omagh site, to whom the technology was a new experience, that actually seeing their U.S. peers made all the difference. They felt that they were dealing with "real people" and could immediately connect on an interpersonal level.

Virtual Field Trips

Case Study 5: Geography, Biology, Physics (Grades 10-12)

I found videoconferencing particularly suitable for providing students with virtual field trips that allowed them to visit parts of the world and enjoy learning experiences that would normally be inaccessible through constraints of distance, time, and expense (Pachnowski, 2002). An example of this was the visit to the Liberty Science Center in New Jersey by grade 10 students studying geography and biology. The visit was in two parts: an outdoor virtual field trip to the Hudson River estuary, and an indoor, interactive lesson

on the effects of erosion. The latter included suggesting alterations to a model of the Hudson River estuary and its environs, already prepared in the center by students working there on special projects. The objective was to explore how erosion might be decreased. The whole experience was an example of how videoconferencing can support a constructivist approach to learning, providing students with authentic "real-world" experiences and exposing them to problem-solving and independent learning (Hayden, 1999). The ability level of the students ranged from middle to high. Much preparation, conducted by e-mail and focusing on maximizing the potential of the technology and involving both teachers and students, had preceded the virtual lesson. This was one of the keys to its effectiveness.

The success of this virtual field trip encouraged the school to offer the experience to advanced-level geography and physics students (grades 11-12). In a similarly constructivist approach, following the virtual tour of the center, these high-level ability students were provided with the skills and the virtual tools to "build their own earthquake" (Martin, 2000, p.19). This was done by allowing the students to enter variables into an earthquake simulator to help them understand the effects of earthquakes of different seismic strengths on different types of structures. Student motivation was high. They described the lesson as "a riveting experience." Kinaesthetic learners found it "a great way of bringing learning to life" (Martin, 2000, p.82) A follow-up lesson was arranged, in the form of a virtual field trip to the Ocean Institute in California, with an interactive discussion of the human experience of earthquakes.

Collaborative Learning

Case Study 6: The Virtual Shared Classroom (Grade 7)

The virtual shared classroom project involved grade 7 students from Northern Ireland and New

Jersey. The project, which was conducted mainly by videoconference, gave all participants the experience of collaborative learning, of becoming part of a larger community of learners, and of having a meaningful and beneficial distance learning experience. Jonassen, Davidson, Collins, Campbell, and Haag (1995, cited in Giuliani, 2001) believe that, with interactive technologies, "the most valuable activity in a classroom of any kind is the opportunity for students to work and interact together and to build and become part of a community" (Giuliani, 2001, p.17). This project provided exactly that type of opportunity to the participating classes. They met once a week by videoconference for a period of six weeks to collaborate on a project on life in the American West. During each shared lesson, the two classes acted as one, dividing into mixed groups of Irish and American pupils. Before each videoconference, these groups researched their topics on the Internet, shared their findings, and prepared their presentations by e-mail. This illustrated the potential of videoconferencing to combine with other technologies to support independent learning and the learning to learn process. The learning experience was further enriched by some team teaching, and by the inclusion of music, dancing, and drama, the latter appealing greatly to the kinaesthetic learner.

Case Study 7: Environmental Studies (Grade 5)

The European Union's (EU) Comenius program promotes collaboration between networks of schools in the K-12 range from different EU countries. As international officer, I encouraged schools to use videoconferencing in order to sustain collaborative working. A typical example involving social interaction and collaborative learning was an environmental project between grade 5 pupils in a small rural school in Northern Ireland and rural and urban schools in Denmark and Italy. I arranged for two- and three-way videoconferenc-

ing between the partner schools. At appropriate stages in their project, the schools "met" virtually. The teachers used the videoconference to plan the next phase, and the pupils enjoyed the exciting social dimension of meeting their European "classmates" face-to-face as well as presenting their work to one another. Their project, which was on the theme of "Who we are/Where we live", was developed as an integral part of the curriculum in each school. Teacher feedback indicated that they found this experience of a virtual staffroom to be a valuable and enjoyable source of professional development, and made them feel part of a wider learning community. Student outcomes included curriculum enrichment, improvement in communication and presentation skills, and language and cultural awareness. What the students most enjoyed was the virtual classroom experience. They had the impression of having visited their partner schools and having received visitors into their own. As one of them expressed it, "We were in their classroom and they were in ours!" The principal pointed out how valuable this experience was to his students, most of whom had never been out of Northern Ireland and were not likely to be in the near future (Martin, 2000, p. 35).

Professional Development

Case Study 8: Professional Development of K-12 Math Teachers

Videoconferencing can greatly enrich the professional development of teachers. One example from my own experience is our school district's math initiative. This was part of a Northern Ireland numeracy initiative aimed at raising the standard of math teaching and learning. Videoconferencing was used to access experts and collaborate with distant peers in a training program for primary (K-6) teachers. I had well-established links with Carlow University (then Carlow College), Pittsburgh, Pennsylvania, and invited math specialists from Carlow to deliver part of the program. A number of elementary teachers from Pittsburgh also agreed to participate. The head of mathematics from Carlow College gave presentations on similar initiatives carried out by the College and on the lessons learned from these. Teachers at both sites shared examples of good practice and arranged to share resources. Use of peripheral technologies, such as the document camera, PowerPoint, and videos provided a high-quality experience. The evaluation highlighted the part played by videoconferencing in enriching the numeracy initiative, widening horizons and promoting self-esteem in teachers.

In a follow-up videoconference, organized as part of the parental involvement in numeracy (PIN) project, teachers, parents, and elementary students on both sides of the Atlantic took part in a highly-interactive workshop. Among the outcomes were a stimulating and mutually-beneficial exchange of ideas and good practice, an increased awareness of the impact of parental involvement in math, both in the classroom and in the home, exchange of resources, and increased self-esteem of the parents and children who participated. This type of videoconferencing illustrates how the technology can facilitate the meaningful application to learners of Vygotsky's principle of the zone of proximal development: "the distance between the actual development level as determined by independent problem-solving and the level of potential development as determined through problem-solving under adult guidance or in collaboration with more capable peers" (Vygotsky, 1978, p. 86). The videoconference-enabled training program was later extended, with similar outcomes, to post-primary (grades 8-12) math teachers.

EXAMPLES FROM OTHER EDUCATORS

In this section, I will deal with three examples of key projects from other parts of Ireland and the UK, with which I have been associated, and which illustrate best practice in the use of videoconferencing in education.

The Dissolving Boundaries Project (K-12)

In Ireland, since 1999, a highly successful project, Dissolving Boundaries through Technology, which is funded by the Department of Education, Northern Ireland, and the Department of Education and Science, Republic of Ireland, has been using computer conferencing and videoconferencing to promote quality learning in schools, and to foster cultural awareness and mutual understanding among children and young people in both parts of the island. A recent report (Austin, Abbott, Mulkeen, & Metcalfe, 2003)) has revealed that, at both primary and post-primary levels, the preferred technology was videoconferencing: 56% at primary level (grades K-5) and 68% at post-primary (grades 6-12). The main reasons given by the students in their responses to questionnaires were the ability to actually see one another, and the immediacy of the medium. Teachers also reported that the virtual face-to-face element made discussion easier, improved listening skills, and led to greater tolerance of other perspectives. Sixty percent also said they found collaborative work more interesting using videoconferencing. Also highlighted in the report was the extent to which videoconferencing improved communication skills.

The Global Leap Project (K-12)

Within the UK, the pace of videoconferencing activity has begun to increase. Many excellent examples of good practice in schools across a wide range of curricular areas are listed in the British Educational Communications and Technology Agency (BECTA) Web site. One of the most significant of the ongoing initiatives in videoconferencing is the global leap project, directed by Mike Griffith, formerly a teacher-adviser working with the Department for Education and Skills (DfES) on its videoconferencing in the classroom project. This project is aimed at raising awareness of the educational value of videoconferencing. I have encouraged schools to enroll in global leap, and have provided examples of good practice, which have been included in the project literature (Arnold et al., 2004). This literature and the global leap Web site offer guidance and support to teachers in the use of the technology. They also provide an extensive list of interested schools with videoconferencing capability in many parts of the world and of a wide range of content providers. In addition, they contain case studies detailing models of good practice from Devon and many other parts of the UK, ranging from the early years classroom, through cross-phase liaison in science, to post-16 courses using an external provider.

I have promoted the annual one-day global leap event among local schools, and, where necessary, facilitated their access to videoconferencing in order to do so. The global leap event enables participating UK schools to "leap" around the globe and participate in a series of lessons and social encounters via videoconferencing. The purpose of this event is to demonstrate what can actually be done now with videoconferencing and to encourage greater uptake of the technology in the day-to-day life of schools.

Connections for Learning Project (Argyll and Bute, Scotland)

Many schools across the UK and Ireland, working on an individual basis, take advantage of the benefits offered by global leap. This reflects the uncoordinated nature of the use of videoconferencing in these islands. However, an excellent example of a systemic approach is the connections for learning project in Argyll and Bute in Scotland (Connected, 2005). Here, the local education authority (school district) has made

videoconferencing "a way of life", a technology that is used in a meaningful way by all schools on a daily basis.

Argyll and Bute Council is the second largest local authority in Scotland in terms of land mass, and one of the smallest in terms of pupil and teacher population and education service personnel. It has 23 inhabited islands, 10 of which have schools. The geography of the area and the difficulties associated with rural and island settings have led to an emphasis on developing effective communication and services through ICT over the last 10 years. In August, 2002, having secured funding from Scotland's New Educational Developments Fund to develop videoconferencing in education, the council began to install the infrastructure. This resulted in the 10 secondary schools being equipped with room-sized videoconferencing equipment; the 42 rural and island primary schools, some of which have only 11 students, receiving desktop videoconferencing systems; the appointment of a full-time project officer (a former primary head teacher); and the appointment of a dedicated technician to support the project officer and schools in the project.

As a result of this impressive infrastructure and dedicated support, schools in this remote and formerly-isolated area can and do now use videoconferencing to enhance learning and teaching across all curricular areas through collaboration within the island schools as well as far beyond. They also use it for distant teaching to fill gaps in staffing; for access to experts; for professional development; and for community involvement in the life of the schools.

PERCEIVED BARRIERS AND FUTURE PROSPECTS

Although we can point to many examples of good practice in the use of videoconferencing in Northern Ireland and elsewhere, it has to be said that, to date, this has been dependent to a large extent on the efforts of individual educators. Videoconferencing is still "a relatively underused technology in schools" (Comber, Lawson, Gage, Cullum-Hanshaw, & Allen, 2004, p.3). Major barriers to its widespread adoption have been, in many cases: the expense involved; previous bad experiences of the technology due to either earlier technical deficiencies or poor preparation and management; a lack of confidence on the part of educators in their own ability to use it; or a lack of awareness of its value in the classroom. I believe that all these barriers have been, or can be, overcome. The robustness and the expense of the hardware are no longer issues, and the advent of Internet Protocol (IP) virtually eliminates connection costs (Martin, 2005). My experience is that videoconferencing is a user-friendly technology that was easily adopted by the teachers with whom I worked, and who, like me in the early stages, had no previous experience and no technical expertise. This ease of use means that only minimal training is required for end-users (Coventry, 1995). The other barriers can be addressed by raising awareness of good practice and by applying some simple guidelines (BECTA, 2005; Illinois Video Network, 2003; Martin, 2000; Rhode Island Network for Educational Technology, 2005).

The future, however, looks brighter. C2k, the body responsible for providing the technology infrastructure to schools, is currently adopting a systemic approach to the provision and implementation of videoconferencing as an educational technology. In the next rollout of the technology infrastructure, a basic videoconferencing system will be provided to all schools. Schools may opt, out of their own budgets, to upgrade to more sophisticated hardware. A number of pilot projects are ongoing, and others are planned for the academic year 2006-2007. These latter involve using videoconferencing to foster curricular collaboration between a number of schools within Northern Ireland, to facilitate fieldwork for preservice teachers and teacher trainers, to enable collaboration and distant teaching between three Irish medium post-primary schools (schools where the curriculum is taught through the Irish/Gaelic language), and to enrich an established link between local schools and schools in Japan. Additionally, Northern Ireland schools can benefit from the new videoconferencing services project provided by the United Kingdom Education and Research Networking Association (UKERNA), involving the Further and Higher Education sectors and the main education institutions in all the UK regions. The aim of the project is to develop a UK-wide videoconferencing service for schools, including infrastructure and the training and support of teachers.

There is, of course, a great need for academic research in this area to inform future use of the technology. Though some research has been done in Higher Education, there is relatively little at K-12 level (Anderson & Rourke, 2005; Heath & Holznagel, 2002). Dissemination of best practice in videoconferencing as a means of "building relationships, supporting collaboration, as well as improving retention and appealing to a variety of learning styles" (Dallas, 2000, p. 292) will also be essential to facilitating the widespread adoption of videoconferencing at this crucial stage. This should speed the day when videoconferencing, based on appropriate pedagogical approaches and in a context of whole-school support, becomes "a way of life" in our schools, helping teachers and students in the process of "learning to learn for a lifetime of change" (Milliband, cited in Claxton, 2003, p. 35).

In the context of brighter prospects, I will now deal with two pilot projects, one recently completed and one still ongoing, that augur well for the future of videoconferencing in Northern Ireland.

Videoconferencing for Students with Severe Learning Difficulties

The first of these is a C2k pilot project involving Grade 7 students in two schools for pupils with severe learning difficulties (SLD). Based on the geography strand of the environment and society area of the Northern Ireland revised curriculum, the project's aim was to raise students' awareness of the world around them, beyond their immediate environment, and give the students a sense of place, their own and that of the students in their partner school. The topic "My Town" provided local interest for students. They also had to create a tourist guide for their partner town. A multimedia approach was used to provide symbol-assisted text conferencing facilities to students according to their ability. I conducted a qualitative evaluation of the project on behalf of C2k. My report focused on videoconferencing in particular and evaluated its robustness, its impact on the learning experiences in the two schools, and the perceptions of this technology by teachers and students. It also considered whether videoconferencing played a role in shifting the current teaching and learning paradigm in these schools.

My findings indicated that videoconferencing is a robust and highly-effective technology for SLD students. The project achieved its aims of using this technology to enhance and enrich the learning experience of SLD students by giving them beyond-the-classroom learning experiences to promote a sense of place within the context of the revised Geography curriculum. There were other important outcomes for both teachers and students. Videoconferencing facilitated teacher professional development through regular virtual collaboration. The students enjoyed the experience. It improved their communication and oral skills, and contributed enormously to their personal and social development. Evidence of this was provided by teachers' responses to questionnaires. They gave examples of particular students, including one with autism and another with Angelmann's

Syndrome, whose self-confidence and social skills had been significantly enhanced by the videoconferencing experience. In the case of the autistic student, the teacher reported that, by the end of the project, he felt sufficiently confident to lead the final presentation to peers from both schools. The student with Angelmann's Syndrome, who frequently displayed difficult behavior, participated happily, using body language as he had no speech, in all the videoconferencing sessions. The teacher noted that his concentration and level of interest during these sessions far surpassed his interest in other class activities.

A number of success factors were identified from this project. A few are specific to the Special Needs environment. Most are relevant to all K-12 schools. They include the support of school principals, whole-school enthusiasm for technology, the robustness and user-friendliness of the videoconferencing technology, technology training for the learning support assistants, as well as for the teachers, in SLD classrooms, and, above all, the teacher factor. Cyrs (1998, cited in Smith, 2004, p. 9) tells us that "students never learn from the technology. They learn from the way instructors communicate or show how to communicate through the technology" (p. 9). From my own experience in general, and from this project in particular, I would say that this is particularly true of videoconferencing technology. The teachers in this project were enthusiastic about the potential of videoconferencing to open up a new, "real-world" learning experience to their disabled and, consequently, somewhat isolated students. They instinctively adapted their methodology to maximize the benefits of the technology. This included adopting a new role as facilitator, designing activities that are learner-centered, interactive, collaborative, and inquiry-based. This latter is most important, because SLD students are traditionally incurious or passive learners. The enlightened use of a constructivist approach to videoconferencing by the teachers in this project allowed their students to construct their own learning about their own town and about their partners' town. The teachers also devised effective inclusive strategies so that even students with poor oral communication skills felt part of the little learning community that was developing.

My research into this project led to an important insight with regard to whether the use of videoconferencing could lead to a paradigm shift in teaching and learning in our classrooms. Traditionally in the SLD classroom, because of the nature of the students' disabilities, collaborative learning and interactivity rarely occur. Yet, the project teachers instinctively and effectively adopted a constructivist, collaborative approach when using videoconferencing. This leads me to suggest that videoconferencing may well be a "disruptive technology"—an innovation that "over time, challenges conventional practices and contributes to new ways of thinking" (Archer, Garrison & Anderson, 1999, cited in Wilson, 2001). Dallas (2001) speaks of videoconferencing as enabling "whole new levels of interaction, and precipitating entirely new communication and ideas" (Dallas, 2001, p. 291). This is particularly significant in view of the fact that technology integration is often undermined by adherence to traditional classroom practice (Bailey, 2003; Pea, 1998).

The Digital Creativity Truck

The second project, the digital creativity truck, is another very exciting project with significant implications for the future use of videoconferencing in education. It is the brainchild of an esteemed colleague, Peter Simpson, an accredited Apple distinguished educator, and assistant technology adviser in the North-Eastern Education and Library Board (NEELB), a large school district in Northern Ireland. The project is funded by The European Union's Interreg program, which aims to promote collaboration among institutions along its border areas. The border, in this

instance, is the border between Northern Ireland and the Republic of Ireland. Nine schools from each jurisdiction are involved in the project. The Truck, which visits them all on a regular basis, is actually a fully-equipped outside broadcast vehicle, based on the model of the vehicle used by a local television network, Ulster Television (UTV). The concept underpinning the project is that of digital literacy. According to Simpson and other enlightened educators, the new breed of students in our schools is demanding this literacy today. They see it as important for them as print literacy. The Truck brings creative digital technology to students where they are in their schools, and opens up to them the world of radio, video and television production, and videoconferencing. Above all, the aim is to help them become creators and shapers of this world, instead of simply passive recipients. The students learn how to edit image and sound and put together a television program. This is then shared by videoconferencing with a partner school, after which, the production process and the quality of the end product are discussed.

Another feature of the project is the emphasis on virtual field trips. Irish schools in the project link with schools in the U.S. and invite them to join their field trips. The truck brings the equipment needed to televise the field experience, for example, a study visit to the Giant's Causeway on Ireland's northern coast. Simpson explains that open space has no ISDN lines or IP connections; however, microwave radio and video links mean that connections can be made from the actual spot to the Truck, from where it can be transferred to the partner school in the U.S. A further example of the use of microwave links to enable videoconferencing from an open-space location in order to share a field trip with a U.S. partner school is the Rathlin Island project. This project linked the island school (off the northeast coast of Ireland) with an elementary school in Fairfax, Virginia. The following excerpt is from a report of the field trip (Rathlin Virtual Field Trip, 2005): "Our environmental expert in Rathlin, Maurice Todd, was able to show live video of what he was finding on the seashore and describe his findings. Pupils in Mantua, Virginia, were able to see this through the videoconference link and ask him questions ...all live. This virtual field trip concept offers the opportunity for pupils to visit places anywhere in the world, with the field trips led by a presenter with local knowledge. In many ways, the pupils in U.S. were joining their friends from Rathlin on their field trip." The report also notes how such projects use videoconferencing technology to nurture the children's natural impulse to learn, to make sense of the world around them, and to express their reactions, and share their discovery. All of this resonates strongly with Dewey's four categories of learning.

A second digital truck will soon be available. It will have satellite broadband facility. This means that the Truck will be able to videoconference from any place in Europe, beam back its output to C2k in Belfast, from where it can be sent to every school in Northern Ireland.

CONCLUSION

The case studies which I have included in this chapter are examples of the range of valuable teaching and learning experiences that are already possible through videoconferencing when educators with imagination and enthusiasm have the courage to push out the boundaries and to exploit its potential. They show how videoconferencing has benefited students over a wide range of learning abilities, from those with severe learning difficulties to the academically-gifted. They demonstrate how it has facilitated learning by inquiry, communication, construction, and expression, Dewey's four categories, in virtual shared classrooms. They illustrate the capability of videoconferencing to offer virtual field trips that bridge the psychological as well as the geographical gap between teachers and students, students and students, and students and materials (Moore,

1989). Taken together, the case studies point up how, through enabling synchronous connections, questioning and immediate feedback, and collaboration across distance, videoconferencing can support constructivist learning (Hayden, 1999) across a range of learning styles (Gardner, 1983). Furthermore, they demonstrate that this technology can enrich a broad range of curricular areas, raise the motivation of both students and teachers, improve the self-esteem and self-confidence of students, promote the enjoyment of learning, and raise awareness and appreciation of cultural diversity.

For me, the most powerful endorsement of videoconferencing in the classroom came from an initially reluctant teacher-user, who, at the conclusion of the trans-Atlantic story- telling project (Case Study 3), wrote: "When we first became involved with this project, I was far from convinced of its true worth, deeming a video link-up a poor second best to the traditional eye contact with a real audience ... I now feel a bit like an evangelist in the school, spreading the 'good news' about videoconferencing with all the redemptive excitement of a new apostle of this technology" (Martin, 2000, p. 83).

My hope is that other educators, encouraged by examples of good practice, will come to share this enthusiasm and excitement as they begin to explore and experience for themselves the enjoyment and the enrichment that videoconferencing can bring to the classroom. My dream is that, in turn, they too will become "evangelists", for I have come to realize that such passion is caught, not taught.

REFERENCES

Anderson, T., & Rourke, L. (2005). *Videoconferencing in kindergarten-to-grade 12 settings: A review of the literature.* Prepared for Alberta Learning by Canadian Association of Distance Education Research. Retrieved September 1,

2005, from http://www.vcalberta.ca/community/litreview.pdf

Arnold, T., Cayley, S., & Griffith, M. (2002). *Video conferencing in the classroom: Communications technology across the curriculum.* Devon, England: Devon County Council.

Austin, R., Abbott, L., Mulkeen, A., & Metcalfe, N. (2003). *The global classroom: Collaboration and cultural awareness in the north and south of Ireland.* Coleraine, Ireland: University of Ulster / Maynooth, Ireland: National University of Ireland.

Bailey, J. (2003). Viewpoint: Overcoming the "achievement paradox": Four lessons from the business world. *eSchool News Online, May 29, 2003.* Retrieved March 10, 2005, from http://www.eschoolnews.com/news/showstory.cfm?ArticleID=4284 Becta. http://www.becta.org.uk

BECTA. (2004). *How to use videoconferencing effectively in your classroom.* Retrieved February 1, 2006, from http://schools.becta.org.uk/index.php?section=tl&catcode=ss_tl_use_02&rid=5223&pagenum=1&NextStart=1&print=1

Bruce, B. C., & Levin, J. A. (1997). Educational technology: Media for inquiry, communication, construction, and expression. *Journal of Educational Computing Research, 17*(1), 79-102.

Claxton, G. (2003). Learning is learnable (and we ought to teach it). In *Learning to succeed: The next decade.* The National Commission on Education Follow-Up Group, Occasional Paper, December 2003, University of Brighton.

Comber, C., Lawson, T., Gage, J., Cullum-Hanshaw, A., & Allen, T. (2004). *Report for schools of the DfES video conferencing in the classroom project.* Retrieved May 1, 2005, from http://www.becta.org.uk/page_documents/research/video_conferencing_report_may04.pdf

Connected (2005). Argyll and Bute online magazine. Retrieved from http://www.ltscotland.org.uk/ictineducation/connected/archivedissues/connected1/video.asp

Coventry, L. (1995). *Videoconferencing in higher education.* Institute for Computer-Based Learning, Heriot Watt University. Retrieved November 14, 2003, from http://www.agocg.ac.uk/reports/mmedia/video3/video3.pdf

Dallas, P. S. (2001). Videoconferencing application to distance education with particular reference to small states. *Distance Education in Small States, 2000 Conference Proceedings. The University of the West Indies/The Commonwealth of Learning.* Retrieved August 14, 2006, from http://www.col.org/colweb/site/pid/3338

Denning, S. (2001). *The springboard: How storytelling ignites action in knowledge-era organizations.* Woburn, MA: Butterworth-Heinemann.

Department of Education Northern Ireland (2004). *Empowering schools in Northern Ireland: Transforming learning, teaching, and leadership through education and technology change.* Bangor, Northern Ireland. Retrieved from http://www.empoweringschools.com

Dewey, J. (1943). *The child and the curriculum / The and school and society.* Chicago: University of Chicago Press.

Gardner, H. (1983). *Frames of mind: The theory of multiple intelligences.* New York: Basic Books Paperback.

Giuliani, J. (2001*). Identification of salient features of videoconferencing instruction.* Unpublished doctoral dissertation, Northern Illinois University. (UMI No. 3013782).

Global Leap Project. *Videoconferencing in the classroom.* Retrieved March 18, 2006 from, http://www.global-leap.com

Hayden, K. L. (1999). *Videoconferencing in K-12 education: A Delphi study of characteristics and critical strategies to support constructivist learning experiences.* Unpublished doctoral dissertation, Pepperdine University. (UMI No. 9934596).

Heath, M. J., & Halznagel, D. (2002). *Interactive videoconferencing: A literature review.* Prepared for the K-12 National Symposium for Interactive Videoconferencing Dallas, Texas, October, 2002.

Illinois Video Network (2003). *Distance learning basics.* Retrieved January 14, 2006, from http://www.state.il.us/cms/ivn/DistanceLearning/Distlearn.htm

Martin, M. (2000). *Videoconferencing in teaching & learning: Case studies and guidelines.* Western Education & Library Board, Omagh, Northern Ireland. Retrieved from http://www.welb-cass.org/site/projects%5Finitiatives/video%5Fconferencing/downloads/VCT&L.pdf

Martin, M. (2005). Seeing is believing: The role of videoconferencing in distance learning. *British Journal of Educational Technology, 36*(3), 397-405.

Moore, M. G. (1989). Three types of interaction. *The American Journal of Distance Education, 3*(2), 1-6.

Pachnowski, L. M. (2002). Virtual field trips through videoconferencing. *Learning and Leading with Technology, 29*(6), 10-13.

Pea, R. (1998, February). *The pros and cons of technology in the classroom.* Speech delivered at Bay Area School Reform Collaborative Funders' Learning Community Meeting, Palo Alto, CA. Retrieved August 18, 2005, from http://tappedin.org/archive/peacuban/pea.html

Rathlin Virtual Field Trip (2005). Retrieved from http://www.neelb.org.uk/cass/ict/videoconferencing/RathlinVirtual%20Fieldtrp.pdf

Rhode Island Network for Educational Technology (2005). Retrieved from http://www.ri.net/RI-NET/products/ivid/polycomuserguide.html

Smith, J. C. (2004). *Effective use of desktop videoconferencing in teacher education and professional development with reference to strategies for adult basic education.* National Center of Adult Literacy, University of Pennsylvania. Retrieved November 3, 2005, from http://www.literacy.org/products/t21_vc_smith_v14.pdf

Vygotsky, L. S. (1978). *Mind and society: The development of higher mental processes.* Cambridge, MA: Harvard University Press.

Wilson, B. G. (2001). Trends and futures of education: Implications for distance education. *Quarterly Review of Distance Education (special issue), October, 2001.* Retrieved March 19, 2006, from http://carbon.cudenver.edu/~bwilson/TrendsAndFutures.html

Section VII
The Future of K–12 Videoconferencing

Chapter XX
Videoconferencing a New Literacy

Stan Silverman
New York Institute of Technology, USA

ABSTRACT

With the advent of broadband telecommunications and affordable equipment, videoconferencing has emerged to replace expensive and elaborate distance learning systems that had been developed in the early 1980's. Yet, as we enter the close of the first decade of the 21st century, videoconferencing has not fulfilled its potential. The following chapter describes and poses solutions to the issues of access, equity, student achievement, pedagogical strategies, and the integration of emerging communication and media technologies that, if deployed, can transform videoconferencing to become a high performance tool for teaching and learning. In addition, as we embrace the millennial generation with unique characteristics that distinguish it from generations that have gone before, we must acknowledge the global, diverse, and politically-charged world. As a result, there is also an urgency to deploy videoconferencing with its fullest capacities; this urgency is an embedded theme in the writings that follow.

INTRODUCTION

As we look to the future of videoconferencing, it is useful to imagine a scene from the early 1900's in which a model a Ford is chugging its ways down main street USA and passes by two blacksmiths' shops on either side of the street. The workers in both shops are drawn outside by the new sounds. In the first shop, the workers have a conversation about how much noise this new technology "thing" makes, and how it will never make it in the world they live in; they retreat back into the shop to make very good horseshoes. The workers in the second shop, while also alarmed by the noise, determine that the world may be changing and that perhaps the best course of business is to add mufflers to their set of products. Fast-forward a few years, and we sadly see that the shop that was only producing very fine horseshoes has been replaced by a fast food restaurant, while the horseshoe/muffler shop has grown and started to franchise.

"As digital media become the dominant means of communication, they will usher in a new paradigm, transforming how we think, behave, relate, and create" (Miller, 2005, p. 31). The visual media of film, video, and television have long made the promise to schools that they will transform the educational system and bring wonder and excitement to classes. The claim was based on the inherent nature of the media. Seels, Fullerton, Berry, and Horn (2004) further state:

These media characteristics of film and television are primarily realism or fidelity, mass access, referability and, in some cases, immediacy. Producers for both of these technologies wanted to make persons, places, objects, or events more realistic to the viewer or listener. The intent was to ensure that the realistic representation of the thing or event was as accurate as possible (i.e., fidelity). The ability to transmit sounds or images to general audiences, or even to present such information to large groups in theaters, greatly expanded access to realistic presentations. In the case of television, the characteristic of immediacy allowed the audience to experience the representation of the thing or event almost simultaneously with its occurrence. The notion of "being there" was a further addition to the concept of realism. (p. 252)

The problem is that historically these media have failed to prove that they can indeed transform the educational landscape. The reason that these media failed to meet their promises was that they were built on a definition of schooling derived from a model of literacy that is 400 years old.

The very nature of literacy is changing. New media surrounds the millennium generation, and their everyday discourses are built on encoding and decoding of information using audio and video technologies. It is more and more common to see students with audio and video players, laptops, and cell phones. These devices have become an extension of their lives in the way that books and magazines are an extension of previous generations. Durrant and Green (2000) commented:

Indeed, we are now able to recognize and acknowledge that, for schooling and education, print is simply one of a range of available technocultural resources. Accordingly, account needs to be taken of a profound media shift in literacy, schooling and society—a broad-based shift from print to digital electronics as the organising context for literate-textual practice and for learning and teaching. Although this does not mean the eclipse of print technologies and cultures, it does mean that we need to employ a rather different, more flexible, and comprehensive view of literacy than teachers are used to in both their work and their lives. Print takes a new place within a reconceptualised understanding of literacy, schooling, and technological practice, one which is likely to be beneficial in moving us and our children into a new millennium. (p. 89)

As we reflect on the success of one of the new uses of visual and audio technologies (videoconferencing) in education, the best way to sum up where we stand is to borrow a phrase from our math colleagues: "Necessary but not sufficient". It is clear from the previous chapters in this book that videoconferencing has made gains on the educational landscape, but it is essential that we confront the political, instructional, and technological issues that still limit its growth and its applications.

In a time of underfunded education and the rise of unfunded mandates as a result of the No Child Left Behind (NCLB) legislation, we are faced with growing skepticism from the general community on the use of instructional technologies. Hidden in our videoconference units are computers; they connect via the Internet or other networks that traditionally are found in the technology budgets of schools. Skepticism has translated to hard questions about the effectiveness of instructional technology and associated questions related to the budget. The world of instructional technology needs to review these perceptions and address the issues. It is imperative that we examine the factors that create the context for the use of current applications and the development of new applications for videoconferencing. These factors include perception of access, equity, applications, and changing technology.

ACCESS

There is a common perception from legislators that the communications highways have been built, and that a significant percentage of schools have the type of access to the Internet that they need to allow for universal deployment of broadband technologies like videoconferencing. An analysis of the data from the Universal Service Program (E-rate) seems to support this view that the schools have significant and pervasive access to broadband connections to the Internet.

One of the first problems with this analysis is that the current definition that the federal government uses for a broadband connection is only 200 kilobytes per second. A reasonable quality videoconference needs 384K connections. Schools that are classified as having broadband connections at 200K will be unable to take advantage of the videoconference applications. So what about schools that have T-1 (1.54 megabytes/sec) connections which, to this point, have been the gold standard for Internet connectivity? On first analysis, it would seem that this type of high-speed connection would allow for easy videoconference connections. The problem with this thinking is the way that the connection is actually used in schools. Generally, that T-1 connection is shared among all the PCs and videoconference equip-

Table 1. Percentage of schools connected to broadband (>200K) (Source: http://nces.ed.gov/surveys/frss/publications/2005015/ - accessed April 30, 2006)

School Category	Percentage connected to Broadband
All School	95%
Elementary schools	94%
Schools < 300 students	97%
Schools 300 to 999 students	90%
Schools with 1,000 or more students	96%
Schools with minority enrollment of 50% or more	97%

ment in the building/district. This sharing reduces the effective bandwidth actually available to a videoconference. In 2001, the average ratio of computers with Internet access to students was 5.4 to 1, with schools with the highest poverty concentration averaging 6.8 to 1 (Cattagni & Farris, 2001). These numbers suggest that even a T-1 connection will be problematic because of the relatively large number of other users sharing the connection. In the case of a school of 600, that would mean that we could have 100 computers connected to the Internet; if only 25 were connected, that bandwidth would be down to 60 kilobytes/sec per connected device.

Clearly, we need to develop a more realistic definition of broadband connectivity and to provision schools and content providers with the access required to support videoconferencing applications. Many groups advocate changing the 200K definition to at least a 10-megabyte minimum standard. The potential solution for this problem may be found in the reauthorization of the Telecommunications Act of 1996. This bill will allow us to change the definition of broadband, provide funding support, and broaden the funding support to cover museums and other content providers.

An area of concern that has recently emerged during the discussions of the reauthorization of the Telecommunications Act is the call for many Internet carriers to establish high-occupancy vehicle (HOV) lanes for video and to charge extra for the video content traveling on these lanes. Currently, all packets of information on the Internet travel as equals (Net Neutrality), but this new effort, if implemented, would single out the video streams and would impose additional fees. This could cripple the Internet protocol (IP) deployment of videoconference equipment into schools. For example, Searls (2005) stated:

(C)arriers subordinate the Net to the pipes that carry it, which they own. To them, the Net is a container cargo system for the stuff we call "con-

tent", and it is subject to whatever traffic control regime they wish to impose on it. That includes tiered service akin to airline service, divided into first class, business, and coach. This brings up doomsday scenarios that are easy for many of us to imagine, if the carriers succeed in lobbying this definition and service regime into law. (http://www.linuxjournal.com//article/8673)

We also must be aware of the push by the Internet carriers to move to an asymmetrical deployment of bandwidth. In the vast majority of situations, the download speed is much greater than the upload speed. This asymmetrical deployment comes out of an old carrier position that they, the carriers, are the holders of the intellectual content, and that schools and homes are simply the receivers of information. Internet roadways must be kept open and flowing equally in both directions, in order to empower the users and not simply have them subject to content that comes "in" from outside their environment, with no ability to interact or create at the school site.

The Internet that we need is an Internet in which all schools, museums, and other content providers has ubiquitous access to symmetrical and robust broadband connections, without additional fees for the type of content that needs to be transmitted.

Dealing with difference is a natural outgrowth of the use of videoconferencing. Differences surface culturally as well as instructionally. The traditional video media is designed for a broadcast environment in which large numbers of individuals view the material and, as such, the content is flattened to accommodate their interests or their needs. Videoconferencing is part of a narrowcast or slithercast delivery of information. In this environment, the content of the programs and instructional strategies can be customized by the provider to meet a narrow band of interests or needs. This customization can focus on the cultural diversity, but can and should be focused on the specific learning needs of the participants.

NCLB has pushed states and local educational agencies to develop data warehouses containing detailed students' test results. Using data mining strategies, we can extract out gaps in student performance. This gap analysis allows us to develop videoconferences specific to the needs of the learner. This type of customization is already occurring in region 1 in New York City, as they work with the Philadelphia Fine Arts Museum and New York Institute of Technology's (NYIT) Culinary Institute to create narrow-cast video conferences designed to meet the specific needs of the students in that region. In the case of NYIT's culinary program, they were given the math results from the region's tests in mathematics and, working with the math specialists in the region, identified that there was a significant gap in performance in the area of fractions. The chefs working with the teachers designed the videoconference around the preparation of pizza and the use of fractions. The students were required to change the recipes for the pizza to accommodate various size groups and to figure out how to cut the pizza to maximize the number of people that could be served. These type of program development laser-focuses the content so that it is targeting specific needs.

In New York State, there is evidence of a growing importance for classroom teachers to link lessons to not only state standards, but to key ideas, performance indicators, and grade bands. In the period of time from November 1, 2005, to October 27, 2006, the MarcoPoloNY Web site (www.nyiteez.org/MarcoPoloNY) had over 11 million hits by teachers seeking to find content that directly matches the instructional needs of their students. It is imperative that we have the ability to design or modify videoconference activities around this level of instructional design.

Another aspect of the issue of equity deals with the content that is covered and the interpreters of the content that are used during the videoconferences. This issue of "Authentic Voices" is not unique to just videoconferencing, as it is a general problem with broadcast forms of media. We often will find artifacts being referenced incorrectly or even sometimes inappropriately. The Educational Enterprise Zone (EEZ) at NYIT has been confronted with this issue a number of times. In one case, a content provider showed planes that they reported were used by the Tuskegee Airmen, while in fact they never flew those specific planes; in another situation, a content provider displayed Native American artifacts in a manner not consistent with cultural norms. As a further example, in a recent training done by a staff member for Navajo teachers on videoconferencing strategies, a pilot connection was made with a prestigious natural history museum and, as a part of the connection, the museum selected the analysis of owl pellets as the core of the videoconference. The Navajo teachers reacted with alarm as, in their culture, the owl is viewed as a symbol of death and should not be displayed or discussed. Our training of museum and other content providers must include sensitivity to cultural norms.

We also must be aware of the need for students to be exposed to a wide range of interpreters of the knowledge base so that the students "see experts" like themselves. The very artifacts selected and how they are treated is an issue that needs to be addressed. We must not only assure that the artifacts are correctly identified, but that they are treated with the reverence and respect that their original cultures demand, and that they are explained in a contextually-appropriate way. This requires the development of strategies to diversify the base of educational specialists at the content provider locations, as well as to develop training strategies for existing educators to help them address cultural and gender issues.

Cultural sensitivity will become even more important as we look towards the globalization of our classrooms. In asynchronous technologies, there is an opportunity for reflection and editing, but in an asynchronous environment, it is important that students and teachers be prepared to interact directly. Our curricula units need to be developed with both broader understandings of culture and use of foreign languages. It is presumptuous to assume that all videoconferences will be in English and will be based entirely on the Western Traditions.

For example, Furstenberg, Levet, English, and Maillet (2001) state:

We, as educators, must prepare our students for this new world and help them develop a deeper understanding of other cultures. This will no doubt be one of the most important skills graduates everywhere will need to possess in this century. So now, more than ever, is the time to search for ways in which this new level of understanding of cultures around the world might be attained. (p. 55)

The barriers for these types of interactions are not technological, but rather are social, political, and organizational in nature. It is imperative that we break through these barriers so that we can use the technologies to foster understanding and cooperation. Priorities must be established to develop these opportunities, and we must work on the creation of specific activities that will broaden the cultural and social experiences of students and teachers. Two examples of existing projects, global nomads and empower peace, help bridge our cultural and historical divides and bring students and teachers together:

- "Founded in 1998, the Global Nomads Group (GNG) is a non-profit organization dedicated to heightening children's understanding and appreciation for the world and its people. Using interactive technologies such as videoconferencing, GNG brings young people together face-to-face to meet across cultural and national boundaries to discuss their differences and similarities, and the world issues that affect them" (http://www.gng.org/about_gng/overview.html).
- "Empower peace seeks to build a worldwide network of high school students and teach-

ers committed to breaking down cultural barriers and misperceptions through open dialogue using videoconferencing and the Internet. Our goal is to bring about a climate of mutual respect and understanding by exposing youth to their contemporaries from abroad. Empower peace also hopes to assist teachers worldwide by enabling their students to learn firsthand about people and countries that they may have only experienced in schoolbooks. Furthermore, through video-conferencing and the Internet, Empower peace hopes to create an arena where students all over the world may engage in a dialogue, sharing insight into their cultures, customs, and lifestyles" (http://www.empowerpeace.com/2005/pages/aboutus/mission.html).

The development of additional activities and the utilization of the potential of this technology must acknowledge and celebrate our differences and build on our common beliefs.

APPLICATIONS

One of the resistance points for videoconferencing is that, in many schools, it has limited use and therefore becomes a budget issue. Most content receivers, who are part of the New York Institute of Technology's EEZ videoconferencing, had to purchase equipment to participate in connections with external connect providers. After that financial outlet, however, one only has to look at the program schedule from any of the major technology conferences to see the interest in these types of connections. Just like any other tool that is placed in the hands of creative people, we have begun to see the emergence of multiple new applications that are pushing the applications horizon. We are seeing students connected from their home to their classrooms when they are unable to attend school, and there is a growing set of classroom-to-classroom applications. These applications range from poetry slams, debates, presentation of research, collaborative project development and cross-class discussions. These types of classroom-to-classroom connections are free and significantly expand the use of the videoconferencing equipment and connections in the buildings.

An often-overlooked area of access deals with how the technology is actually used in the classroom. It is critical that we view the pedagogy of videoconferencing in the same way that we view the technology of videoconferencing. We rejoice in the bidirectional transmission of video, and in the same way, we also rejoice in the talents of all of our schools by creating opportunities for the students to be both the creators of information as well as its receivers.

All too often for underserved schools, there is a perception that the school is missing something, and that the technology will fill the void. This narrow approach also marked the early days of the deployment of computer technology to schools; the computers in suburban schools were used for creation, while the computers in underperforming schools were simply used for remediation. The deployment of videoconferencing creates the ability to unlock the talents of students, and can be used to turn them into creators and deliverers of content, not just recipients. To accomplish this, we must build activities based on a constructivist platform, so that the creation of knowledge is a major part of our videoconferencing efforts.

In a recent pilot, project elementary students on Long Island connected with National Park Service rangers at the Parks of New York Harbor for a videoconference on the Statue of Liberty. The videoconference had two components. In the first videoconference, students worked on decoding the symbols on the statue and learning the historical context during the planning, creation, and installation. In this first connection, the students were recipients of knowledge. In preparation for the second connection, the students were asked to review the current social, economic, and political environment, and to design a statue that would be the equivalent symbol for today.

Another growing use of videoconferencing is in the area of mentoring for both students and teachers. It is possible to establish connections so that students working on research projects can easily connect to college faculty and researchers in commercial and government laboratories. A critical advantage of this electronic mentoring environment is that it allows students to connect to people like themselves in business and industry by using the videoconferencing equipment already available in many locations.

Equally exciting is the ability for our educational communities to utilize the technology to establish mentoring environments for our teachers. Some states are instituting mandatory mentoring requirements for new teachers, but have encountered scale and distribution issues. A small district may hire a new physics teacher, but will have no one that can provide comprehensive mentoring in the district. The videoconferencing capability allows the district to reach out to other districts or to colleges and universities, and link the new teacher to an appropriate mentor. In a safe environment, the mentor can work with the teacher by observing classroom practice and making suggestions.

Videoconferencing also is being used within districts for administrative meetings. This use allows for meetings to be held as needed and to meet the "just-in-time" and "just-enough" needs of the participants, while at the same time reducing the out-of-building time required by face-to-face meetings. Equally as important as increasing the efficiency of meeting, the videoconferencing/hybrid environment will open the opportunities for more varied groups to meet to address dynamically-occurring issues. The technologies will allow for groups of para- professionals to meet to discuss issues; joint planning sessions with teachers across buildings and districts; and a gathering of building safety officers so that they can deal with emerging security concerns.

Finally, the use of videoconferencing as a means to increase participation of the community with our potential for educational systems cannot be overstated. InterCounty Teacher Center, a consortium of eleven school districts covering a distance of 45 miles in the densely-populated Long Island region (where traveling 10 miles can take 45 minutes), had been having trouble with the attendance of board members at the bimonthly meetings. The Board decided to use two locations connected by videoconferencing and, as a result, the average attendance at the meetings increased by 100%. We can further open the walls of all our community meetings by connecting to local libraries, community centers, and individual school buildings. This will allow us to bring the meetings to people instead of people to the meetings. It is a national imperative to increase the participation rate of our parents and community in the schools, and videoconferencing can help facilitate that process.

New Applications of Technologies

This is an exciting point in the world of videoconferencing. There are a series of technologies that are being melded together, with videoconferences either as part of the software or as bolt-on-the-side technologies. These technologies allow us to create hybrid environments that significantly expand the scope of what is possible.

The first area of impact for videoconferencing will be in the area of access. Already, there is a growing deployment of I2 (Internet2) networks. These very high-speed fiber-based networks will significantly increase the number of schools that can receive high-speed and high-quality videoconferences, including the new high-definition videoconferences. High-definition videoconferencing will not only open up more possibilities for videoconferencing, but also will enable existing videoconference providers to display artifacts at much higher levels of detail.

At the same time that tethered videoconferencing will experience the benefits of higher available bandwidth, we are seeing the deployment of new high-speed wireless systems by the telecommunications industry. These cell-based access technologies will be joined by new satellite units using small-profile antennas with low-cost high-speed access. This will allow the providers to deliver content inexpensively from locations far removed from traditional broadband tethered connections constructed by placement issues. Zoos and science museums will be able to routinely transmit from the actual locations without being bound by the limitations of finding an Ethernet jack in which to plug their units. As an example, most content providers belonging to NYIT's EEZ began their programs with a videoconferencing unit as their whole technology implementation. Shortly after starting their delivery of programs, the EEZ began to receive requests for peripherals that could help with the display of the artifacts or other visual media. The first requests were for document cameras that could be attached to the main videoconferencing unit, and which would allow the content provider to show objects in a way that could be better viewed by the remote participant. In the same way that the document cameras expanded the scope of what would be displayed, a new set of peripherals is opening possibilities. These new peripherals include wireless cameras that can be placed in remote locations, handheld microscopes that can be used to examine fine details, digital microscopes to examine cells, and annotation devices for marking up the video image. These annotation devices allow the content provider to have the same capabilities as a sportscaster or weatherperson on TV.

The biggest changes in the videoconferencing environment will occur as a result of the merging of traditionally stand-alone communications tools. These tools fall into two general categories, asynchronous and synchronous. Asynchronous communications systems are those in which the participants do not have to be online at the same time. In the past twenty years, there has been a significant growth in the types of communication systems available. They include text discussion boards, course management systems, blogs, Wikis, video e-mail, and audio discussion boards. In each of these cases, the system allows for an expansion of discourse, both before and after a videoconference session. The content providers and teachers will no longer be limited to a one-hour single connection, but instead can use the connection as the driving agent for building ongoing investigations and discussions. This will allow for the content to be explored at a greater depth and for students to take greater ownership of the investigations without incurring greater costs. This also allows the content provider to link a number of schools that have scheduled separate videoconferences to work together on projects. The schools that are linked together can be from varied locations around the world. While a number of schools already have asynchronous tools in place, there are a growing number of free products that are readily available.

Pushing our instructional options even further is the asynchronous technology currently referred to as video on demand (VOD). By using video on demand, students, teachers, and content providers have, at their disposal, huge databases of actual video content that can be incorporated into their projects as well as used by the content providers as program material. An exciting aspect of this technology is that it will allow both the content provider and the receiver to each add their own content. VOD can then be used by the content providers to store programs that are one-of-a-kind in nature (i.e., guest speakers), and allow the content to be delivered at another time to a different audience. These stored video programs can be delivered either as a stand-alone or as part of another program.

These asynchronous products readily serve as companions, extensions, and support for video-conferencing which, as a synchronous product, requires the users to be available at the time of the connection. There are also products that are synchronous in nature and can serve to push the boundaries of videoconferencing in terms of what can be done, and also have the potential to significantly increase the number of people who are able to participate. One such category of product is Webinar software. The products in this category of software create a seminar environment using a suite of tools. One such product, Elluminate, used by the Educational Enterprise Zone, has voice, instant messaging, shared whiteboards, guided Web tours, polling for understanding, quiz capabilities, application sharing, and the ability to display rich media, including live video. Webinar software can be used as an "on the side technology" used in conjunction with an existing videoconference, as a means of extending the discourse in much the same way as the synchronous products, or even as a replacement for existing videoconferencing systems. When used as an "on the side" technology, the Webinar toolsets significantly increase the potential for dynamic interactions between the participants. For schools, content providers, and other participants to use the Webinar systems, they would simply need inexpensive "eyeball" cameras and access to the Internet.

MOVING FORWARD

As we look forward, we need to make sure that we include the use of MP3 players, video Ipods, and small-format tablet computing devices. Content sources will need to incorporate these devices and develop strategies for pushing content into these devices. Already schools are utilizing podcasts in their instructional programs, and soon there will be an expectation that support information will be delivered using this type of distribution. Schools also will be looking for an outcome of videoconference activities to be the requirement for students to push their knowledge out to a broader community.

The key to the future of videoconferencing will be in our understanding of the nature of interactive communications as it relates to an evolving set of tools and cultural experiences. As a community, we need to address the issues of access in a way that makes all participants able to be creators of knowledge as well as receivers. It is imperative that we develop our programs and our instructional strategies so that they push the limits for students and let them participate in a global society. The tools of the technology will constantly be in change, as is the nature of technology, but good, sound instructional practices must set the foundation for all our collective works.

REFERENCES

Cattagni, A., & Farris, E. (2001). *Internet access in U.S. public schools and classrooms: 1994– 2000* (NCES 2001–071). U.S. Department of Education. Washington, DC: National Center for Education Statistics.

Durrant, C., & Green, B. (2000). Literacy and the new technologies in school education: Meeting the l(IT)eracy challenge? *Australian Journal of Language and Literacy, 23*(2), 89.

Empower Peace (1999). Empower peace Web site. Retrieved April 30, 2006, from http://www. empowerpeace.com/2005/pages/aboutus/mission.html

Furstenberg, G., Levet, S., English, K., & Maillet, K. (2001). Giving a virtual voice to the silent language of culture: The cultura project. *Language, Learning & Technology, 5*(1), 55.

Institute of Educational Services (2003). *Internet access in U.S. public schools and classrooms: 1994–2003*. Retrieved April 30, 2006, from http://nces.ed.gov/surveys/frss/publications/2005015/

Mack, K. (2005). *Marco Polo in New York*. Retrieved April 30, 2006, from http://www.nyiteez.org/MarcoPoloNY

Miller, M. R. (2005). The digital dynamic: How communications media shape our world. *The Futurist, 39*, 31.

No Child Left Behind Act (2001). 20 U.S.C. 70 [section] 6301

Searls, D. (2005, Nov). Saving the Net: How to keep the carriers from flushing the Net down the tubes. *LINUX Journal, Article 8673*. Retrieved December 3, 2006, from http://www.linuxjournal.com//article/8673

Seels, B., Fullerton, K., Berry, L., & Horn, L. J. (2004). 12 Research on learning from television. In D. H. Jonassen (Ed.), *Handbook of research on educational communications and technology, 2nd ed.* (pp. 249-320). Mahwah, NJ: Lawrence Erlbaum Associates.

Telecommunications Act (1996). Pub. LA. No. 104-104, 110 Stat. 56

Yestrau, C. (2004). Retrieved April 30, 2006, from http://www.gng.org/about_gng/overview.html

Compilation of References

Abdal-Haqq, I. (1989). The influence of reform on inservice teacher education. *Eric Digest*. Retrieved November 30, 2006, from http://www.thememoryhole.org/edu/eric/ed322147.html

Abrahamson, C. (1998). Issues in interactive communications in distance education. *College Student Journal, 32*(1), 33-43.

Access Center (2006). Webinars. Retrieved August 1, 2006, from http://www.k8accesscenter.org/online_community_area/Webinar.asp

Adams, S. (2002). Cost effective real-time video conferencing for instruction and collaborative learning in music and the performing arts via next generation Internet powered virtual laboratory environment. In G. Richards (Ed.), In *Proceedings of World Conference on E-Learning in Corporate, Government, Healthcare, and Higher Education, 2002* (pp. 2531-2532). Chesapeake, VA: AACE.

Adcock, P., & Austin, W. (2002, March). *Alternative classroom observation through two-way audio/video conferencing systems*. Paper presented at the Society for Information Technology and Teacher Education Conference.

Amirian, S. (2003). Pedagogy and videoconferencing: A review of recent literature. In *Proceedings of the First NJEDge.NET Conference*, Plainsboro, NJ, October 31, 2003. Retrieved April 10, 2006, from http://www.iclassnotes.com/amirian_handout.pdf#search='NJEDge.NET%20Conference%20%20Amirian' and http://www.iclassnotes.com/amirian_megacon.pdf

Amirian, S. (2003, October). Pedagogy and videoconferencing: A review of recent literature. In *Proceedings of the First NJEDge.NET Conference*, Plainsboro, New Jersey.

Anderson, T., & Rourke, L. (2005). *Videoconferencing in kindergarten-to-grade 12 settings: A review of the literature*. Prepared for Alberta Learning by Canadian Association of Distance Education Research. Retrieved September 1, 2005, from http://www.vcalberta.ca/community/litreview.pdf

Anderson, T., & Rourke, M. (2005). *Videoconferencing in kindergarten-to-grade 12 settings: A review of the literature*. Retrieved April 1, 2006, from http://www.d261.k12.id.us/VCing/curriculum/design.htm

Andrews, K., & Marshall, K. (2000). Making learning connections through telelearning. *Educational Leadership*, 53-56.

Arnold, T., Cayley, S. & Griffith, M. (2002). *Videoconferencing in the classroom: Communications technology in the classroom*. Retrieved May 16, 2006, from http://www.becta.org

Arnold, T., Cayley, S., & Griffith, M. (2004). *Video conferencing in the classroom: Communications technology across the curriculum*. Devon, England: Devon County Council.

Ashton, T. (2002). New virtual field trips (Book). *Roeper Review, 24*(4), 236-238.

AT&T Knowledge Explorers (2006). Videoconferencing directories. Retrieved April 6, 1946, from http://www.kn.pacbell.com/wired/vidconf/directory.cfm

Austin, R., Abbott, L., Mulkeen, A., & Metcalfe, N. (2003). *The global classroom: Collaboration and cultural awareness in the north and south of Ireland.* Coleraine, Ireland: University of Ulster / Maynooth, Ireland: National University of Ireland.

Author. (1997). California school district employs videoconferencing units for global studies. *T H E Journal, 25*(3), 38.

Awbrey, S. M. (1996). Successfully integrating new technologies into the higher education curriculum. *Educational Technology Review, 5.*

Ba, H., & Keisch, D. (2004). *Bridging the gap between formal and informal learning: Evaluating the SeaTrek distance learning project.* Center For Children and Technology, New York, New York: Education Development Center, Inc. Retrieved August 14, 2006, at http://www2.edc.org/CCT/Publications_report_summary.asp?numPubId=177.

Bailey, J. (2003). Viewpoint: Overcoming the "achievement paradox": Four lessons from the business world. *eSchool News Online, May 29, 2003.* Retrieved March 10, 2005, from http://www.eschoolnews.com/news/showstory.cfm?ArticleID=4284 Becta. http://www.becta.org.uk

Baldenhorst, Z., & Axmann, M. (2002). The educational use of videoconferencing in the arts faculty: Shedding a new light on puppetry. *British Journal of Educational Technology, 33*(3), 291-299.

Barbanell, P., Falco, J., & Newman, D.L. (2003). *New vision, new realities: Methodology and mission in developing interactive videoconferencing programming.* Paper presented at the annual meeting of the Museum and the Web, 2003. Retrieved November 14, 2006, from http://www.archimuse.com/ mw2003/papers/barbanell.barbanell.html

Barbanell, P., Newman, D. L., & Falco, J. (2003, March). *New vision, new realities: Methodology and mission in developing interactive videoconferencing programming.* Paper presented at the Museums and the Web, Charlotte, NC.

Barker, B. O., & Taylor, D. R. (1993). *An overview of distance learning and telecommunications in rural schools.* Paper presented at the 58th Annual Conference of the National Association of Counties, Chicago, IL.

BECTA. (2004). *How to use videoconferencing effectively in your classroom.* Retrieved February 1, 2006, from http://schools.becta.org.uk/index.php?section=tl&catcode=ss_tl_use_02&rid=5223&pagenum=1&NextStart=1&print=1

Beilin, R., & Rabow, J. (1981). Status value, group learning, and minority achievement in college. *Small Group Behavior, 12,* 495-508.

Belcheir, M. J. & Cucek, M. (2001). *Student perceptions of their distance education courses.* Boise State University, Office of Institutional Assessment. ED 480 923.

Bennet, F. (2002). The future of computer technology in K-12 education. *Phi Delta Kappan, 2*(8), 621-625.

Bethpage Community. Retrieved April 26, 2006, from http://www.bethpagecommunity.com/Schools/technology/Videoconferencing%20Manual.pdf

Bethpage Union Free School District (n.d.) Videoconferencing manual: Content providers.

Blanck, G. (1990). Vygotsky: The man and his cause. In L. C. Moll (Ed.), *Vygotsky and education: Instructional implications and applications of sociohistorical psychology* (pp. 31-58). Cambridge, MA: Cambridge University Press.

Boccia, J., Fontain, P., Lucas, F. Michael. (2002, March). *Looking into classrooms: A technology mediated observation program for preservice teachers.* Paper presented at Society for Information Technology and Teacher Education Conference.

Bradshaw, L. (2002). Technology for teaching and learning: Strategies for staff development and follow-up support. *Journal of Technology and Teacher Education, 10*(1), 131-150.

Bruce, B. C., & Levin, J. A. (1997). Educational technology: Media for inquiry, communication, construction, and expression. *Journal of Educational Computing Research, 17*(1), 79-102.

Bruce, B. C., Dowd, H., Eastburn, D. M., & D'Arcy, C. J. (2005). Plants, pathogens, and people: Extending the classroom to the Web. *Teachers College Record, 107*(8), 1730-1753.

Bruner, J. (1985). Vygotsky: An historical and conceptual perspective. In Wertsch, J. (Ed.) *Culture, communication, and cognition: Vygotskyan perspectives* (pp.21-34). London: Cambridge University Press.

Burgstahler, S. (2001). Use of telecommunications products by people with disabilities. *Do-It. University of Washington.* Retrieved April 11, 2006, from http://www.washington.edu/doit/brochures/pdf/telcom.pdf

Cannavina, G., Stokes, C. W., & Cannavina, C. (2004). Evaluation of video-conferencing as a means to facilitate outreach and work-based learning. *Work-Based Learning in Primary Care, 2,* 136-47.

Carter, K. (2004). Online training: What's really working? *Technology & Learning, 24*(10), 32-37.

Cattagni, A., & Farris, E. (2001). *Internet access in U.S. public schools and classrooms: 1994– 2000* (NCES 2001–071). U.S. Department of Education.

Washington, DC: National Center for Education Statistics.

Cavanaugh, C. (2001). The effectiveness of interactive distance education technologies in K-12 learning: A meta-analysis. *International Journal of Educational Telecommunications, 7*(1), 73-88.

Cavanaugh, C., Gillian, J. K., Kromrey, J., Hess, M., & Blomeyer, R. (2004). *The effects of distance education on K-12 student outcomes: A meta-analysis.* Naperville, IL: Learning Point Associates.

CEO Forum on Education and Technology (2001). *Educational technology must be included in comprehensive education legislation.* Retrieved November 14, 2006, from http://www.ceoforum.org

CEO Forum on Education and Technology (2001). Key building blocks for student achievement in the 21st century: Assessment, alignment, accountability, access, and analysis. *The CEO Forum Schools Technology and Readiness Report Year 4.* Washington DC: CEO Forum.

Chadwick, K., & Shrago, J. (2001). How Tennessee successfully motivated and supported teachers' skill development in meaningful classroom Internet use. In D. Grisham (Ed.), *Teacher professional development and technology.* Multi-paper presentation conducted at the Annual Meeting of the American Educational Research Association, Seattle, WA.

CILC: Center for Interactive Learning and Collaboration (n.d.). Retrieved August 22, 2006, from http://www.cilc.org

Clark, K., Hosticka, A., Schriver, M., & Bedell, J. (2002). Computer-based virtual field trips. *ERIC Document.* Retrieved April 1, 2006, from EBSCOHost

Classroom and Media Services Information Services and Technology of the University of Manitoba (n.d.). Videoconferencing manual. *University of Manitoba.* Retrieved April 27, 2006, from http://umanitoba.ca/campus/ist/cms/video-conferencing/manual/index.shtml

Claxton, G. (2003). Learning is learnable (and we ought to teach it). In *Learning to succeed: The next decade.* The National Commission on Education Follow-Up Group, Occasional Paper, December 2003, University of Brighton.

Cochrane, C. (1996). The use of videoconferencing to support learning: An overview of issues relevant to the library and information profession. *Education for Information, 14*(4), 317-330.

Cochran-Smith, M. (1995). Uncertain allies: Understanding the boundaries of race and teaching. *Harvard Education Review, 56,* 541-570.

Comber, C., Lawson, T., Gage, J., Cullum-Hanshaw, A., & Allen, T. (2004). *Report for schools of the DfES video conferencing in the classroom project.* Retrieved May 1, 2005, from http://www.becta.org.uk/page_documents/research/video_conferencing_report_may04.pdf

Connected (2005). Argyll and Bute online magazine. Retrieved from http://www.ltscotland.org.uk/ictineducation/connected/archivedissues/connected1/video.asp

Cooper, M. (1996). *Universal service: A historical perspective and policies for the twenty-first century.*

Coventry, L. (1995). Video conferencing and learning in higher education. A report to the advisory group on computer graphics. SIMA Report Series ISSN 1356-5370. Retrieved March 15, 2006, from http://www.agocg.ac.uk/mmedia.htm

Coventry, L. (1995). *Videoconferencing higher education.* Institute for Computer-Based Learning, Heriot Watt University. Retrieved November 14, 2003, from http://www.agocg.ac.uk/reports/mmedia/video3/video3.pdf

Cox, S. E., & Su, T. (2004). Integrating student learning with practitioner experiences via virtual field trips. *Journal of Educational Media, 29*(2), 113-123.

Cradler, J. (1994). Summary of current research and evaluation findings on technology in education. Retrieved November 17, 2005, from http://www.wested.org/techpolicy/refind.html

Cronk, R. (1996). *The television mystique: Electronic synchrony and the television totem.* Retrieved November 30, 2006, from http://www.westland.net/venice/art/cronk/tv.htm

Cross, K. P., & Angelo, T. A. (1988). *Classroom assessment techniques: A handbook for faculty.* Ann Arbor, MI: National Center for Research to Improve Postsecondary Teaching and Learning.

Dallas, P. S. (2001). Videoconferencing application to distance education with particular reference to small states. *Distance Education in Small States, 2000 Conference Proceedings. The University of the West Indies/The Commonwealth of Learning.* Retrieved August 14, 2006, from http://www.col.org/colweb/site/pid/3338

Darling-Hammond, L. (1992). Accountability for professional practice. In M. Levine (Ed.), *Professional practice schools: Linking teacher education and school reform* (pp. 81-104). New York: Teachers College Press.

Darling-Hammond, L. (1994). *Professional development schools: Schools for developing a profession.* New York: Teachers College Press.

Darling-Hammond, L. (1999). Target time toward teachers. *Journal of Staff Development, 20*(2), 35-42.

Darling-Hammond, L. (2006). Constructing 21st-century teacher education. *Journal of Teacher Education, 57*(3).

Davis, B. G. (1993). *Tools for teaching.* San Francisco: Jossey-Bass.

Davis, J. (1996). Computer-assisted distance learning, part II: Examination performance of students on and off campus. *Journal of Engineering, 85*(1), 77-82.

Dede, C. (2001). A new century demands new ways of learning. In D. T. Gordon (Ed.), *The digital classroom* (pp.171-174). Cambridge, MA: Harvard Education Letter.

DeFord, K., & Dimock, V. (2002). *Interactive video conferencing: A policy issues review.* Retrieved February 6, 2006, from: http://neirtec.terc.edu/k12vc/resources/ivc%20policy%review%june%2002.pdf

Denning, S. (2001). *The springboard: How storytelling ignites action in knowledge-era organizations.* Woburn, MA: Butterworth-Heinemann.

Department of Education Northern Ireland (2004). *Empowering schools in Northern Ireland: Transforming learning, teaching, and leadership through education and technology change.* Bangor, Northern Ireland. Retrieved from http://www.empoweringschools.com

Dewey, J. (1943). *The child and the curriculum / The and school and society.* Chicago: University of Chicago Press.

Dieker, L.A., & Monda-Amaya, L. E. (1997). Using problem solving and effective teaching frameworks to promote reflective thinking in preservice special educators. *Teacher Education and Special Education, 20*(1), 22-36.

Digital Handbook (2003). *A videoconferencing guide for teachers and students.* Retrieved April 11, 2006, from http://www.d261.k12.id.us/VC-ing/curriculum/design.htm

Dishongh, K. (2005, December 28). Ideas bubble up when students put their heads together. *USA Today,* 8d.

Distance Learning (n.d.). Retrieved August 22, 2006, from http://www.discoverycenter.org/distancelearning.php

Doherty, K., & Skinner, R. (2003, January 9). States of the states. Quality count 2003: "If I can't learn from you…" *Education Week, 22*(17), 75-78.

DoIt Support Services of George Mason University (n.d.). Videoconferencing. Retrieved April 25, 2006, from http://www.doit.gmu.edu/portfolio/2004/CT/VTC04.htm

Dubois, J. R. (1996). Going the distance: A national distance learning initiative. *Adult Learning, 8*(1), 19-21.

DuCharme-Hansen, B. A., & Dupin-Bryant, P. A. (2005). Distance education plans: Course planning for online adult learners. *TechTrends, 49*(2), 31-39.

Durrant, C., & Green, B. (2000). Literacy and the new technologies in school education: Meeting the l(IT)eracy challenge? *Australian Journal of Language and Literacy, 23*(2), 89.

Dutton, J., Dutton, M., & Perry, J. (2001). Do online students perform as well as lecture students? *Journal of Engineering Education, 90*(1), 131-136.

Dyke, M., Harding, A., & Lajeunesse, S. (2006, April). *Digital observation of teaching practice.* Paper presented at the Annual Conference of the American Educational Research Association, San Francisco, CA.

Edens, K. M. (2001). Bringing authentic K-12 classrooms and teachers to a university classroom through videoconferencing. *Journal of Computing in Teacher Education, 17*(3), 26-31.

Education. *HighBeam Research.* Retrieved September 15, 2005, from http://www.highbeam.com

Empower Peace (1999). Empower peace Web site. Retrieved April 30, 2006, from http://www.empowerpeace.com/2005/pages/aboutus/mission.html

European Studies Project. http://www.europeanstudies.freeserve.co.uk

Ezarik, M. (2001). Charting the technology explosion. *Curriculum Administrator, 37*(7), 36-41.

Falco, J., Barbanell, P., Newman, D., & DeWald, S. (2005). In L. T. Wee Him & R. Subramaniam (Eds.), *E-learning and virtual science centers.* Hershey, PA: Idea Group, Inc.

Falk, J. H., & Dierking, L. D. (2000). *Learning from museums: Visitor experiences and the making of meaning.* Walnut Creek, CA: AltaMira.

Farrell, G. M. (1999). *The development of virtual education: A global perspective.* Vancouver, British Columbia: The Commonwealth of Learning.

Federal Communications Commission (1996). Telecommunications act of 1996. Public law 104-104. 110 statute 56 (hereafter, 1996 Act, or the conference report). *Washington, DC.* Retrieved April 17, 2006, from http://www.fs.fed.us/recreation/permits/commsites/pl-104-104.pdf

Federal Communications Commission (1999). Section 504: Programs and activities accessibility handbook. *Washington, DC.* Retrieved April 11, 2006, from: http://www.fcc.gov/cgb/dro/section_504.html

Federal Communications Commission (2004). E-rate. *Washington, DC.* Retrieved April 11, 2006, from: http://www.fcc.gov/learnnet/

Federal Legislation and Education in New York State (2006). University of the State of New York (pp. 22-23). The State Education Department.

Fels, D. I., & Weiss, P. L. (2006). *Video-mediated communication in the classroom to support sick children: A case study.* Retrieved May 16, 2006, from www.ryerson.ca/pebbles/publications/ijie-pebblesfinal.pdf

Ferrer, G. (in press 2006). Videoconferencing brings world to CdA students. *The Spokesman-Review.*

Filby, N. (1995). Analysis of reflective professional development models. ED 393 057.

Flavell, J. H. (1992). Cognitive development: Past, present, and future. *Developmental Psychology, 23,* 998-1005.

Floyd, M. (2002). More than just a field trip: Making relevant curricular connections through museum experiences. *Art Education, 55*(5), 39-45.

Fountain, C., & Evans, D. (1994). Beyond shared rhetoric: A collaborative change model for integrating preservice and in-service urban education delivery systems. *Journal of Teacher Education, 45,* 218-227.

Freeman, M. (1998). Videoconferencing: A solution to the multi-campus large classes problem? *British Journal of Educational Technology, 29*(3), 197-210.

Fullan, M. (2000). The return of large-scale reform. *Journal of Educational Change, 1,* 1-23.

Fullan, M. (2003). *The moral imperative of school leadership.* Thousand Oaks, CA: Corwin Press.

Furst-Bowe, J. A. (1997). Comparison of students in traditional and videoconferencing courses in training and development. *International Journal of Instructional Media, 24*(3), 197-206.

Furstenberg, G., Levet, S., English, K., & Maillet, K. (2001). Giving a virtual voice to the silent language of culture: The cultura project. *Language, Learning & Technology, 5*(1), 55.

Gabbert, B., Johnson, D. W., & Johnson, R. (1986). Cooperative learning, group-to-individual transfer, process gain, and the acquisition of cognitive reasoning strategies. *Journal of Psychology, 120,* 265-278.

Gage, J., Nickson, M., & Beardon, T. (2002). *Can videoconferencing contribute to teaching and learning? The experience of the motivate project.* Paper presented at the Annual Conference of the British Educational Research Association. Retrieved November 14, 2006, from http://www. leeds.ac.uk/educol/ documents/00002264.htm

Galloway, W., Boland, S., & Benesova, A. (2002). *Virtual learning environments.* Retrieved May 16, 2006, from http://www.dcs.napier.ac.uk/~mm/socbytes/feb2002_i/3.html

Gardner, H. (1983). *Frames of mind: The theory of multiple intelligences.* New York: Basic Books.

Garrett, J., & Dudt, K. (1998). Using video conferencing to supervise student teachers. *Proceedings of the SITE 98: Society for Information Technology & Teacher Education International Conference, Washington, DC: Vol. 9* (pp. 142-150).

Gernstein, R. B. (2000). Videoconferencing in the classroom: Special projects toward cultural understanding. *Integration of Technology in the Classroom, 16*(3-4), 177-186.

Gibson, S., & Nocente, N. (1999). Computers in the schools. *Computers in social studies education: A report of teachers' perspectives and students' attitudes, 15*(2), 73-81. New York: Haworth Press.

Giuliani, J. (2001*). Identification of salient features of videoconferencing instruction.* Unpublished doctoral dissertation, Northern Illinois University. (UMI No. 3013782).

Glazer, E., Hannafin, M. J., & Song, L. (2005). Promoting technology integration through collaborative apprenticeship. *Educational Technology Research and Development, 53*(4), 57-68.

Global Leap Project. *Videoconferencing in the classroom.* Retrieved from http://www.global-leap.com

Gokhale, A. A. (1995). Collaborative learning enhances critical thinking. *Journal of Technology Education, 7,* 1045-1064.

Good, R. (2003). *The future of Web conferencing: Good interviews with Keith Teare.* Retrieved May 18, 2006, from http://www.masternewmedia.org/2003/11/24/ the_future_of_web_conferencing.htm

Granger, C. A., Morbey, M. L., Lotherington, H., Owston, R. D., & Wideman, H. H. (2002). Factors contributing to teachers' successful implementation of IT. *Journal of Computer Assisted Learning, 18,* 480-488.

Green, J. N. (1999). Interactive videoconferencing improves performance of limited English proficient students. *T.H.E. (Technological Horizons in Education) Journal, 26*(4), 69-70. Retrieved November 14, 2006, from http://thejournal.com/articles/14095

Greenberg, G. (1998). Distance education technologies: Best practices for K-12 settings. *Technology and Society Magazine, 17*(4), 36-40.

Greenburg, A. (2003). Best practices in live content acquisition by distance learning organizations: Enhancing primary- and secondary-school classrooms by tapping content resources via two-way interactive video. *Wainhouse Research.* Retrieved February, 2006, from http://www.wainhouse.com/files/papers/wr-content-acq.pdf

Greenburg, A. (2004). Navigating the sea of research on video conferencing-based education: A platform for understanding research into the technology's effectiveness and value. *Wainhouse Research.* Retrieved February, 2006, from http://www.wainhouse.com/files/papers/wr-navseadistedu.pdf

Greenwood, A. (1998). Learning science at a distance: Using interactive television to work with schools. *Education, 118*(3), 349-352.

Groulx, J. (2001). Changing preservice teacher perceptions of minority schools. *Urban Education, 36*, 60–92.

Guskey, T. (2000). *Evaluating professional development.* Thousand Oaks, CA: Corwin Press, Inc.

Haga, M., & Heitkamp, T. (2000). Bringing social work education to the prairie. *Journal of Social Work Education, 36*(2), 309-324.

Halal, W. E., & Liebowitz, J. (1994). Telelearning: The multimedia revolution in Education. *The Futurist, 28*(6), 21-26.

Hamza, M., Checker, C., & Perez, B. (2001). Creative leaps in distance education technologies. *International Society for Technology in Education, SIGTel Bulletin, Archives.* Retrieved March, 2006, from http://www.iste.org/Content/Navigation-Menu/Membership/SIGs/SIGTel_Telelearning_/SIGTel_Bulletin2/Archive/20012/2001_June_-_Hamza.htm

Hatton, N., & Smith, D. (1995). Reflection in teacher education towards definition and implementation. *Teaching and Teacher Education, 11*(1), 33-49.

Hayden, K. L. (1999). *Videoconferencing in K-12 education: A Delphi study of characteristics and critical strategies to support constructivist learning experiences.* Unpublished doctoral dissertation, Pepperdine University. (UMI No. 9934596).

Hayne, P. (2001). New virtual field trips (Book Review). *Media and Methods, 37*(7), 30-36.

Hearnshaw, D. (2000). Towards an objective approach to the evaluation of videoconferencing. *Innovations in Education and Training International, 37*(3), 210-217.

Heath, M. J., & Halznagel, D. (2002). *Interactive videoconferencing: A literature review.* Prepared for the K-12 National Symposium for Interactive Videoconferencing Dallas, Texas, October, 2002.

Heaviside, S., Riggins, T., & Farris, E. (1997). Advance telecommunications in U.S. public elementary and secondary schools. *Fall, 1996 (NCES 97-854), U.S. Department of Education, Washington, DC: National Center for Education Statistics.* Retrieved March 16, 2006, from http://www.anchoragepress.com/archives-2006/news-2vol15ed13.shtml

Heifetz, R. A. (1994). *Leadership without easy answers.* Cambridge, MA: The Belknap Press of Harvard University Press.

Hein, G. E. (1995). The constructivist museum (electronic version). *Journal for Education in Museums, 16*, 21-23. Retrieved August 3, 2006, from http://www.gem.org.uk/pubs/news/hein1995.html

Hein, G. E., & Alexander, M. (1998). *Museums: Places of learning.* Washington, DC: American Association of Museums.

Heitkamp, T. (1995). *Social work education at a distance: An innovative approach.* A paper presented at the Annual Program Meeting of the Council on Social Work Education, San Diego, CA.

Hiltz, S. (1997). Impacts of college-level courses via asynchronous learning networks: Some preliminary results. *Journal of Asynchronous Learning Networks, 1*(2), 1-19.

Holznagel, D. (2003). *Access and opportunity policy. Options for interactive video in K-12 education* (pp. 25-46). Northwest Regional Educational Laboratory, Portland OR.

Hoot, J., Massey, C., Barnett, M., Henry, J., & Ernest, J. (2001). A former church as a center of excellence for children. *Childhood Education, 77*(6), 386-392.

Howard-Kennedy, J. (2004). Benefits of video-conferencing in education. *Media and Methods, 41*(1), 17.

Howard-Kennedy, J. (2004). Middle school videoconferencing fosters global citizenship. *Center Digital.* Retrieved April 25, 2006, from http://www.centerdigitalgov.com/international/story.php?docid=90700

Hudson, J. A., & Fivush, R. (1991). As time goes by: Sixth graders remember a kindergarten experience. *Applied Cognitive Psychology, 5,* 347-360.

Hung, D., & Nichani, M. R. (2002). Bring communities of practice into schools: Implications for instructional technologies from Vygotskian perspectives. *International Journal of Instructional Media, 29*(2), 171-183.

Hung, D., Tan, S. C., & Chen, D.T. (2005). How the Internet facilitates learning as dialog: Design considerations for online discussions. *International Journal of Instructional Media, 32*(1), 37-46.

Hunter, M. (1984). *Mastery teaching.* El Segundo, CA: TIP Publications.

Huyssen, A. (1995). *Twilight memories: Marking time in a culture of amnesia.* New York: Routledge.

Illinois Video Network (2003). Retrieved from http://www.state.il.us/cms/ivn/DistanceLearning/Distlearn.htm

Institute of Educational Services (2003). *Internet access in U.S. public schools and classrooms: 1994–2003.* Retrieved April 30, 2006, from http://nces.ed.gov/surveys/frss/publications/2005015/

Instructional Services of Penn State (2003). *Etiquette and tips for a successful videoconference.* Retrieved April 23, 2006, from http://www.hbg.psu.edu/iit/mw2/etiquette.htm

International Society for Technology in Education (2004). Use of NETS by state. National education technology standards (NETS) and the states (updated May 19, 2004). Retrieved April, 2006, from http://cnets.iste.org/docs/States_using_NETS.pdf investment. Retrieved April 8, 2004, from http://www.wested.org/online_pubs/learning_return.pdf

Irele, M. (1999). Cost-benefit analysis in distance education. *Lucent Technologies and the World Campus, Pennsylvania State University.*

Irving, K. (2001). Innovations in observing children: Use of new technologies. In *Promoting meaningful learning: Innovations in educating early childhood professionals* (pp. 77-83). Washington, DC: National Association for the Education of Young Children.

Jerome School District (2003). Strategies for using video conferencing technology in the K-12 classroom: A teacher's digital handbook. Retrieved April 11, 2006, from http://www.d26/k12.id.us/vcing/index.htm

JKC (2006). *Video conferencing and video conferencing systems–Video conferencing trends and the future?* Retrieved May 16, 2006, from http://www.jkcit.co.uk/video-conferencing-future-trends.htm

Johnson, D. W., & Johnson, R. T. (1996). Cooperation and the use of technology. In D. H. Jonassen (Ed.), *Handbook of research for educational communications and technology* (pp.1017-1044). New York: Simon and Schuster Macmillan.

Johnson, S., Aragon, S., Shaik, N., & Palma-Rivas, N. (2000). Comparative analysis of learner satisfaction and learning outcomes in online and face-to-face learning environments. *Journal of Interactive Learning Research, 11*(1), 29-49.

Jonassen, D. H. (2002). Engaging and supporting problem solving in online learning. *The Quarterly Review of Distance Education, 3,* 1-13.

Jonassen, D. H. (2002). Engaging and supporting problem-solving in online learning. *The Quarterly Review of Distance Education, 3,* 1-13.

Jonassen, D. H., Carr, C., & Yueh, H. (1998). Computers as mindtools for engaging learners in critical thinking. *Tech Trends, 43,* 24-32.

Jones, K. C. (2007). *No Child Left Behind could get boost for tech: New legislation would invest in classroom technology to prepare U.S. students for work in the information economy.* Retrieved from, http://www.informationweek.com/industries/showArticle.jhtml?articleID=199701868&subSection= p.1

Joyce, B., & Showers, B. (1995). *Student achievement through staff development: Fundamentals of school renewal (2nd ed.).* New York: Longman.

Keasley, G. (2005). Social developmental theories - L. Vygotsky. Retrieved April 22, 2006, from http://tip.psychology.org/vygotsky.html

Kerka, S., & Wonocott, M. E. (2000). Online assessment: Continuous and interactive. Retrieved April 20, 2006, from http://www.calpro-online.org/eric/docs/pfile03.htm

Kleiner, A., & Farris, E. (2002). Internet access in U.S. public schools and classrooms, 1994-2001. *U.S. Department of Education, Fall, 2002 (NCES 2002-018), Washington, DC: National Center for Education Statistics.* Retrieved March 23, 2006, from http://nces.ed.gov/pubs2002/2002018.pdf

Klemm, B. E., & Tuthill, G. (2003). Virtual field trips: Best practices. *International Journal of Institutional Media, 30*(2), 177-193.

Knipe, D., & Lee, M. (2002). The quality of teaching and learning via videoconferencing. *British Journal of Educational Technology, 33*(2), 301-311.

Knowledge Network Explorers (2006). Videoconferencing directories. Retrieved April 6, 2006, from http://www.kn.pacbell.com/wired/vidconf/directory.cfm

Knowledge Network Explorers (2006). Videoconferencing evaluation. Retrieved April 15, 2006, from http://www.kn.pacbell.com/wired/vidconf/eval.html

Kosak, L., Manning, L., Dobson, E., Rogerson, L., Cotnam, S., Colaric, S., & McFadden, C. (2004). Prepared to teach online? Perspectives of faculty in the University of North Carolina system. *Online Journal of Distance Learning Administration, VII-III.* Retrieved April 10, 2006, from http://www.westga.edu/~distance/ojdla/fall73/kosak73.html

Kraft, N. P. (1997). Components for effective professional development. *RMC Research Corporation.* Retrieved April 8, 2006, from http://www.starcenter.org/articles/effectivepd.html

Lai, W., Pratt, K., & Grant, A. (2003). *State of the art and trends in distance, flexible, and open learning.* Retrieved April 10, 2006, from http://hedc2.otago.ac.nz/TLI/distance_learning_pdf/distance_lit_review.pdf#search='review%20of%20the%20literature%20videoconference%20learning

LaRose, R., Gregg, J., & Eastin, M. (1998). Audio graphic telecourses for the Web: An experiment. *Journal of Computer-Mediated Communication [On-line], 4*(2). Retrieved March 18, 2006, from http://www.ascusc.org/jcmc/vol4/issue2/larose.html

Lehman, J. D., & Richardson, J. (2004). *Making connections in teacher education: Electronic portfolios, videoconferencing, and distance field experiences.* Paper presented at Association for Educational Communications and Technology. Retrieved August 1, 2006, from http://p3t3.soe.purdue.edu/AECT%202004.pdf

Leinhardt, G., & Knutson, K. (2004). *Listening in on museum conversations.* Walnut Creek, CA: AltaMira.

Lesley University (2005). Interview questions for teachers. Retrieved December 4, 2006, from http://www.lesley.edu/services/crc/interview-forteachers.html

Levin, R. (1990, November). *An unfulfilled alliance. The lab school in teacher education: Two case students, 1910-1980.* Paper presented at the Annual Meeting of the History of Education Society, Atlanta, GA.

Levine, M. (1992). *Professional practice schools: Linking teacher education and school reform.* New York: Teachers College Press.

Lewis, L., Snow, K., Farris, L., & Levin, D. (1999). *Distance education at postsecondary education institutions: 1997-98.* Washington, DC: U.S. Department of Education, National Center for Educational Statistics.

Li, Q., & Akins, M. (2005). Sixteen myths about online teaching and learning in higher education: Don't believe everything you hear. *TechTrends, 49*(4), 51-60.

Library of Congress (2002). *Copyright law.* Retrieved April 11, 2006, from: http://www.copyright.gov

Lim, J. (2006). Ask donut. *Word Press.* Retrieved April 12, 2006, from http://bcisdvcs.wordpress.com/2006/03/23/ask-donuthead

Lou, Y. (2004). Understanding process and affective factors in small group versus individual learning with technology. *Journal of Educational Computing Research, 31*(4), 337-369.

Loveman, S. (2004). Bartley would have enjoyed this: Explorations in online/distance learning at an independent school. *Independent School, 63*(4), 72-77.

Mack, K. (2005). *Marco Polo in New York.* Retrieved April 30, 2006, from http://www.nyiteez.org/MarcoPoloNY

MacNaughton, R., & Johns, F. (1993). The professional development school: An emerging concept. *Contemporary Education, 64*(4), 215-218.

Marshall, J. M. (2002). *Learning with technology: Evidence that technology can and does, support learning.* A white paper prepared for Cable in the Classroom.

Martin, M. (2000). *Videoconferencing in teaching & learning: Case studies and guidelines.* Western Education & Library Board, Omagh, Northern Ireland. Retrieved from http://www.welb-cass.org/site/projects%5Finitiatives/video%5Fconferencing/downloads/VCT&L.pdf

Martin, M. (2005). Seeing is believing: The role of videoconferencing in distance learning. *British Journal of Educational Technology, 36*(3), 397-405.

Matthews, D. (1999). The origins of distance education and its use in the United States. *THE Journal, 27(2),* 54-60.

McAlpine, L. (2000). Collaborative learning online. *Distance Education, 21,* 66-80.

McDermon, L. (2005). Distance learning: It's elementary! *Learning and Leading with Technology, 33*(4), 28-30.

McKenzie, J. (1999). Scaffolding for success. *From Now On: The Technology Journal, 9*(4). Retrieved April 17, 2006, from http://fno.org/dec99/scaffold.html

Menlove, R., Hansford, D., & Lignugaris-Kraft, B. (2000). Creating a community of distance learners: Putting technology to work. In *Proceedings of the American Council on Rural Special Education (ACRES) Annual Conference March, 2000, Alexandria, VA. Capitalizing on leadership in rural special education: Making a difference for children and families* (pp. 247-253).

Merriam, S. B. (2001). Andragogy and self-directed learning: Pillars of adult learning theory.

New Directions for Adult and Continuing Education, 89, 3-13.

Merrick, S. (2005). Videoconferencing primary and secondary: The state of the art. *Innovate, 2*(1). Retrieved April, 2006, from http://www.tandberg.net/ind_focus/education/index.jsp

Merrill, H. S. (2004). Best practices for online facilitation. *Adult Learning, 14*(12), 13-16.

Miller, M. R. (2005). The digital dynamic: How communications media shape our world. *The Futurist, 39*, 31.

Moore, M. G. (1989). Three types of interaction. *The American Journal of Distance Education, 3*(2), 1-6.

Motagna, M., & Carlton, M. (1998). *Bell labs helps Clinton students make a video call to Russia*. Retrieved April 15, 2006, from: http://www.bell-labs/news/1998/june14/1.html

Motamedi, V. (2001). A critical look at the use of videoconferencing in United States distance education. *HighBeam Research.* Retrieved on September 15, 2005, from http://www.highbeam.com

Motamedi, V. (2001). A critical look at the use of videoconferencing in the United States distance education. *Education, 122*(2), 386-394.

Mouza, C. (2003). Learning to teach with new technology: Implications for professional development. *Journal of Research on Technology in Education, 35*(2), 272-289.

Mueller, M. (1993). Universal service in telephone history: A reconstruction. *Telecommun. Policy, 17*(5), 352-369.

Mulrine, A. (2003). Skipping the formaldehyde: Virtual frogs, videoconferencing teachers - and vital lessons. *U.S. News and World Report, 135*(13), 64.

National Council for Accreditation of Teacher Education (NCATE) (2002). Professional standards for the accreditation of schools, departments, and colleges of education (p. 4). Retrieved March 19, 2006, from http://ncate.org/documents/unit_stnds_2002.pdf

National Informatics Centre (2006). Faqs. Retrieved May 16, 2006, from http://vidcon.nic.in/faq.htm

National Research Council (2000). *Inquiry and the national science education standards.* Washington, DC: National Academy Press.

Newman, D. (2006). *The impact of multi-media videoconferencing on children's learning: Positive outcomes of use.* Paper presented at the Annual Meeting of the American Educational Research Association. San Francisco, CA.

Newman, D. L. (2003). *The virtual informal education Web project: Formative evaluation of the Schenectady City School District technology innovation challenge grant* (Schenectady Component, Year 3 Report (2002-2003) - Tech. Rep.). Albany, NY: Evaluation Consortium University at Albany, SUNY.

Newman, D. L. (2004). *The virtual informal education Web project: Formative evaluation of the Schenectady City School District technology innovation challenge grant* (New York Institute of Technology Component, Year 4 Report - Tech. Rep.). Albany, NY: Evaluation Consortium University at Albany, SUNY.

Newman, D. L. (2005). *Beyond the barriers: Benefits of K-12 teacher participation in collaborative classroom videoconferencing training.* A paper presented at the Annual Conference of the Society for Technology in Teacher Education (SITE), Phoenix, AZ.

Newman, D. L. (2005). *The virtual informal education Web project: Formative evaluation of the Schenectady City School District technology innovation challenge grant* (Schenectady Component, Year 5 Report - Tech. Rep.). Albany, NY: Evaluation Consortium University at Albany, SUNY.

Newman, D. L. (2005). *The virtual information education Web project: Summative evaluation of the technology innovation challenge grant end of the grant report 2000-2005.* SUNY Albany, NY: Evaluation Consortium. Retrieved November 14, 2006, from http://www.projectview.org/Project-VIEW.Endof GrantReport.2000-2006.pdf

Newman, D. L. (2005, March). *Beyond the barriers: Benefits of K-12 teacher participation in collaborative classroom videoconferencing training.* Paper presented at the annual meeting of the SITE, Phoenix, AR.

Newman, D. L. (2006). *The virtual information education Web project: Summative evaluation of the Schenectady city school district technology innovation challenge grant, Schenectady component, Five year report.* SUNY Albany, NY: Evaluation Consortium.

Newman, D. L., & Goodwin-Segal, T. (2003). *Evaluation of a technology integration challenge grant program: Using technology to connect museums and classrooms.* A paper presented at the 2003 Annual Meeting of the American Educational Research Association, Chicago, IL.

Newman, D. L., & Goodwin-Segal, T. (2004). *Civics mosaic: Cooperative civic education and economic education exchange program evaluation report* (October 2003-June 2004). Albany, NY: University at Albany/SUNY, Evaluation Consortium.

Newman, D. L., & King, J. (2004). *The virtual information education Web project: Formative evaluation of the Schenectady city school district technology innovation challenge grant* (New York Institute of Technology Component, Year Four 2003-2004 Report). Albany, NY: University at Albany/SUNY, Evaluation Consortium.

Newman, D. L., & Spaulding, D. T. (2001). *Evaluation of the science research in the high-school program: 2000-2001 program implementation* (Evaluation Report). State University of New York at Albany: The Evaluation Consortium.

Newman, D. L., Barbanell, P. & Falco, J. (2005). Documenting value-added learning through videoconferencing: K-12 classrooms' interactions with museums. In G. Richards (Ed.), *Proceedings of World Conference on E-Learning in Corporate, Government, Healthcare, and Higher Education 2005* (pp. 389-401). Chesapeake, VA: AACE.

Newman, D. L., Barbanell, P., & Falco, J. (2006). Videoconferencing communities: Documenting online face-to face user interactions. In N. Lambropoulos & P. Zaphiris (Eds.), *User-centered design of online learning communities* (p. 122-140). Hershey, PA: Idea Group Publishing.

Newman, D. L., Barbanell, P., & Falco, J. (2007). Videoconferencing communities: Documenting online user interactions. In N. Lambropoulos & P. Zaphiris (Eds.), *User-centered design of online learning communities* (pp. 122-140). Hershey, PA: Idea Group, Inc.

Newman, D. L., Catapano, N., & Spaulding, D. T. (2002). *The virtual informal education Web project: Formative evaluation of the Schenectady City School District technology innovation challenge grant* (Ball State Report, March, 2002 - Tech. Rep.). Albany, NY: University at Albany/SUNY, Evaluation Consortium.

Newman, D. L., Du, Y., Bose, M., & Bidjerano, T. (2006). *A content analysis of videoconference integration plans.* Paper presented at the annual meeting of SITE , Orlando, FL.

Newman, D. L., Gligora, M. A., King, J., & Guckemus, S. (2005, April). *Breaking down the classroom walls: The impact of external videocon-*

ferencing on children's cognition. Paper presented at the annual meeting of the American Educational Research Association, Montreal, Canada.

Newman, D. L., King, J. A., Gligora, M. A., Guckemus, S. M., & Pruden, J. M. (2004). *Evaluating the impact of videoconferencing: Documenting teacher outcomes and changes in instructional strategies.* Paper presented at the Annual Meeting of the American Evaluation Association, Atlanta, GA.

Newman, D., Barbanell, P., & Falco, J. (2004). *Documenting value-added learning through videoconferencing: K-12 classrooms' interactions with museums.* Paper presented at the annual meeting of E-Learn Conference, Washington, D.C.

Newman, D., Barbanell, P., & Falco, J. (2005). Achievement of student cognitive growth: Results of integrating interactive museum videoconferencing. In J. Trant & D. Bearman (Eds.), *Museums and the Web 2005: Proceedings.* Toronto: Archives Museum Informatics. Retrieved on April 20, 2006, from http://www.archimuse.com/mw2005/papers/newman/newman.html

Newman, D., Barbanell, P., & Falco, J. (2005). Documenting value-added learning through videoconferencing: K-12 classrooms' interactions with museums. In G. Richards (Ed.), *Proceedings of World Conference on E-Learning in Corporate, Government, Healthcare, and Higher Education, 2005, Chesapeake, VA* (pp. 389-401).

Newmann, F. M. (1992). *Student engagement and achievement in American secondary schools.* New York: Teachers College Press. Retrieved November 14, 2006, from http://eric.ed.gov/ERICDocs/data/ericdocs2/content_storage_01/0000000b/80/26/c2/ 2b.pdf

Newmann, F. M., Secada, W. G., & Wehlage, G. G. (1995). *A guide to authentic instruction and assessment: Vision, standards, and scoring.* Madison, WI: Wisconsin Center for Education Research.

Nkrumah, W. (in press 2003). Portland, Oregon, Museum puts students in touch with NASA. *The Oregonian.*

No Child Left Behind Act (2001). 20 U.S.C. 70 [section] 6301

Nobel, D. F. (1998). *Digital diploma mills: The automation of higher education.* Retrieved April 4, 2006, from http://www.firstmaonday.dk/issues/issue3_1/noble/index.html

Norman, G., & Schmidt, F. (1992). The psychological basis of problem-based learning: A review of the evidence. *Academic Medicine, 67,* 557-565.

Norman, K. I., & Hayden, K. L. (2002). K-12 instruction in the United States: Integrating national standards for science and writing through emerging technologies. In *Proceedings of the 10th International Organization for Science and Technology Education Symposium, Foz do Iguacu, Parana, Brazil: Vol: 1 & 2* (pp. 323-333).

Northwestern University Information Technology (2004). *Videoconferencing at Northwestern.* Retrieved April 2, 2006, from http://www.it.northwestern.edu/bin/news/vidconf_pr2.pdf

Northwestern University Information Technology (2005). *Understanding videoconferencing.* Retrieved April 6, 2006, from http://www.it.northwestern.edu/videoconferencing/understand/index.html

Northwestern University Information Technology (2005). *Videoconferencing examples.* Retrieved April 22, 2006, from http://www.it.northwestern.edu/videoconferencing/understand/examples.htm

North Dakota State Government (2006). Internet filtering policy. Education Technology Services. Retrieved June 11, 2007, from http://www.edutech.nodak.edu/support/policies/filtering/

O'Connor, D. (2003). Application sharing in K-12 education: Teaching and learning with Rube Goldberg. *TechTrends, 47*(5), 6-13.

Omatseye, J. N. (1999). Teaching through tele-conferencing. *Learning and Leaning with Technology, 29*(6), 10-13.

Omatseye, J. N. (1999). Teaching through tele-conferencing: Some curriculum challenges. *College Student Journal, 33*(3), 346-353.

Pace, S. & Tesi, R. (2004). Adult's perceptions of field trips taken within grades K-12: Eight case studies in the New York metropolitan area. *Education, 125*(1), 30. Retrieved November 29, 2006, from http://web.ebscohost.com/ehost/delivery?vid=7&sid=46751b8

Pachnowski, L. M. (2002). Virtual field trips through technology. *Learning and Leading with Technology, 29*(6), 10-13.

Packard Bell (1995). *Video conferencing for learning.* Retrieved April 17, 2006, from www.kn.pacbell.com/wired/vidconf/vidconf.html

PBSOnline (n.d.). *Before I die.* Retrieved April 13, 2006, from http://www.thirteen.org/bid/pevalhost.html

Pea, R. (1998, February). *The pros and cons of technology in the classroom.* Speech delivered at Bay Area School Reform Collaborative Funders' Learning Community Meeting, Palo Alto, CA. Retrieved August 18, 2005, from http://tappedin.org/archive/peacuban/pea.html

Penn, M. (1998). Videoconferencing one-to-one but far from home. *Technology Connections, 5*(2), 22-23.

Peters, O. (1993). *Understanding distance education.* In K. Harry, M. Hohn, & D. Keegan (Eds.). *Distance education: New perspectives.* London: Routledge.

Peterson, R. (1998). The NASA Lewis Research Center's learning technologies project. *T.H.E. Journal, 26*(4), 63-66.

Peterson, R. (2000). "Real-world" connections through videoconferencing—We're closer than you think! *TechTrends, 44*(6), 5-11.

Petracchi, H., & Patchner, M. (2000). Social work students and their learning environment: A comparison of interactive television. *Journal of Social Work Education, 36*(2), 335-347.

Plymouth (2006). The future of video conferencing. Retrieved May 16, 2006, from http://www.2.plymouth.ac.uk/distancelearning/vidconf.html#future

Raider-Roth, M. B. (2005). Trusting what you know: Negotiating the relational context of classroom life. *Teachers College Record, 107*(4), 587-628.

Rathlin Virtual Field Trip (2005). Retrieved from http://www.neelb.org.uk/cass/ict/videoconferencing/RathlinVirtual%20Fieldtrp.pdf

Rhode Island Network for Educational Technology (2005). Retrieved from http://www.ri.net/RINET/products/ivid/polycomuserguide.html

Rice, K. (2006). A comprehensive look at distance education in the K-12 context. *Journal of Research on Technology in Education, 38*(4), 425-448.

Richardson, V. (2003). The dilemmas of professional development. *Phi Delta Kappan, 84*(5), 401-406.

Rideout, V., Vandewater, E., & Wartella E. (2003). Zero to six: Electronic media in the lives of infants, toddlers, and preschoolers. *The Henry J. Kaiser Family Foundation,* 1-38. Retrieved April, 2006, from http://www.kff.org/entmedia/upload/Zero-to-Six-Electronic-Media-in-the-Lives-of-Infants-Toddlers-and-Preschoolers-PDF.pdf

Ringstaff, C., & Kelley, L. (2002). The learning return on our educational technology investment. Retrieved April 8, 2004, from http://www.wested.org/online_pubs/learning_return.pdf

Robinson, C. F., & Kakela, P. J. (2006). Creating a space to learn: A classroom of fun, interaction, and trust. *College Teaching, 54*(1), 202-206.

Rodes, P., Knapczyk, D., Chapman, C., & Chung, H. (2000). Involving teachers in Web-based professional development. *T.H.E. Journal, 27*(10), 95-102.

Rogoff, B., et al. (2003). Firsthand learning through intent participation. *Annual Review of Psychology, 54*, 175-203.

Rothstein, R., Jacobsen, R., & Wilder, T. (2006). 'Proficiency for all' is an oxymoron: Accountability should begin with realistic goals that recognize human variability. *Education Week, 26*(13), 42.

Rotman, L. (2006). Internet2 survey finds over 46,000 K20 institutions connected to its next-generation network. *Internet2*. Retrieved April 21, 2006, from https://mail.internet2.edu/wws/arc/i2-news/2006-03/msg00004.html

Roush, N. (2004). Colonial Williamsburg virtual field trips. *Social Studies and the Young Learner, 16*(4), 29-32.

Roybal-Allard, L. (2007). Congresswoman Lucille Roybal-Allard (CA-34) testifies about her legislation to improve student academic achievement through technology. U.S. House of Representatives, Washington D.C. Retrieved June 14, 2007, from http://www.house.gov/list/press/ca34_roybal-allard/pr070516.html p.1

Russell, T. L. (1999). *The no significant difference phenomenon: A comparative research annotated bibliography on technology for distance education*. North Carolina State University, N.C: IDECC.

Sallis, E., & Jones, G. (2002). *Knowledge management in education: Enhancing learning and education*. London: Kogan Page Ltd.

Satterlee, B. (2002). *Applications of technology, currently being used in business and industry, to education*. Retrieved November 7, 2006, from http://eric.ed.gov/sitemap/ html_0900000b8017a8a8.html

SBC Knowledge Network Explorer (1995). *Videoconferencing: Introduction*. Retrieved March 16, 2006, from http://www.kn.pacbell.com/wired/vidconf/intro.html

Schrock, K. (2006). Kathy Schrock's guide for educators–Assessment and rubrics. Retrieved April 17, 2006, from http://school.discovery.com/schrockguide/assess.html

Schrum, L. (1996). Teaching at a distance: Strategies for successful planning and development. *Learning and Leading with Technology, 23*(March), 30-33.

Schunk, D. H. (1999). Social self interaction and achievement behavior. *Educational Psychologist, 34*(4), 219-227.

Schutte, J. G. (1997). *Virtual teaching in higher education: The new intellectual superhighway or just another traffic jam?* Retrieved February 13, 2003, from http://www.csun.edu/sociology/virexp.htm

Search Grant Opportunities (n.d.). Retrieved August 22, 2006, from http://www.grants.gov/search/basic.do

Searls, D. (2005, Nov). Saving the Net: How to keep the carriers from flushing the Net down the tubes. *LINUX Journal, Article 8673*. Retrieved December 3, 2006, from http://www.linuxjournal.com//article/8673

Seels, B., Fullerton, K., Berry, L., & Horn, L. J. (2004). 12 Research on learning from television. In D. H. Jonassen (Ed.), *Handbook of research on educational communications and technology, 2nd ed.* (pp. 249-320). Mahwah, NJ: Lawrence Erlbaum Associates.

Seifert, B. (2006, March). The Internet just got a lot faster. *Anchorage Press, 15*(13). Retrieved April 21, 2006, from http://www.anchoragepress.com/archives-2006/news2vol15ed13.shtml

Sembor, E. C. (1997). Citizenship, diversity, and distance learning: Videoconferencing in Connecticut. *Social Education, 61*(3), 154-159.

Senge, P. (1990). *The fifth discipline*. New York: Doubleday.

Sergiovanni, T. J. (2001). *The principalship: A reflective practice perspective*. Boston: Allyn & Bacon.

Sherron, G. T., & Boettcher, J. V. (1997). Distance learning: The shift to interactivity. *EDUCAUSE* (pp. 23-24). Retrieved April 9, 2006, from http://www.educause.edu/LibraryDetailPage/666?ID=PUB3017

Silverman, S., & Silverman, G. (1999). The educational enterprise zone: Where knowledge comes from! *T.H.E. Journal, 26*(7), 56.

Smeaton, A., & Keogh, G. (1999). An analysis of the use of virtual delivery of undergraduate lectures. *Computers and Education, 32*(1), 83-94.

Smith, J. C. (2004). *Effective use of desktop videoconferencing in teacher education and professional development with reference to strategies for adult basic education*. National Center of Adult Literacy, University of Pennsylvania. Retrieved November 3, 2005, from http://www.literacy.org/products/t21_vc_smith_v14.pdf

Smith, S. (2003). Online video conferencing: An application to teacher education. *Journal of Special Education Technology, 18*(3), 62-64.

Smyth, R. (2005). Broadband videoconferencing as a tool for learner-centered distance learning in higher education. *British Journal of Educational Technology, 36*(5), 805-820.

Souder, W. E. (1993). The effectiveness of traditional vs. satellite delivery in three management of technology master's degree programs. *The American Journal of Distance Education, 7*(1), 37-53.

Sparks, D., & Hirsh, S. (1997). *A new vision for staff development*. Alexandria, VA: Association for Supervision and Curriculum Development.

Speck, M. (1996). Best practice in professional development for sustained educational change. *ERS Spectrum, 14*(2), 33-41.

Speltz, C. A., & Shaugnessy, M. F. (1990). Human interactions in education: The museum as an experimental learning center. (ERIC Document Reproduction No.ED328493).

Spicer, J. I., & Stratford, J. (2001). Student perceptions of a virtual field trip to replace a real field trip. *Journal of Computer Assisted Learning, 17*, 345-354.

Spillane, J. P. (2000). *District leader's perceptions of teacher learning* (Rep. No. OP-05). University of Pennsylvania, Consortium for Policy Research in Education.

Sprague, D., & Dede, C. (1999). If I teach this way, am I doing my job? Constructivism in the classroom. *Learning and Leading with Technology, 27*(1), 6-9.

Springer, L., Stanne, M. E., & Donovan, S. S. (1999). Effects of small-group learning on undergraduates in science, mathematics, engineering, and technology: A meta-analysis. *Review of Educational Research, 69*, 21-51.

Stainfield, J., Fisher, P., Ford, B., & Solem, M. (2000). International virtual field trips: A new direction? *Journal of Geography in Higher Education, 24*(2), 255-262.

Staples, A., Pugach, M. C., & Himes, D. (2005). Rethinking the technology integration challenge: Cases from three urban elementary schools. *Journal of Research on Technology in Education, 37*(3), 285-311.

Strudler, N., & Wetzel, K. (1999). Lessons from exemplary colleges of education: Factors affecting technology integration in preservice programs. *Educational Technology Research and Development, 47*, 63-81.

Sullivan, L., & Smith, S. A. (2001). Charting your journey to distance learning. *Multimedia Schools, 8*(5), 12. Retrieved from http://www.infotoday. com/mmschools/oct01/sullivan&smith.htm

Teitel, L. (1999). Looking toward the future by understanding the past: The historical context of professional development schools. *Peabody Journal of Education, 74*(3/4), 6-15.

Telecommunications Act (1996). Pub. LA. No. 104-104, 110 Stat. 56

Telemedicine Information Exchange (2006). Telemedicine and tele-health articles. Retrieved August 1, 2006, from http://tie.telemed.org/articles.asp

The Institute for the Advancement of Research in Education at AEL (2004, April). *Review of research: Nine components of effective professional development.* Prepared for Texas Instrument Educational and Productivity Solutions Division.

Thomson/West (1997). United States code annotated title 47. Telegraphs, telephones, and radiotelegraphs. Communications act of 1934, 47 U.S.C.A. 151. Retrieved April 11, 2006, from www.fcc.gov/omd/pra/docs/3060-1-41-07.doc

Tillett, T. (2005). Virtual school. *Environmental Health Perspectives, 113*(10), A668.

Totten, S., Sills, T., Digby, A., & Russ, P. (1991). *Cooperative learning: A guide to research.* New York: Garland.

Tucker, S. (2001). Distance education: Better, worse, or as good as traditional education? *Online Journal of Distance Learning Administration, 4*(4). Retrieved February 23, 2006, from http://www/westga.edu/~distance/ojdla/winter44/tucker44.html

Truesdell, K. S. (1998). Broadening professinal development through school-university collaboration. Thesis (Ed.)—State University of New York at Buffalo, 1998.

Tufts University, Educational Media Center (n.d.). Glossary. Retrieved September 15, 2005, from http://www.tufts.edu/orgs/edmedia/gloss.shtml

Tuthill, G., & Klemm, E. B. (2002). Virtual field trips: Alternatives to actual field trips. *International Journal of Instructional Media, 29*(4), 453-468.

Tuttle, H. G. (2003). *Maximizing student learning in a videoconference.* Paper presented at the New York State Association for Computers and Technology in Education Annual Conference. Rochester, NY.

Tuttle, H. G. (1996). Learning: The star of video-conferencing. *MultiMedia Schools, 3*(4), 37-41.

Tuttle, H. G. (1998). *Improving student learning in videoconferences.* Paper presented at National Educational Computer Conference, San Diego, CA.

Tuttle, H. G. (2004). *Learning and technology assessments for administrators.* Ithaca, NY: Epilog Visions.

Tweedell, C. B. (2000, October). *A theory of adult learning and implications for practice.* Paper presented at the Annual Meeting of the Midwest Educational Research Association, Chicago, IL. ED 446 702.

U.S. Department of Education (2004). *National education technology plan. Tear down those walls: The revolution is underway.* Retrieved November 23, 2005, from http://nationaledtechplan.org/theplan/TearDownThoseWalls.asp

U.S. House of Representatives (1996). Committee on the judiciary. Subcommittee on courts and intellectual property. Fair use guidelines for educational multimedia. Retrieved April 11, 2006, from http://www.ccumc.org/copyright/cguides.html

Ullman, E. (2006). Students in Michigan connect with authors. *District Administration, 42*(3), 106.

University of Ulster (n.d.). Videoconferencing manual. Retrieved April 24, 2006, from http://www.ulster.ac.uk/isd/itus/media/vcmanual.pdf

University of Virginia Information Communication and Technology (2006). Videoconferencing examples. Retrieved April 22, 2006, from http://www.itc.virginia.edu/videoconf/video-info/vr-sec8.html

Visual Understanding in Education (2006). What is VTS? Retrieved April 18, 2006, from http://www.vue.org/whatisvts.html

Vygotsky, L. (1978). *Mind in society: The development of higher psychological processes.* Cambridge, MA: Harvard University Press.

Wade, R. (1984). What makes a difference in in-service teacher education? A meta-analysis of research. *Educational Leadership, 42*(4), 48-54.

Watkins, C. (2002). Videoconferences can bridge the gap. *American Libraries, 33*(11), 14.

Weinstein, I. M. (2006). The ISDN to IP migration for videoconferencing: Real world options that make both dollars and sense. *Wainhouse Research.* Retrieved March, 2006, from http://www.tandberg.net/ind_focus/education/index.jsp

Weiss, N. E. (1998). *True needs true partner: 1998 survey highlights.* Washington, DC: Institute of Museum and Library Services. (ERIC Document Reproduction Service No. ED434 848).

Wenzel, G. C. (2000). Center for Puppetry Arts GSAMS outcomes: Survey assessment instrument results for distance education. Retrieved February

2006, from http://www.puppet.org/edu/distance.shtml

Wetzel, K., Zambo, R., Buss, R., & Padgett, H. (2001, June). *A picture of change in technology rich K-8 classrooms.* Paper presented at National Educational Computing Conference, "Building on the Future". Retrieved November 8, 2006, from http://www.eric.ed.gov/ ERICDocs/data/ericdocs2/content-storage-01/0000000b/80/0d/d0/48.pdf

Wheeler, S. (2000). User reactions to videoconferencing: Which students cope best? *Education Media International, 37*(1), 31-38.

Whipp, J. L. (2003). Scaffolding critical reflection in online discussions. *Journal of Teacher Education, 54*(4), 321-333.

Wiggins, G., & McTighe, J. (1998). *Understanding by design.* Alexandria, VA: Association for Supervision and Curriculum Development.

Wikipedia (2006). Children's Internet protection act. Retrieved April 21, 2006, from: thttp://en.wikipedia.org/wiki/children's_internet_protection_ac

Wilcox, J. (2006). Less teaching, more assessing. *Association for Supervision and Curriculum Development Education Update, 48*(2) 1, 2, 6, 8.

Wilcox, J. R. (2000). *Video conferencing and interactive multimedia: The whole picture.* New York: Telecom Books.

Wilkerson, L. (2004). *The history of video conferences—Moving ahead at the speed of video.* Retrieved April 15, 2006, from www.ezinearticles.com

Wilkerson, L. (2006). *The history of video conferencing.* Retrieved April 25, 2006, from http://www.video-conferencing-guide.com/history-of-video-conferencing.htm

Wilkinson, D. (2001). *Project VIEW videoconference integration training.* Project VIEW, Schenectady City School District.

Willis, B. (n.d.). *Distance education at a glance: Evaluation for distance educators.* Retrieved April 10, 2006, from http://www.uidaho.edu/eo/dist4.html

Wilson, B. G. (2001). Trends and futures of education: Implications for distance education. *Quarterly Review of Distance Education (special issue), October, 2001.* Retrieved March 19, 2006, from http://carbon.cudenver.edu/~bwilson/TrendsAndFutures.html

Wilson, K. (2000). Virtual seminars in European studies: A model for collaborative learning. *Computer and the Humanities, 34,* 345-347.

Windschitl, M., & Sahl, K. (2002). Tracing teachers' use of technology in a laptop computer school: The interplay of teacher beliefs, social dynamics, and institutional culture. *American Educational Research Journal, 39*(1), 165-205.

Witherspoon, J. P. (1996). *Distance education: A planner's casebook.* Boulder, CO: Western Interstate Commission for Higher Education.

Wood, D. (1988). *How children think and learn.* New York: Basil Blackwell, Inc.

Woodruff, M., & Mosby, J. (1996). *A brief description of videoconferencing: Videoconferencing in the classroom and library.* Retrieved April 15, 2006, from http://www.kn.pacbell.com/wired/vidconf/description.html#what

Woods, T. J. (2005). *Instructor and student perceptions of a videoconference course.* Retrieved April 11, 2006, from http://www.uleth.ca/edu/grad/pdf/thesis_woods.pdf

Woolfolk, A. (2004). *Educational psychology* (9th ed.). Boston: Pearson Education, Inc.

World Intellectual Property Organization (2006). *Copyright and related rights.* Retrieved April 17, 2006, from http://www.wipo.org

Worthen, B. (2006, April 15). *The net neutrality debate: You pay, you play? CIO.* Retrieved April 24, 2006, from http://www.cio.com

Worthington, V., & Ellefson, N. (n.d.). Electronic field trips: Theoretical rational. *LETSNet, Michigan State University.* Retrieved on September 15, 2005, from http://commtechlab.msu.edu/sites/letsnet/noframes/bigideas/bl/blthor.html

Wulff, D. H., Nyquist, J. D., & Abbott, R. D. (1987). Students' perceptions of large classes. In M. G. Weimer (Ed.), *Teaching large classes well* (pp. 17-30). *New Directions for Teaching and Learning, 32,* (Winter). San Francisco: Jossey-Bass.

Yestrau, C. (2004). Retrieved April 30, 2006, from http://www.gng.org/about_gng/overview.html

Yorks, L. (2005). Adult learning and the generation of new knowledge and meaning: Creating liberating spaces for fostering adult learning through practitioner-based collaborative action inquiry. *Teacher College Record, 107*(6), 1217-1244.

Yost, D. S., Sentner, S. M., & Forlenza-Bailey, A. (2000). An examination of the construct of critical reflection: Implications for teacher education programming in the 21st century. *Journal of Teacher Education, 51*(1), 39-49.

About the Contributors

Dianna L. Newman is associate professor at the University at Albany/SUNY, USA, and director of the Evaluation Consortium at Albany. Dr. Newman has served on the board of directors for the American Evaluation Association; assisted in writing the "Guiding Principles for Evaluators," which function as the professional guidelines for practice; and served on the national Joint Committee for Standards in Educational Evaluation. She has been an evaluator for several federal- and state-funded technology-based curriculum integration grants and, currently, she is developing an innovative model of evaluation that will document systems change resulting from technology-based curriculum integration in K-12 and higher-education settings. Dr. Newman is widely published in the areas of technology innovation and K-12 curriculum practices.

John Falco currently serves as the director of The Institute for New Era Educational Leadership and Innovation at The College of Saint Rose, Albany, New York. He has served education as teacher, principal, and superintendent in K-12 public schools. Dr. Falco was the director and principal investigator of Project VIEW, a $10 million U.S. Department of Education Technology Innovation Grant that focused on interactive videoconferencing collaboration between schools and museums. He also has served as director and co-principal investigator for a National Science Foundation Grant, and was named Outstanding Superintendent in Technology for 2000-2001 by New York State Computer and Technology Educators. He has been a presenter and requested speaker at numerous conferences, including the National Summit for Technology in 2003 in Washington, D.C. He has received degrees from Columbia University, The City College of New York, Long Island University, and earned his doctorate at Seton Hall University.

Patricia Barbanell has 30 years of K-12 and museum education experience in multicultural and technology integration. She serves the NYS Education Department as a member of the Technology Policy and Practices Council, the Middle School Reform Advisory Committee, and the Arts Curriculum and Assessment Committee. She has worked as museum/school education coordinator for Project VIEW, and has taught visual arts. Dr. Barbanell is past president of both the NYS Art Teachers and the NYS Council of Educational Associations. She has presented at scores of professional conferences, and has been published in arts and technology journals. She received her Doctorate from Columbia University.

Stan Silverman, of the New York Institute of Technology, is widely regarded as a pioneer and national leader in distance learning and educational technology. He combines a physicist's knowledge of technological hardware with a teacher's insight into how they can be applied to enhance learning. He is a professor in the School of Education and Professional Services and director of the school's Technology-Based Learning Systems Department and Educational Enterprise Zone. He is a nationally-known speaker on technology and education, serves on the NYS Regents Technology Council and chairs the NYS Teacher Center Technology Committee. He is the author of numerous publications concerning technology and education, and has served as the project director for many research and technology innovation projects funded by a wide variety of organizations. He has been honored by inclusion in the USDLA Hall of Fame, and was the September, 2003, profile winner of the Center for Digital Education's "In the Arena" program.

* * *

Gel Alvarado was born and raised in Zamboanga City, Philippines. As a Fulbright scholar at the University of Washington, Alvarado conducted research on environmental education in marine protected areas in the Philippines. She has worked as a research assistant for a Michigan Department of Natural Resources-funded project, the Fisheries Stewardship, and Heritage Outreach/Research Initiative. Alvarado is currently completing her dissertation research, in which she will investigate the influence of different teaching pedagogies on fourth-grade students' capacity to identify an environmental problem in the Great Lakes Region, find possible solutions, and attempt to implement these solutions.

Marion Barnett is an associate professor who teaches early childhood education within the Department of Elementary Education and Reading at Buffalo State College. Prior to her 24 years in higher education, she was a head start, Pre-K, Kindergarten, and First-Grade teacher for 10 years. Dr. Barnett's research interests include working with preservice teachers on issues of family involvement in education. A collaboration with an early childhood higher-education colleague /charter school director led to a distance learning project and two subsequent PT3 grants (Preparing Tomorrow's Teachers to use Technology), which have become the focus of her research for the last five years.

Temi Bidjerano has a doctorate in educational psychology and methodology at the University at Albany/SUNY with a concentration in measurement and educational research. Her major research interests are in investigating, from a cross-cultural perspective, fourth-grade children's emotional experiences with student report cards. She has numerous presentations at both national and regional conferences, and a number of her manuscripts are currently being considered for publication in referred journals.

Denice Blair Leach has worked as a museum educator at the Michigan State University Museum in East Lansing, Michigan, developing and presenting videoconference programs in the social studies for K-12 audiences. She is also a private curriculum consultant and developer. Her research interests include historic sites and buildings, especially how people learn in historic environments, what educational practices are currently used by historic sites (including technology), and how these practices may be improved to benefit communities. Blair Leach is active as a volunteer for local museums and historic preservation organizations.

Mohua Bose is a specialist in learning theory and educational psychology. She has served as an evaluator for multiple-technology integration programs, and has written and presented numerous papers on the role of technology in K-12 environments. Ms. Bose is currently completing her dissertation at the University at Albany/SUNY, where she is investigating the role of professional development in K-12 videoconferencing.

Joseph Bowman, Jr. is a service associate professor in the Department of Educational Theory and Practice and the director of Center for Urban Youth and Technology (CUYT) at the University at Albany, State University New York. Dr. Bowman's research focuses on questions of access and equity to technology and content for urban and rural communities. His research interests also include the influence of video production technology and videoconferencing on youth and teachers as forms of expression and instruction. Dr. Bowman has a committed interest in education, community development, technology, and economic development nationally and internationally.

Sal DeAngelo has numerous years of experience as a technology specialist in K-12 districts and served as the technology service coordinator and program coordinator for Project VIEW. In this role, he assessed over 100 school districts and providers in establishing the infrastructure needed to support videoconferencing. He has taken this experience "on the road" via online and in-person conferences, and continues to advocate for equity through technology.

Felix Fernandez has a PhD from the University at Albany, has taught at the College of St. Rose, and held an internship position at the Office of Career Education and Instructional Technology, New York State Education Department; he is currently working for a major consulting firm as an educational specialist. His research interests include educational technology, technology integration, teacher professional development, and gender differences.

Jennifer Hahn has served as a middle-school and math teacher in a suburban district for over five years. She attended multiple technology trainings through Project VIEW and, using this training, she has integrated technology into her classroom and conducts multiple videoconferences with outside providers on an annual basis. She also has worked firsthand in the development of two videoconferences through Project VIEW.

Emily Diekemper Hansen never imagined she would live in Indiana. She attended school at North Carolina State University and graduated in 2000 with a BS in zoology and a BA in multidisciplinary studies. Her willingness to travel landed her at the Indianapolis Zoo, where she became a member of the Education Department, doing "a little bit of everything". In 2001, she became the coordinator of the zoo's distance learning program, and has enjoyed connecting with over 130,000 students across the United States since accepting the position. In addition to her videoconferencing role, she has participated in Project Iguana, a partnership with zoos, schools, and NGOs in the Dominican Republic that is committed to the research and conservation of critically-endangered Ricord's iguana. She is also currently pursuing a Master's degree in museum studies from Indiana University. As for her favorite animal in the zoo, it is a toss-up between a scruffy little screech owl named Zeus and the giant Pacific octopus.

Melaine C. Kenyon is the associate director for instructional technology. She is an electronic learning specialist and oversees the staff members who provide educational technology training, support, and resources to the college's faculty, staff, and students. She is currently spearheading efforts to upgrade classroom technology as well as the campus's distance learning facilities. Along with teaching college courses online, Melaine has developed and taught online and hands-on professional development workshops on instructional design, incorporating information literacy in Web-based courses, and course management systems. Melaine holds a BA in history and an MLS from the University at Buffalo.

Marie Martin is a former teacher of modern languages and international officer with a school district in Northern Ireland. For the past ten years, she has promoted the use of videoconferencing and other technologies to enrich and extend learning in K-12 classrooms. She is currently advising on educational videoconferencing projects in Northern Ireland, and is a doctoral candidate in the Instructional Technology program in Duquesne University, Pittsburgh, Pennsylvania. She has contributed on videoconferencing to education journals and conferences in Ireland, the UK, and the U.S., and is the author of *Videoconferencing in Teaching and Learning: Case Studies and Guidelines,* published in 2000.

Dennis G. Mike has a background in both special education and reading education. Prior to becoming an associate professor for the Department of Elementary Education and Reading at Buffalo State College (SUNY), he served as a resource room teacher, reading specialist, curriculum developer, adaptive and assistive technologies specialist, director of special education, and policy-maker for the NYS Education Department. Dr. Mike's primary research interest is the use of technology to promote the literacy development of children with disabilities. His PhD in reading education is from the University at Albany/SUNY.

Sharon Miller-Vice graduated from the University at Albany, Albany, New York, in 2004, with a Masters degree in curriculum development and instructional technology. She is finishing her Certificate of Advanced Studies in Curriculum and Instruction at the University (2006). She works for the New York State Education Department and is a research associate for the Center for Urban Youth and Technology in the Department of Educational Theory and Practice, School of Education, University at Albany. Her research interests include online learning, technology integration, and youth development programs.

Leigh Mountain is a PhD candidate currently in the process of completing a dissertation on the impact of videoconferencing on student learning at the University at Albany/SUNY. She works as a project director at the Evaluation Consortium where she conducts program evaluations for several U.S. Department of Education, NYS Department of Education, National Science Foundation, and other foundation grants. She was an evaluator on a project that evaluated the implementation of videoconferencing into the classroom; her interest in videoconferencing and its impact on education has grown since then.

Patty Petrey Dees is the distance learning program director at the Center for Puppetry Arts in Atlanta. Dees founded the Center's IVC program in 1998, and developed nationally-recognized programs that adhere to state and national curriculum standards. Dees served as chair of the Georgia K-12 Videoconferencing Resource Group from 1999-2002. Dees has presented workshops at state and regional educational technology conferences such as the National Educational Computing Conference and the

Keystone Conference. She is a member of the United States Distance Learning Association and International Society for Educational Communications and Technology. She currently serves on the content provider advisory board for the Center for Interactive Learning and Collaboration.

Patricia A. Ranney holds an MA in communication from the State University of New York at Albany, and is completing her MS in educational psychology with a focus in program evaluation at the College of St. Rose in Albany, New York. She also has a BS in marketing and management from Siena College, which led her to the corporate world for more than 20 years. After observing the decline in basic skills of just-out-of-high-school employees entering the corporate world, she decided to enter the field of education, where she hopes to bring "out-of-the-box" thinking that will ultimately assist teachers in their efforts to educate a culturally-diverse and socially-dynamic classroom.

Dean Spaulding serves on The College of Saint Rose faculty in the Department of Educational Psychology, in Albany, New York. He also teaches extensively in the department's Master's in program evaluation. He is the former chair for Teaching Program Evaluation for the American Evaluation Association. Dr. Spaulding is also one of the authors of *Methods in Educational Research: From Theory to Practice,* published in 2006, by Jossey-Bass Wiley, San Francisco, and the author of *Program Evaluation in Practice: Core Concepts and Examples for Discussion and Analysis* (in press), to be published by Jossey-Bass Wiley.

Harry Grover Tuttle has been the president of the International Society for Technology in Education (ISTE)'s Technology Coordinator SIG and of the New York State Association for Computers and Technology in Education. He has been a district coordinator of technology and a technology integration teacher. He presents at national conferences, and publishes many articles on technology and learning. Dr. Tuttle's book, *Learning and Technology Assessments for Administrators,* identifies over fifty aspects of technology integration. He currently works in Syracuse University's School of Education. His focus is on improving student learning through technology.

Kim Truesdell is an assistant professor in the Department of Elementary Education and Reading at Buffalo State College. Besides teaching literacy classes for elementary and secondary teacher candidates, she is involved in a PT3 grant looking at reflective mediation through the use of distance learning and electronic discussion. Dr. Truesdell's research interests include reflection and the development of teachers and teacher candidates, and the reading motivation and self-efficacy of 6th graders through a Book Buddy program. She has been a professor and college administrator for 15 years. Prior to that time, she taught for 10 years in the public schools.

Sharon Vatsky is the senior education manager for school, teacher, and family programs at the Solomon R. Guggenheim Museum in New York City. Her previous experience includes 10 years as curator of education at the Queens Museum of Art, where she formulated programming for dozens of exhibitions of modern and contemporary art for audiences of all ages. She has taught courses in visual arts and arts education at St. John's University, the University at Albany/SUNY, City University of New York, and Teachers College, Columbia University.

Fawn Warner earned a Bachelor of Science in professional writing and a Master of Arts in writing from Missouri State University. Fawn has worked for Discovery Center of Springfield, Inc, an interactive science and technology center, since December of 2001. In her role as education director, Fawn helped expand the Discovery Center's distance learning program through extended marketing efforts, building partnerships, and educator training.

Diane Wilkinson has several years of experience as a teacher, a K-12 instructional technology support staff member, and a provider of technology professional development. She served as instructional support coordinator for Project VIEW, where she provided both training and on-site support for teachers and building-level technology staff. An advocate of collaborative classrooms and constructivist learning, she is responsible for major innovations in collaborative classroom videoconferencing and the development of effective training and support methods for that process.

Index